CAFÉ SOCIETY

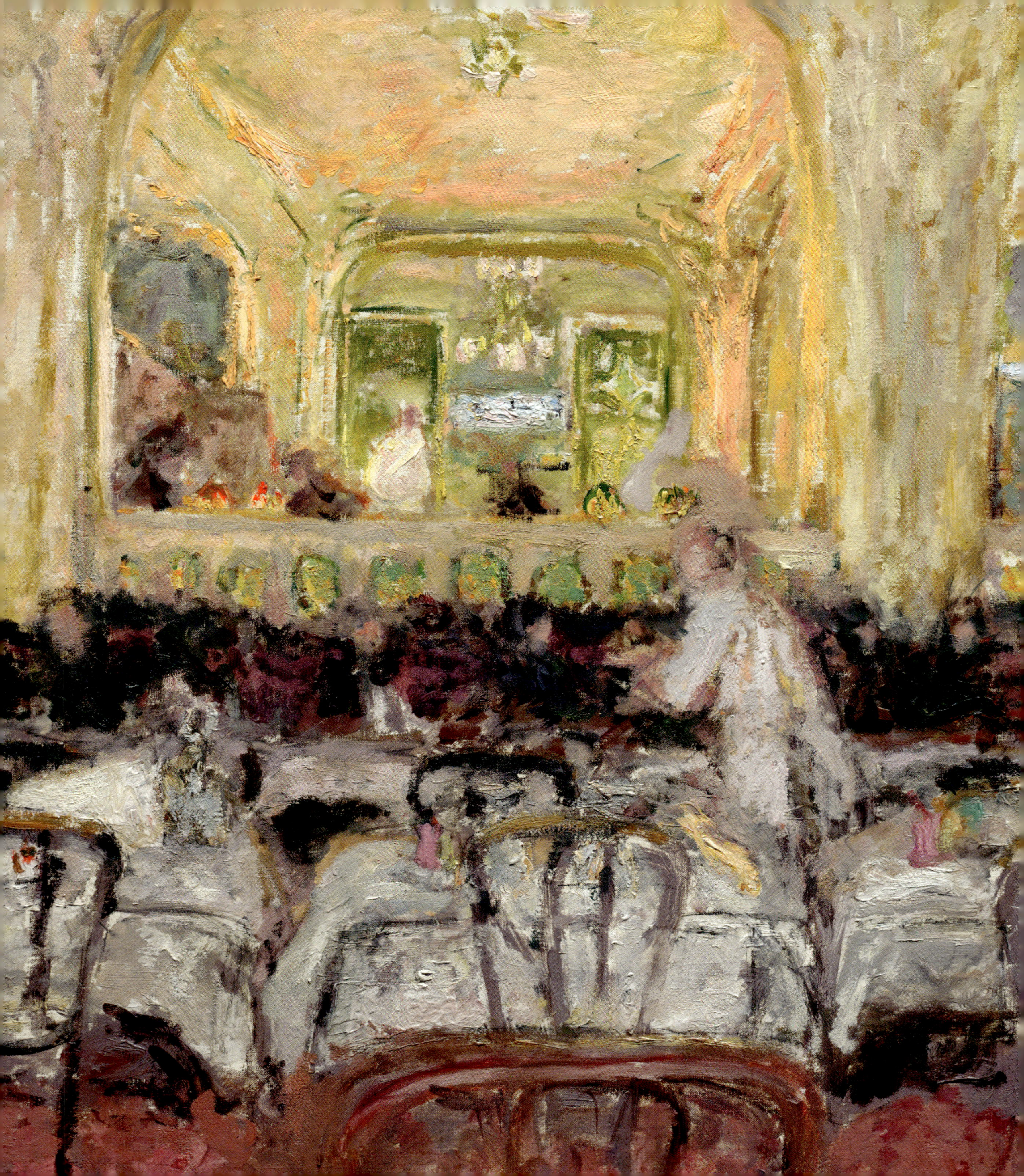

CAFÉ SOCIETY

Art and Sociability in Belle Époque Paris

Edited by Julie Pierotti
Foreword by Jack Becker, Gertrud Oelsner, and Kevin Sharp
Contributions by Taylor J. Acosta, Ellen Daugherty, W. Scott Haine, Jeffrey H. Jackson,
Julie Pierotti, Corkey Sinks, and Dorthe Vangsgaard Nielsen

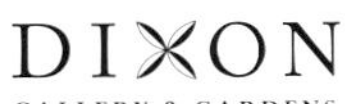

THE JOSLYN   ORDRUPGAARD   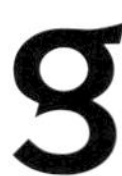

Dixon Gallery and Gardens, Memphis, in association with D Giles Limited

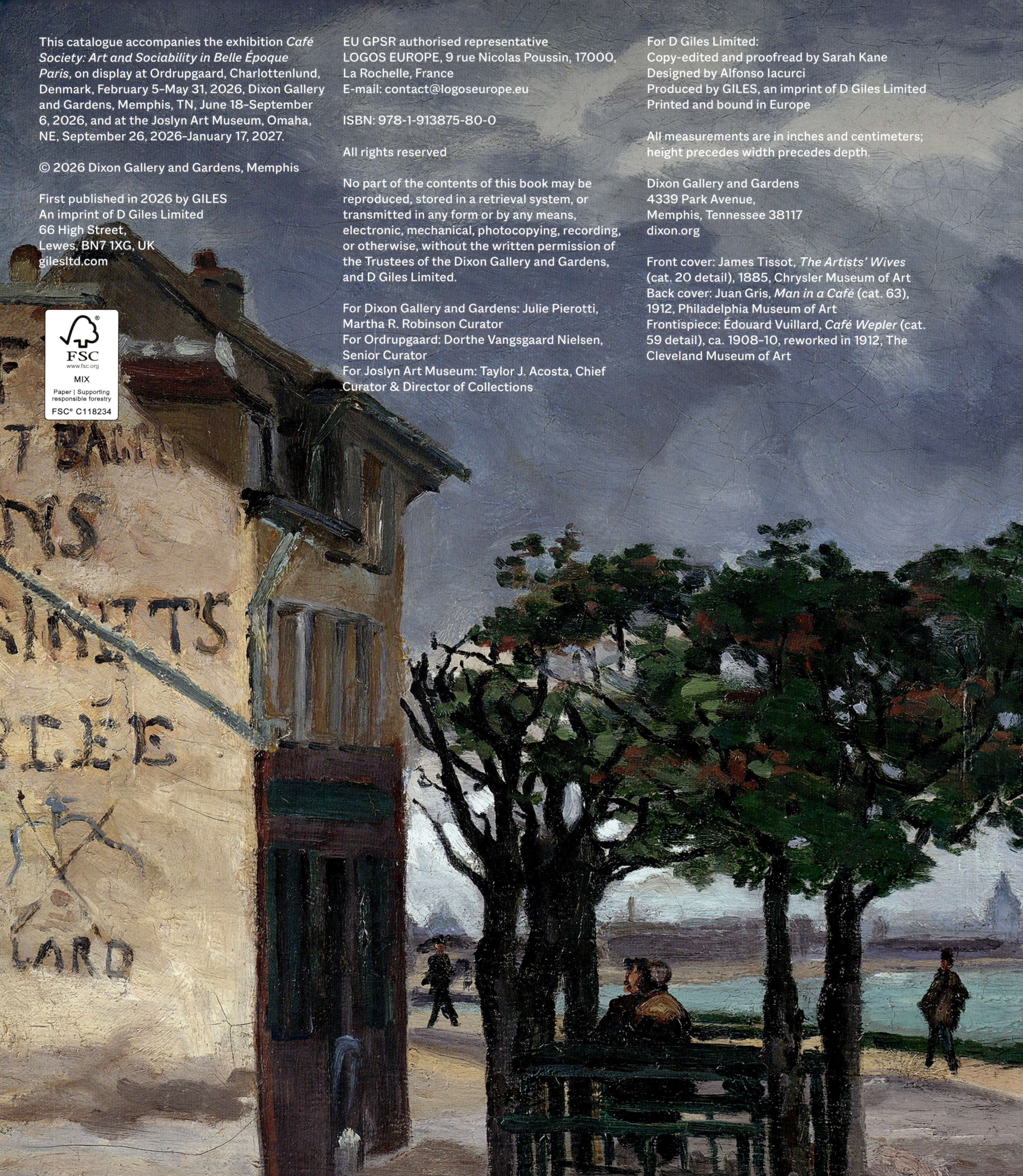

This catalogue accompanies the exhibition *Café Society: Art and Sociability in Belle Époque Paris*, on display at Ordrupgaard, Charlottenlund, Denmark, February 5–May 31, 2026, Dixon Gallery and Gardens, Memphis, TN, June 18–September 6, 2026, and at the Joslyn Art Museum, Omaha, NE, September 26, 2026–January 17, 2027.

First published in 2026 by GILES
An imprint of D Giles Limited
66 High Street,
Lewes, BN7 1XG, UK
gilesltd.com

EU GPSR authorised representative
LOGOS EUROPE, 9 rue Nicolas Poussin, 17000,
La Rochelle, France
E-mail: contact@logoseurope.eu

ISBN: 978-1-913875-80-0

For Dixon Gallery and Gardens: Julie Pierotti, Martha R. Robinson Curator
For Ordrupgaard: Dorthe Vangsgaard Nielsen, Senior Curator
For Joslyn Art Museum: Taylor J. Acosta, Chief Curator & Director of Collections

For D Giles Limited:
Copy-edited and proofread by Sarah Kane
Designed by Alfonso Iacurci
Produced by GILES, an imprint of D Giles Limited
Printed and bound in Europe

All measurements are in inches and centimeters; height precedes width precedes depth.

Dixon Gallery and Gardens
4339 Park Avenue,
Memphis, Tennessee 38117
dixon.org

Front cover: James Tissot, *The Artists' Wives* (cat. 20 detail), 1885, Chrysler Museum of Art
Back cover: Juan Gris, *Man in a Café* (cat. 63), 1912, Philadelphia Museum of Art
Frontispiece: Édouard Vuillard, *Café Wepler* (cat. 59 detail), ca. 1908–10, reworked in 1912, The Cleveland Museum of Art

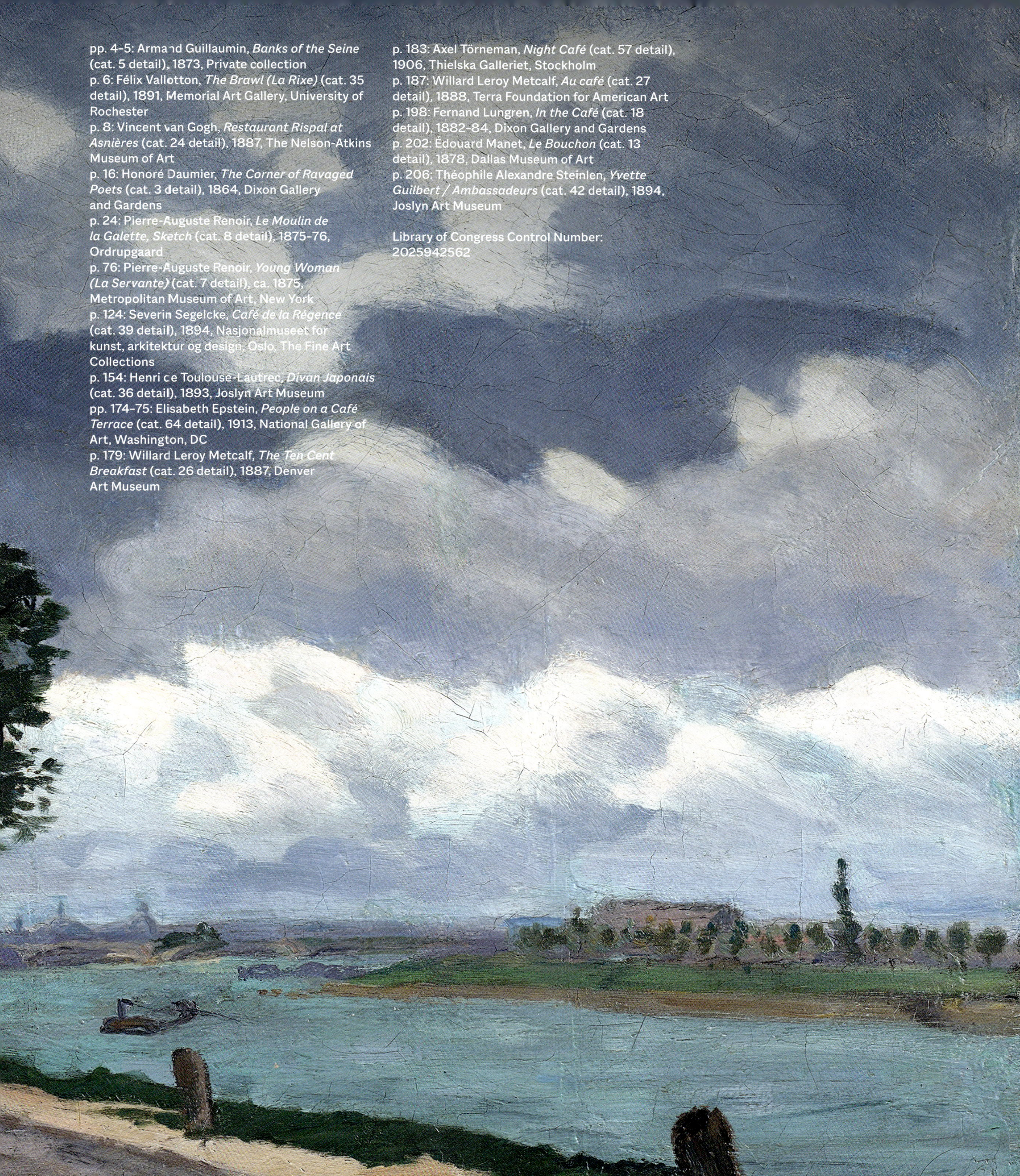

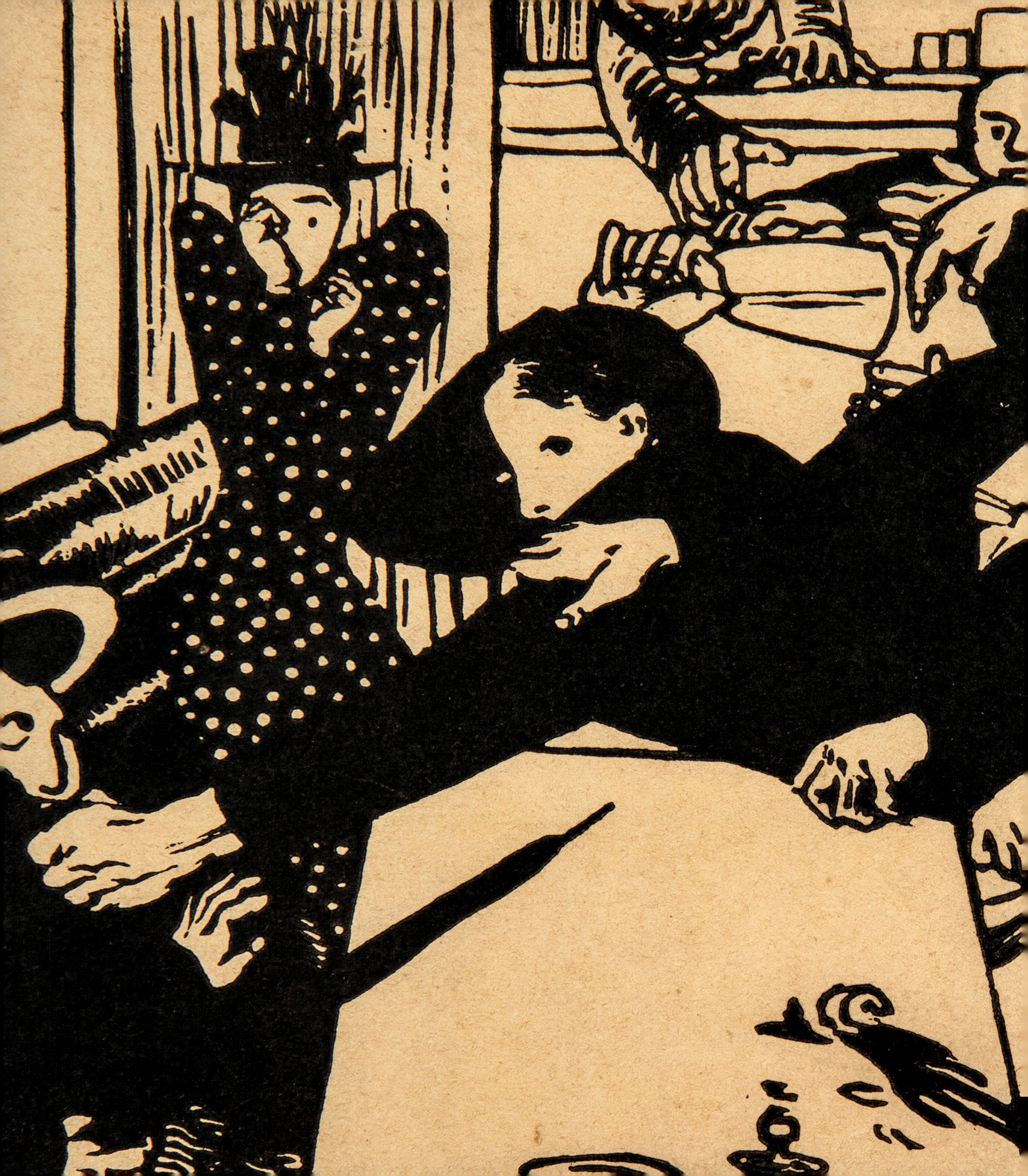

CONTENTS

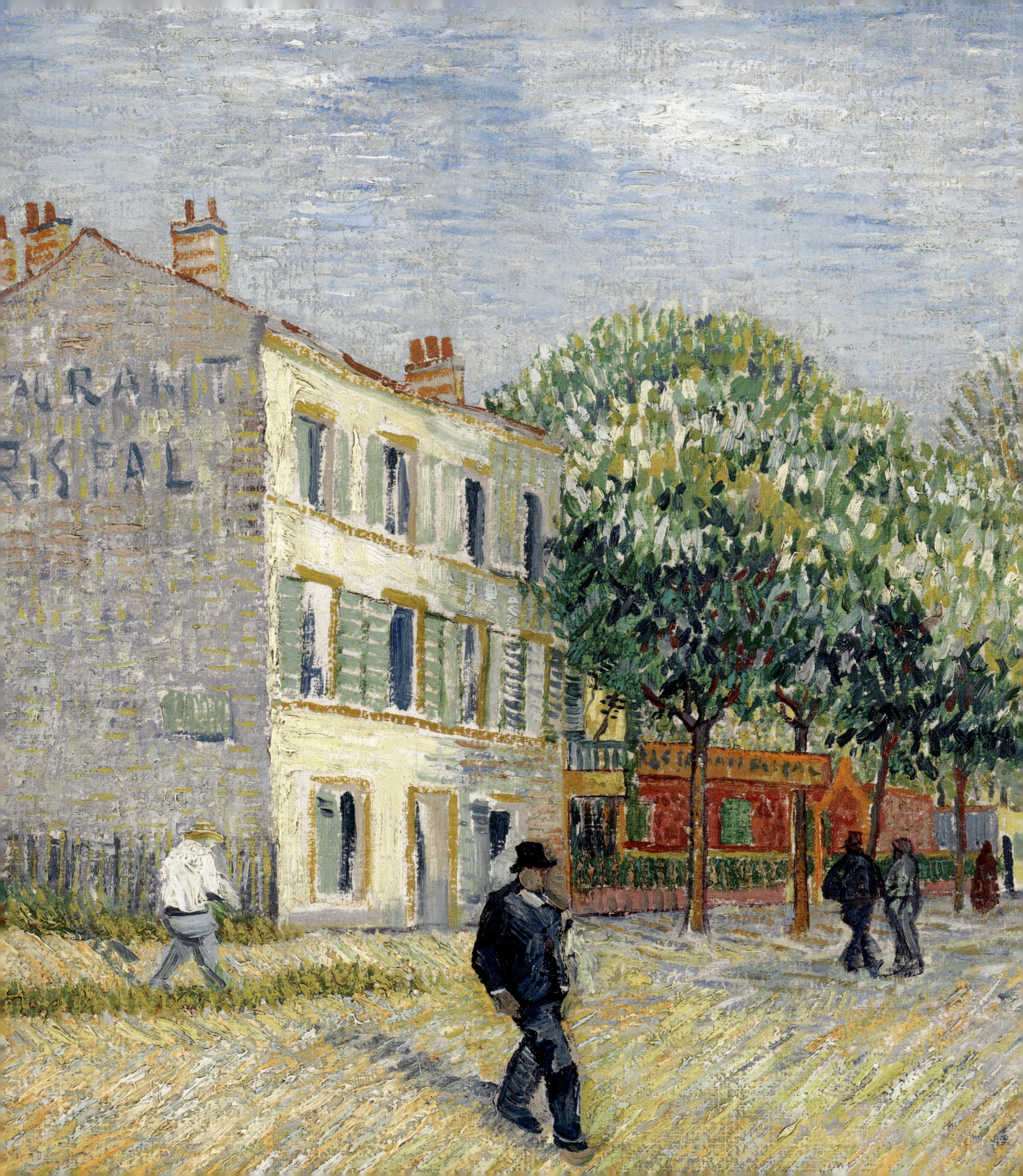
AURANT
RISPAL
RESTAURANT RISPAL

L'ADDITION, S'IL VOUS PLAÎT

Jack Becker, Gertrud Oelsner, Kevin Sharp

Some of the most resonant and compelling exhibitions produced by art museums in recent years have not been the familiar career retrospectives of well-known artists or group shows that illuminate a particular segment of art history. Lately, it has rather been the thematic exhibitions that have caught our interest, and, at the same time, captured the public imagination. These projects have placed many of those same well-known artists and their lesser-known colleagues into absorbing contexts that were and are relevant to their times and to ours.[1] *Café Society: Art and Sociability in Belle Époque Paris*, we believe, will be a significant addition to that roster of exhibitions.

At the Dixon Gallery and Gardens in Memphis, the curatorial team has been discussing the possibility of a show about café culture in Paris for at least fifteen years. It probably started with a small but marvelous Jean-Louis Forain gouache and watercolor painting called *Café Interior* (ca. 1879, cat. 14) that had entered the Dixon collection in 1993. The artist thought enough of the work that he included it among his submissions to the fourth Impressionist exhibition in 1879 (his debut with the group). The Dixon in turn featured it prominently in the Forain retrospective we organized in 2011 with the Musée du Petit Palais in Paris.[2] This charming, but also caustic and revealing work may have launched our interest in cafés as creative incubators of late nineteenth- and early twentieth-century French painting.

Despite our interest in the subject, no such café-themed exhibition ever quite materialized at the Dixon. Other projects, artists, shows, and opportunities seemed to repeatedly push "Café Society" deeper onto our exhibition calendar. Then, in 2018, an intriguing canvas of a Parisian café interior by a relatively little-known American painter named Fernand Lungren turned up on the New York art market. Lungren was best remembered as a landscapist, painting in the American

West. But for a brief interval in the early 1880s, he was charmed by the Parisian demimonde and the cafés that were so often their haunts. Lungren's *In the Café* (1882–84, cat. 18) entered the Dixon collection in 2018 and more or less instantly sealed our commitment to "Café Society."[3]

Although the notion of a show called *Café Society* originated at the Dixon Gallery and Gardens, the project has been very much a collaboration between the three outstanding art museums that are hosting the exhibition. Ordrupgaard, in Charlottenlund just outside of Copenhagen, Denmark, possesses world-class collections of French and Danish paintings and a long history of producing groundbreaking shows. Among those stellar projects was the 2024 exhibition *Impressionism and Its Overlooked Women*, to which the Dixon loaned paintings from its collection by Mary Cassatt and Berthe Morisot. It was one of the more compelling and thoughtful shows to commemorate the 150th anniversary of the first Impressionist exhibition in 1874.[4]

The loan of the Cassatt and Morisot paintings to *Impressionism and Its Overlooked Women* helped kindle a dialogue between Ordrupgaard and the Dixon, which quickly turned into an eager conversation about working together on some future exhibition. Discussions between the curators of both institutions about sharing *Café Society* began almost immediately and came together, we are pleased to report, with astonishing swiftness.

By then, the Joslyn Art Museum in Omaha, Nebraska, had already signed on with the Dixon to co-organize *Café Society*. Having just completed a major expansion of their facilities, designed by the international architecture firm Snøhetta, the Joslyn staff were eager to develop meaningful exhibitions both to coincide with the opening of their new building and in the years that followed. Joslyn and Dixon had worked together or shared no fewer than four exhibitions between 2013

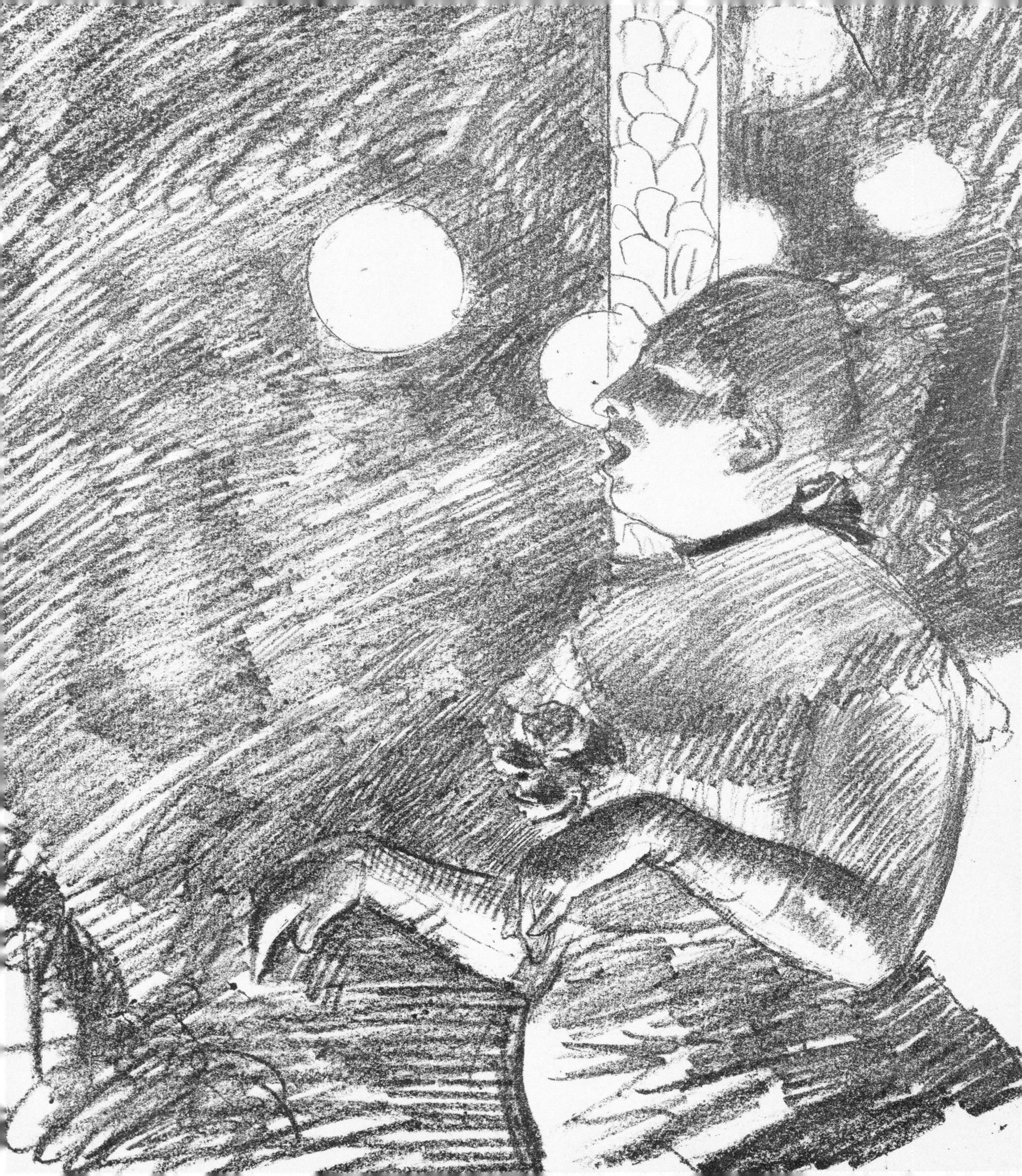

and 2025, and the opportunity to collaborate on *Café Society*, to once again bring the strength of each institution's collection to the service of an important exhibition, was an attractive opportunity for both museums.[5]

As it happened, Snøhetta, the architecture firm, had also designed an important and much-discussed expansion of the Ordrupgaard facilities that was only completed in 2021.[6] It was mere coincidence that two institutions on two different continents, Ordrupgaard and Joslyn, found themselves planning an exhibition together after recently working with one of the more celebrated design firms in the world. It may have had nothing to do with Ordrupgaard's and Joslyn's decision to become co-organizers of *Café Society* with the Dixon, but in building international art museum partnerships—typically the sole province of very large institutions—any shared experience and common ground can make a difference. Regardless of the no doubt many complex reasons why Ordrupgaard, Dixon, and Joslyn elected to work together on *Café Society*, the leadership and staffs of these three potent institutions are pleased to have entered into this collaboration and hope it may be the first of many to follow.

Their exceptionally high degree of difficulty and startling expense make international loan exhibitions such as *Café Society* some of the most challenging undertakings any art museum can embrace—which is why this arena is often left to just a handful of very large institutions in most countries. But complexity and costs are only part of it. To bring this type of project to successful completion requires vision, expertise, resourcefulness, and resolve. We are pleased and proud to have these qualities on the curatorial teams of Ordrupgaard, Dixon, and Joslyn. From its first glimmer

of life, going as far back as 2011, *Café Society* has been championed by Julie Pierotti, the Dixon's Martha R. Robinson Curator. We feel deeply gratified that this project she believes in so strongly is now finally coming to fruition. At Ordrupgaard, Senior Curator Dorthe Vangsgaard Nielsen advocated for the exhibition from the first proposal and has introduced brilliant Scandinavian artists and their Parisian travels into the discussion of the city's cafés. Taylor J. Acosta, the Chief Curator and Director of Collections at the Joslyn Art Museum, has shown similar faith in the project, and brought another strong and effective curatorial voice to the exhibition.

From our opening in 1976, leaders of the Dixon Gallery and Gardens have wisely known that the kind of energy generated from self-organized exhibitions cannot be replicated or understated. Since 2007, the Dixon has organized more than sixty of our own exhibitions, many of which have traveled to no fewer than fifty museums around the world. This incredible feat for a small museum in Memphis, Tennessee, means that we have leaned heavily on our colleagues in the art world over and over again. This was especially true for *Café Society*, when we were asking for major works of art from major institutions for a three-venue project. We were so gratified by the generosity of our colleagues and the consideration they have shown us in the planning of this project. Therefore, we would like to thank Guillaume Ambroise, Sylvain Amic, Agustín Arteaga, Temma Balducci, Andrea Barnwell Brownlee, Emily Beeny, Peter Bell, Andreas Bertman, Juliane Betz, Paula Binari, Sofia Biondi, Rachel Bradshaw, Galerie Brame & Lorenceau, Virginia Brilliant, Heather Lemonedes Brown, Hannah Byers, Thomas P. Campbell, Laura Cantone, André Cariou, Cailin Carter, Mark Castro, Åsa Cavalli-Björkman,

Johan Cederlund, Harry Cooper, Sharon Corwin, Philipp Demandt, Ghislain d'Humieres, Angelica Daneo, Kimberly Davis, Katrina and Steve Denegri, Christiane Dole, Katherine Drake, Ela Dutta, Tricia Earl, Alexander Eiling, Kaywin Feldman, Emily Foss, Turry Flucker, Valérie Fours, Tucker Garrison, Kristin Margrethe Gaukstad, Tracee Glab, Emilie Gordenker, Dunia Grandi, Anne Gregersen, William M. Griswold, Gloria Groom, Maud Guichané, Katie Hanson, Christoph Heinrich, Max Hollein, Sarah Jesse, Susan and Darryl Johnson, Georgina Kelman, Holly Keris, Thomas Kinservik, John Kirkland, Cameron Kitchin, Alicja Knast, Sarah Kohn, Samantha Koslow, Catherine Le Guen, Kimmo Levä, Isabella Lores-Chavez, Lisbeth Lund, Natalie Mead, Asher Miller, Gretchen Shie Miller, Tomi Moisio, Betty and Jack Moore, Janet Moore, Nicole Myers, Asma Naeem, Erik Neil, Melanie Neil, Riitta Ojanperä, Regina Palm, Guillaume Parage, Pam Parry, Isolde Pludermacher, Laura Quintrell, Verena Rayer, Chris and Dan Richards, Katharine Richardson, Penelope Riley, Fleur Roos Rosa de Carvalho, Valerio Mazzetti Rossi, William Rudolph, Ingrid Røynesdal, Salvador Salort-Pons, Polly Sartori, Jamiee Shim, Janne Sirén, Pauli Sivonen, Jessica Smith, Anne-Laure Sol, Barbi Spieler, Molly Stark, Alexandra Suda, Erno Tainio, Pierre Terjanian, Gary Tinterow, Grace Trumbo, Møyfrid Tveit, Vic Verhasselt, Eric Weider, Jørgen Westad, Ortrud Westheider, Elizabeth Williams, Emily Willkom, and Julián Zugazagoitia.

The Dixon's ambitious exhibition program is supported each year by a dedicated community of donors who believe in our curatorial program and in the power of exhibitions to enrich our city. We would like to express our gratitude to the Joe Orgill Family Fund for Exhibitions, Kathy and Ben Adams, the Armstrong Company, Susan and Damon Arney, Amelia and Mike Bailey, Kathy and Jack Blair, Fran and Rusty Bloodworth, Paul and Suzanne Rhea Burgar, Alice and Phil Burnett, Kate and Michael Buttarazzi, Marilyn Rhea Cheeseman, Holly and Paul T. Combs, Jane and Mike Coop, Alice and Matt Crow, Robert Dodge and Patti McNeil, Karen and Preston Dorsett, the William B. "Billy" Dunavant Foundation, the Theodore W. and Betty J. Eckels Foundation, Andrea and Doug Edwards, First Horizon Bank, Marylon Rogers Glass, Amanda and Nick Goetze, Jenny and Ellis Haddad, Martha and Mike Hess, Julie and Rob Hussey, Rose M. Johnston, Anne and Mike Keeney, Nell R. Levy, Kay and Jim Liles, Gloria and Doug Marchant, Debbie and Chip Marston, Mabel and Phil McNeill, Snow and Henry Morgan, Brandon and Joe Morrison, Nancy and Steve Morrow, Opus East Memphis, Irene Orgill, Gwen and Penn Owen, Linda Pelts, Chris and Dan Richards, Trish and Carl Ring, the Scheidt Family Foundation, the Mary and Jeff Simpson Charitable Trust, Irene and Fred Smith, Kaki and Vince Smith, Dorothy Stevenson, Susan Adler Thorp, Ainslie and Hardy Todd, Shirley and Bob Turner, Adele Wellford, Barbara and Lewis Williamson, and Lucy Woodson and Bob Berry for making this exhibition and publication possible through their generosity.

Over the many years of its gestation, *Café Society* has been overseen with advice and enthusiasm by the Dixon's Visual Arts Committee, a sub-committee of the Board of Trustees that provides essential supervision of the museum's curatorial activities. Julie Pierotti would like to thank members Markova Reed Anderson, Essie Arrindell-Williams, Debi Havner, John Horseman, Rose Johnston, Anne Keeney, JJ Keras, Barbara Lapides, Kay Liles, Linda Mallory, Suzanne Mallory, Jackie Mandell, Steve Ross, Susan Adler Thorp, and Barbara Williamson for their kind and wise counsel throughout the development of this exhibition.

The catalogue you are holding is a true collaboration between historians, curators, and a talented group of designers. We are grateful to have Dr. W. Scott Haine and Dr. Jeffrey H. Jackson, two historians noted internationally for their groundbreaking research on Parisian café culture, as contributors to this publication. Both Scott and Jeff have been enthusiastic supporters of this exhibition, and we are so pleased to have had the opportunity to work with them. Taylor J. Acosta, Dorthe Vangsgaard Nielsen, and Julie Pierotti have all contributed essays to this publication that illuminate the connections between cafés and the visual arts in nineteenth- and early twentieth-century Paris. Ellen Daugherty and Corkey Sinks, the Dixon's Assistant Curator and Graphic Designer respectively, worked creatively and meticulously to produce the map of important Parisian cafés for artists in the appendices of this book, and Camryn Moore, Rae and Bill Dyer Curatorial Assistant at the Joslyn, provided support on the map and on the Exhibition Checklist. Dixon Registrar Kristen Kimberling's great work managing images for this publication was also vital to its success.

In producing *Café Society*, Dan Giles has been an eager and encouraging friend from the beginning, and we thank him and his team, including Liz Japes, Allison McCormick, and Louise Ramsay, for their organization and creativity in designing and printing this attractive catalogue.

The staff of the Ordrupgaard, Dixon Gallery and Gardens, and Joslyn Art Museum put their hearts and souls into ensuring that each exhibition has the greatest impact possible on our community. At the Ordrupgaard, we would like to acknowledge Malene Anthon, Dorthe Vangsgaard Nielsen, Signe Kristensen Stranddorf, Johannes Preetzmann, and Babette Honoré for their excellent work and collegiality in the planning of this exhibition. For his extensive and thorough work on the translation of this catalogue into Danish, the Ordrupgaard team would like to thank René Lauritsen. Finally, the Ordrupgaard would like to express their gratitude to the A.P. Møller Fonden, Augustinus Fonden, Ny Carlsbergfondet, and Aage og Johanne Louis-Hansens Fond for their support.

For their dedication to the Dixon, we would like to thank Miguel Alcantar, Christan Allen, Melvin Avendano, Juliana Bjorklund, Jake Blair, Marlin Burnwatt, Cindy Cobb, Ellen Daugherty, Jenny Duggan, Chris Emanus, Erika Fuller, Wanda Gaines, Jeff Goggans, Dan Goodwin, Rebekah Hedges, Braden Hixson, Anna Hood, Gail Hopper, Susan Johnson, Hope Jones, Robert Jones, Shawn Jones, Kristen Kimberling, LaArie King, Sarah Lorenz, Kyle McLane, Jorden Miernik-Walker, Lacy Mitcham, Norma Montesi, David Pender, Lorenzo Perez, Julie Pierotti, Adam Queen, Kristen Rambo, Hannah Reasons, Della Rhodes, Christine Ruby, Margarita Sandino, Corkey Sinks, Dale Skaggs, Sarah Stobbe, Rachel Sturch, Dorothy Svgdik, Stephanie Valentine, Cameron Waters, Shawna White, Jessie Wiley, and Charlene Williams.

At the Joslyn Art Museum, we offer our sincere thanks to Taylor J. Acosta, Candace Berger, Kristin Bergquist, Jordan Cairncross, Kristy Durkin, Jennifer Gleason Gillen, Sarah Haines, Rebecca Manning, Graycen Marquart, Camryn Moore, Julie Oberlies, Nancy Round, Amy Rummel, Kevin Salzman, and Jim Sullivan.

Finally, for the unwavering support they have given us in the planning and execution of this exhibition, we reserve our greatest thanks for Lester Katz, Matthew Loftus, Ronald Pierotti, and Erin Riordan.

Dr. Jack Becker
Executive Director & CEO
Joslyn Art Museum

Gertrud Oelsner
Director
Ordrupgaard

Kevin Sharp
Linda W. and S. Herbert Rhea Director
Dixon Gallery and Gardens

Endnotes

1. Among the many notable exhibitions and publications that we could cite are: *Splendeurs et Misères: Images de la Prostitution, 1850–1910* at the Musée d'Orsay, Paris (2015–16); *World War I and the Visual Arts* at the Metropolitan Museum of Art, New York (2017–18); and *Soul of a Nation: Art in the Age of Black Power 1963–1983* at Tate Modern, London, and other venues (2017–20).

2. *Jean-Louis Forain: La Comédie parisienne*, with a catalogue edited by Florence Valdès-Forain.

3. The Dixon acquired Fernand Lungren's *In the Café* from Questroyal Fine Art in New York. The purchase was supported by a bequest from Cecil Williams Marshall.

4. The exhibition, which later traveled to the National Gallery of Ireland in Dublin, was accompanied by a catalogue edited by Dorthe Vangsgaard Nielsen.

5. The Dixon and Joslyn worked together on *Renoir to Chagall: Paris and the Allure of Color* (2013); *Wild Spaces, Open Seasons: Hunting and Fishing in American Art* (2016–17); *Illuminating the Word: The Saint John's Bible* appeared at both institutions (2019–20); and *All Aboard: The Railroad in American Art* (2024–25).

6. The literature on Snøhetta is large and varied. But see, for example, *Snøhetta: Collective Intuition* (New York: Phaidon Press, 2019).

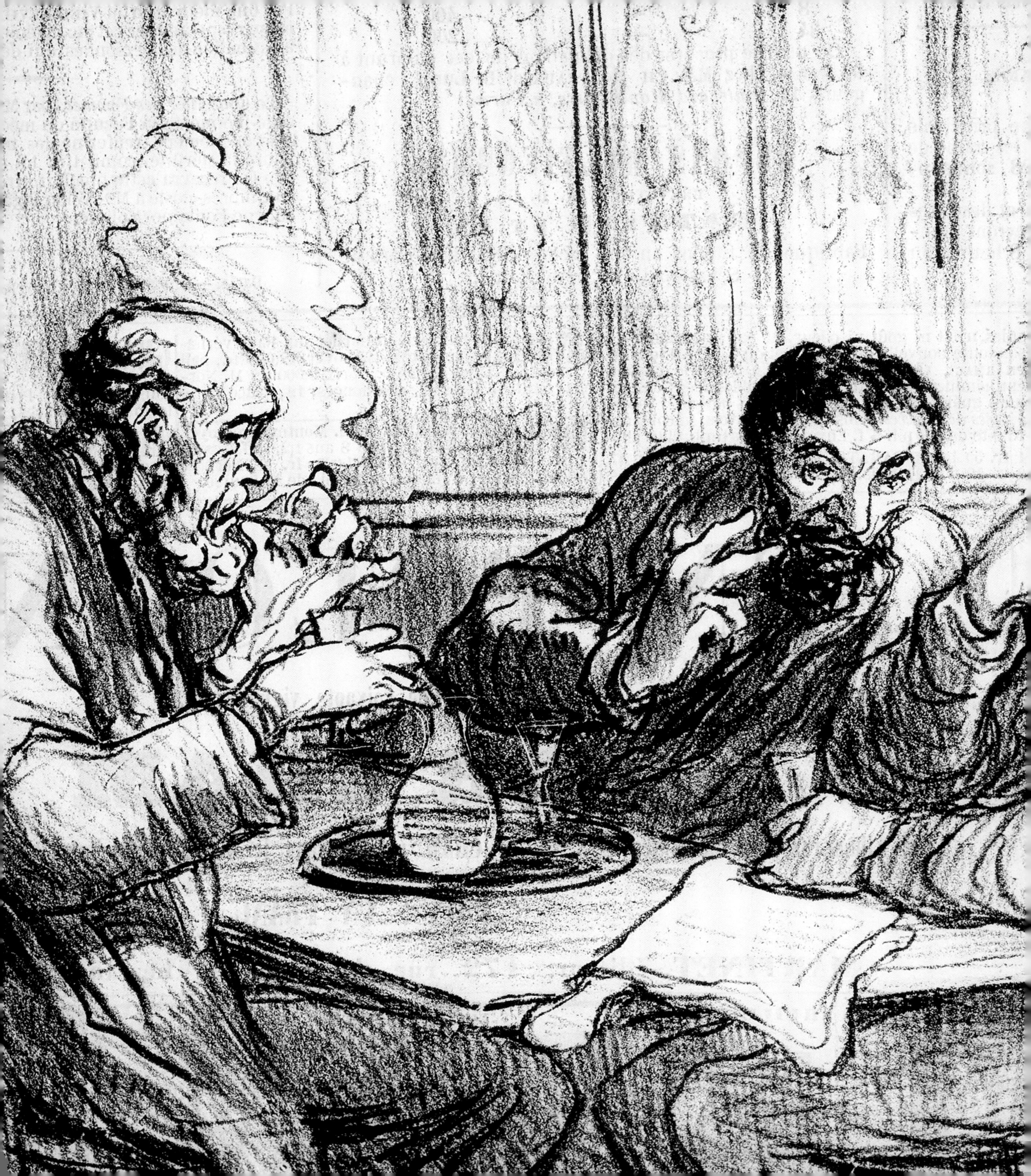

THE CAFÉ IS A "THINKING SPACE"

W. Scott Haine & Jeffrey H. Jackson

What can cafés teach us in an age of internet connectivity? Born in seventeenth-century London, the modern café has long allowed people to spend the day reading, thinking, or relaxing for only the price of a drink. But they have also done something more crucial: as hubs of activity, cafés allow patrons to find others with whom to share and debate their thoughts. Cafés created the first social networking sites.

A twenty-first-century creative economy thrives on precisely these kinds of places that we have dubbed "thinking spaces."[1] The best offer two key elements: time for individual thought and the ability to enjoy in-depth conversations. Innovation comes from a balance of both social engagement and quiet time.

Many offices, especially in the high-tech sector, have discovered the power of the thinking space. Years ago, Apple founder Steve Jobs insisted that a corporate headquarters should allow random, spontaneous, serendipitous sociability. Such well-designed offices have proven to be some of the most creative places around. The phenomenon of "co-working," where freelancers or business travelers focus on different projects for different employers while using a common space, is based on the premise that we work best when we are in a community, even when our ideas are heading in different directions. Shifts brought about by the 2020 global pandemic and other economic trends, including office downsizing and remote work, have altered the patterns of where and when people work. Yet they haven't changed the need for collaboration, whether in person or in a video meeting.

These may seem like recent ideas, but the original model for the "thinking space" was the café, and, in cities like Paris, Vienna, Rome, and New York, such venues became famous for helping birth cutting-edge artistic movements and fervent political ideologies. Revolutionaries, philosophers, and artists all had their favorite haunts, each with its own flavor—there was

a café for everyone and every interest. They were the incubators of "bohemianism," the avant-garde practice of living on the edge for the sake of one's highly idiosyncratic ideas. In many ways, that artistic ingenuity was the origin point of our internet-based world because in a creative economy we're all bohemians or "content creators" now.

The images in this exhibition capture the range of people, places, activities, and interactions that made the café such an important space throughout history. Take a look at the human variety in these depictions of Parisian cafés: artists, musicians, and writers; dandies, oddballs, and lovers; laborers, socialites, and prostitutes; dancers, singers, and actors; partiers, alcoholics, and loners. All shared the desire to be with others, and the artists who captured their lives on paper or canvas have enabled us to see just how the café fulfilled their needs. Jean-Louis Forain shows the range of society and silence that made a thinking space in his watercolor *Café Interior* (ca. 1879, cat. 14). Groups sit around in conversation while the man in the lower left corner appears to be alone in quiet contemplation. The men on the painting's right ogle the standing woman, but she looks away—whether playing hard-to-get or simply to entertain thoughts of her own. One can envision groups and individuals ebbing and flowing throughout the evening, speaking for a while and then moving on to new arrangements. Imagine the millions of conversations taking place on the night Forain shows us, as this diverse mix of people watched, listened to, brushed against, and argued with one another. How many new ideas or relationships might have come from this particular combination of people?

And yet, as they mingled, café-goers were also able to pull themselves out into their own world. Émile-Othon Friesz captures the thinking space dynamic very clearly in *Scene in a Parisian Brasserie* (ca. 1905–6, cat. 56). Here, two women and a man sit "alone together." One reads a book, one sips a drink,

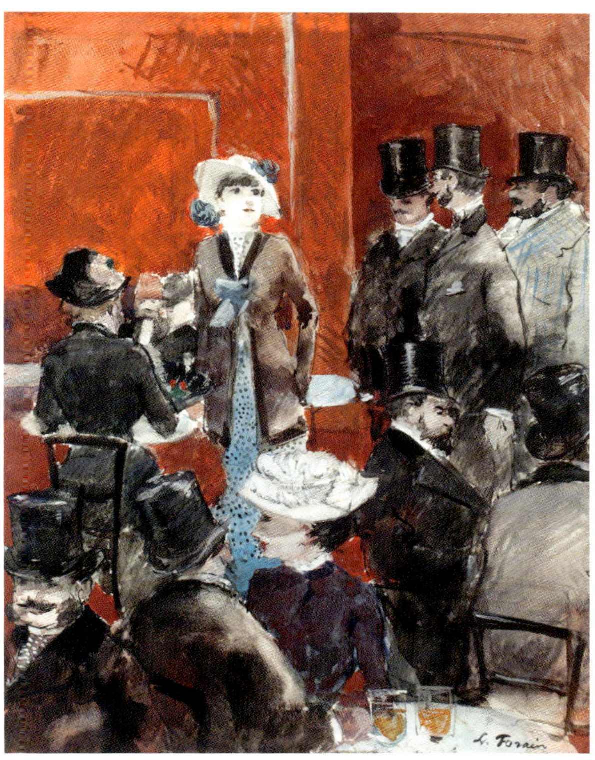

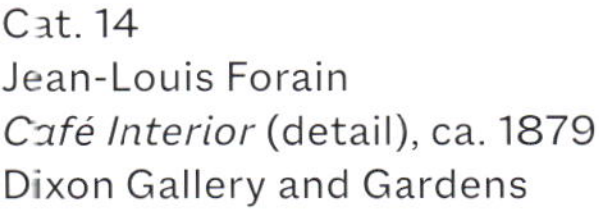

Cat. 14
Jean-Louis Forain
Café Interior (detail), ca. 1879
Dixon Gallery and Gardens

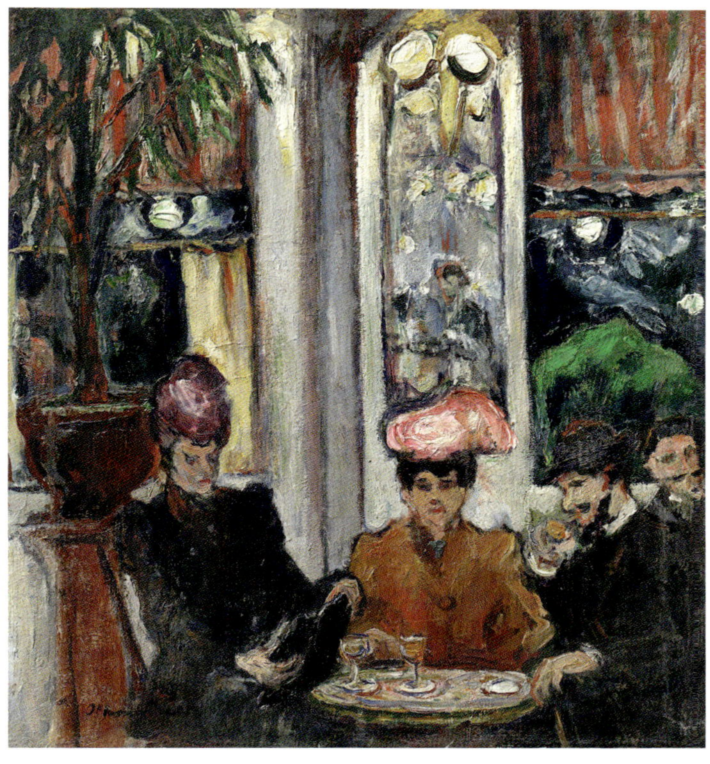

Cat. 56
Émile-Othon Friesz
Scene in a Parisian Brasserie (detail),
ca. 1905–6
Museum Barberini

and the third looks straight ahead. Each seems to be isolated, and yet the table they share keeps them connected. In the moment Friesz captures, these people seem to have little to do with one another, but in the next they could easily resume a conversation or share a joke. The woman with the book could put down her tome and relate what she has just read to her companions. The café has brought them together in the same place and time, allowing them to engage and disengage, perhaps numerous times over the course of an afternoon's leisure.

Spanish painter Santiago Rusiñol also shows a thinking space in his *Café des Incohérents* (1889–90, fig. 1). This Parisian artist's hangout is basic and dim, much like the faces of the customers, among which artist Maurice Utrillo in the background and fellow Spaniard Ramon Casas staring at the woman across

the table. The place has brought together a strange mix of objects—including the scale model of the Eiffel Tower, various Asian masks, and several paintings by younger artists—and a diverse group of people seated across the long, thin tables that bring them face-to-face with other bohemians engaged in artistic pursuits.[2]

Yet those creative conversations have not always been always easy or straightforward, and several artists in this exhibition give powerful glimpses of the complexities of cafés as thinking spaces. André Devambez depicts an important and very recognizable figure crucial to the art world, the over sixty-year-old Victorine Meurent. A singer and cancan dancer who was a youthful model for numerous artists (she was the scandalous nude at the center of Manet's boundary-breaking *Olympia*), she later became an established painter in her own right and showed work

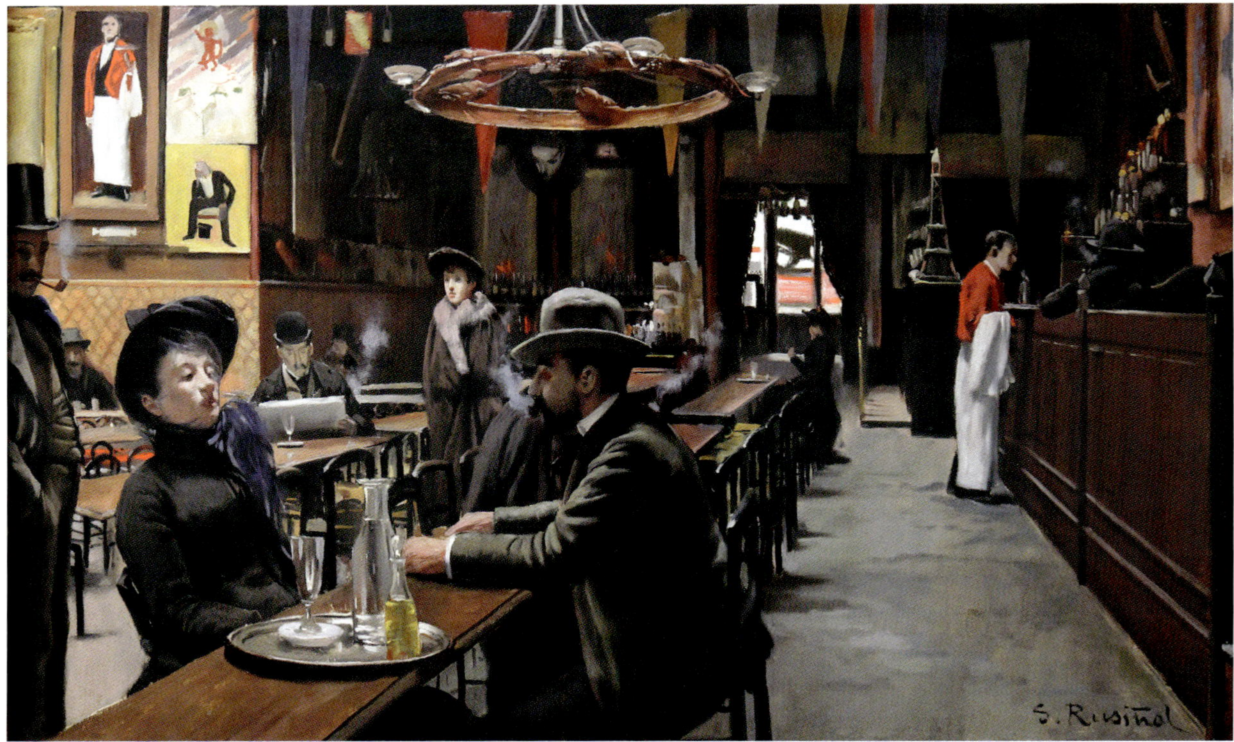

Fig. 1
Santiago Rusiñol
Spanish, 1861–1931
Café des Incohérents, 1889–90
Oil on canvas
31 ½ × 45 ⅝ in. (80 × 116 cm)
Museu de Montserrat; Gift of J. Sala Ardiz,
R.N. 200.532

at the Paris Salon. The figure slumped over his beer is likely the Symbolist poet Paul Verlaine.[3] The unknown others in the image, busy drinking and arguing, suggest the creative give-and-take of café debate. But Devambez titles this piece *Les Incompris* (ca. 1904, cat. 52), which means "the misunderstood," echoing the title of Rusiñol's painting which translates as "the incoherent ones." These names imply that confusion, uncertainty, and a willingness to confront hard truths are part of the creative process. They also remind us that bohemian artists were often the rebellious outsiders because their challenging ideas did not fit comfortably with most conventional wisdom. The once shockingly beautiful Meurent has aged to a masculine-looking figure, her

infamously nude body now obscured by a bulky red coat. Verlaine's poetry dwelled on themes of decay, decadence, and oddly emotional experiences in veiled, impressionistic language. Perhaps the difficulties of life that these figures represent—the vagaries of ageing, the power of the irrational—could only be hashed out in the café with others whose worldviews did not sit comfortably with those of the mainstream. Those are often precisely the kinds of ideas that require a dedicated thinking space.

In *Au Café* (ca. 1877–80, fig. 2), Edgar Degas shows how the need for isolation and society can coexist in a creative tension. The two women in the painting are talking, perhaps about something urgent given the

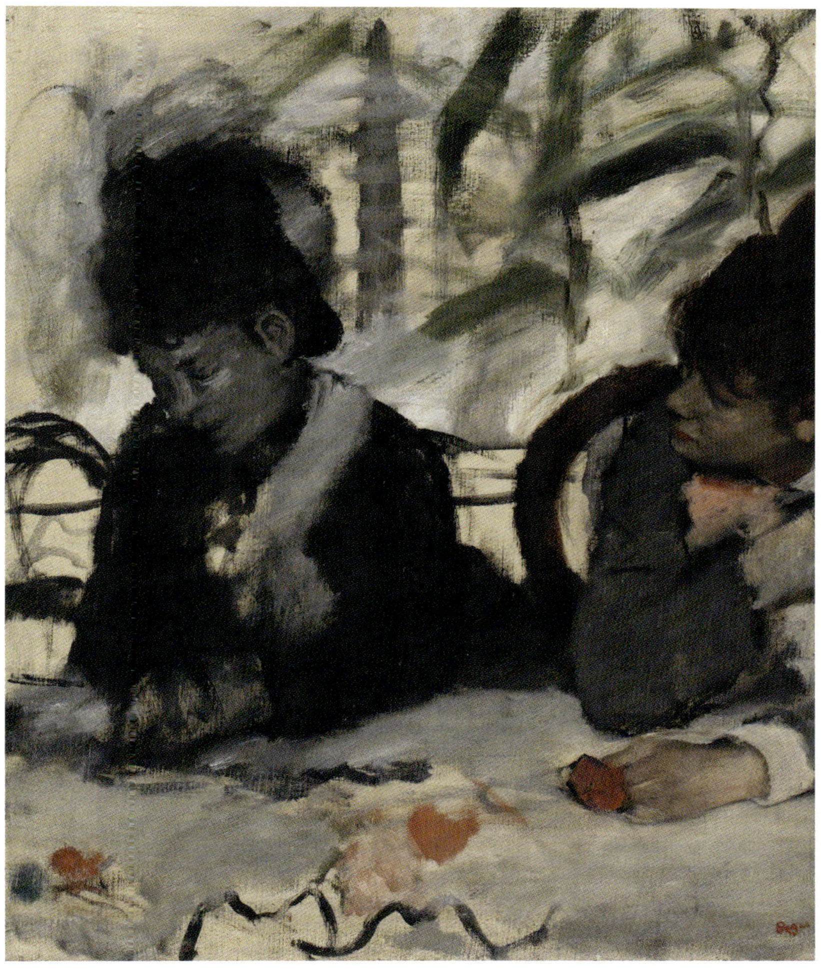

Fig. 2
Edgar Degas
French, 1834–1917
Au Café, ca. 1875–77
Oil on canvas
25 ⅞ × 21 ½ in. (65.7 × 54.6 cm)
Fitzwilliam Museum, Cambridge;
Bequeathed by Frank Hindley Smith, 1939

concerned looks on their faces. Yet as one stares at her companion, the other turns away. They are sharing intense thoughts and feelings, but the power of their conversation almost seems too much to bear for the woman on the left. Likely surrounded by a café full of people, they "huddle together in a conspiratorial manner" in a bubble of their own which Degas highlights by making us watch a private moment taking place

in a room full of strangers.[4] But when the time is right, they could leave that privacy and seek out others who are just beyond the frame of Degas's canvas.

The power of cafés is not relegated to the past nor has it shifted entirely to the workplace. Cafés can still be the incubators of innovation, yet ironically, despite the growing number of coffee shops and their historic role, places that offer a blend of isolation and sociability have been replaced by sites where we are alone in public. Starbucks and many other chains have brought elements of the café tradition into the present, but customers in these places cut themselves off with earbuds and laptops; outside the cities where people walk or take mass transit, the bulk of Starbucks' business takes place at the drive-through window. For those who go inside, how many people truly discuss ideas with someone at Starbucks on a regular basis? Each of us still needs privacy to cultivate our own unique voice and generate ideas, but we must also refine those notions through conversation, brainstorming, and exchanges. Without that balance, great ideas can suffer in silence or be subsumed in groupthink.

It doesn't have to be this way, and cafés can still offer inspiration. When one New Haven, Connecticut, coffee shop banned laptops, business boomed as people came in for human interaction rather than the wi-fi. Some cafés offer patrons a sign to place on their table that invites others to sit down and talk. Nearly all university libraries and many office buildings provide a café where people gather to study or converse. Meet-ups often happen in cafés and bars to bring people together and share new ideas. And, just like the historic venues in Paris which attracted particular clienteles, themed venues—from knitting cafés to cat cafés to chess and board game cafés—now unite people with common interests.

These new approaches to re-creating the café represent a self-conscious effort to combat the

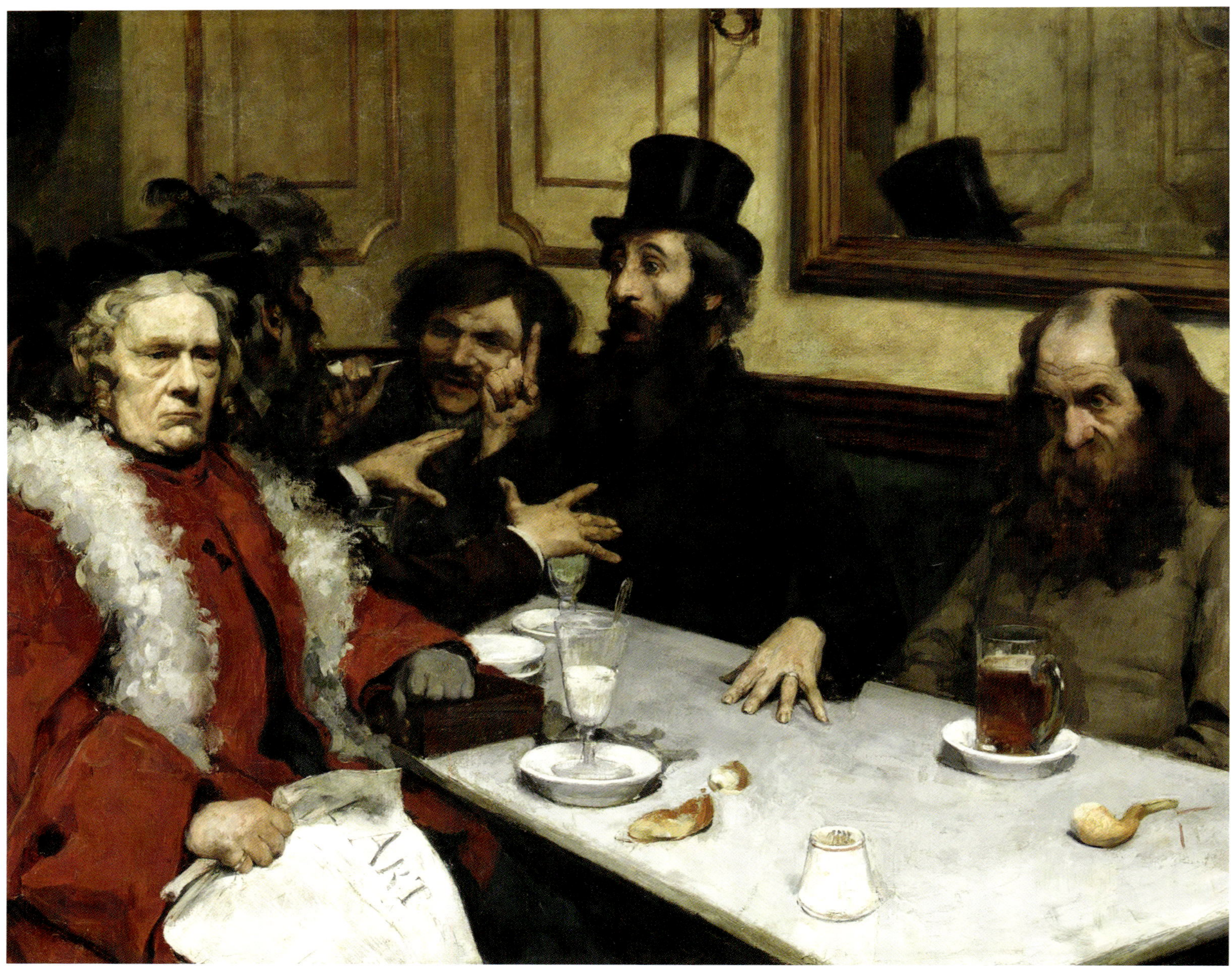

Cat. 52

André Devambez
French, 1867–1944
Les Incompris, ca. 1904
Oil on canvas
36 ¼ × 44 in. (92 × 112 cm)
Musée des Beaux-Arts de Quimper, Bequest
of Corentin-Guyho, 1936

tendency toward isolation and allow for that crucial balance of private thoughts and public conversation. An old-fashioned activity like talking is not efficient in modern technological terms, and it certainly requires more than a social media post. But as creativity increasingly becomes a necessity at work, the tried-and-true model of the café as a thinking space may provide a way to update an old idea for a new era.

And the images in this exhibition remind us of what a truly powerful and transformative place a good café can be.

Endnotes

1. For more on this concept, see Leona Rittner, W. Scott Haine, and Jeffrey H. Jackson, eds., *The Thinking Space: The Café as a Cultural Institution in Paris, Italy and Vienna* (London: Routledge, 2013).

2. Gabriel P. Weisberg, "Discovering Sites: Enervating Signs for the Spanish *Modernistas*," in *Montmartre and the Making of Mass Culture*, ed. Gabriel Weisberg (New Brunswick, NJ: Rutgers University Press, 2001), 247–72.

3. https://www.mbaq. fr/fr/nos-collections/ ecole-francaise-du-19e-siecle/andre- devambez-les-incompris-434.html.

4. https://artuk.org/discover/ stories/edgar-degas-at-the-cafe.

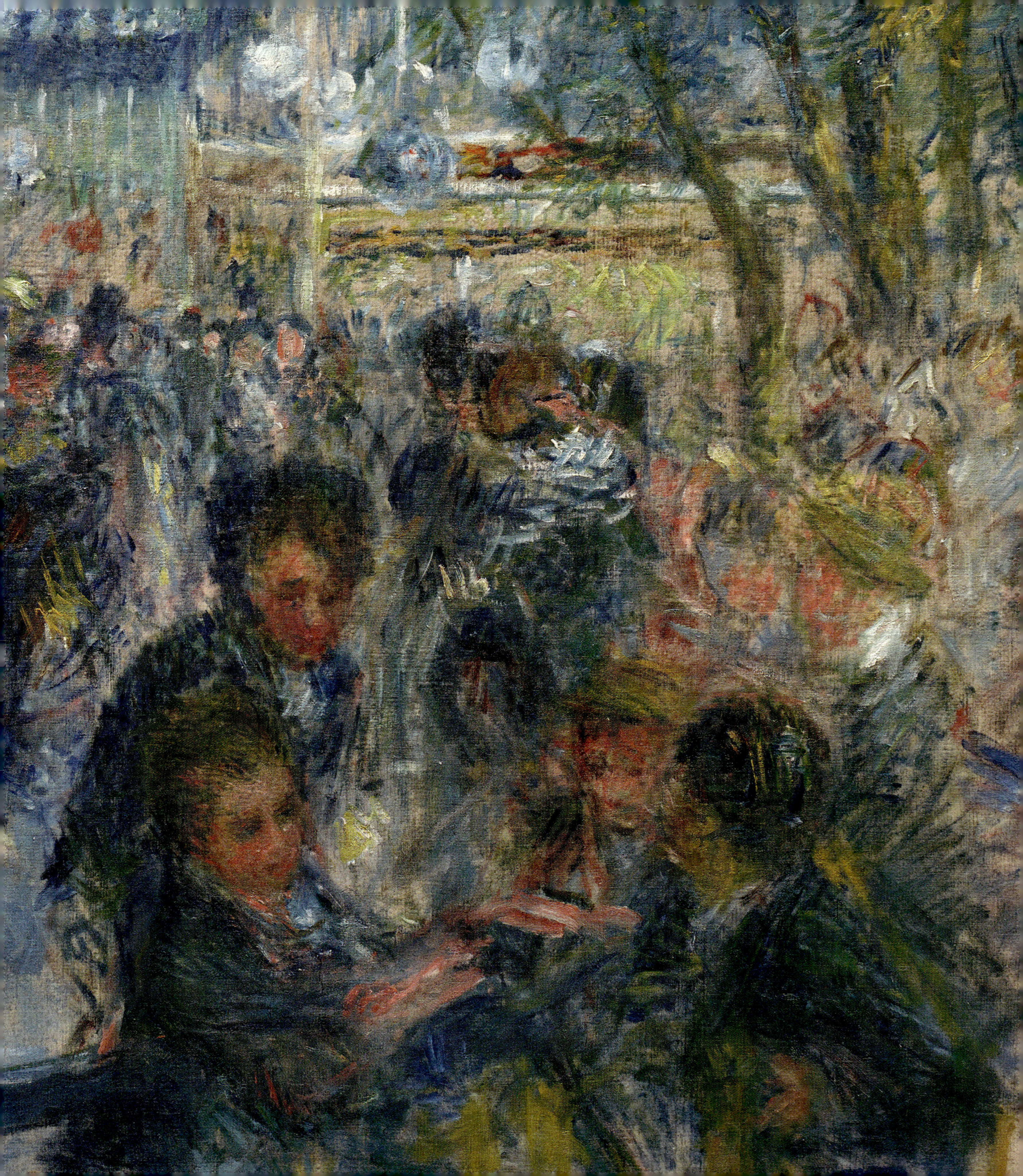

CAFÉS AND THE CITY OF PARIS

Jeffrey H. Jackson

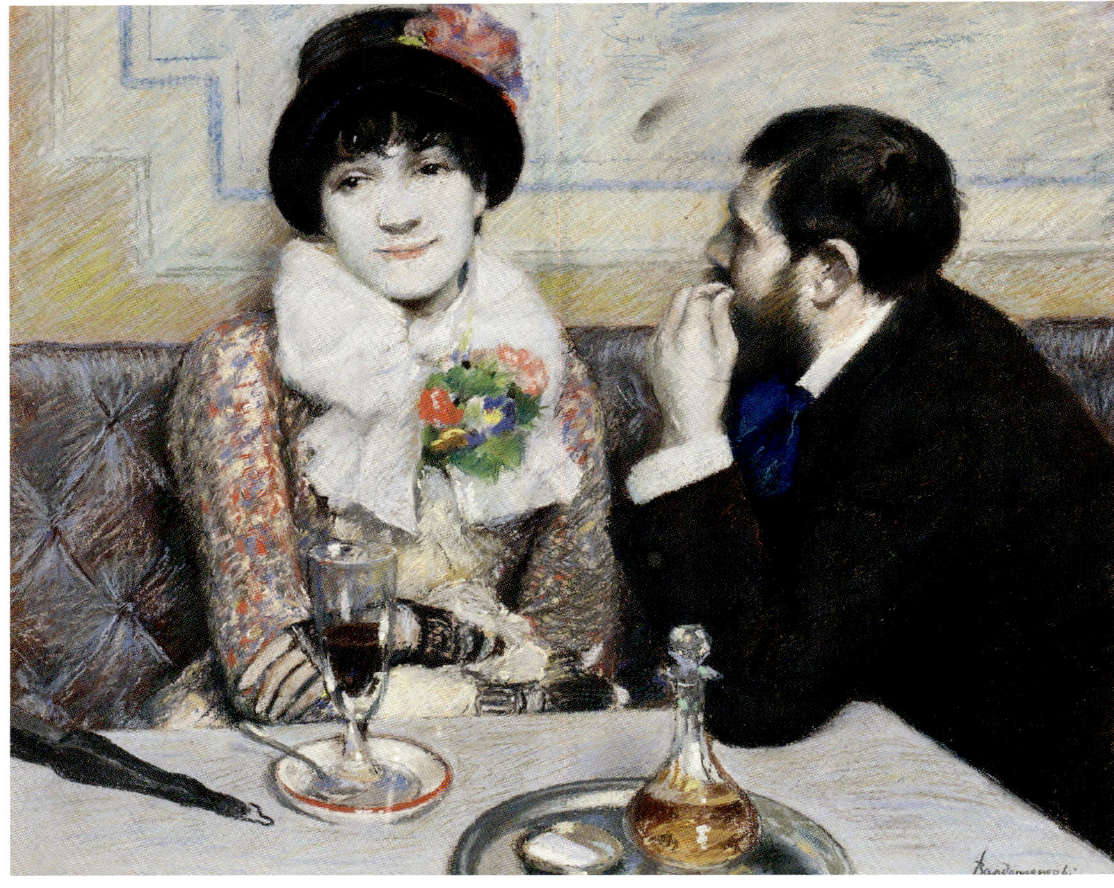

Fig. 3
Federico Zandomeneghi
Italian, 1841–1917
Couple in a Café (*At the Café*), ca. 1885
Pastel on paper
17 ½ × 21 ¼ in. (44.5 × 54 cm)
Foundation Francesco Federico Cerruti for the Arts Collection, Rivoli

Lovers court in a back booth while philosophers debate at sunny sidewalk tables a few feet away. Businessmen hammer out a deal next to a family sharing a meal at a long banquette. Painters, writers, musicians, and poets—more commonly known as "bohemians"—gather to imagine their art while coffee or wine stimulates their conversation. For centuries, characters like these have inhabited the cafés that dot the City of Light. Because such gathering places are at the heart of Parisian life, paintings and illustrations of cafés provide a crucial window into the city's history. They also document the rich variety of human experiences for which cafés provided the backdrop. Federico Zandomeneghi puts a delicate moment of seduction on display in *Couple in a Café* (ca. 1885, fig. 3). Politics comes to the fore in Jean-Émile Laboureur's sketch *Menu pour le 14 juillet au 65ᵉ régiment d'infanterie* (1899, cat. 46) commemorating the storming of the Bastille prison during the French Revolution. Art itself is at the center of Honoré Daumier's comic take on would-be poets attempting to compose their verses through a cloud of cigarette smoke and the haze of alcohol in *The Corner of Ravaged Poets* (1864, cat. 3). Depictions of cafés bring all sides of the city into view—from beauty to ugliness, from love to anger, from connection to loneliness. And they allow us to explore how the urban space of Paris—its architecture, streets, infrastructure, and traffic—has evolved, revealing the daily workings of this ever-changing metropolis.

The Café and the Street

Most cafés have doors and windows that can be closed, but quite frequently they are opened to allow light, air, customers, and staff to move freely inside and

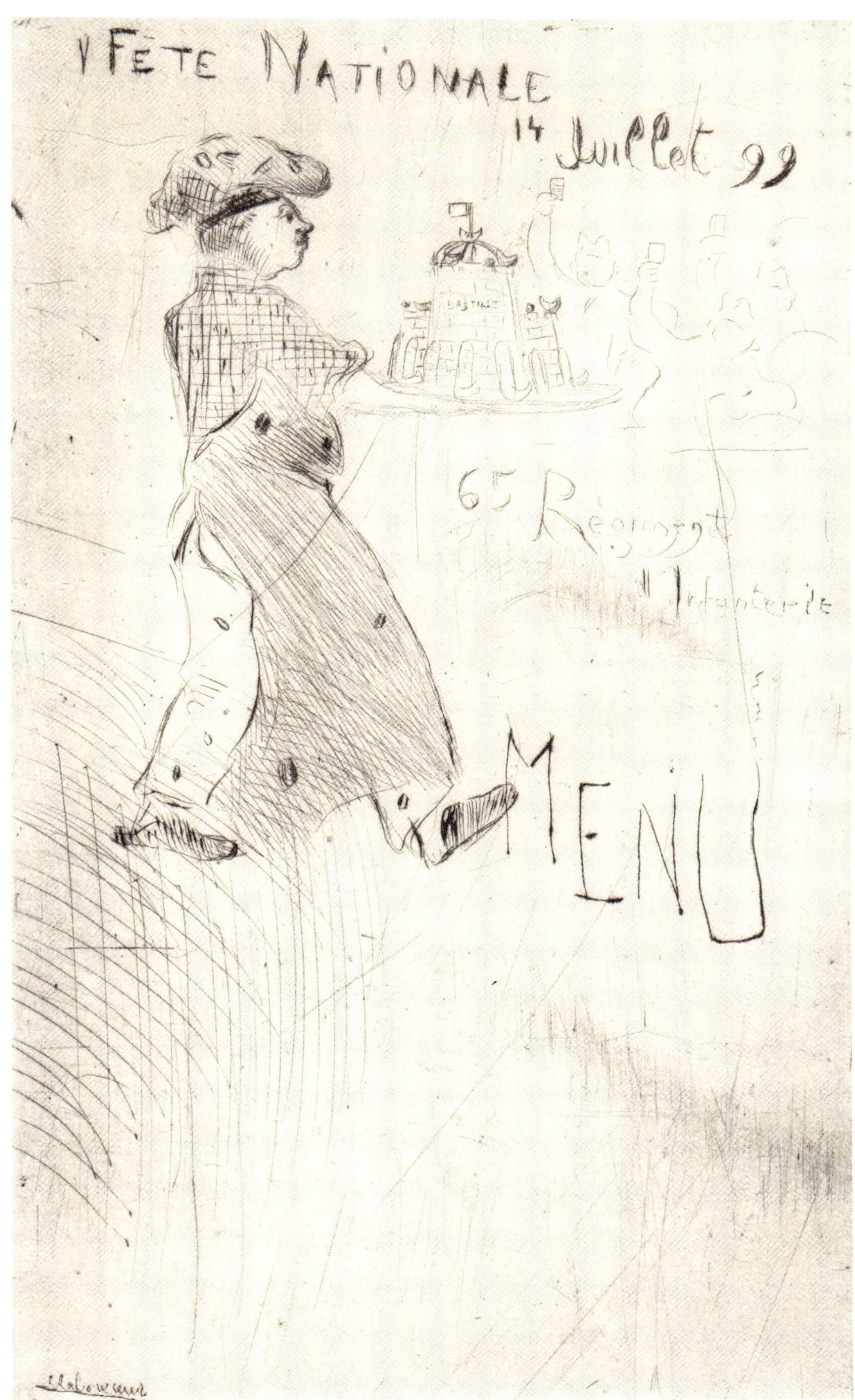

Cat. 46

Jean-Émile Laboureur
French, 1877–1973
*Menu pour le 14 juillet au 65e
régiment d'infanterie*, 1899
Drypoint
7 ¾ × 4 ¾ in. (19.7 × 12.1 cm)
Georgina Kelman Works on Paper

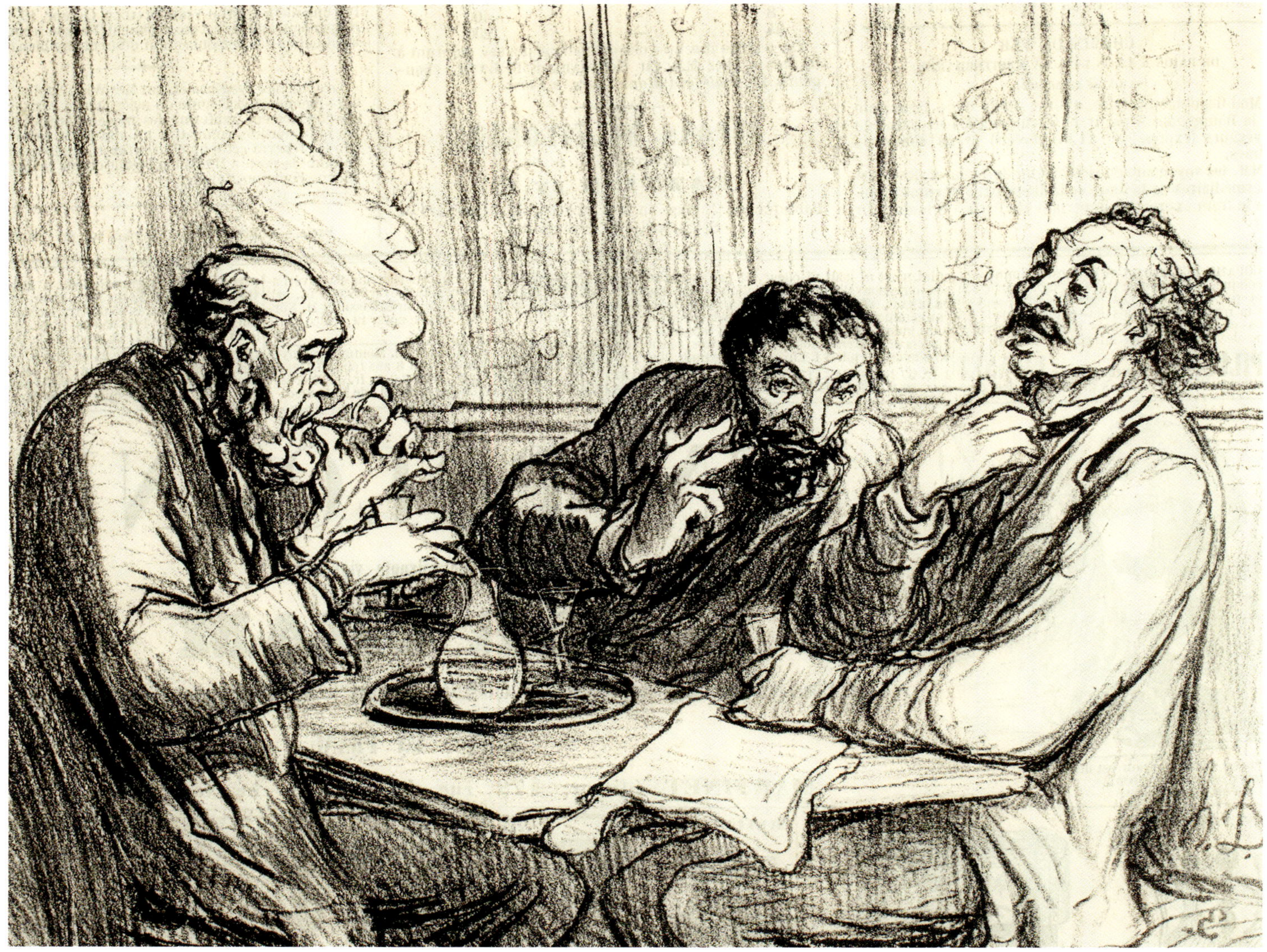

Cat. 3

Honoré Daumier
French, 1808–1879
The Corner of Ravaged Poets, 1864
Lithograph on newsprint
9 ¼ × 10 ³⁄₁₆ in. (23.5 × 25.9 cm)
Dixon Gallery and Gardens; Gift of
Dr. Armand Hammer, 1987.86

out. Noise, pollution, and curious pets may follow, but the café's porousness creates an essential connection between its patrons and the city around them. Café customers often do not face one another, but instead look outward to the street. That public orientation is a great equalizer of cafés both chic and shabby. No matter who visits, whether dressed in finery or in work clothes, most café-goers are on display. By looking outward, they become part of the streetscape. And because the weather in north-central France is mild, sitting out of doors is possible for much of the year. The city's latitude allows for long summer days averaging more than sixteen hours of daylight. Even in the coldest months of winter, café owners provide braziers that, combined with warm drinks, keep customers content.

Henri Gervex's *Café Scene in Paris* (1877, see cat. 11)—which includes the artist himself lighting his pipe alongside his well-dressed friends at their neighborhood café—illustrates this café-to-street connection. Although we cannot see the street, Gervex's use of bright, natural light to highlight his subjects implies that they are either near the wide-open front of the café or behind a large picture window facing outward. By contrast, he leaves the interior of the establishment dark and remote with only dimly glowing lamps inside to suggest the depth of the space. For Gervex, the action was clearly at or near the front of the café, not deep in its interior. Gervex and his friends relax, share news and conversation, smoke, and drink. The simple space is cozy and welcoming, both for the people pictured and for the viewer who perhaps spies the empty seat on the leather banquette and might wish to occupy it.

From the street, cafés often have a similar look. Bright awnings push out onto the sidewalk; waiters dance between tight round tables and colorful chairs while balancing trays packed with glasses and plates. Yet, despite common characteristics, each café has its own atmosphere depending on the owner, the regular clients, and the fare on offer. Each of the city's twenty *arrondissements* (wards or administrative districts) has its own unique character. Within each of these sections, smaller *quartiers* (best translated as "neighborhoods") have a distinctive, local feel. Cafés are very much part of what makes each area its own city-within-a-city, reinforcing the link between these businesses and the urban space around them. Nevertheless, many paintings in this exhibition treat both the café and the city in generic terms. Unless a café is named in the title of the work, as is the case with Vincent van Gogh's view of the Restaurant Rispal in the Parisian suburb of Asnières (cat. 24), the viewer is simply left to see its depiction as representative of any such establishment anywhere in Paris. Such a choice implies that any café is quintessentially "Parisian" no matter where one might go in the city.

Café interiors, varying widely in their décor, traditionally reflected the mood of different neighborhoods. Some were simple spots with plain décor and a handful of regulars. Georges Bottini's etching *Les Rouliers* (1903, cat. 51) depicts two wagon drivers in their local tavern enjoying a drink and the company of the *patron*, the word often used for the café owner. Although we don't know where in the city the artist found this dark but homey working-class watering hole, he depicts it with affection as a place for familiar faces and conversation. The viewer feels as if they are witnessing a scene that has unfolded day by day in this neighborhood café for years as ordinary Parisians take a break from the work of keeping this corner of the city running. American painter Willard Leroy Metcalf's *The Ten Cent Breakfast* (1887, cat. 26) shows us a slightly more well-appointed venue, complete with white tablecloths and a cozy fire. However, his title suggests that these artists, including the Scottish novelist Robert Louis Stevenson on the far right of the image, are enjoying café hospitality as cheaply as possible,

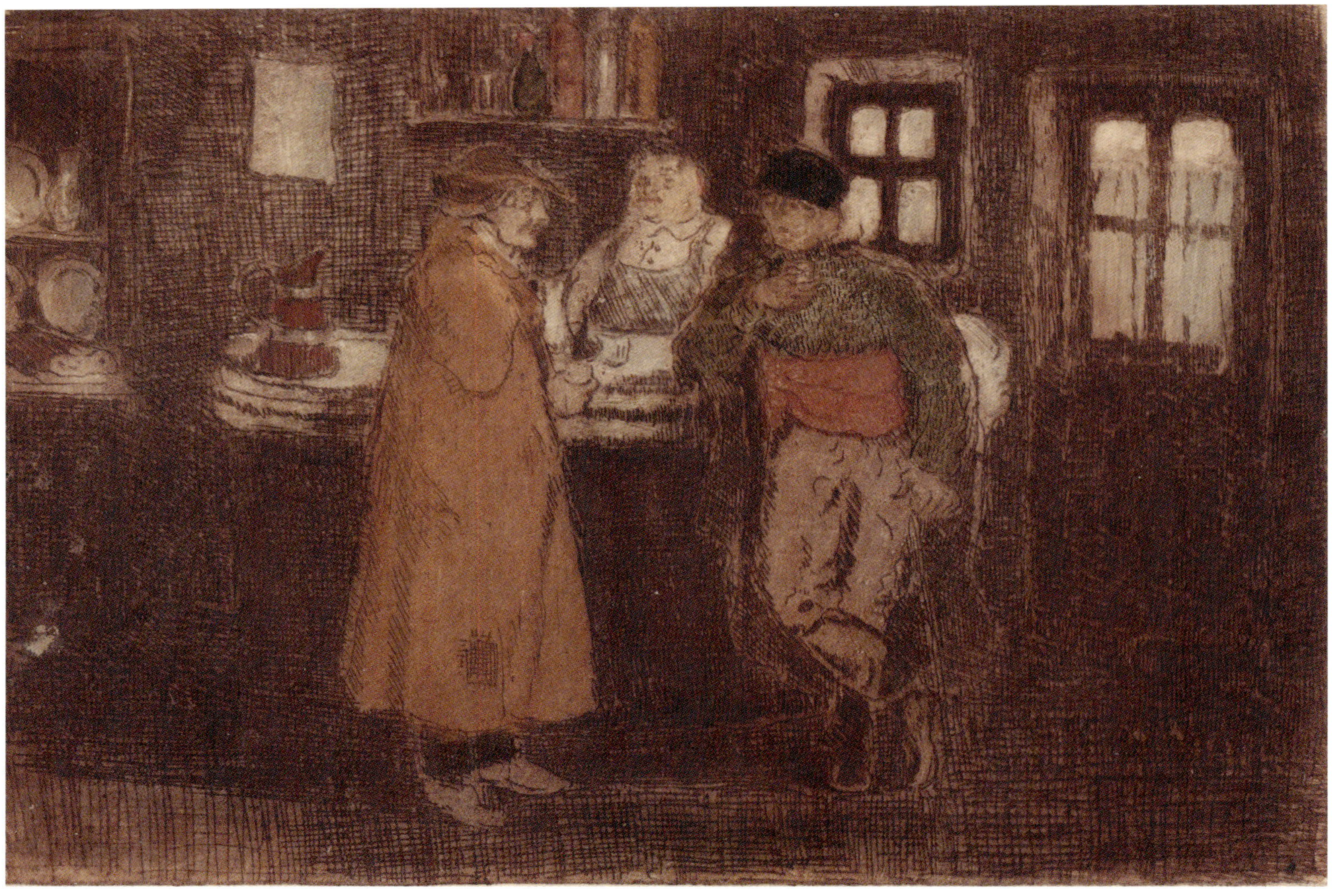

Cat. 51

George Bottini
French, 1874–1907
Les Rouliers (Southard 56), 1903
Etching printed in colors, edition of 15
5 ⅞ × 8 ½ in. (14.9 × 21.6 cm)
Georgina Kelman Works on Paper

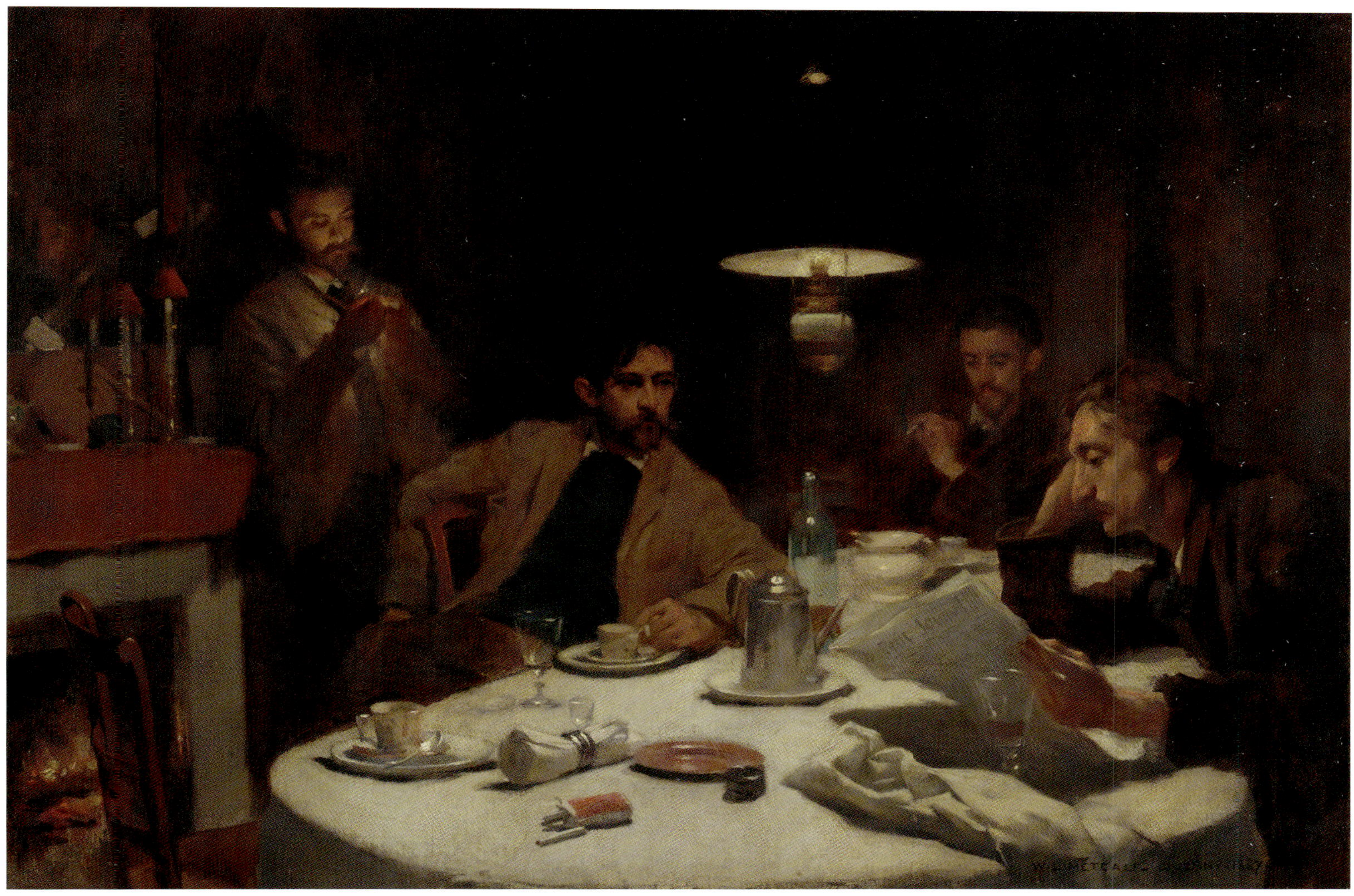

Cat. 26

Willard Leroy Metcalf
American, 1858–1925
The Ten Cent Breakfast, 1887
Oil on canvas
14 ¾ × 21 ½ in. (37.5 × 54.6 cm)
Denver Art Museum; Gift of T. Edward &
Tullah Hanley Collection, 1974.418

something that such venues offered to artists whether successful or struggling.

Meanwhile, in some posher parts of Paris, owners turned cafés into lush, mirrored palaces to attract well-dressed customers who enjoyed expensive food and drinks. Unlike his depiction of artists eating on the cheap, Metcalf's *Au café* (1888, cat. 27) takes the viewer into a glowing world of fashion, fantasy, and seduction lit by gaslights that seem to lift the ceiling higher. Even more powerfully, Édouard Vuillard's *Café Wepler* (ca. 1908–10, cat. 59) depicts the famous establishment located at 14 Place de Clichy. Vuillard had been a theater decorator and interior designer who brought the influence of post-Impressionism and Japanese art to his paintings.[1] In his evocation of the Wepler—the largest oyster house in the city—Vuillard focuses on the café's high ceilings filled with light that would draw elegant Parisians into its dramatic interior, itself like a stage. Under the soaring, illuminated archways that resembled the proscenium of a theater, life's dramas would unfold.

Whether fancy or plain, cafés grew in number and popularity in the late nineteenth century at a time of rapid change in Paris. Napoleon III—nephew and namesake of the original emperor—took power in an 1848 coup and crowned himself emperor in 1851. He pushed forward previous decades' worth of city planning efforts aimed at making Paris a showpiece of urban design and, in the process, cemented his own political power. Much of the modern look and feel of the Paris we know today dates from the 1850s and 1860s. The emperor directed his chief government official for the Paris region, Baron Georges-Eugène Haussmann, to rebuild the city from top to bottom. He also expanded the city limits in 1860, bringing what had been independent suburban communities into Paris proper.

The process of "Haussmannization," as it has been called ever since, meant ripping up whole neighborhoods and rebuilding them to strict specifications, including height restrictions; unlike many cities filled with towering skyscrapers, one can still see the sky throughout Paris. Cleanliness and public health were also part of the plan. Haussmann created new public parks to allow contact with nature, offering these "clean" spaces outside the city's "dirty" streets and polluted air. The two expansive green spaces on the eastern and western edges were dubbed "the lungs of Paris." He also installed a modern sewer system to take away street runoff and later household waste. The sewers became so famous as an engineering marvel that people toured them in boats up to the 1970s, and walking tours still exist today. Many Parisians paid the price for this large-scale gentrification. Construction pushed thousands of working-class people to the city's outskirts. Losing their homes and communities politically radicalized them, thus setting up deep conflicts for decades to come. But for the wealthy who inhabited (and still inhabit) the city's center, the result was a renovated urban space where people could move more freely and experience beautiful new buildings. The Opéra Garnier—the opera house designed by architect Charles Garnier—was only one of many architectural marvels on the updated *grand boulevards*, the wide, straight streets that replaced hundreds of small, centuries-old, winding paths throughout the city center.

Although the boulevards are not visible in the images in this exhibition, they are often implied by lavish interiors; Café Wepler, for example, sat on the new Boulevard de Clichy. The *Menu for Restaurant Larue* (ca. 1912, cat. 61) by Georges Lepape captures the excitement of boulevard life with its bright colors. One of the most fashionable eateries of the day—frequented by politicians as well as wealthy French and American customers—Restaurant Larue was situated near the Church of La Madeleine at the convergence of two of Haussmann's new avenues.[2] Its sophisticated dishes, many of which exhibited a Russian influence, became

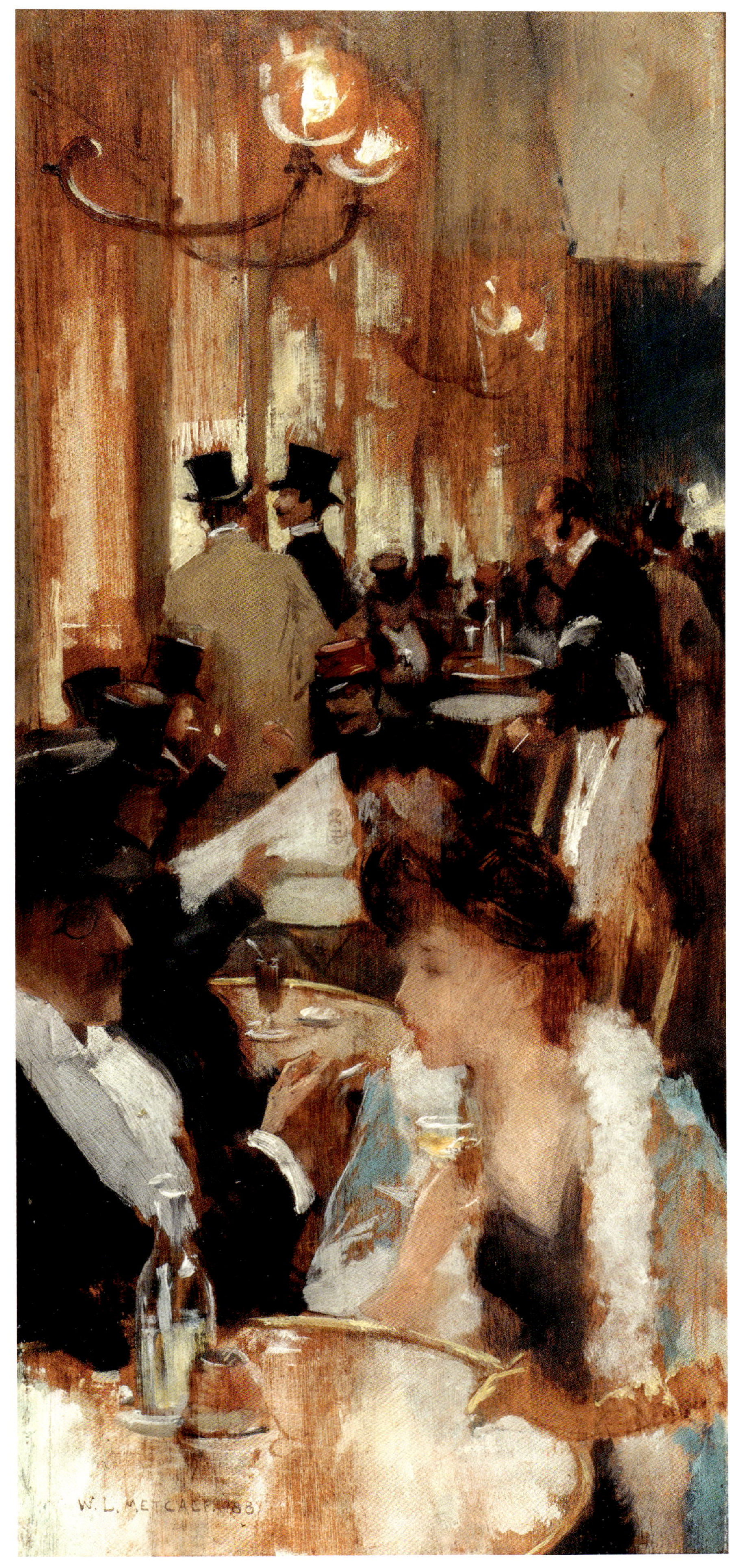

Cat. 27

Willard Leroy Metcalf
American, 1858–1925
Au café, 1888
Oil on panel
13 ¹¹⁄₁₆ × 6 ¹⁄₁₆ in. (34.8 × 15.4 cm)
Terra Foundation for American Art, Daniel
J. Terra Collection, 1992.10

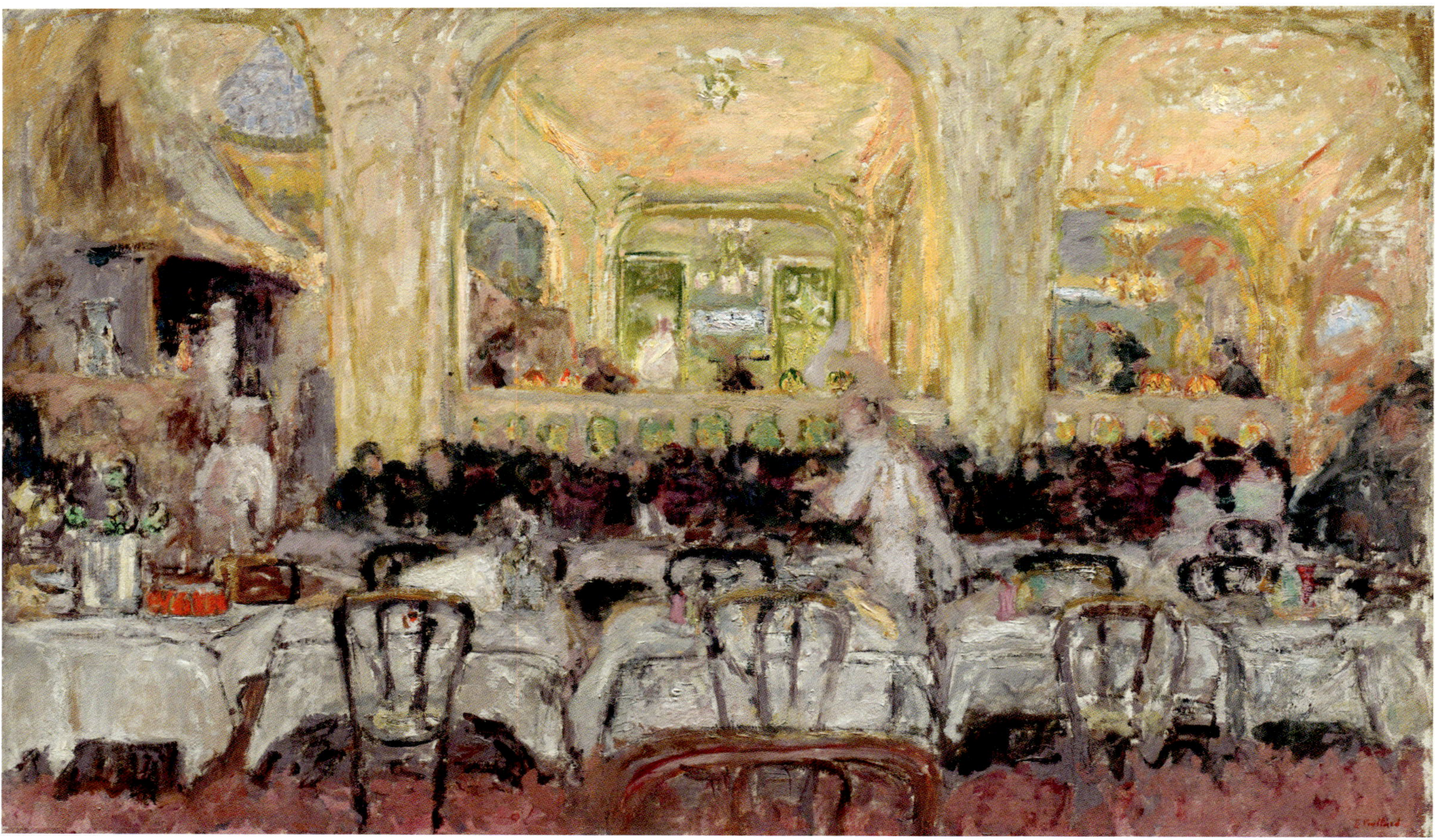

Cat. 59

Édouard Vuillard
French, 1868–1940
Café Wepler, ca. 1908–10, reworked in 1912
Oil on fabric
24 ½ × 40 ⅝ in. (62.2 × 103.2 cm)
The Cleveland Museum of Art, Gift of the
Hanna Fund, 1950.90

the talk of the city's elites, such as the elegantly dressed woman at the center of the image. Lepape offers a scene of boulevard drama among the well-to-do as the woman grapples with a lusty patron under the judgmental gaze of another.

Urban renewal, Haussmann thought, was also good for business because the boulevards promoted exchange throughout Paris. Historically, cities were the places where farmers brought their goods to market, and business remains integral to all urban life. To make the economy function more smoothly, traders came to rely upon social relationships, and cafés soon became the hubs of those networks. The presence of waitstaff and café owners in many images remind us that cafés—which are first and foremost money-making enterprises—are also part of a larger urban economy of labor, property, and profit. Édouard Manet's *gillotage* engraving, titled *At the Café* (1874, cat. 6), offers a quick sketch of Impressionist painters drinking at the Café Guerbois (9 Avenue de Clichy). A waiter in his dark coat with towel draped across his arm hovers nearby, looking down on this table full of artists watching to see what they might need, but also perhaps with a certain skepticism as to whether they will pay.[3] In Jean-Émile Laboureur's *Ernest, garçon de restaurant* (1902–11, cat. 50), a waiter who would normally be invisible to patrons is named and celebrated in a dignified portrait.

The boulevards—hundreds of feet wide and lined with new, fashionable homes and shops—led to the large department stores that began to replace smaller, family-owned outlets. Le Bon Marché, followed by Le Printemps and Galeries Lafayette, became the most important stores in the fin-de-siècle era, as they still are today. Innovations in steel and glass production allowed for large display windows, thus giving birth to the idea of "window shopping." Strolling along these new thoroughfares, whether for commerce or recreation, became increasingly common especially for the expanding middle classes (known in French as *la bourgeoisie*). Office workers, file clerks, bank employees, telegraph operators, and stock traders now had money to spend. These *grands magasins*, as department stores were called, helped blur the lines between middle- and upper-class Parisians since the ready-to-wear clothing they offered made it possible for members of the bourgeoisie to afford the kind of fashion previously reserved for aristocrats and the wealthy. New clothes also gave the rising middle classes confidence to enter new upscale cafés where they could spend their growing disposable income.

Paris has been known as the "City of Light" for many reasons, including its association with the eighteenth-century intellectual movement known as the Enlightenment, but even earlier it had been one of the first European cities to adopt streetlighting beginning in 1667. In the nineteenth century, new, stronger gaslights installed on the boulevards meant that after dark, even during the shorter winter days, the life of these streets could continue. Along with more rigorous nighttime policing, these new illuminations led to the "blurring [of] boundaries between day and night," according to historian A. Roger Ekirch, and "altered the pace and scope of people's lives."[4] Gaslights also encouraged an expanded nightlife found in newly established music halls, dance halls, and cabarets. A large part of that social life was also found in the cafés that opened on these boulevards, catering to a wealthier, or socially climbing, clientele.

Édouard Vuillard gives a vision of the nighttime boulevard in his lithograph *The Pastry Shop* (*Outdoor Café at Night*) (ca. 1898–99, fig. 4). Set in a café after dark, Vuillard shows how activity continued throughout the city even after sunset. Much like his depiction of the Café Wepler, the image focuses on light and height. Patrons sit underneath a large, soaring awning, mixed

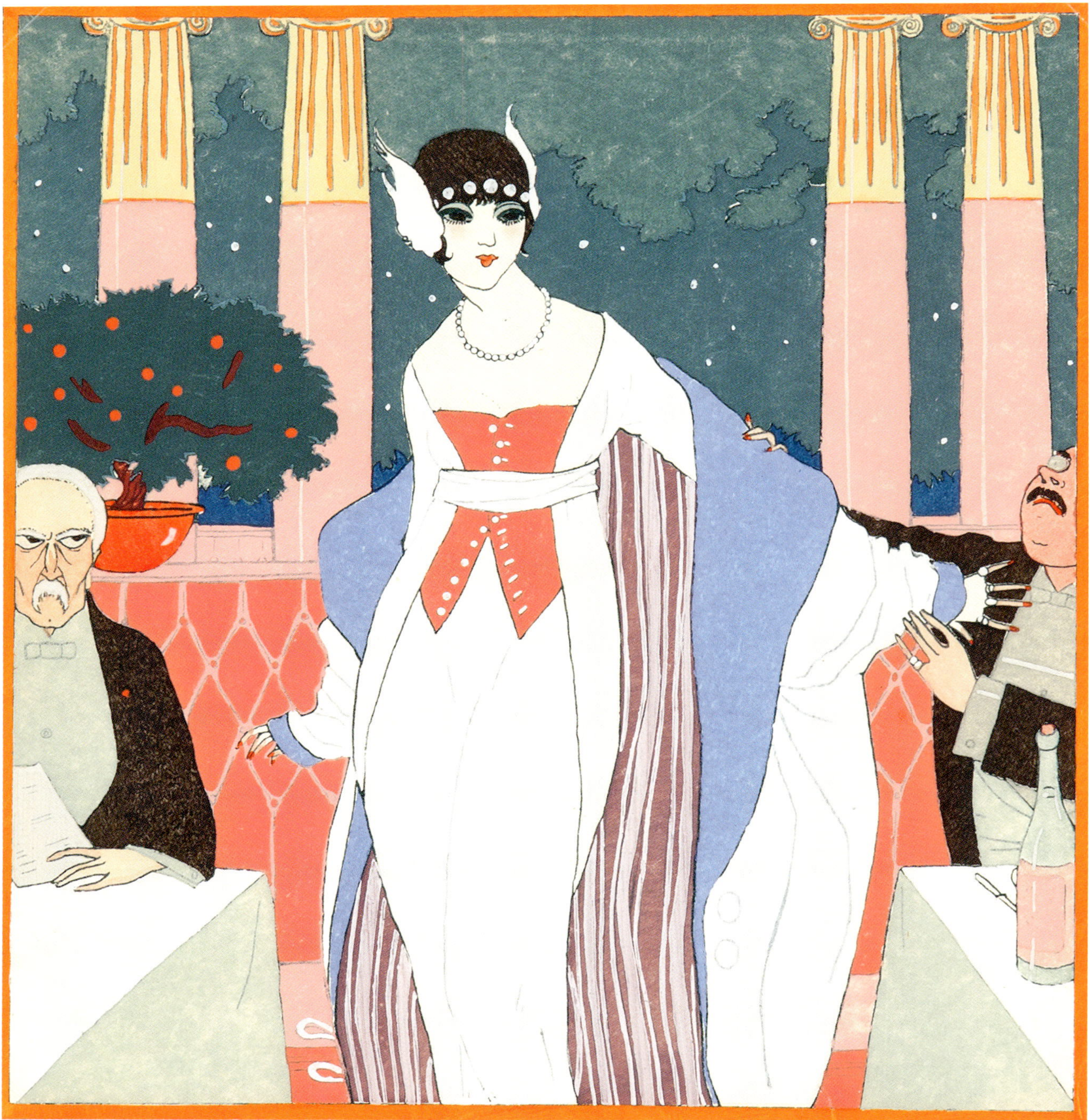

Cat. 61

Georges Lepape
French, 1887–1971
Menu for Restaurant Larue, ca. 1912
Pochoir
6 ¼ × 5 ¹⁵⁄₁₆ in. (15.9 × 15.1 cm)
Private collection, Memphis

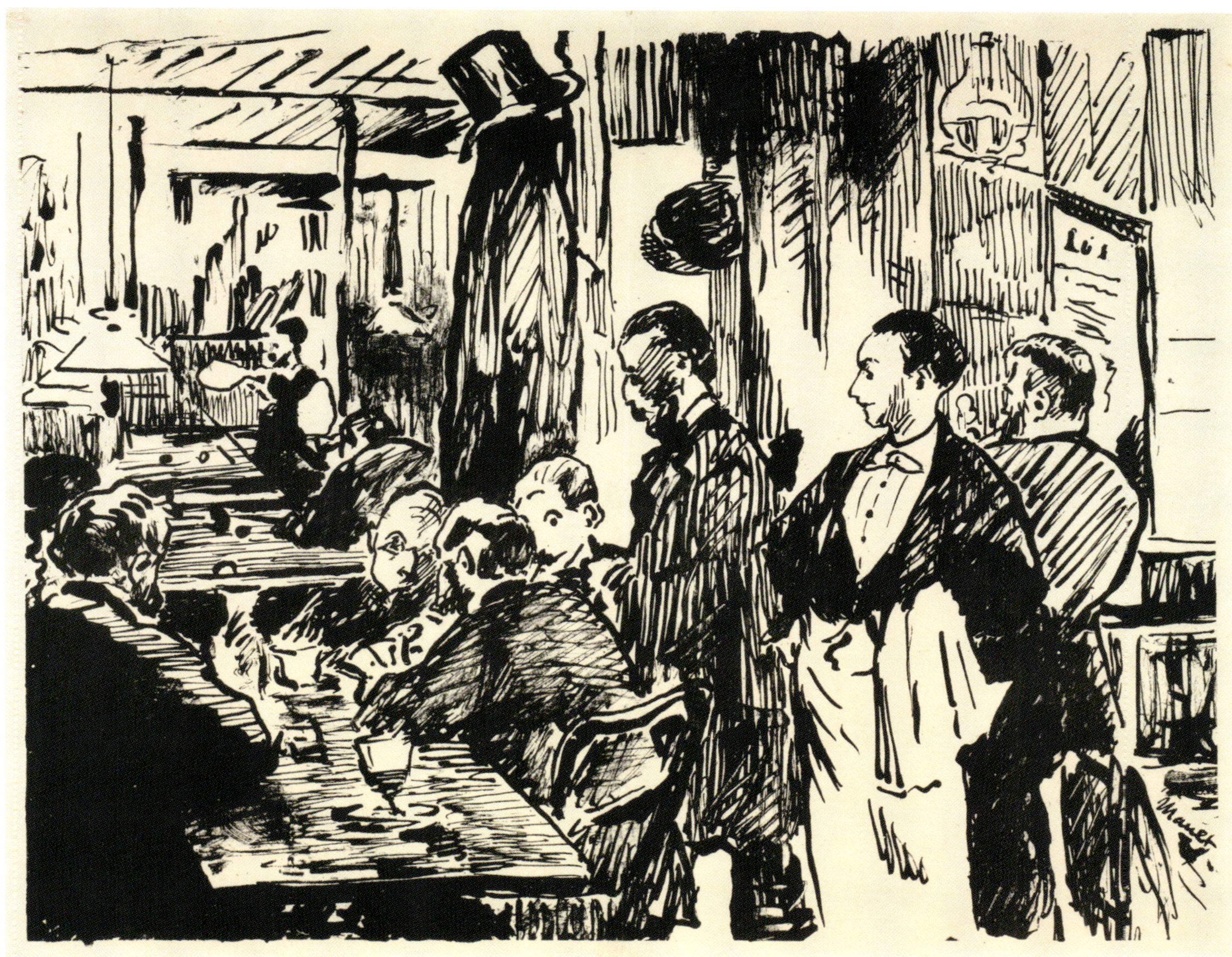

Cat. 6

Édouard Manet
French, 1832–1883
At the Café, 1874
Brush and ink transfer relief plate
image: 10 ⅜ × 13 ⅛ in. (26.4 × 33.3 cm)
sheet: 10 ⅞ × 13 ¹¹⁄₁₆ in. (27.6 × 34.8 cm)
Baltimore Museum of Art; The George
A. Lucas Collection, purchased with funds
from the State of Maryland, Laurence and
Stella Bendann Fund, and contributions
from individuals, foundations, and
corporations throughout the Baltimore
community, BMA 1996.48.18058

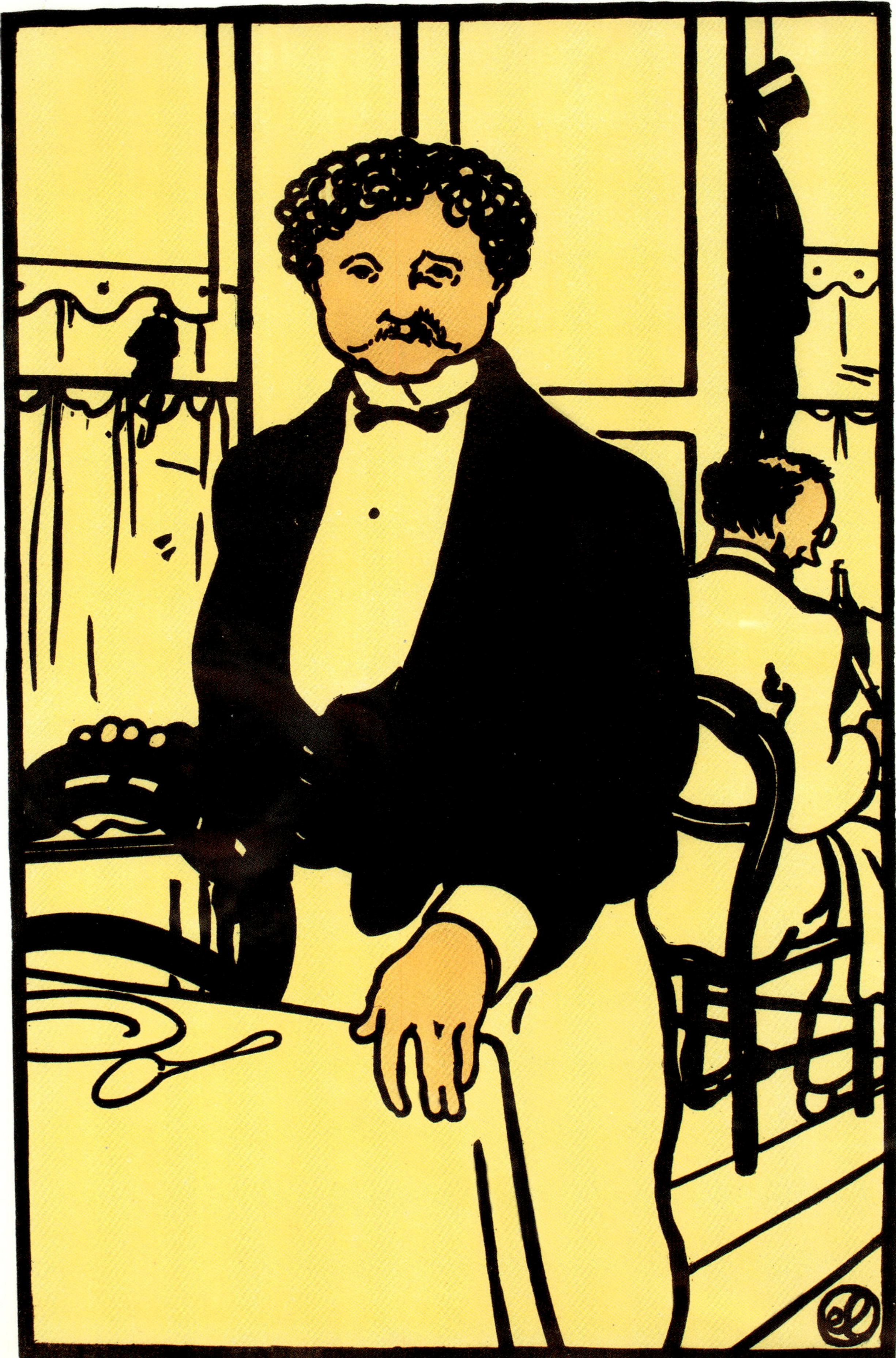
laboureur

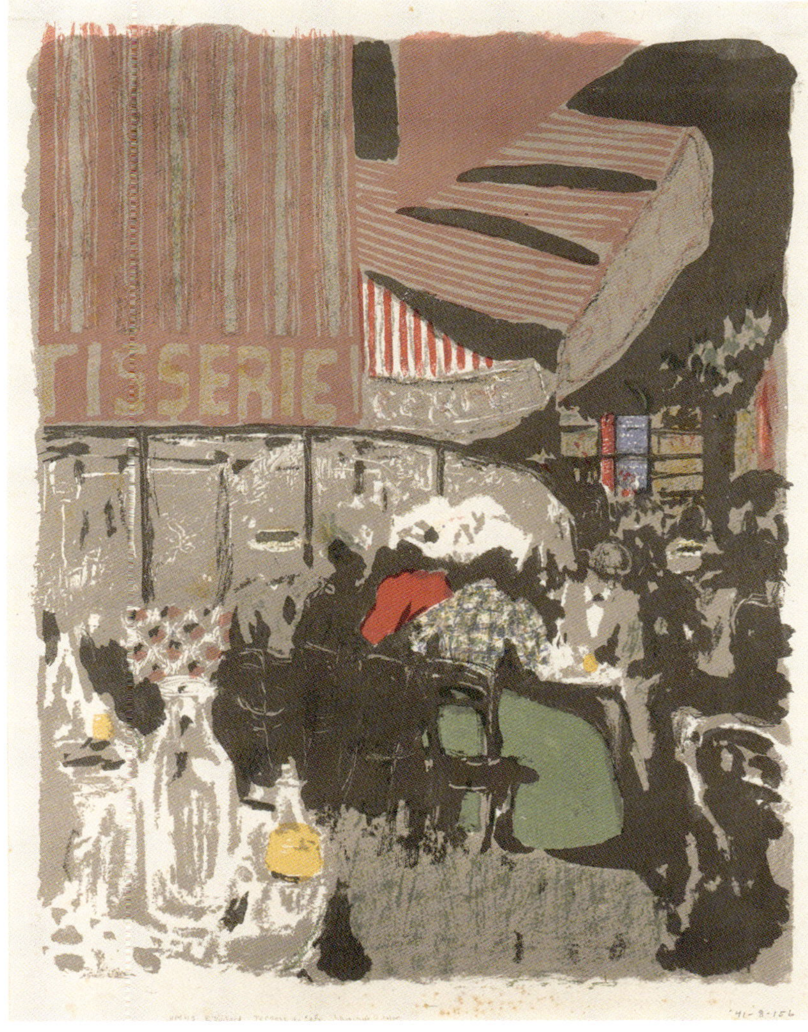

Fig. 4
Édouard Vuillard (French, 1868–1940)
Published by Ambroise Vollard, Paris (1867–1939)
Printed by Auguste Clot (French, 1858–1936)
The Pastry Shop (*Outdoor Café at Night*),
ca. 1898–99
Color lithograph (transfer lithograph)
14 × 10 ¾ in. (35.6 × 27.3 cm)
Philadelphia Museum of Art; Purchased with the
John D. McIlhenny Fund, 1941

Cat. 50

Jean-Émile Laboureur
French, 1877–1973
Ernest, garçon de restaurant, 1902–11
Woodcut printed in black with lithographic
transfer in yellow and orange
image: 17 ⅜ × 11 in. (44.1 × 27.9 cm)
Dixon Gallery and Gardens; Museum
purchase with funds provided by Peggy
and Keith Kunkel and an anonymous
donor, 2024.9

with other elements of the urban setting. The contrast
between the night sky in the upper right-hand corner
and the brightness of the café that shines onto the
boulevard to illuminate the patterns and colors of the
customers' clothes suggests how the café could interact
with and transform the city at all times of day. The
glassware in the foreground glows in the café's lights,
emphasizing the purpose for someone's visit. This
lithograph was part of a series titled "Landscapes and
Interiors," and Vuillard clearly presents this nighttime
setting to the viewer as an urban landscape scene.

A Lonely Crowd

For all the changes that made Paris a more modern
city, many late nineteenth-century social thinkers
began to worry that the growing metropolis could have
consequences for urban dwellers. Critics instilled a belief
that cities were degenerate, dangerous "urban jungles."
Parisian newspapers ran sensationalized stories about
criminal gangs known as "Les Apaches" terrorizing
law-abiding citizens (fig. 5). (They used the name of the
Native American tribe to emphasize a racialized view
of "savagery.") Most of these stories had little basis
in fact, but they sold newspapers in the age of a booming
popular press. In the 1890s, the father of French
sociology Emile Durkheim diagnosed the *anomie*—the
loneliness that comes from fraying communities—that
accompanied city life. He believed it often led
to suicide. At the turn of the century, German thinker
Georg Simmel argued that growing cities made their
inhabitants numb to the world around them. He equated
city life with what he called the *blasé* attitude, a kind
of indifference to others that was unique to urbanites.

Among the images in this exhibition are many
depictions of loneliness, often women sitting alone
at a café table with a drink, suggesting that alcohol was

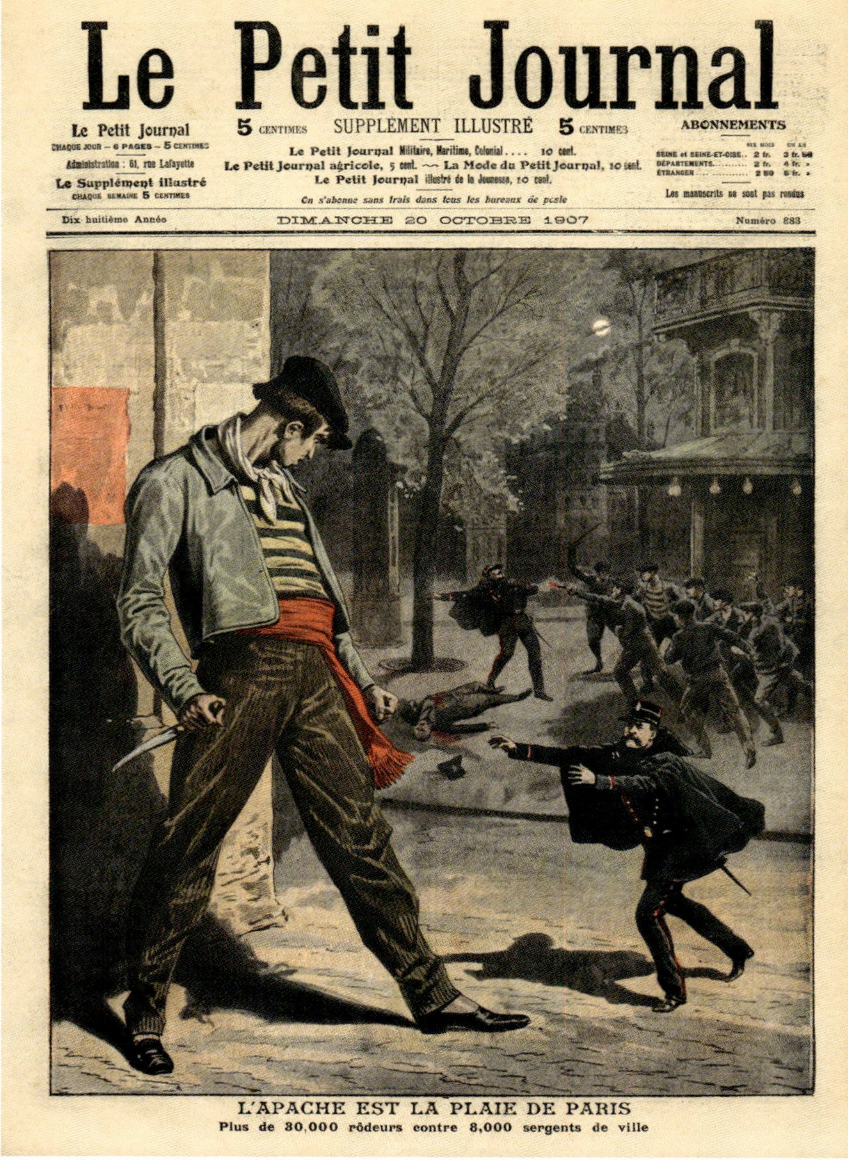

Fig. 5
"The Apache is a Nuisance for Paris", cover
of *Le Petit Journal*, October 20, 1907
Color lithograph
Private collection

a common way to handle social isolation. Jean-Louis Forain's *Woman in a Café* (ca. 1885, see cat. 19) depicts a well-dressed woman (perhaps a high-class prostitute) alone at a table with a drink at the ready and a plate which she has perhaps emptied of a morsel of food. She looks around the room, but we cannot know what she sees. Her expression, "slightly too sharp-eyed for comfort," according to art historian Souren Melikian, suggests an active mind busy taking in all that she sees, but only at a distance.[5]

Forain provides a different view of anomie in his depiction of one of the city's most famous cafés, the Nouvelle Athènes at 66 Rue Pigalle, which was known as a famous gathering place for artists and is often credited as the birthplace of Impressionism. In both his etching *Café de la Nouvelle Athènes* (ca. 1876, cat. 9) and the painting *Au café de la Nouvelle Athènes* (n.d., fig. 6), the place is packed, but in neither of Forain's renderings do the patrons engage with one another. Instead, each sits alone in his or her own world,

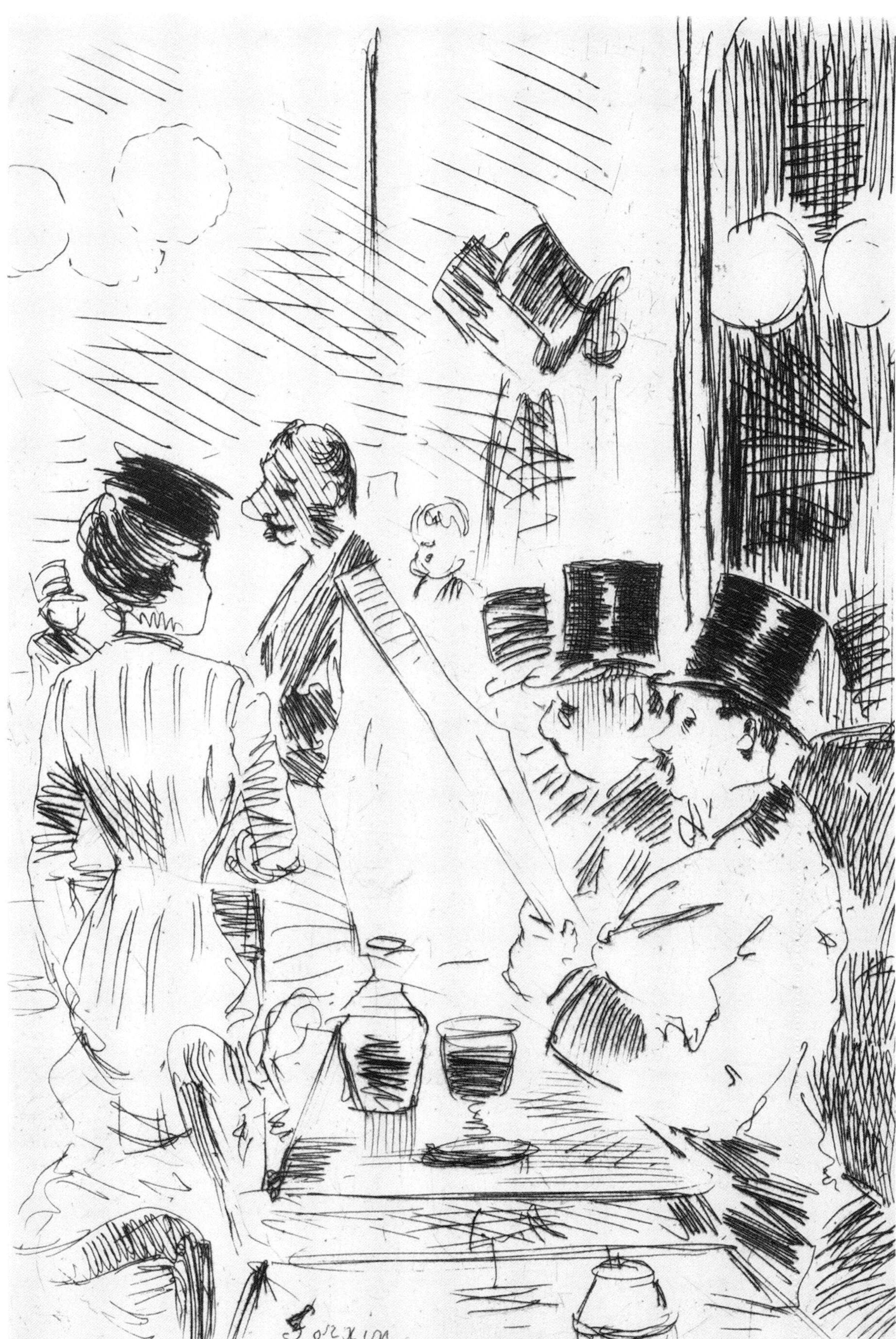

Cat. 9

Jean-Louis Forain
French, 1852–1931
*Café de la Nouvelle
Athènes*, ca. 1876
Etching
image: 6 ⅛ × 4 ⅝ in.
(15.6 × 11.7 cm)
sheet: 11 ½ × 9 ½ (29.2 × 24.1 cm)
Dixon Gallery and Gardens;
Museum purchase, 2022.3

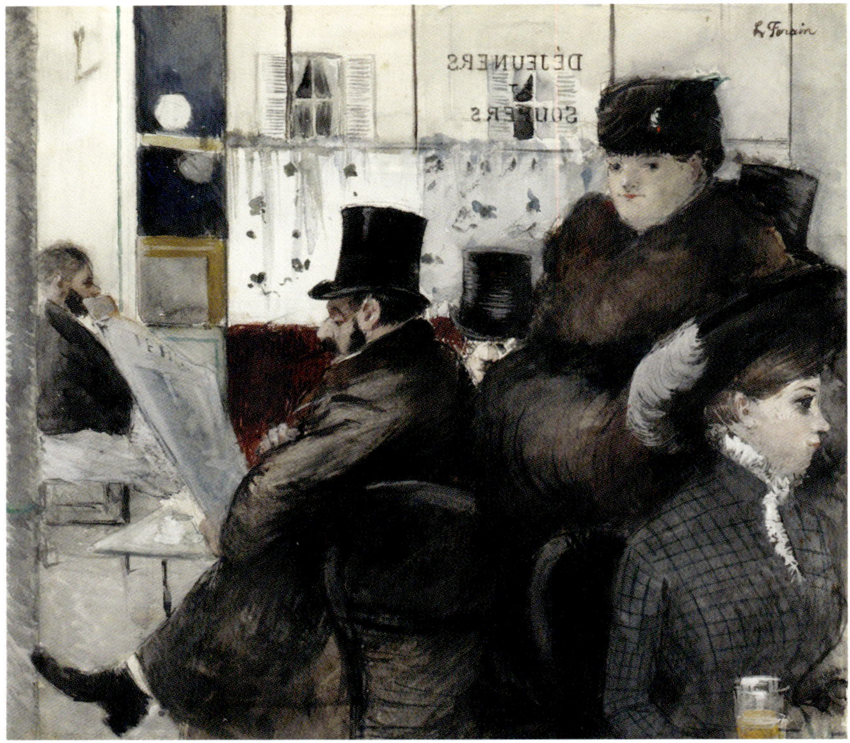

Fig. 6
Jean-Louis Forain
French, 1852–1931
Au café de la Nouvelle Athènes, n.d.
Watercolor, gouache, Chinese ink, graphite
14 ¼ × 15 ⅜ in. (36.2 × 39 cm)
Musée d'Orsay, Paris, RF30038

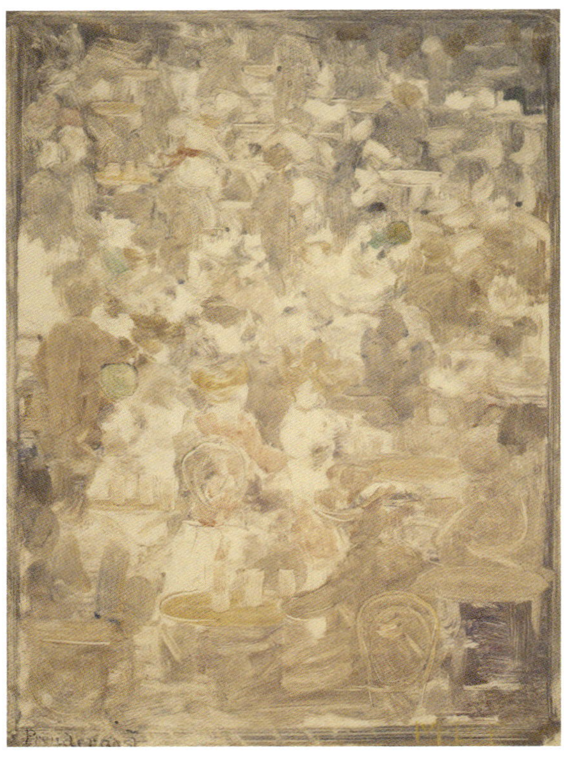

Fig. 7
Maurice Brazil Prendergast
American, 1858–1924
Outdoor Café Scene, 1900–5
Monotype
National Gallery of Art, Washington,
DC, Rosenwald Collection, 1964.8.1403

some reading a newspaper or gazing off into the distance. No one's eyes meet, and no one speaks to anyone else.

Some artists captured the changes in Paris by showing the crush of people in the swelling metropolis. Maurice Brazil Prendergast's *Outdoor Café Scene* (1900–5, fig. 7) depicts a crowded café not through a realistic representation of bodies and faces but by offering a largely abstract blur to evoke rapid motion and intense busyness. Tables, chairs, drinking glasses, women's hats, and other details peek through the muted colors, but the overall sense is one of confusion and a mass of humanity churning inside the café. Likewise, Félix Vallotton's woodcut *The Brawl* (*La Rixe*) (1892, cat. 35) may have frightened some viewers by exposing the violent underbelly of urban

life. Well-dressed patrons have devolved into animals. Their civilized façades are stripped away as they lunge at one another's throats, likely due to a loss at a card game.[6]

Vallotton's image speaks to widespread concerns in the late nineteenth century about the growing influence of crowds and mobs on the streets and at political rallies. One of the most famous books in France during the era, Gustave Le Bon's *Psychologie des foules* (Crowd Psychology, 1895), described how individuals could become lost inside larger groups and surrender their capacity for rational thought when captivated by the passions of the masses. Le Bon's ideas would anticipate the fascist groups already forming across Europe by this era that would challenge

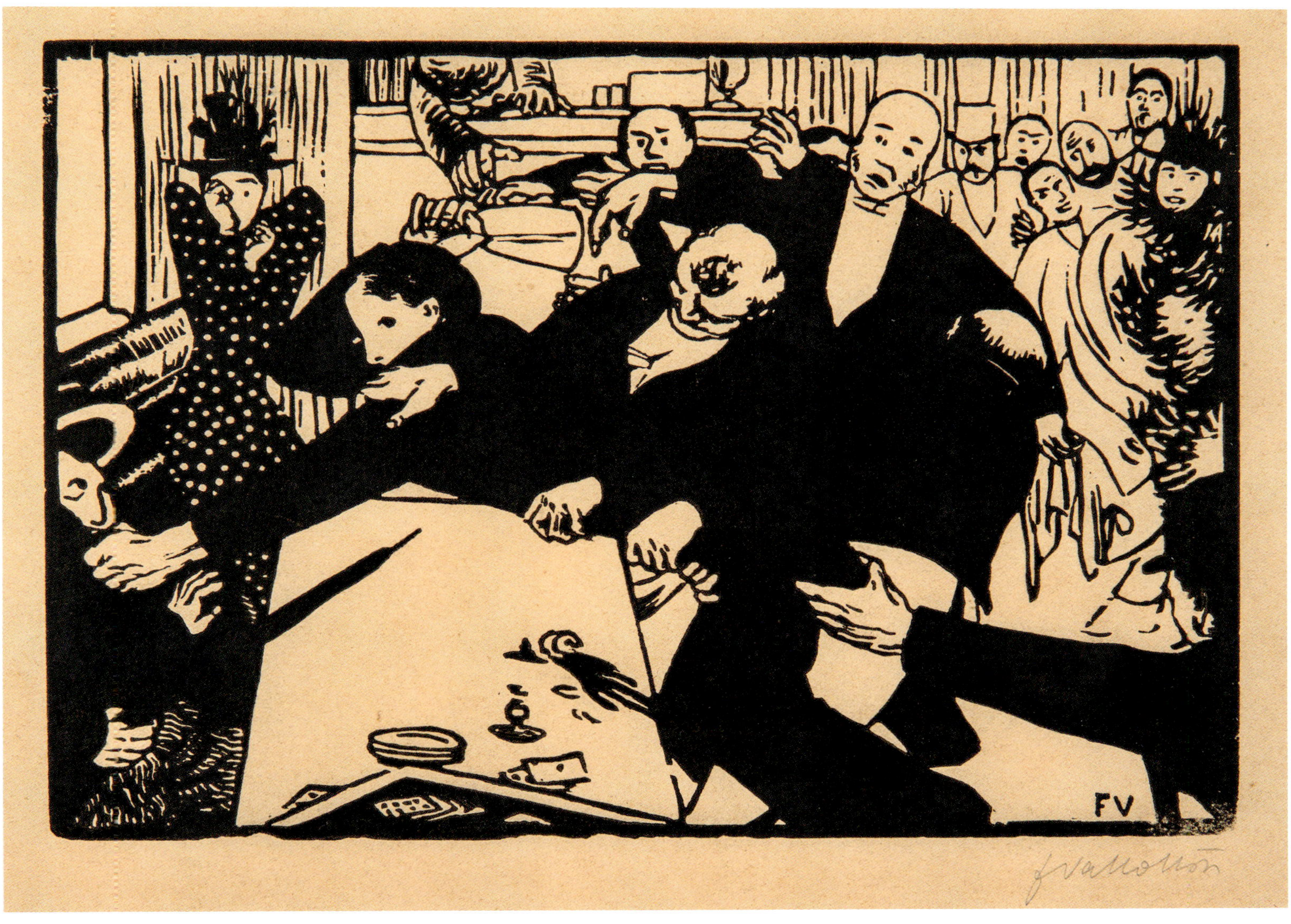

Cat. 35

Félix Vallotton
Swiss, 1865–1925
The Brawl (*La Rixe*), 1892
Woodcut in black on wove paper, sole state
10 ⅝ × 14 ⅛ in. (27 × 35.9 cm)
Memorial Art Gallery, University
of Rochester; General Acquisitions
Fund, 1984.17

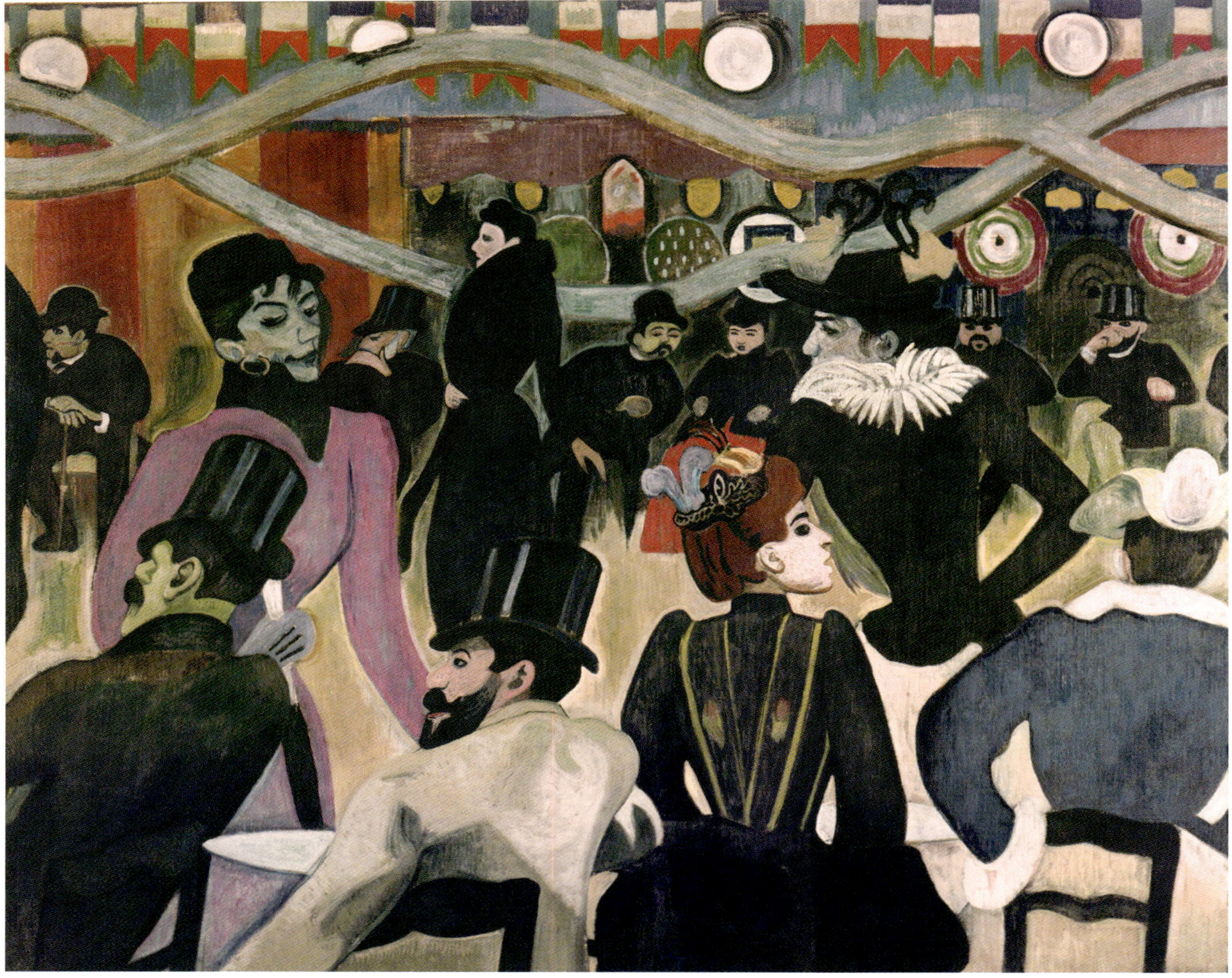

Fig. 8
Jens Ferdinand Willumsen
Danish, 1863–1958
Montagnes-Russes, 1890
Oil on canvas
49 ¼ × 58 ¾ in. (125 × 149.2 cm)
Nasjonalmuseet, Oslo, NG.M.02423

democratic governments in the 1920s and '30s. Fascists would offer a sense of communal identity and belonging to many who felt left out by the city's anonymity.

Cafés could be lonely, or they could be so busy that an individual might easily be ignored by the people around. But they could also shrink urban life down to manageable human scale. Visitors could be part of the city yet escape the rush by watching the throngs from the quiet comfort of a seat with a coffee or a glass of wine in hand. And for all the artistic images of loneliness reinforcing fears about the city's dangers, many other paintings and drawings showcase the vibrancy of the café's social world. Cafés could also become the focus for the very social connection that critics feared was missing in cities.

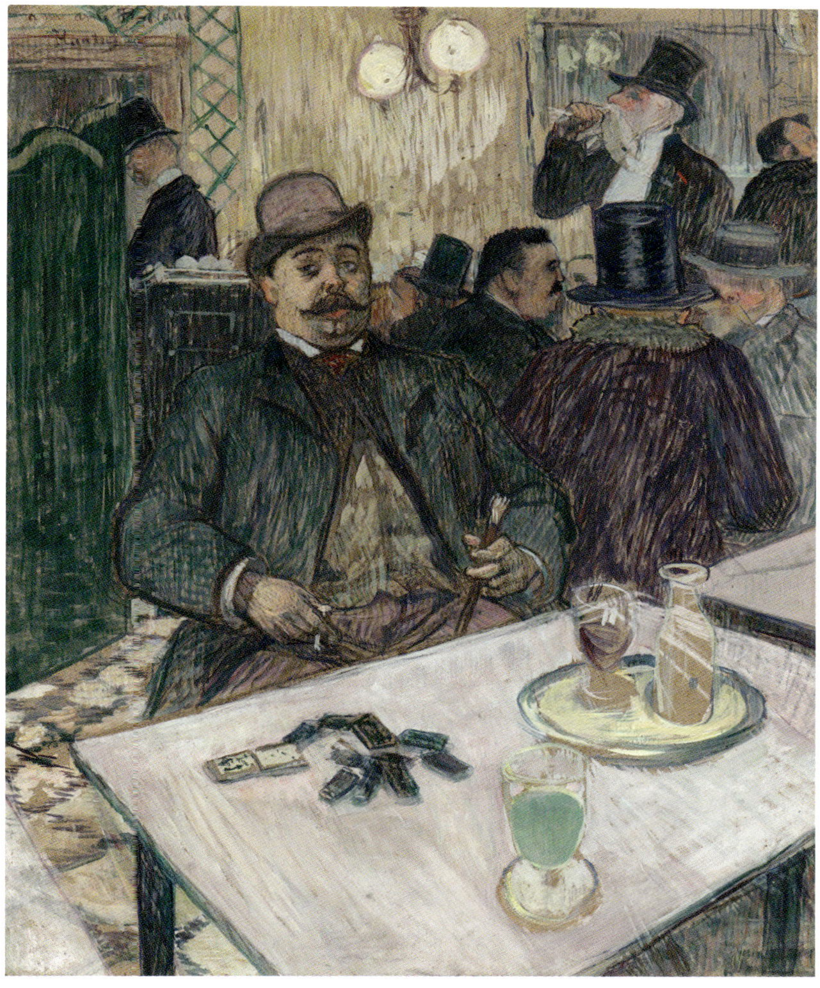

Fig. 9
Henri de Toulouse-Lautrec
French, 1864–1901
Monsieur Boileau at the Café, 1893
Oil and tempera with charcoal on millboard
31 5/8 × 25 9/16 in. (80.3 × 65 cm)
The Cleveland Museum of Art, Hinman
B. Hurlbut Collection, 1925.1409

Having a place to encounter others was especially important in the 1870s and 1880s as the population of Paris grew, thanks in large part to migration from the countryside. Immigrants from the same town or region elsewhere in France might meet at a particular café frequented by people from back home. The newly arrived could find a job, look for a place to live amidst a housing crunch, and learn news (and gossip) to help them navigate a new life in Paris. Tourists and expatriates from other countries also found cafés a home away from home. Workers from the same trade or factory could gather after hours. The politically engaged could connect with other like-minded thinkers in establishments known to cater to certain ideologies or parties. A person could make friends, debate new ideas, and fall in love in the café—perhaps all in one day. The café reknitted communities and created new ones.[7] Since entertaining guests in a small Parisian apartment could be difficult, the café often became an extension of the home. And as in any public space, the dinner party sometimes expanded as friends strolled by on the sidewalk or as people struck up a conversation with those at the neighboring table.

Danish artist Jens Ferdinand Willumsen captures this café sociability in his *Montagnes-Russes* (1890, fig. 8). The title makes reference to a popular amusement hall in Paris that at the time included a roller coaster (in French, *montagnes russes*). Willumsen shows the undulating tracks at the top of the image in curving blue hues and a shooting gallery in the background. Prostitutes move through the space in search of clients, and top-hatted men look, chat, and drink amidst the unfolding scene.[8] Likewise, American Fernand Lungren shows two women engaged in deep conversation over glasses of wine in an elegant and brightly lit venue that illuminates their lovely attire in his painting *In the Café* (1882–84, see cat. 18). In Henri de Toulouse-Lautrec's *Monsieur Boileau at the Café*

(1893, fig. 9), the painting's namesake, a gossip columnist known for his heavy drinking, looks outward with a welcoming expression, seeming to invite the viewer to join him in a game of dominoes.[9] Behind him, another group of men clearly enjoys one another's company.

Often music, dance, or performance facilitated café sociability by providing an occasion to gather. American artist Richard E. Miller shows that most clearly in his *Café L'Avenue, Paris* (ca. 1906–10, cat. 58; the precise location of "the avenue" on which this café was located is unknown). A small ensemble of piano, violin, and double bass entertains the evening's crowd. The music seems to lighten the mood, as does Miller, who makes the interior of the café bright with light and convivial conversation in the foreground and background. A dancer in motion fills the right half of the canvas of Jean Metzinger's Cubist take on a music-filled café in *Danseuse au café* (1912, fig. 10). On the other half of the canvas, a couple watches with glee at a table filled with drinks. The "jerky staccato motion suggested by the dancing figure"[10] and the fractured figures of the café-goers help illuminate the dark space lit with the glow of a few electric globes. The painting "captures the social mood and tempo of Paris prior to World War I,"[11] yet the scene itself—Parisians gathered for a fun night out—is also timeless.

Seeing the City

Paris often becomes a kind of theater for café patrons who look out into the street. As they drink their coffee or wine, café-goers may see a fleeting, unintended fashion show, or they might become the audience of a spontaneous drama of passers-by fighting or kissing—or both. Before the introduction of cars around 1900, pedestrians, bicycles, pushcart vendors, horses pulling wagons loaded with goods, and horse-drawn omnibuses (an early form of mass transit) all packed

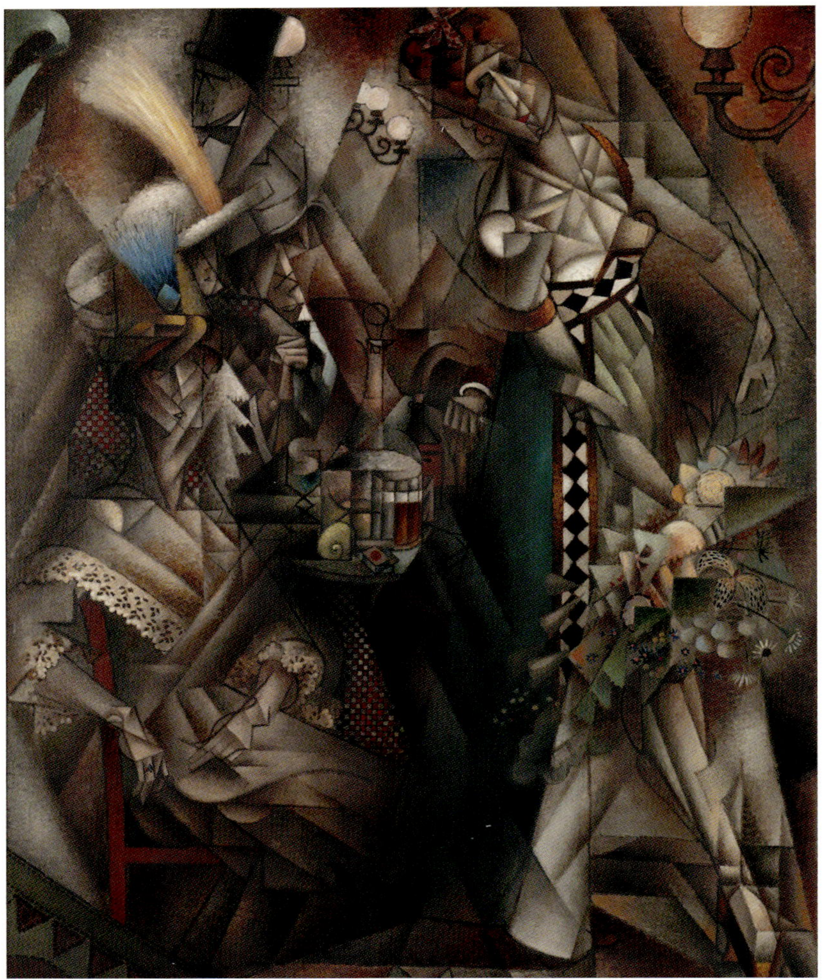

Fig. 10
Jean Metzinger
French, 1883–1956
Danseuse au café (*Dancer in a Café*), 1912
Oil on canvas
57 ½ × 45 in. (146 × 114.3 cm)
Collection Buffalo AKG Art Museum;
General Purchase Funds, 1957, 1957:1

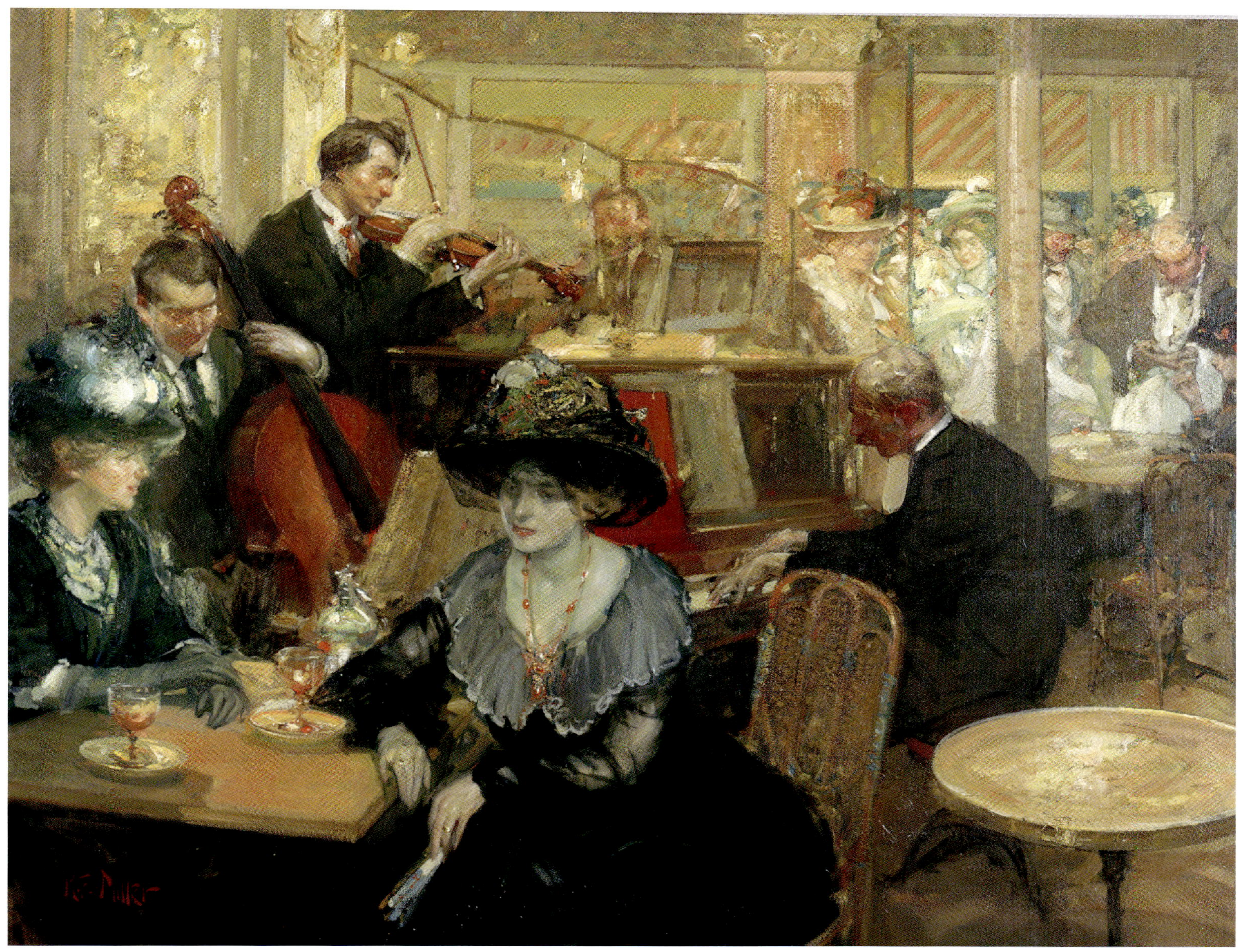

Cat. 58

Richard E. Miller
American, 1875–1943
Café L'Avenue, Paris, ca. 1906–10
Oil on canvas
44 ⅞ × 57 ½ in. (114 × 146.1 cm)
Cummer Museum of Art & Gardens,
Jacksonville, Florida; Purchased with funds
from the Cummer Council, AP.1985.1.1

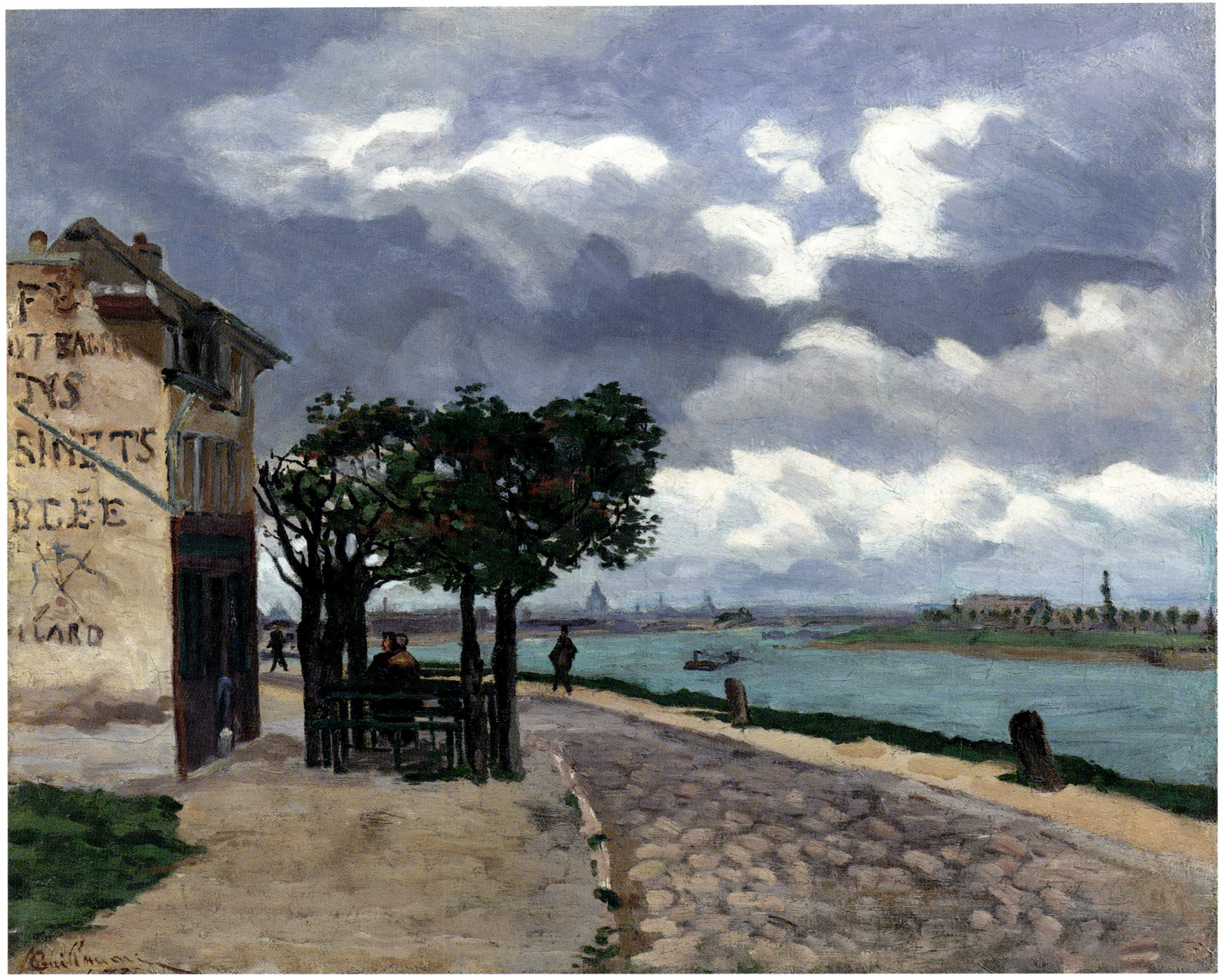

Cat. 5

Armand Guillaumin
French, 1841–1927
Banks of the Seine, 1873
Oil on canvas
21 ¼ × 25 ⅝ in. (54 × 65.1 cm)
Private collection

Cat. 24

Vincent van Gogh
Dutch, 1853–1890
Restaurant Rispal at Asnières, 1887
Oil on canvas
28 ⅞ × 23 ⅝ in. (73.3 × 60 cm)
The Nelson-Atkins Museum of Art, Kansas
City; Gift of Henry W. and Marion H. Bloch,
2015.13.10

Jeffrey H. Jackson

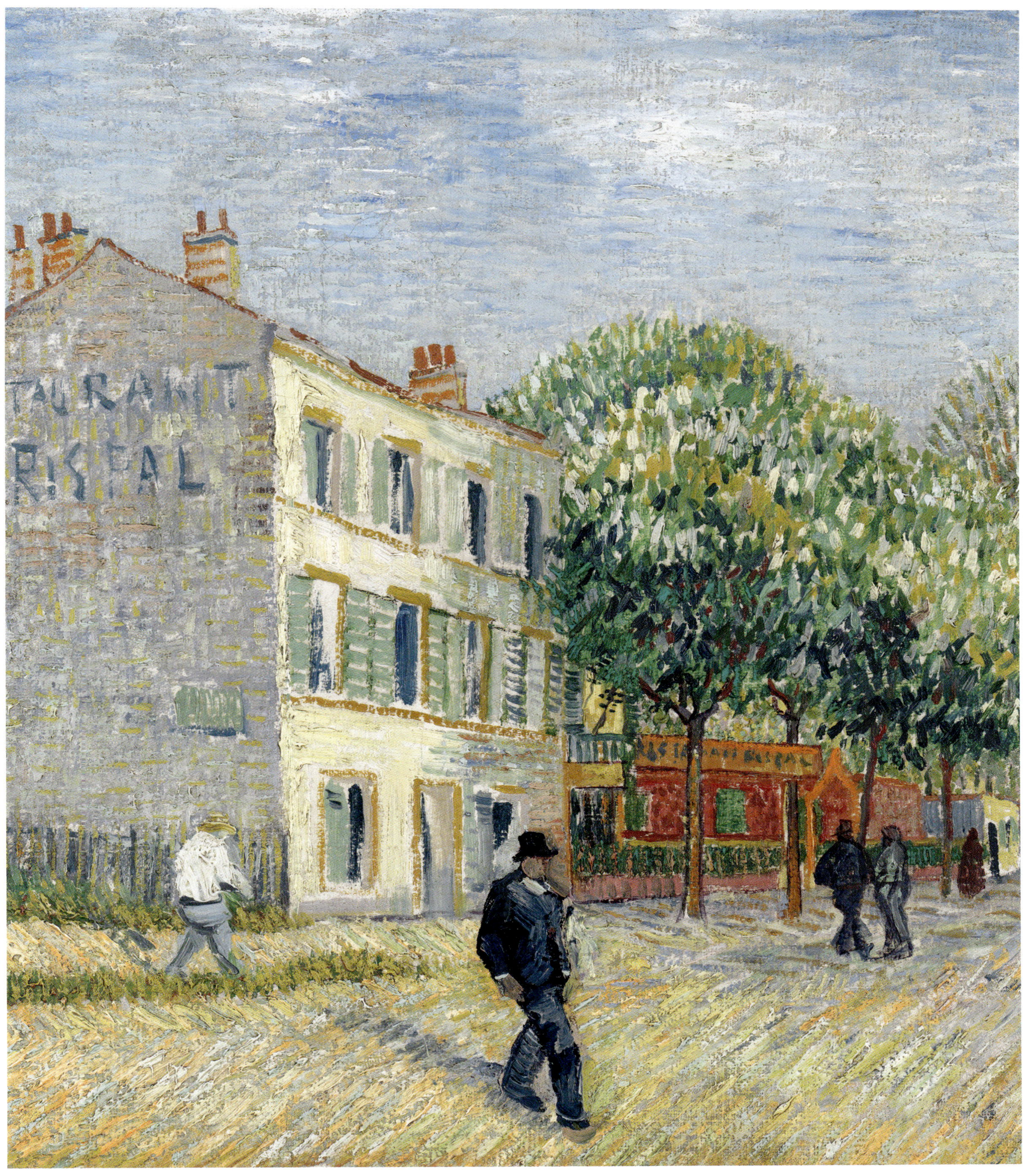

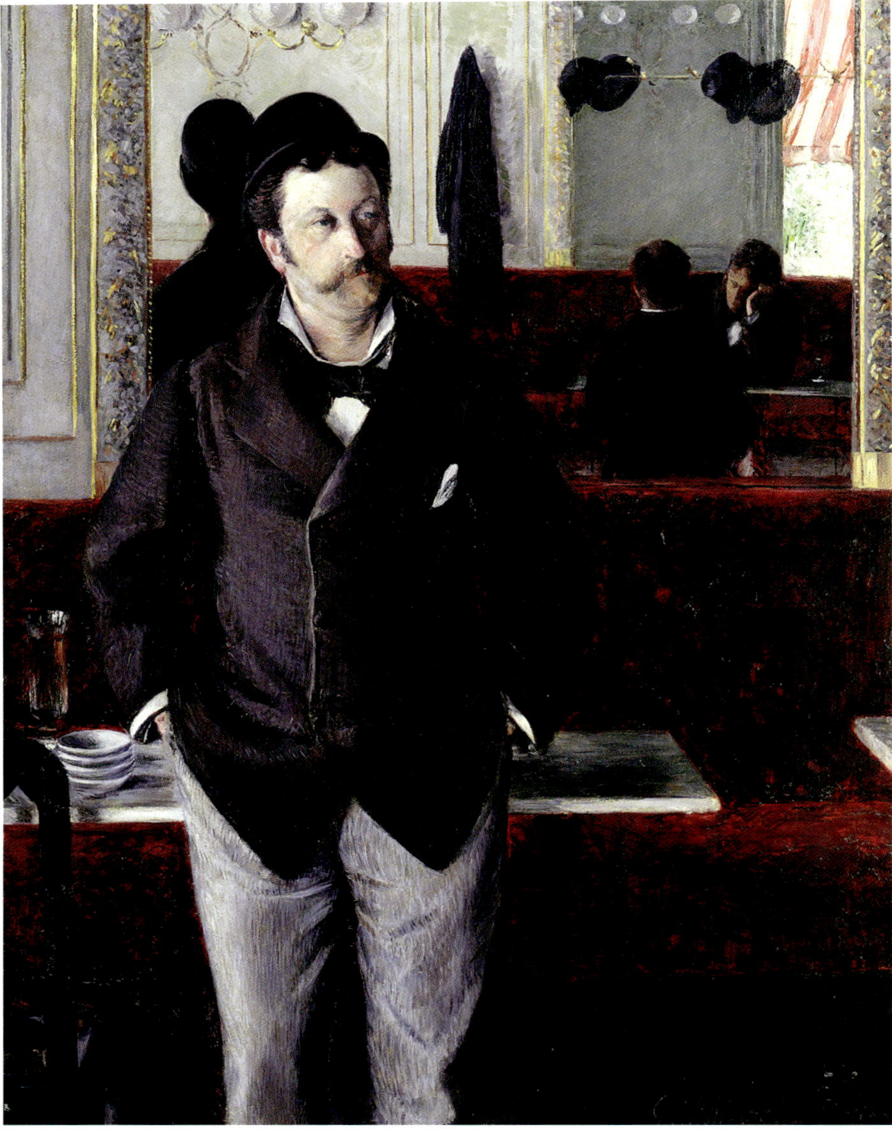

Fig. 11
Gustave Caillebotte
French, 1848–1894
In a Café, 1880
Oil on canvas
60 ¼ × 44 ⅞ in. (153 × 114 cm)
Musée des Beaux-Arts, Rouen, D.946.1

Parisian thoroughfares—allowing the café visitor to observe the ebb and flow of this complicated and at times chaotic traffic, complete with near misses and tragic accidents as vehicles weaved through the streets. Depending on the neighborhood, each show unfolding before their eyes would look different because the physical shape of streets and buildings—including the café's own layout—altered the café–street relationship. Large boulevards produced different spectacles than the maze of medieval streets of the Marais neighborhood (3rd arrondissement) that largely escaped Haussmann's demolition. For example, the scene outside the humble collection of quiet tables along the riverbank in what was likely a suburban working-class establishment depicted in Armand Guillaumin's *Banks of the Seine* (1873, cat. 5) would be quite unlike what passed by the doors of the more upscale venue, likely on a busy street, depicted in Gervex's *Café Scene in Paris*. Even in the relatively quiet riverside suburb of Asnières, Vincent van Gogh observed a steady trickle of patrons, dressed in such a manner to indicate their diversity of classes, strolling toward and away from the towering Restaurant Rispal on a clear sunny day (cat. 24). But no matter what street one may have chosen, its cafés provided the opportunity to watch the city, in all its diverse comedy and drama, travel past.

In this respect, the café turned the famous notion of the "flâneur" on its head. The term refers to someone, usually a man of leisure, who saunters through the city appreciating the complexity of urban life in all its beauty and ugliness. In his landmark 1860 essay "The Painter of Modern Life," French poet and art critic Charles Baudelaire described the artist as a flâneur who takes creative inspiration from the vibrancy of the city itself. Baudelaire's painter meanders through the streets to catch glimpses of Parisian life, and then turns the faces and stories into art. The idea of "modern art" was born as artists turned away from biblical or classical themes to create work about the city, especially Paris.

The café customer did not stroll through the city, rather the city moved past his eyes (or hers, although the flâneur and the artist were almost always thought of as male at that time). Those sitting at café tables could be flâneurs because they watched the passing faces of Parisians and could turn them into art. Cafés were long known as places where creative people gathered, and it would come as no surprise to learn that many of the observations that have inspired poems, songs, or paintings have unwittingly come from those who merely walked past a café.

Gustave Caillebotte's *In a Café* (1880, fig. 11) gives us a typical image of the flâneur. A plainly dressed, mustachioed man blends in with the café interior where he stands, his curious gaze exploring the world around him. "The scene is set in a fancy establishment on the great Parisian boulevards, around noon, as can be seen from the sunny reflections of leaves and the red and white awning in the mirror."[12] The man studies two others whom the viewer sees in the mirror. They look a lot like our flâneur but seem to be deep

in thought or conversation—or perhaps "playing cards or dominoes"[13]—with one man resting his head on his hand. Meanwhile, the watcher keeps his distance, pondering the scene and perhaps inventing a story or sketching in his mind's eye based on what he sees. The bright sunlight penetrates the dark café in the upper right-hand corner, but it is only a slice of the outside world entering into this otherwise pensive, interior scene.

Even as cafés allowed Parisians to view the city and its people, they also became the subject of works of art. Artists acting as flâneurs recognized cafés as important sites in a rapidly changing city and, therefore, a crucial part of "modern life." Modern artists found urban subjects—railroads, architecture, streetscapes, cafés—especially fascinating as the city transformed rapidly in the last decades of the nineteenth century. Paintings and illustrations of cafés offer microcosms of Paris that document the urban space and the lives that Parisians lived at a time of population change, urban renewal, and a growing middle class. They capture Paris at the very moment when it began to look like what we now think of as classic Paris. The art of this era helped create the very "Parisian" feel that would later be amplified by photography and motion pictures. That city-café relationship is especially pronounced in Albert André's *The Café* (1917, cat. 67), which shows the view from inside a café in the southern French port city of Marseilles looking out to a rain-soaked street. Other paintings look from the street into the café itself, as though the artist were standing in the road with an easel and catching a moment from someone's life or a fleeting scene of social interaction happening at the café's tables.

Ilya Repin's *A Parisian Café* (1875, fig. 12) illustrates the café as the subject of the flâneur's gaze by depicting a crowd that spills out onto the boulevard itself. The barrier between the interior and exterior of the café is negligible as the patrons in the foreground sit on the sidewalk facing out to the rest of Paris to see and be seen

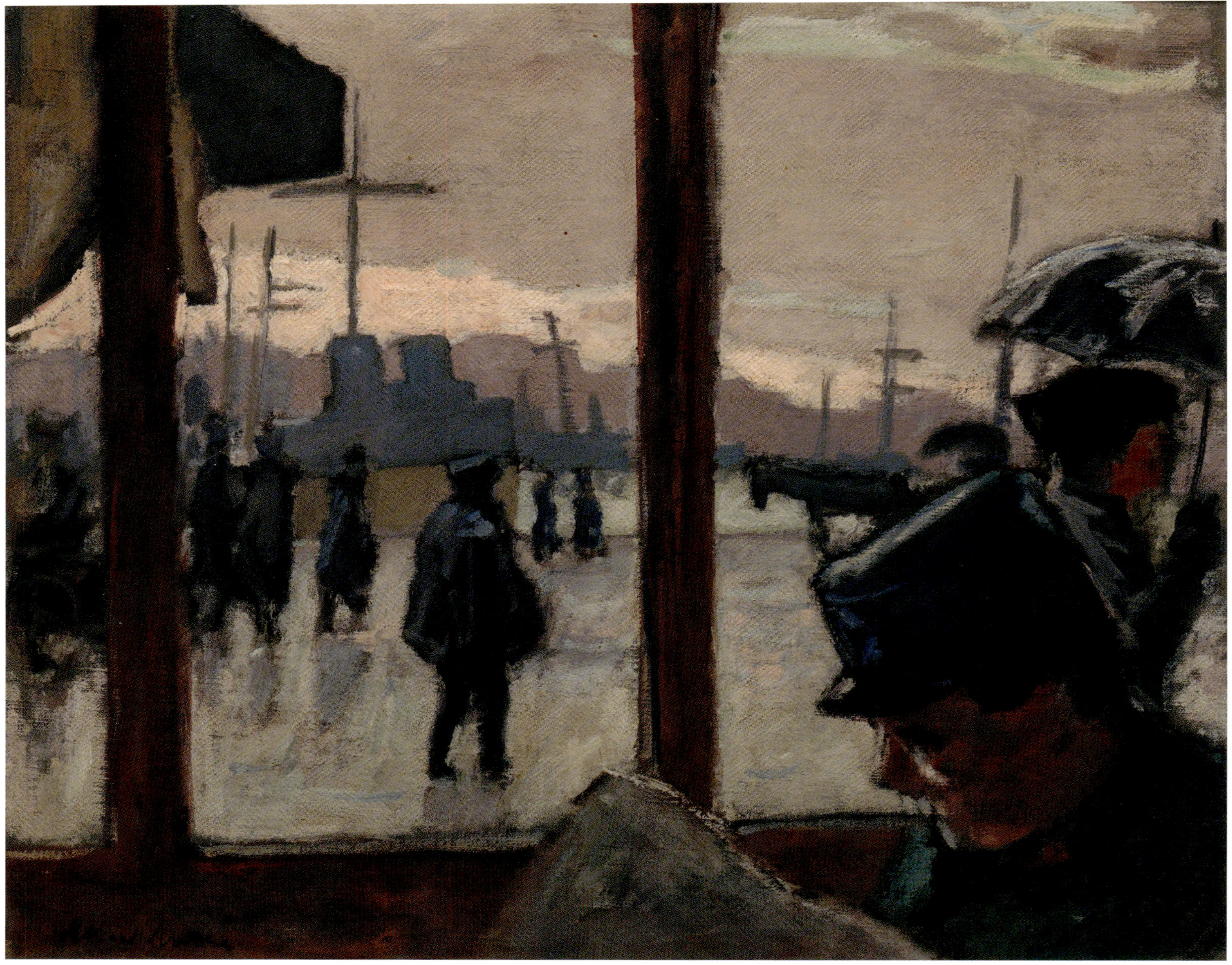

Cat. 67

Albert André
French, 1869–1954
The Café, 1917
Oil on canvas
15 × 18 in. (38.1 × 45.7 cm)
Joslyn Art Museum; Gift of the American
Federation of Arts, 1943.60

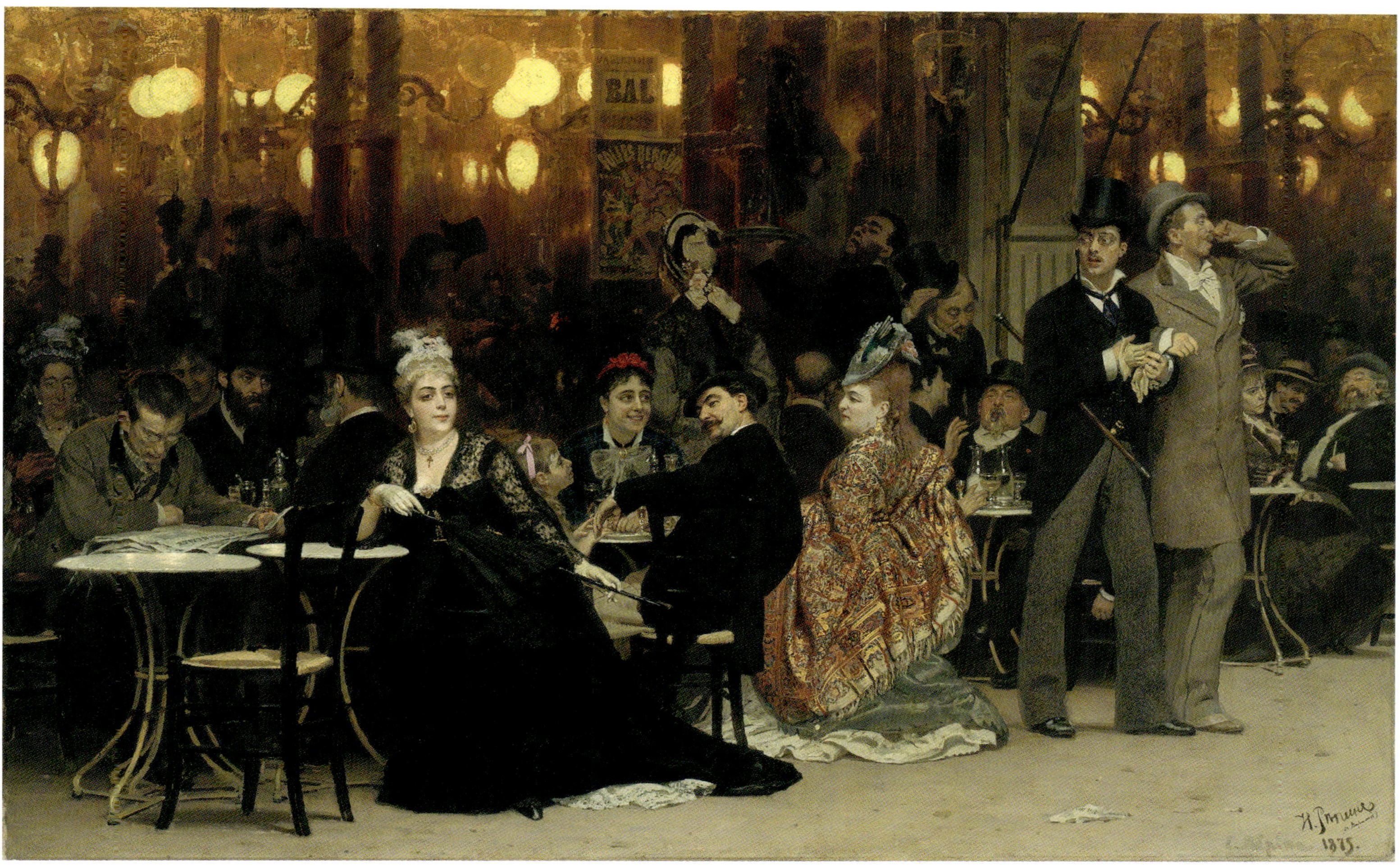

Fig. 12
Ilya Repin
Russian, 1844–1930
A Parisian Café, 1875
Oil on canvas
47 ½ × 75 ½ in. (120.6 × 191.8 cm)
Private collection

by passersby. Repin depicts a cross-section of social groups, from top-hatted gentlemen to homburg-sporting men further down the social scale. All of them inhabit the same café, even if they do not interact with one another. Customers talk and drink, one man reads a newspaper—a reminder that the café has long been the heart of intellectual as well as social life—and a family dines in the middle of the image. In the dim glow of the interior space, faces in the painting are much less finished than those in the foreground. The city intrudes in the form of two advertisements for popular entertainments of the time: a *bal* (or dance hall) and the Folies Bergère, one of the great music halls of the late nineteenth century; the poster Repin depicts is not unlike that by Jules Chéret included in this exhibition featuring the American dancer Loïe Fuller famous for her flowing gowns and scarves illuminated on stage by dramatic theatrical lighting (1893, see cat. 37).

Amidst several well-known figures of the day, three women form a compositional triangle at the center of the painting. One woman looks inside the café; we only see her back. In some ways she stands in for the viewer who is also peeking in. The two seated women wear different, yet equally striking fashions. The bejeweled one dressed in black is the prominent actress Anna Judic. The other wears an exotic scarf imported from "the East" in a nod to French fascination with exoticism in this era of imperial expansion and conquest in Africa and Asia. Despite the difference in clothing, both are on display for anyone walking past the café to see and attract the viewer. Madame Judic has certainly caught the eye of the gentleman in the dark suit and top hat as he gazes across the length of the canvas at her beauty. Or perhaps he is aghast at what art historian David Jackson called the "liberality and license of Paris as the unchaperoned and worldly figure of Anna Judic draws the attention and excitement of those about her."[14] Either way, Repin offers this scene as just one of the many dramas that might be captured at this café on any given day.

A Decadent Escape

There has always been a push-and-pull in the relationship between the café and the city. Cafés could bring people together and inspire great art, but they could also provide a quiet respite from the city's noise and crowds. In many images, Paris is present but only hinted at on the edge even as pairs or groups of people talk, flirt, or simply share one another's presence. Jean-François Raffaëlli's *Bohèmes au café* (1886, fig. 13), which depicts the Café Guerbois, provides an example of the café as an escape from urban life. Raffaëlli gives the viewer a group of "bohemians," the word commonly used for creative thinkers—painters, poets, musicians, writers. For them the café was a locale to encounter other like-minded people and a cheap place for "starving artists" to sit all day for the price of a drink or two. But the city, although

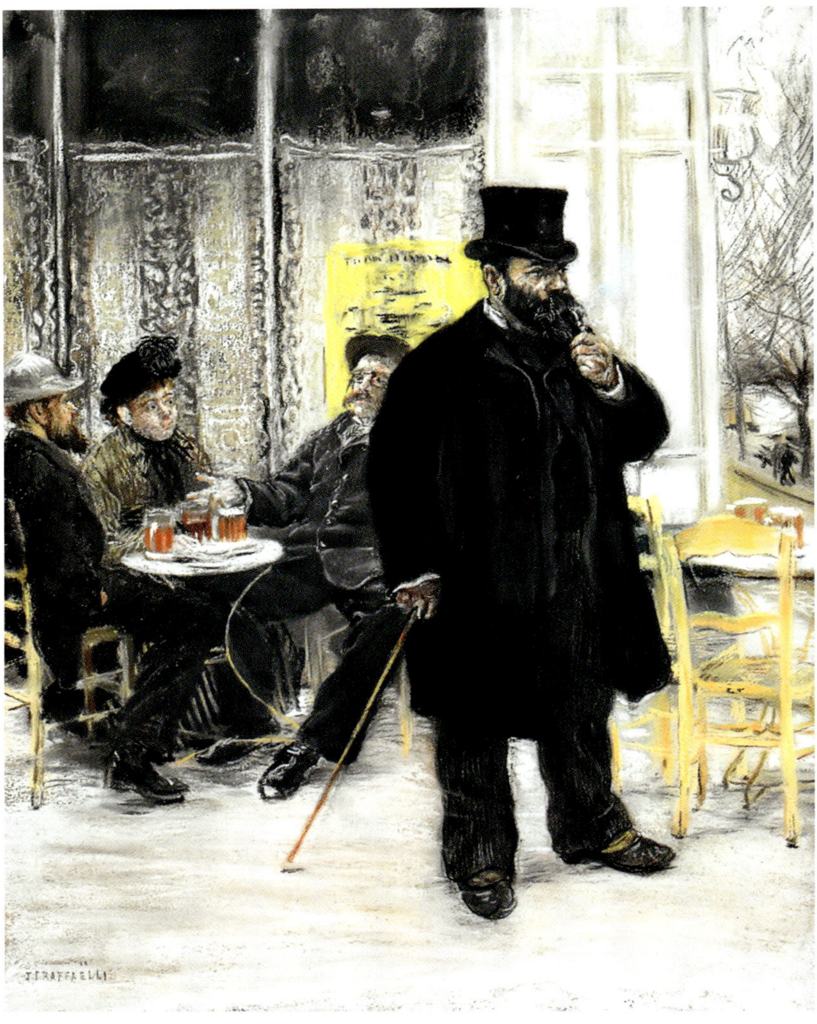

Fig. 13
Jean-Francois Raffaëlli
French, 1850–1924
Bohèmes au café, 1886
Pastel on canvas
21 ⅞ × 17 ¼ in. (55.5 × 43.7 cm)
Musée des Beaux-Arts, Bordeaux, Bx E 985

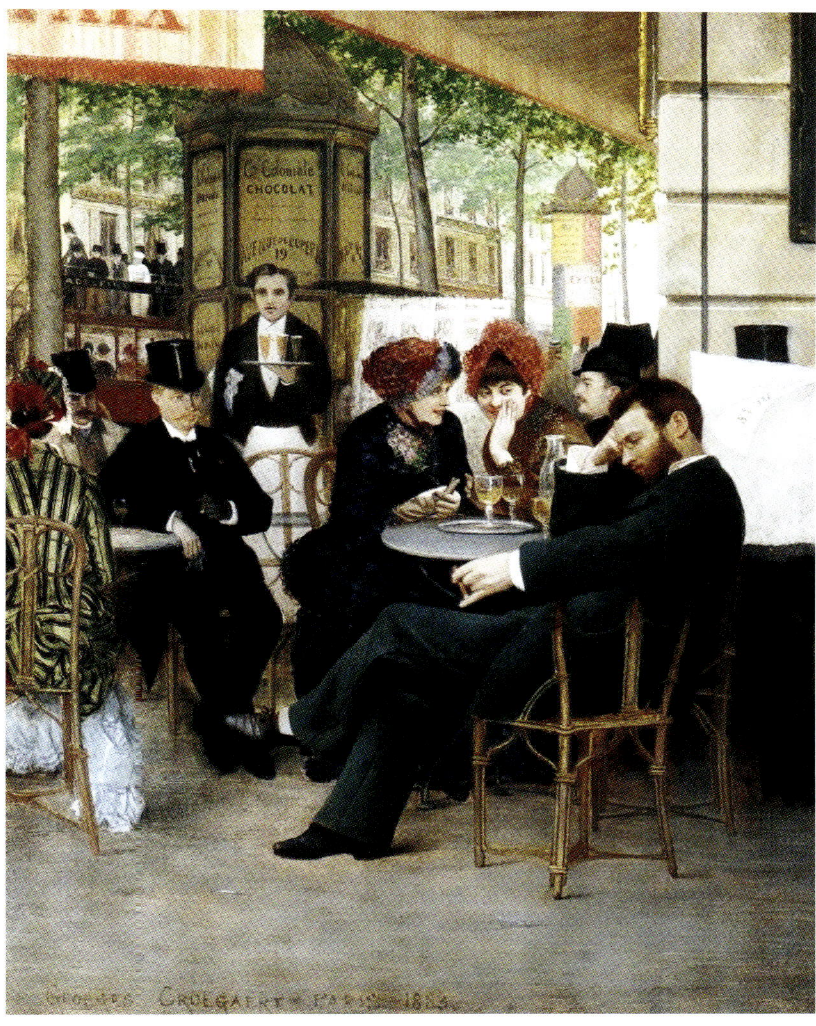

Fig. 14
Georges Croegaert
French, 1848–1923
Le Café, 1883
Oil on panel
13 ⅜ × 10½ in. (34 × 26.5 cm)
Private collection

present in the painting, is on the margin; a mere sliver of the streetscape is visible on the right-hand side of the canvas. The café has provided a quiet cocoon in which these artists can pursue their conversations.

Belgian artist Georges Croegaert shows a very different group of people in *Le Café* (1883, fig. 14), who are likewise enjoying the quiet space set apart from the urban fray. The city is clearly present in the form of an omnibus in the painting's background; we see passengers riding on the top level of this double-decker vehicle and the staircase leading upwards on the left-hand edge of the canvas. Croegaert's refined crowd in fashionable attire flirts and gossips under the awning outside this upscale café. Yet even though they are sitting only a few feet from the busy roadway, Croegaert makes the urban space feel far away, thus allowing the painting's action to take place in an atmosphere of relative isolation.

Pushing the city to the fringes of the painting points out visually how cafés could also provide privacy even though visitors often sat in full view of others. Édouard Manet captures this kind of public intimacy in *Chez le Père Lathuille* (1879, see fig. 35) as lovers look into one another's eyes. The model for the man in the painting was the son of the café's owner wearing Manet's own coat.[15] The café owner himself stands in the background as the waiter but looks at the viewer rather than at the couple. The couple's gaze is the center of the painting, not the city street on the right-hand side. The greenery inside the café and the trees outside further shut out the urban setting.

Likewise, Italian painter Giovanni Boldini's *Conversation in a Café* (ca. 1879, fig. 15) depicts another type of couple. The two well-dressed women, purportedly artist Berthe Morisot and Countess Gabrielle de Rasty, rest amidst a sea of café tables and chairs on a Parisian boulevard in full view of anyone passing by. Yet Boldini frames the images so that the street is off to the side, thus

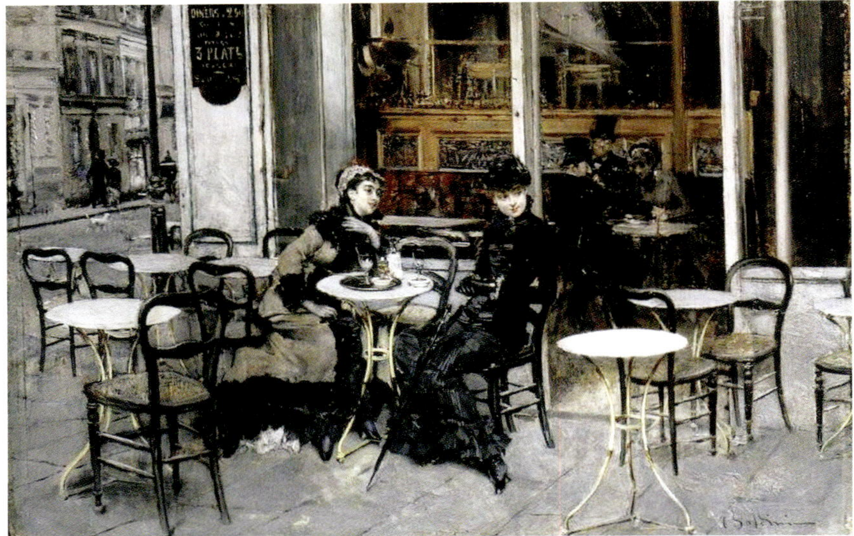

Fig. 15
Giovanni Boldini
Italian, 1842–1931
Conversation in a Café, ca. 1879
Oil on panel
11 × 16 ⅛ in. (28 × 41 cm)
Private collection

creating the sense that these women are alone and that their conversation is contained completely within their own private space. Although they look curiously into the distance, perhaps at something or someone on the street, the viewer does not know what has captured their attention. Despite being in public, the café has allowed them to be in a world of their own.

A similar kind of privacy also emerges in Raffaëlli's *The Absinthe Drinkers* (1881, cat. 17). Yet this image of being cut off from Paris also speaks of the dangers of social isolation: "Raffaëlli excelled at capturing the coarse milieu of the Parisian *banlieue*—the marginal areas beyond the city then being colonized by industrialization and urban sprawl."[16] The men he depicts here are outsiders, alienated from others, and unable to rouse energy for a day's activity or even to look one another in the eye. They are also likely drunk, seated beneath a cluster of grapes painted on the café wall representing the allure of wine. But Raffaëlli has told us that they are drinking absinthe, the popular licorice-flavored spirit. One contemporary critic called the pitiable subjects of this work "poverty-stricken wrecks" who had succumbed to absinthe's strength with "such a particular character of suffering and of revolt, such a poignant color of melancholy." The café gave them privacy, but it also condemned them to alcoholic loneliness.[17]

Anxieties about the power of absinthe were strong in France, and it was ultimately banned by the French government in 1915 for fear that it caused insanity and would undermine the military during World War I. The drink was highly controversial in part because artists swore by its ability to open their minds to new ways of seeing. Vincent van Gogh's abusive relationship with absinthe was notorious, and some believe its hallucinogenic properties inspired his famous paintings such as *The Starry Night* (1889).[18] Van Gogh thought enough of the drink to paint its "portrait" in *Café Table with Absinthe* (1887, fig. 16). A full glass of the greenish-grey liquid, paired with a carafe of water, sits on a table next to the window. The two vessels are almost personified as a "couple," or as lovers who sit close together in an intimate café rendezvous. Juan Gris offers a Cubist scene of a Parisian dandy enjoying his glassful of absinthe which appears so prominently in the foreground in his *Man in a Café* (1912, cat. 63) that

Cat. 17

Jean-François Raffaëlli
French, 1850–1924
The Absinthe Drinkers, 1881
Oil on canvas
42 ½ × 42 ½ in. (108 × 108 cm)
Fine Arts Museums of San Francisco; Museum purchase, Roscoe and Margaret Oakes Income Fund, Jay D. and Clare C. McEvoy Endowment Fund, Tribute Funds, Friends of Ian White Endowment Fund, Unrestricted Art Acquisition Endowment Income Fund, Grover A. Magnin Bequest Fund, and the Yvonne Cappeller Trust, 2010.16

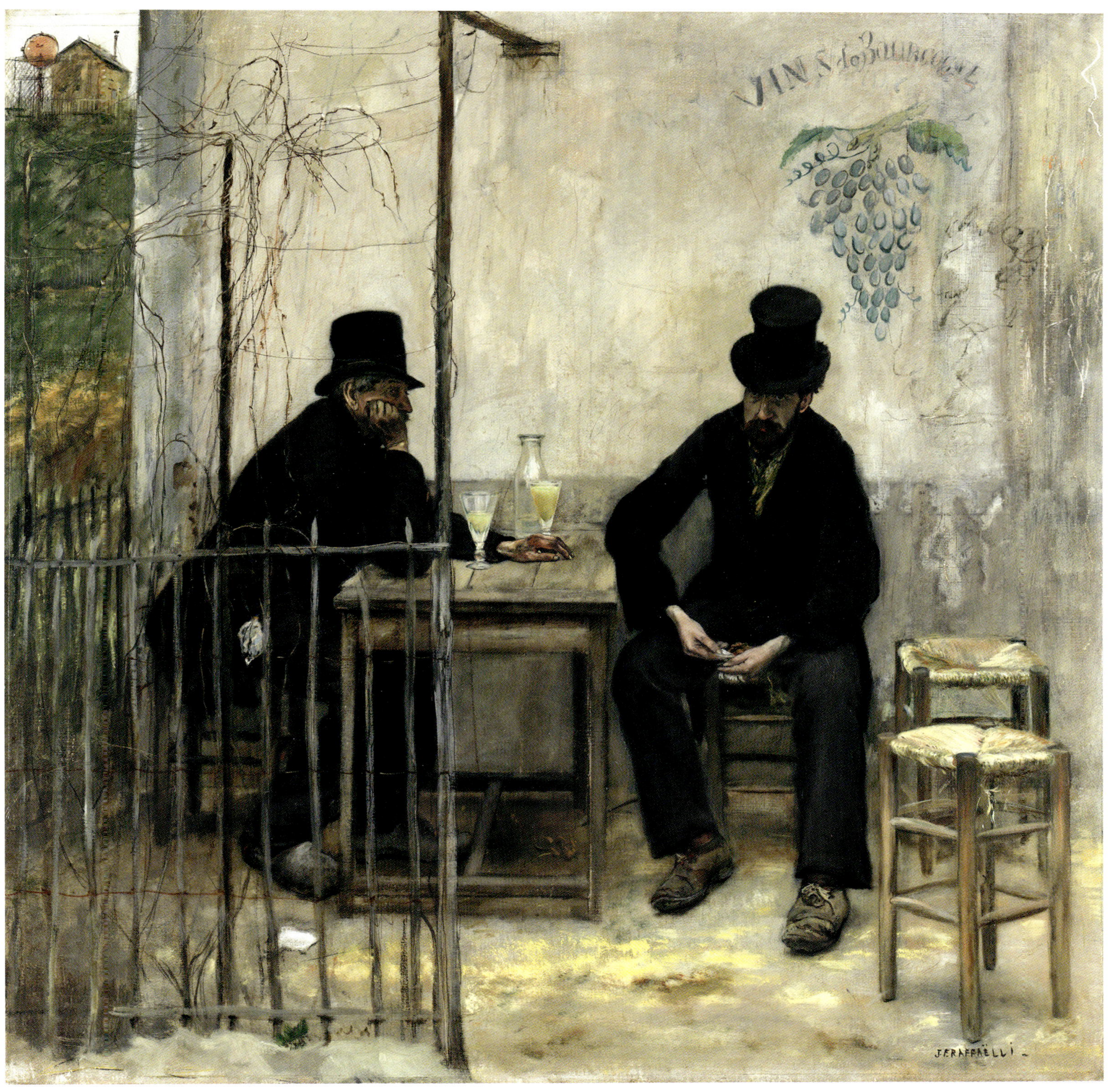

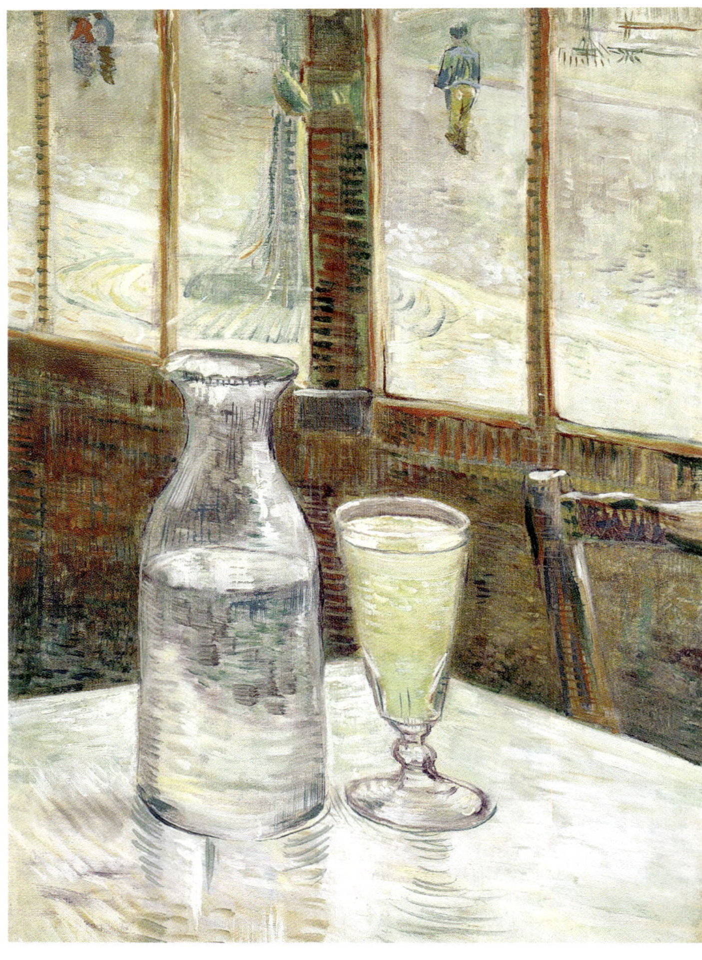

Fig. 16
Vincent van Gogh
Dutch, 1853–1890
Café Table with Absinthe, February–
March 1887
Oil on canvas
18 ¼ × 13 ⅛ in. (46.3 × 33.2 cm)
Van Gogh Museum, Amsterdam (Vincent
van Gogh Foundation)

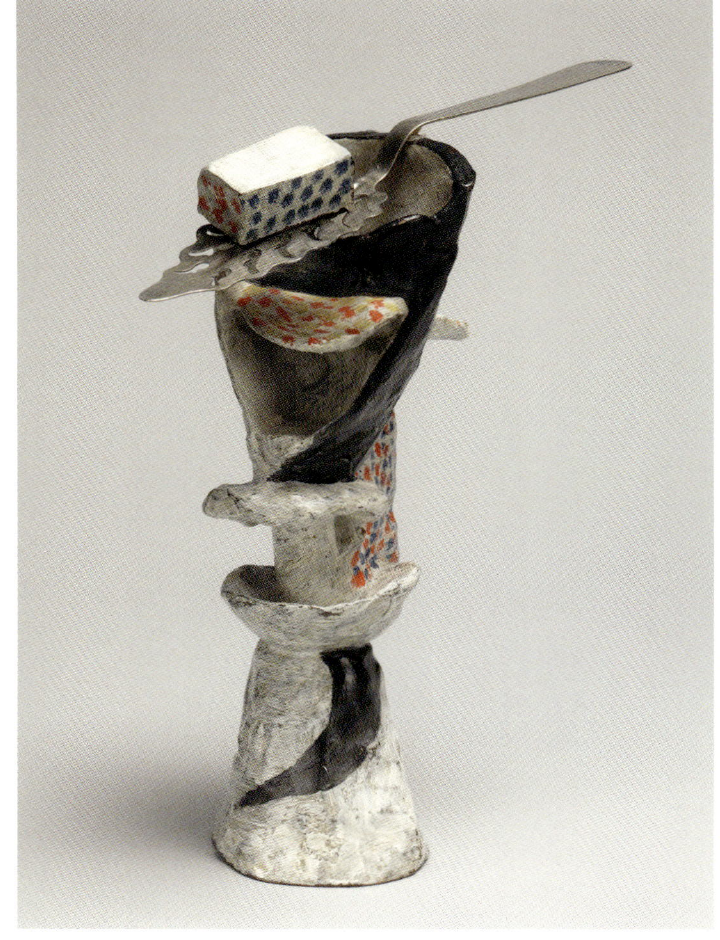

Fig. 17
Pablo Picasso
Spanish, 1881–1973
Glass of Absinthe, spring 1914
Painted bronze with absinthe spoon
8 ½ × 6 ½ × 3 ⅜ in. (21.6 × 16.4 × 8.5 cm),
diameter at base 2 ½ in. (6.4 cm)
The Museum of Modern Art, New York; Gift
of Louise Reinhardt Smith, 292.1956

it seems to be his companion. Gris showed appreciation to Cubism's champion, the poet Guillaume Apollinaire, by including his initials (AP) in the background along with the first letters of Pablo Picasso's (PIC). Like Gris, Picasso also paid tribute to the appeal of the elixir in his sculpture *Glass of Absinthe* (1914, fig. 17), including the ritual of pouring water over a sugar cube that sits on a slotted spoon. The gaps in the spoon allow the

melted sugar to flow into the glass to dilute the bright green liquor. Picasso incorporated an actual spoon into his work, merging artistic representation and an object of daily life.[19] That attention to the details of everyday Parisian experience appears in many of Picasso's "café still-lifes" (cat. 60) where he painted bottles of liquor, coffee pots, café tables, and, in *La Glace* (1912, cat. 62), a bowl of ice cream he likely ate at the

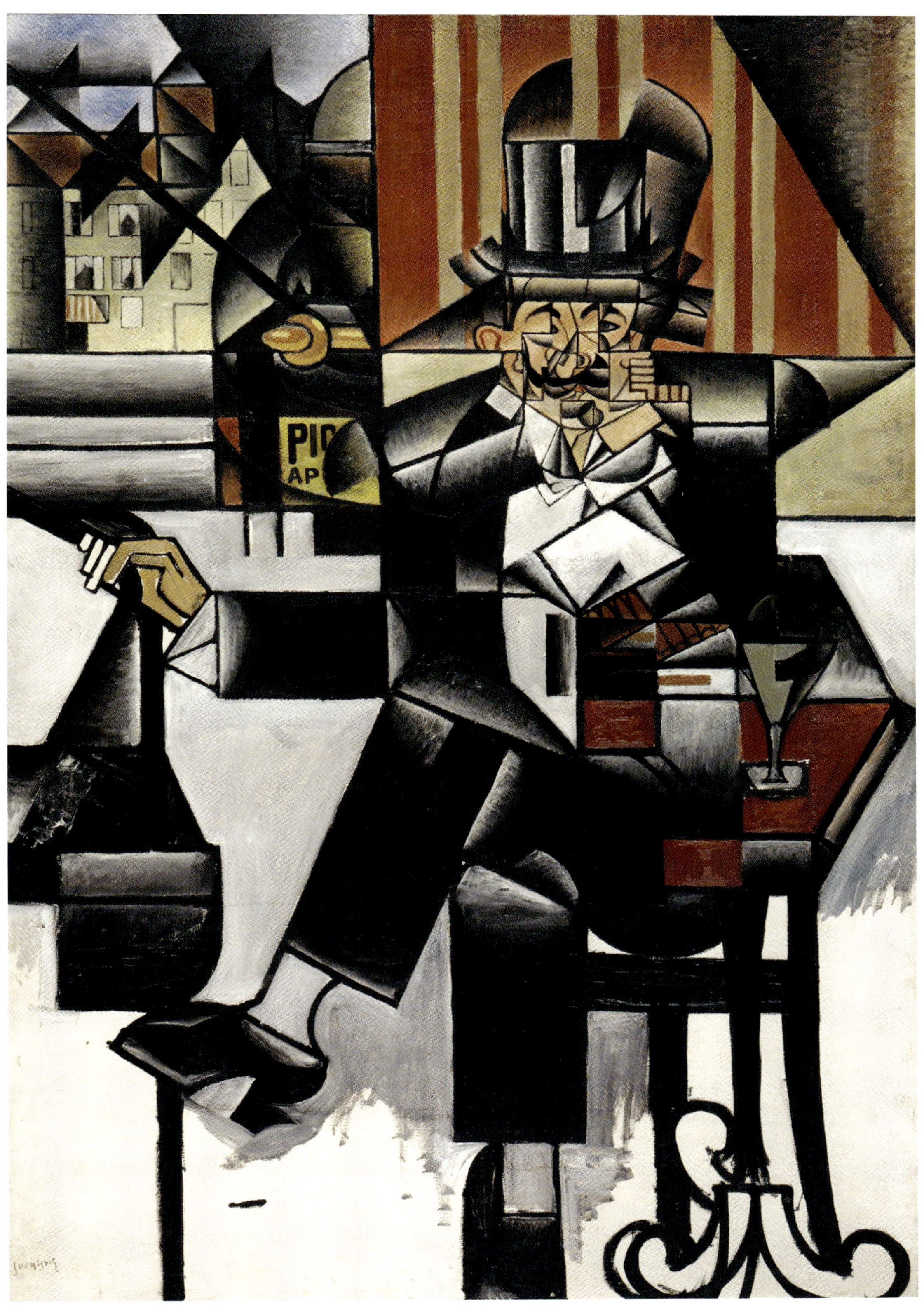

Cat. 63

Juan Gris
Spanish, 1887–1927
Man in a Café, 1912
Oil on canvas
50 ¼ × 34 ¾ in. (127.6 × 88.3 cm)
Philadelphia Museum of Art, The Louise
and Walter Arensberg Collection, 1950,
1950-134-94

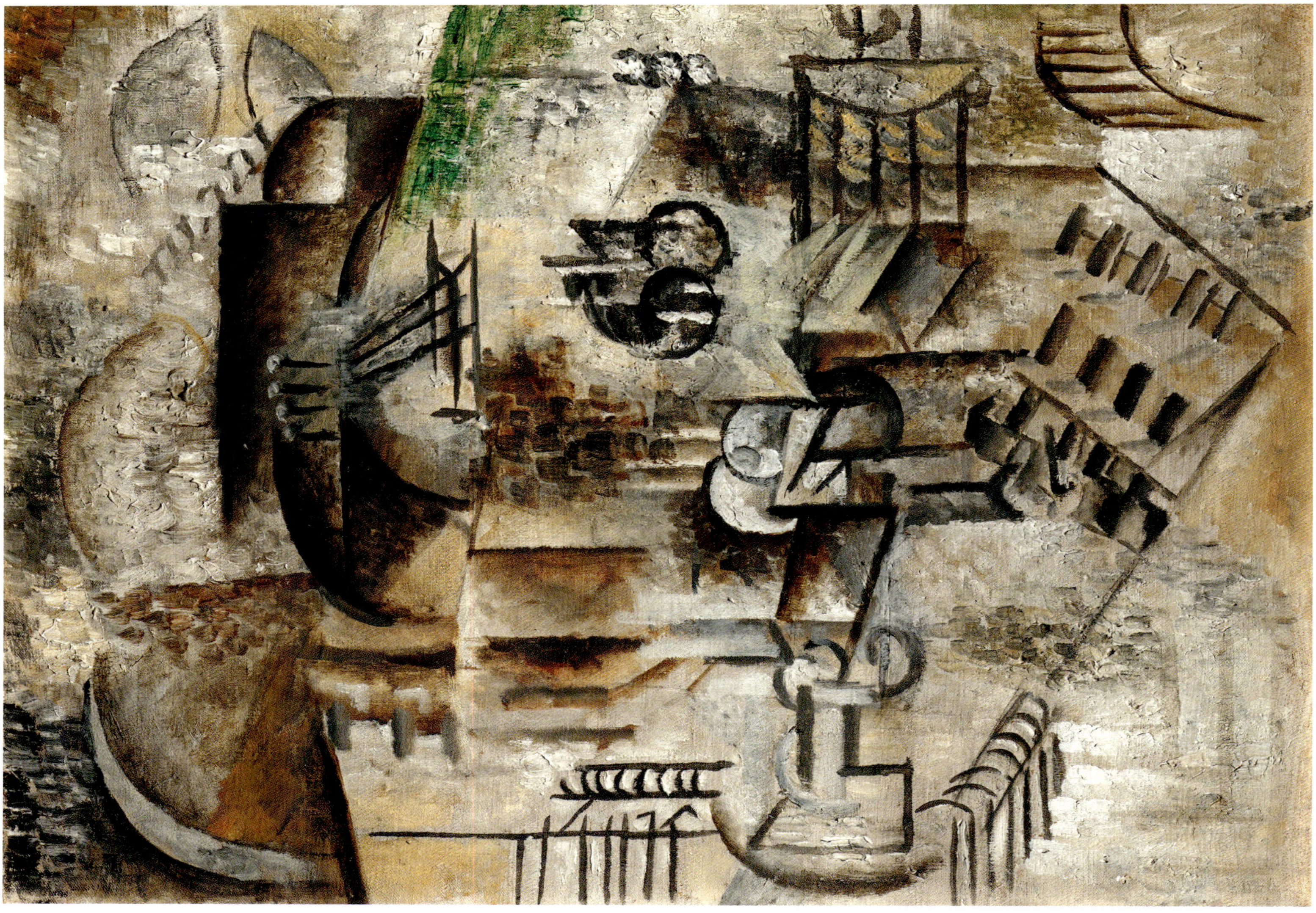

Cat. 60

Pablo Picasso
Spanish, 1881–1973
Mandolin and a Glass of Pernod, 1911
Oil on canvas
13 × 18 ½ in. (33 × 47 cm)
National Gallery, Prague, O 14818

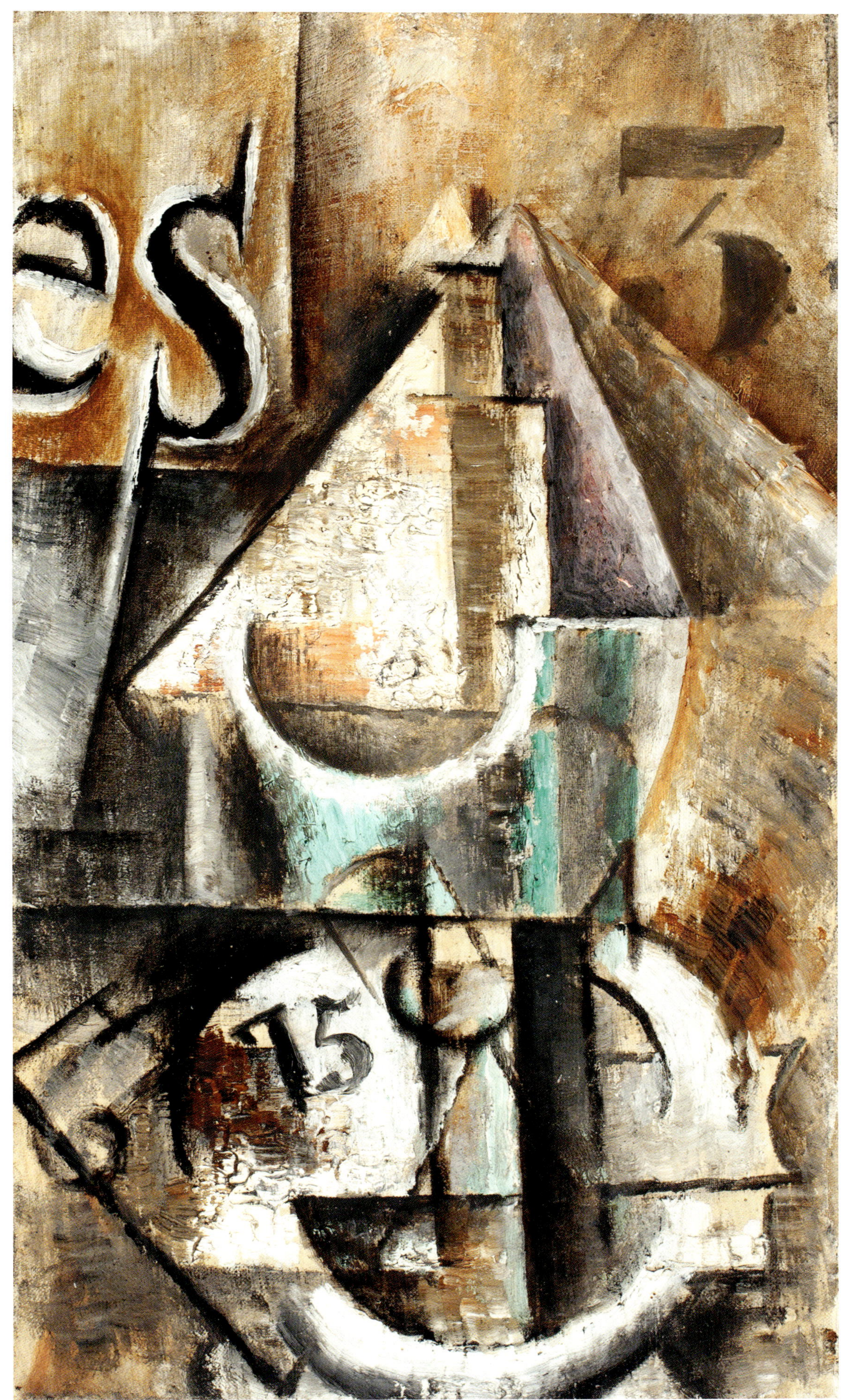

Cat. 62

Pablo Picasso
Spanish, 1881–1973
La Glace, January–March 1912
Oil on canvas
9 ½ × 5 ½ in. (24.1 × 14 cm)
Kirkland Family Collection

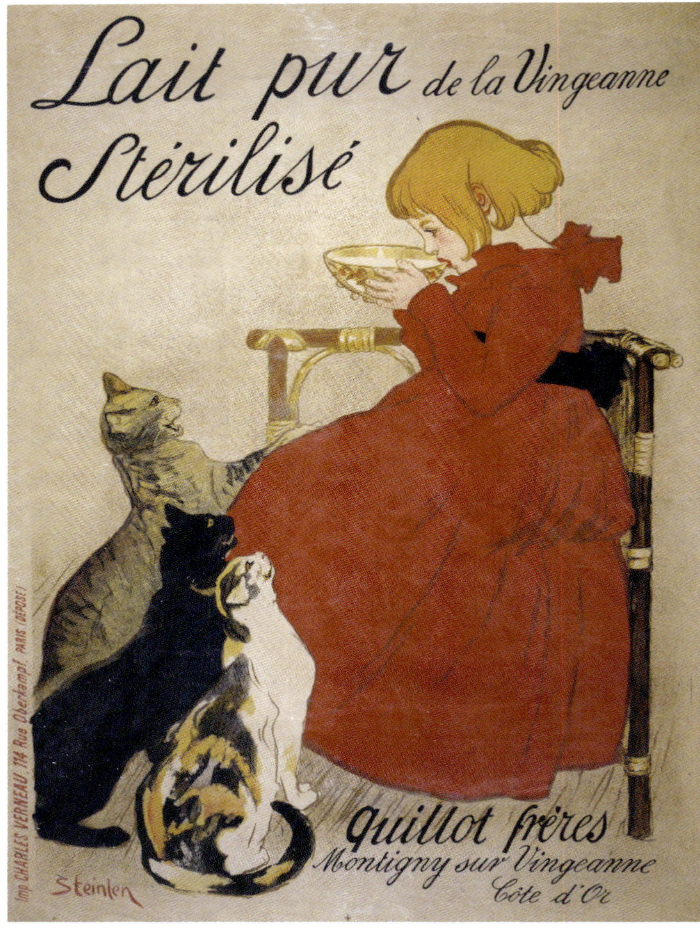
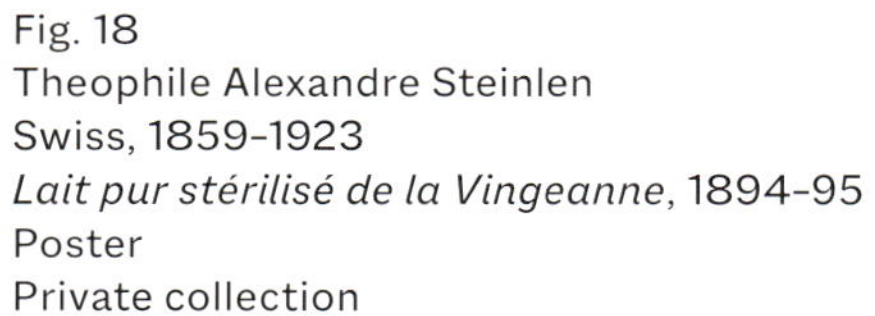

Fig. 18
Theophile Alexandre Steinlen
Swiss, 1859–1923
Lait pur stérilisé de la Vingeanne, 1894–95
Poster
Private collection

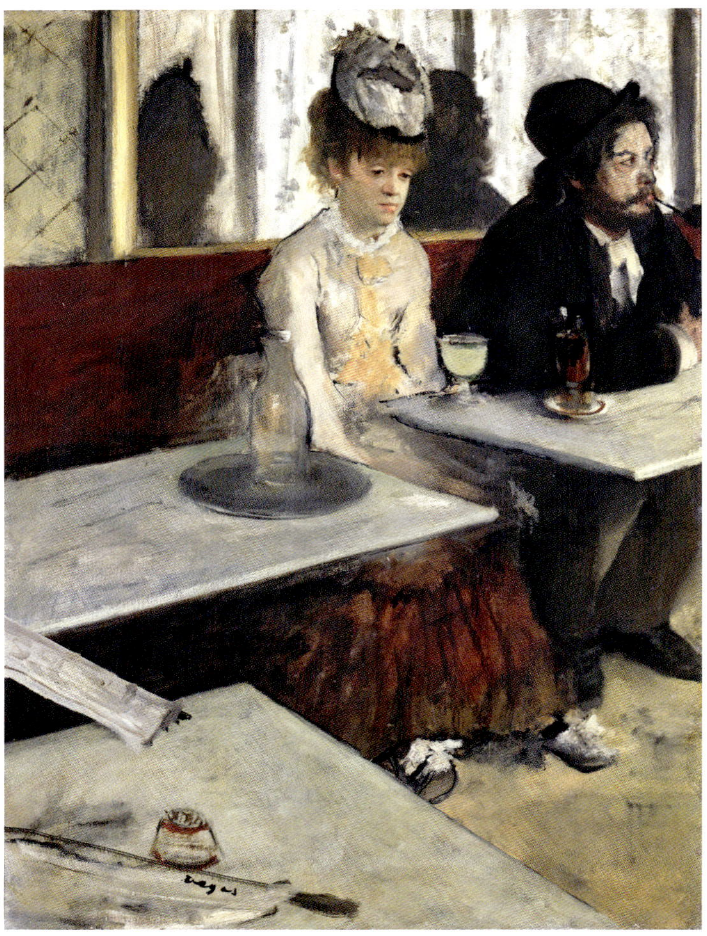

Fig. 19
Edgar Degas
French, 1834–1917
Dans un café, 1875–76
Oil on canvas
36 ¼ × 27 in. (92 × 68.5 cm)
Musée d'Orsay, Paris, RF 1984

Taverne de l'Ermitage, the Montmartre gathering place near his home where numerous artists and entertainers gathered. For Picasso, anything from dessert to alcohol could become art.

Worries about absinthe's potency were part of a larger moral panic in the late nineteenth century. Political and social change sparked fears of France's "degeneracy" both in terms of declining values but also of French citizens' physical bodies. France underwent a lengthy period of soul-searching in the wake of the

Franco-Prussian War of 1870–71. The capital was besieged, the French army humiliated, Napoleon III taken prisoner, and a new unified German empire spitefully declared in the halls of Versailles. The conquering Germans absorbed the eastern French territories of Alsace and Lorraine. Many in the newly established democratic government, the Third Republic, worried that French people were becoming weak and unable to defend the nation in a future conflict that some believed to be inevitable. That concern was aggravated by the fact that large numbers of soldiers had come home from the war addicted to the morphine given by surgeons as an anesthetic. As a result, the government passed welfare legislation to assist families financially and promote a higher birthrate so that mothers could produce the next generation of soldiers. Medical experts touted physical exercise routines to toughen up French men. They also advocated children drinking "pure sterilized milk," thus inspiring the famous 1894 advertising poster by Théophile Alexandre Steinlen which features that phrase (fig. 18).[20] This same concern for physical health also led to the anti-absinthe campaign.

Paintings such as Raffaëlli's highlight these concerns about alcohol as well as larger worries about Paris as a place of moral decline. There is a strong connection between such images of isolation, related to Durkheim's fears of anomie, and alcohol consumption in many of the paintings in this exhibition. That fear was perhaps most famously expressed in Edgar Degas's *Dans un café* (1875–76, fig. 19) of a woman drinking on her own. Ignoring the man next to her, her eyes are glazed over as she stares off into the distance, suggesting her mental state at drinking too much of "the green fairy," as absinthe was sometimes known. The angle of the shadow entering the Nouvelle Athènes, where the scene takes place, suggests that the painting is set in the morning hours; the woman is drunk well before noon.

A City of Neighborhoods

Depictions of cafés were most likely to be set in one of the two most famous neighborhoods in the modern history of the arts in Paris: Montmartre or Montparnasse. Unsurprisingly, painters and illustrators routinely depicted these *quartiers* because they were home. Not only did French artists—whether Parisian or new migrants from the provinces—find their way there, so

did the Dutch artist Vincent van Gogh, the American Robert Henri, the Italian Federico Zandomeneghi, and the Spaniard Pablo Picasso. These foreign artists often highlight Montmartre or Montparnasse as their subject matter in their work.

Before the city limits expanded in 1860, Montmartre was a rural village on a hilltop just outside Paris's urban boundary to the north. That meant it was also outside the wall where Parisian taxmen collected a duty on goods being imported. As a result, food and alcohol were cheaper there and in the other settlements surrounding the capital. Business was brisk for restaurants and cafés in these areas as Parisians looked for less expensive fare, and cost-conscious artists were among the most regular customers. Père Lathuille's café depicted in Manet's painting was just beyond the tax wall on the way to Montmartre located at 7 Avenue de Clichy, as was the Café Guerbois next door. The Café Wepler would be founded in 1881 just a few meters down the street.

Montmartre was also a beautiful place that inspired painting, verse, and song (cat. 68). Set on a promontory, Montmartre has some of the most stunning views of the rest of the city, which lies in the lowland along the Seine to the south. It was also connected to the fields and vineyards in the countryside to the north. The higher altitude allowed millers to set up windmills (*moulins*). Those picturesque structures are still nostalgic symbols of Montmartre today.

Spaniard Ramon Casas's painting *Plein air* (ca. 1890–91, fig. 20) depicts a human dynamic like those set in other cafés yet locates it in Montmartre, something made clear by the windmill. Only two people occupy the canvas, and, although we do not see their faces, they are in relationship to one another through the woman's gaze at the man in the distance. Such a moment in the lives of these two people could easily take place in a café on one of the city's boulevards. But Casas stayed in Montmartre with other artists, especially the

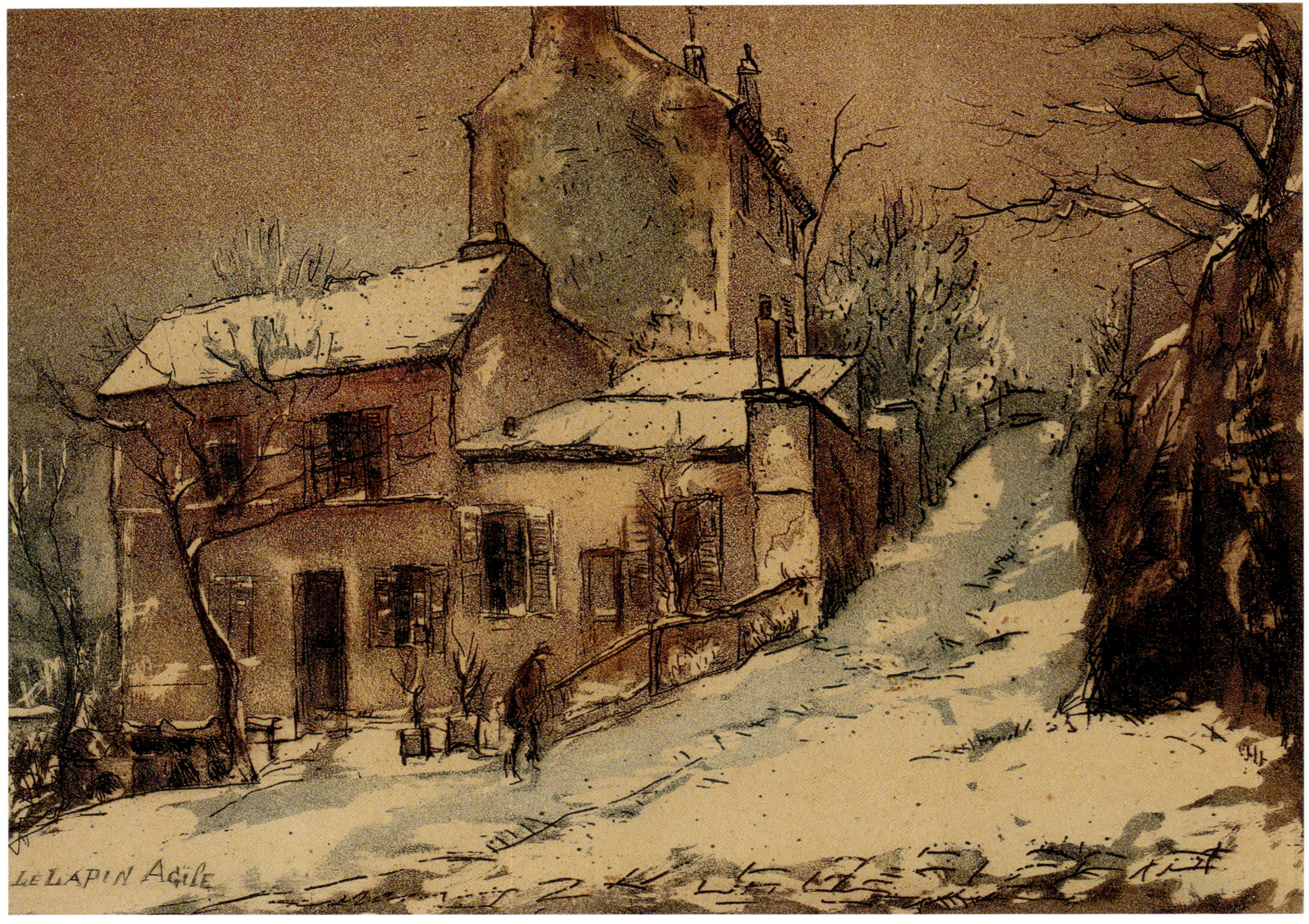

Cat. 68

Gen Paul (Paul Trelade)
French, 1895–1975
Le Lapin Agile, ca. 1920
Aquatint
image: 5 ¾ × 8 in. (14.6 × 20.3 cm)
sheet: 9 ¾ × 11 ⅝ in. (24.8 × 29.5 cm)
Private collection

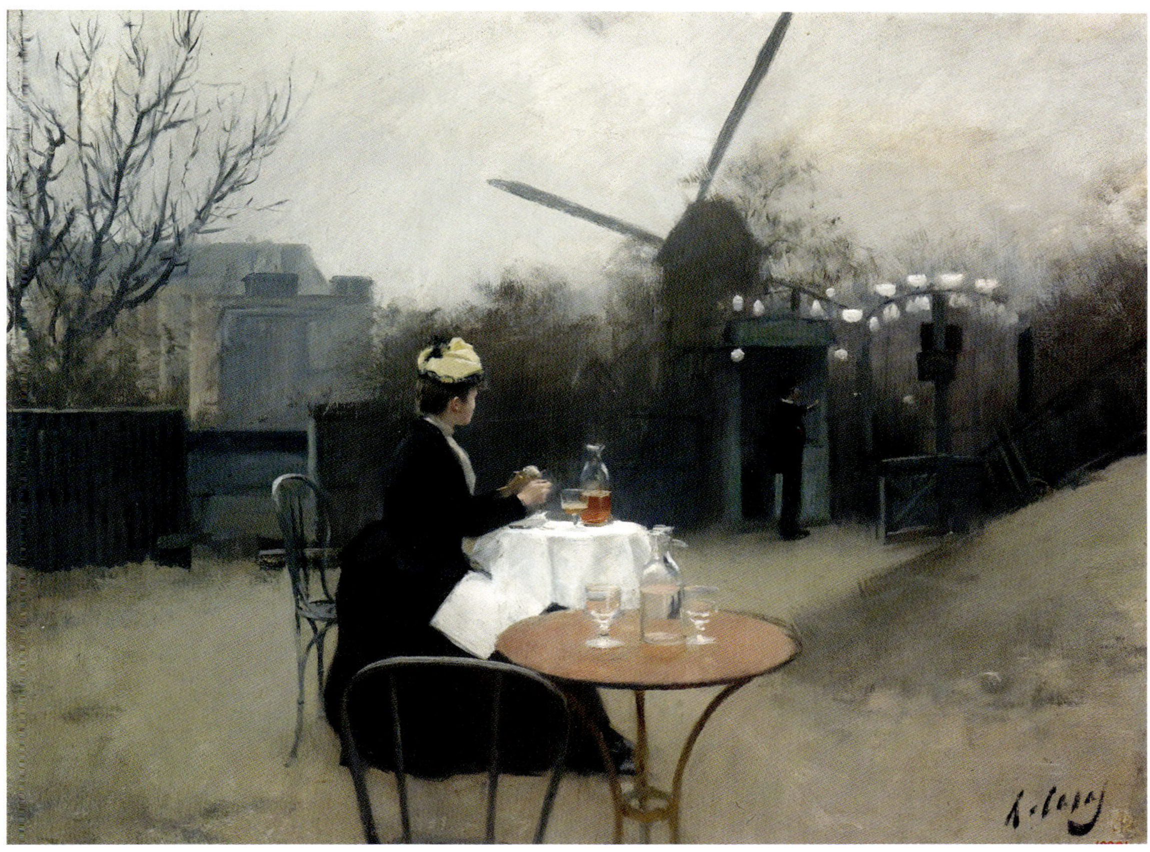

Fig. 20
Ramon Casas
Spanish, 1866–1932
Plein air, ca. 1890–91
Oil on canvas
19 ⅞ × 25 ¾ in. (50.5 × 65.5 cm)
Museu Nacional d'Art de
Catalunya, Barcelona

Impressionists, whenever he traveled from Spain, and this painting pays tribute to his particular neighborhood rather than to the city as a whole.

In the last decades of the nineteenth century, after Montmartre became part of Paris through Haussmann's expansion of the city, urban growth followed new residents up the hillside. Authorities began cutting roads into the area, making it easier to reach and encouraging more people to visit. Developers built apartment buildings with the most modern conveniences including "gas and water on every floor," as many of the new structures advertised. With more customers climbing the hill, many of the already established venues began advertising performances by the bohemians who spent time there, thus giving birth to the *cabaret artistique*. Paintings and posters created by artists including Toulouse-Lautrec and Steinlen immortalized the most famous of such venues, such as Le Chat Noir and Le Mirliton. Soon, nightly performances of music, poetry readings, dramas, or shadow theater (made when cut-out shapes were backlit onto a screen facing the audience) entertained throngs who came from throughout the city.

Vincent van Gogh's *La Guinguette à Montmartre* (1886, cat. 23) is an homage to the heritage of Montmartre at a moment when the neighborhood was changing. In this painting of a local watering-hole (a *guinguette* was an outdoor tavern), we do not see Paris as a city, but rather glimpse an older vision of semi-rural Montmartre slowly being pushed aside by gentrification. The scene is quiet and sparsely populated with only a

65

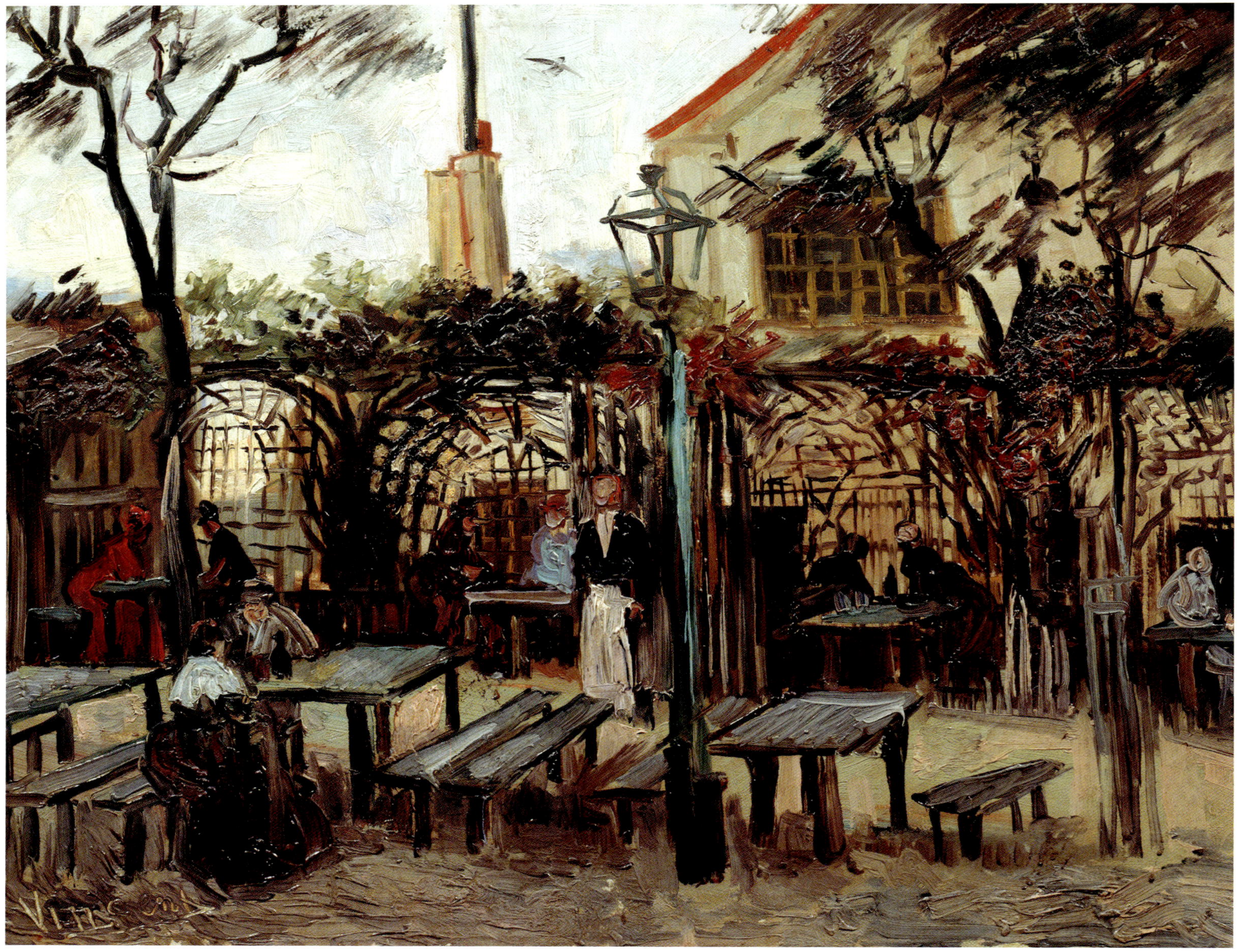

Cat. 23

Vincent van Gogh
Dutch, 1853–1890
La Guinguette à Montmartre, October 1886
Oil on canvas
9 ¹¹⁄₁₆ × 25 ³⁄₈ in. (50 × 64.5 cm)
Musée d'Orsay, Paris; Bequest of Pierre
Goujon in memory of his father Dr. Etienne
Goujon, 1915

few patrons sitting at tables tucked into the arbors as a waiter in a white apron stands at the ready. Buildings in the background are nondescript, but typical of the area's modest structures. The rough wooden tables in the foreground, suggesting the more rustic character of the area, often hosted many of Van Gogh's fellow painters.

Van Gogh's paintings of Montmartre featured fields, gardens, and working windmills, further emphasizing the area's traditional rural character even though Montmartre had been incorporated into the city of Paris for more than twenty-five years by the time he and his brother Theo lived there between 1886 and 1887. Although he did turn his attention southward to the city below in several paintings, in most of his images there is no sign of a growing metropolis. Instead, Van Gogh's Montmartre paintings more often reflect a longing for the return of the village's countryside character, hearkening back to the days when it was a refuge outside of Paris. That sort of nostalgia would climax a few years later when several groups of artists declared that Montmartre had broken off from the rest of Paris and would now become its own self-governing city-state (although Van Gogh was not involved in these efforts). Such announcements of secession were largely made in jest, but they contained a core of anger at the transformation of the area that had long inspired so much artwork.[21]

As the entertainment economy grew, many windmills were converted into cabarets or dance halls since show business was more profitable than grinding grain or pressing grapes. Van Gogh shows the exterior of one of the most famous Montmartre sites in two paintings, *Moulin de la Galette* (1886, fig. 22) and *Le Moulin de la Galette* (1886–87, fig. 21), the latter of which shows the windmill closely connected with the nearby rural surroundings of Montmartre. Turned in 1814 from a mill into a *guinguette* by the family that owned it, the venue became a cabaret in 1830 to take advantage

of Parisians' desire to slip outside the tax wall. In 1870 it became an outdoor dance hall, a change which Pierre-Auguste Renoir demonstrates in his *Le Moulin de la Galette, Sketch* (1875–76, see cat. 8). By the time of Renoir's painting, fashionable Parisians frequently headed to Montmartre. Men and women, illuminated by the glow of hanging gas lamps that highlights many shades of their colorful clothing, dance in the outdoor space surrounded by those eating, drinking, and socializing. This painting reminds us too that the category of "café" could be broadened to other types of spaces beyond the traditional tables-chairs-and-drinks establishment. Cabarets, café-concerts, bistros, and brasseries each had their own character—some focusing more on food and others on entertainment—but all were part of the broader category of the "café" as a place where people came together to meet and spend time with one another in public.

Yet none of the patrons Renoir depicted at the Moulin de la Galette would have lived in Montmartre. The neighborhood was still a bit edgy, in part because of its long history of sitting just outside the city's administrative reach, and was still home to many poor and working-class people. Part of Montmartre was known as *le maquis* (meaning "scrubland"), an impoverished area filled with ramshackle houses and lean-tos that housed some of Paris's most destitute residents. It was also home to criminals, prostitutes, and gay and lesbian bars, making it a place that many respectable bourgeois avoided. But for those who thrived on the thrill of danger or sought out new experiences, traveling there meant "slumming" at the Moulin de la Galette or other sites with the knowledge that they could return to the safety of their middle- or upper-class homes after living for a few hours on the edge.

By the turn of the twentieth century, Montmartre was beginning to lose some of its luster as an artistic

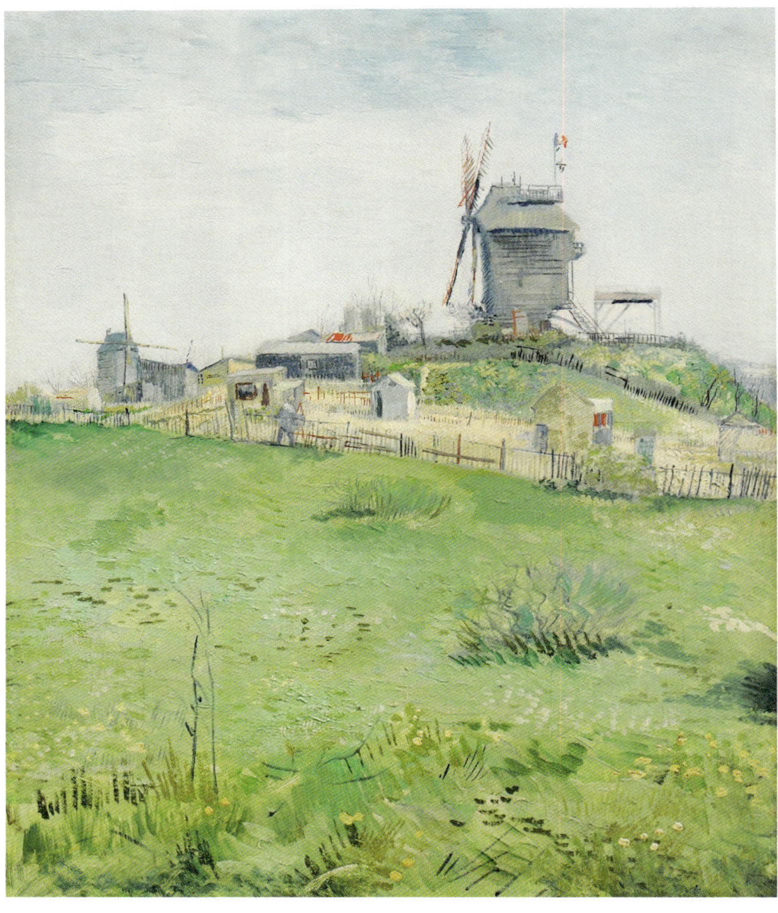

Fig. 21
Vincent van Gogh
Dutch, 1853–1890
Le Moulin de la Galette, 1886–87
Oil on canvas
18 ⅝ × 15 ½ in. (47.31 × 39.37 cm)
Carnegie Museum of Art; Acquired through
the generosity of the Sarah Mellon Scaife
Family, 67.16

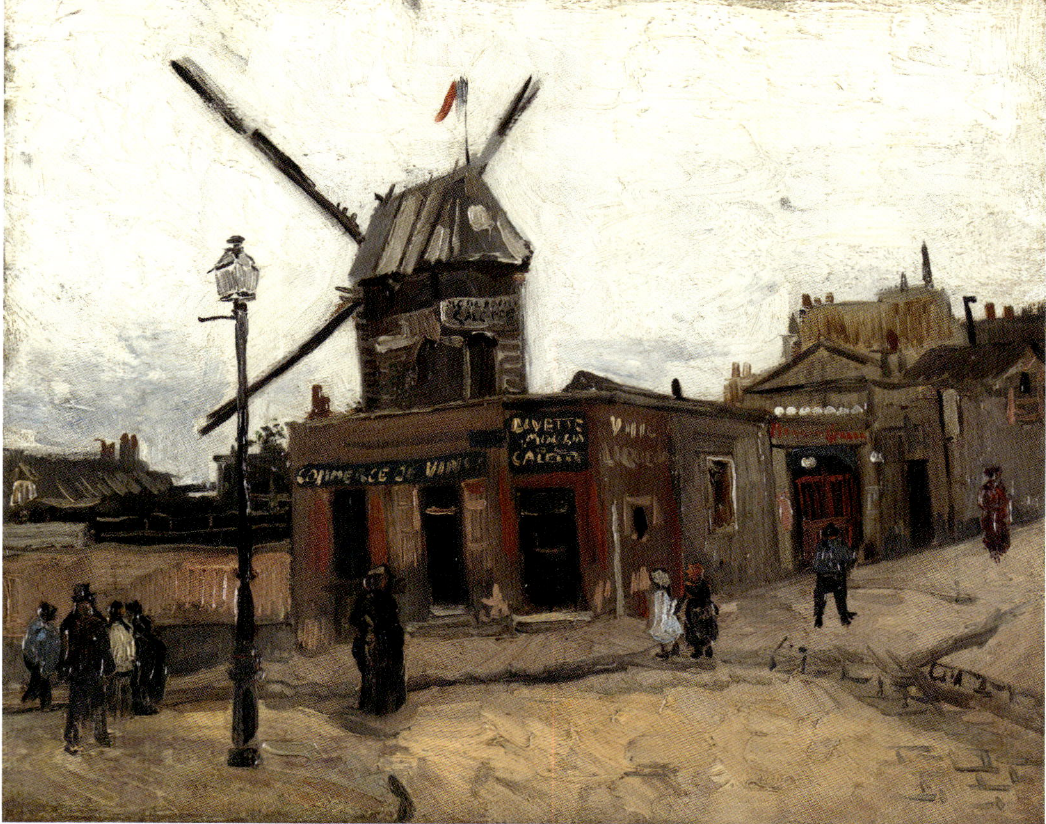

Fig. 22
Vincent van Gogh
Dutch, 1853–1890
Moulin de la Galette, mid-October 1886
Oil on canvas
15 ⅛ × 18 ⅛ in. (38.4 × 46 cm)
Collection Kröller-Müller Museum, Otterlo,
The Netherlands, KM 103.198

neighborhood, in part because it had become too touristy and commercial. Haussmann's boulevards at the bottom of the hill replaced the city's former boundary and the tax wall. Along those wide streets, music halls including the Moulin Rouge sprang up, using the now-famous symbol of the windmill to draw visitors to the neighborhood for flashy showbiz entertainment complete with semi-nude dancers which, for naysayers, departed from the more authentic artistry of previous generations. Even places like the Moulin de la Galette were evolving. After a renovation that lit up the entrance with the words "Bal Dubray" (after the name of the family who owned it), "the place was festooned," according to historian Sue Roe, "with coloured lights, rivalling the cabarets at the bottom of the hillside which flashed their neon strips and flashy new electric lighting." Palm trees now framed the bandstand.[22]

Although the Eldorado and Folies-Bergère music halls were located in other parts of the city, the advertising posters for these venues by Jules Chéret (1893 and 1894, cats. 41 and 37) are excellent examples of a type of image that would have been posted on walls and advertising pillars (also known as Morris columns), to tell viewers about shows in Montmartre as well as other establishments throughout the city. The Eldorado, at 4 Boulevard de Strasbourg, was one of the largest and lushest music halls of the day, featuring big stars and packing in huge crowds. The dazzling image in the poster does not promote a specific performance but the theater itself. It tells the viewer that whatever show they see will be a fabulous spectacle likely to combine music, dance, comedy, and sex.[23] The leggy dancer in a flowing dress trimmed in gold appeared so frequently in Chéret's posters that she came to be known as the *chérette*, described by historian Marcus Verhagen as "the dancing, nymphlike woman who dominated his designs." In this poster for the Eldorado, Verhagen notes, "she was

illuminated from below, like an actress standing in the glare of a series of footlights, but she dispensed with the stage, hovering restlessly against the background," and above a musician in a clown costume playing the banjo.[24] The spread of chromolithography made such brightly colored posters cheap to produce so they became ubiquitous across the urban landscape as a mass-produced form of imagery that would have been seen by thousands every day as they walked down the street.[25] The same techniques used to advertise music halls, circuses, and café-concerts also promoted a wide variety of consumer products; a Morris column with advertisements for chocolate appears in the background of Croegaert's *Le Café*. But, for many critics, these flashy ads only confirmed that art in Montmartre, and Paris more generally, had abandoned the age-old (and largely fictional) idea of "art for art's sake" and sold out to the forces of commerce. As Verhagen puts it, the "*chérette* laughed with the entrepreneur, not at him."[26]

As Montmartre changed, the artistic center of the city began to shift southward, across the river to Montparnasse which, like Montmartre, was on higher ground (*mont* means mountain in French). Both areas also had mythical origins. Montmartre was, according to most accounts, the "Mount of the Martyr" where the Roman governor of Gaul decapitated Saint Denis, the bishop of Paris and the patron saint of France, around 250 CE. Montparnasse's name came from classical mythology as Mount Parnassus, the place where the Greek muses lived and inspired literature, science, and art. This part of Paris got its name thanks to seventeenth-century students from the nearby Sorbonne who went there to recite poetry. Much of Montparnasse was leveled during building projects of that era, but it remained a popular location for cafés and dance halls, especially during the time of the French Revolution.

By the time American Robert Henri painted *Paris Café, Montparnasse* (fig. 23) in 1898, he had already been visiting France off-and-on for a decade, and he stayed in Montparnasse where he could witness the bohemian migration toward that part of town. That change would also facilitate the influx of American tourists, expatriate writers, and artists into the neighborhood in the 1920s where they spent hours at the famous cafés dotting the four corners of the Boulevard Raspail and Boulevard Montparnasse. At the time of Henri's painting, only one of those cafés existed (Le Dôme, founded in 1898), and it quickly became a gathering spot. Henri does not identify the café that forms the backdrop for the mother and child walking down the street; the Terra Foundation speculates that it was one near his studio. The painting clearly reflects Henri's debt to Impressionism, but also showcases the dim colors and "gritty realism" that he would champion as a leader of the American urban realists (sometimes called the "Ash Can" school) back in New York. Once again, the city is on display, but it is not a bright or happy place—not a "city of light"—except for the glow coming from the café's red awning. Rather, Henri's vision is dark, mottled, and overcast. Yet, like paintings of Montmartre cafés, this image seems to be more about a specific neighborhood than Paris as a whole. There is nothing distinctively Parisian about the scene; no landmarks or symbols suggest we are in the French capital: "In the distance buildings give way to an undefined vista of trees and roofs, furthering the impression of a village scene rather than a corner of a vast metropolis."[27] Henri's vision is so localized as to cut the viewer off from the rest of Paris. Henri's *Café Terrace* (1899, cat. 47) included in this exhibition continues the theme of dark, moody colors and the disassociation of the café he depicts from the rest of the city. But this space is brighter with social activity, showing how such establishments bring people together in public spaces.

Cafés in a Changing Society

In the cafés of Paris, one could observe the evolution of the city and its inhabitants. Paintings of cafés, then, serve as historical documents which capture snapshots of Parisian life to reveal how the city was changing. For example, Boldini's painting of Berthe Morisot and Gabrielle de Rasty sitting together illustrates a shift in the ability of women to be in public without male accompaniment, something taboo in earlier generations. The presence of so many single women in the paintings of this exhibition demonstrates how artists highlighted modern gender roles. The last decades of the nineteenth century are often associated with the birth of the "new woman" who would take her fullest form as the liberated woman of the 1920s; Americans would call her the "flapper." Boldini's painting prefigures Maurice-Louis Branger's famous photograph of American writers Djuna Barnes and Solita Solano sitting side by side in a Parisian café ca. 1925 (fig. 24), an image that has become ubiquitous in books and films about that era. In Boldini's time, this modern woman was still coming into being, but seeing these two commanding the public urban space of the sidewalk café forecasts changes to come.

The late nineteenth century was also a time of growing class conflict and heated urban politics throughout France. Working-class people pushed to the city's edge by Haussmannization embraced socialist and communist parties in the hope that taking power away from the rich might improve the lives of the poor. A series of strikes rocked France during these decades as industrial development and mechanization transformed older businesses. On canvas, Raffaëlli's depiction of class conflict in *Bohèmes au café* is more subtle. The "starving artists" at the table are in a world of their own while an elegantly dressed wealthy man has turned his back on them. Both rich and poor occupy the same social space, but they are visibly at odds with one another.

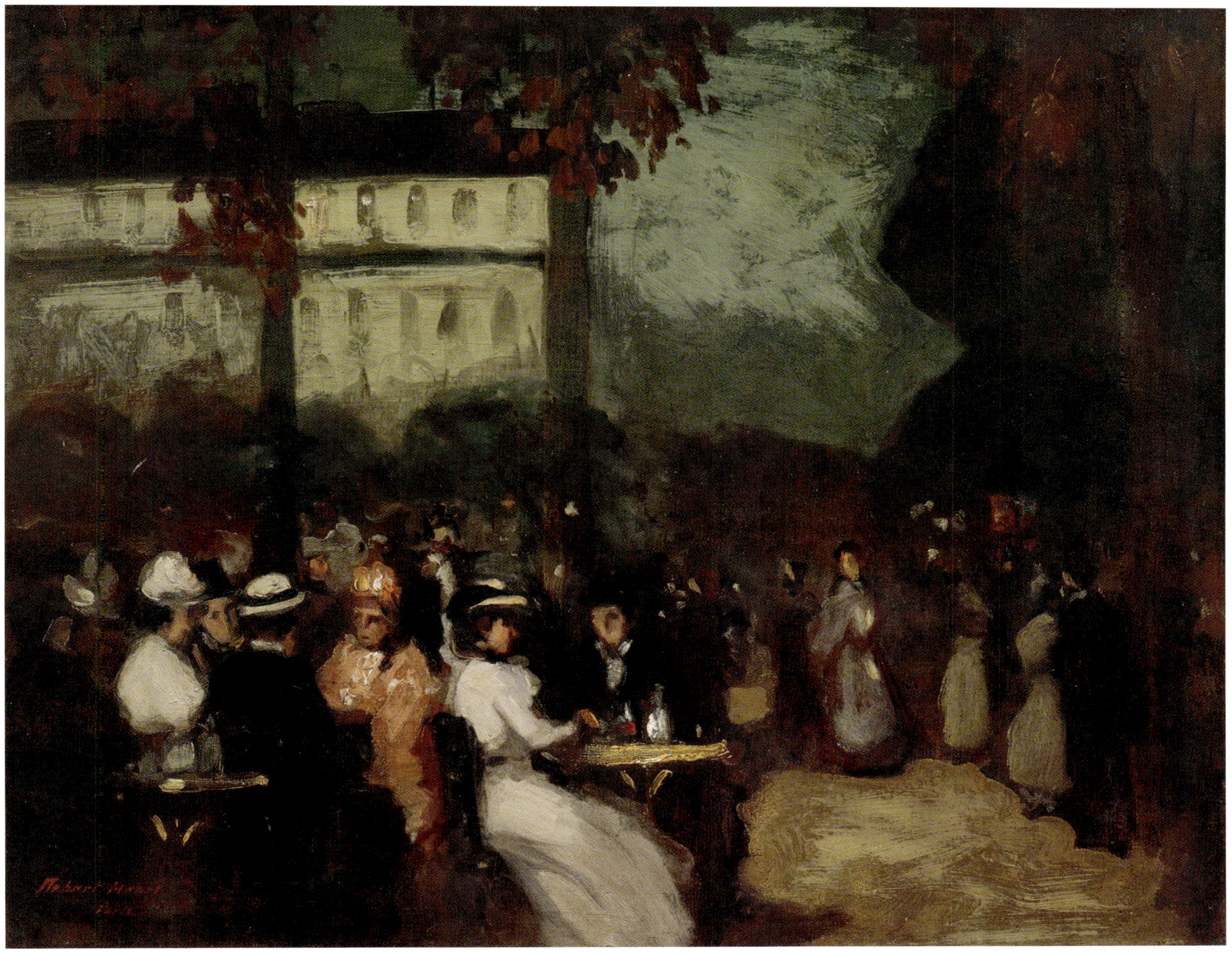

Cat. 47

Robert Henri
American, 1865–1929
Café Terrace, 1899
Oil on canvas
25 ¾ × 32 ⅛ in. (65.4 × 81.6 cm)
Fayez S. Sarofim Collection, FSC 2022.064

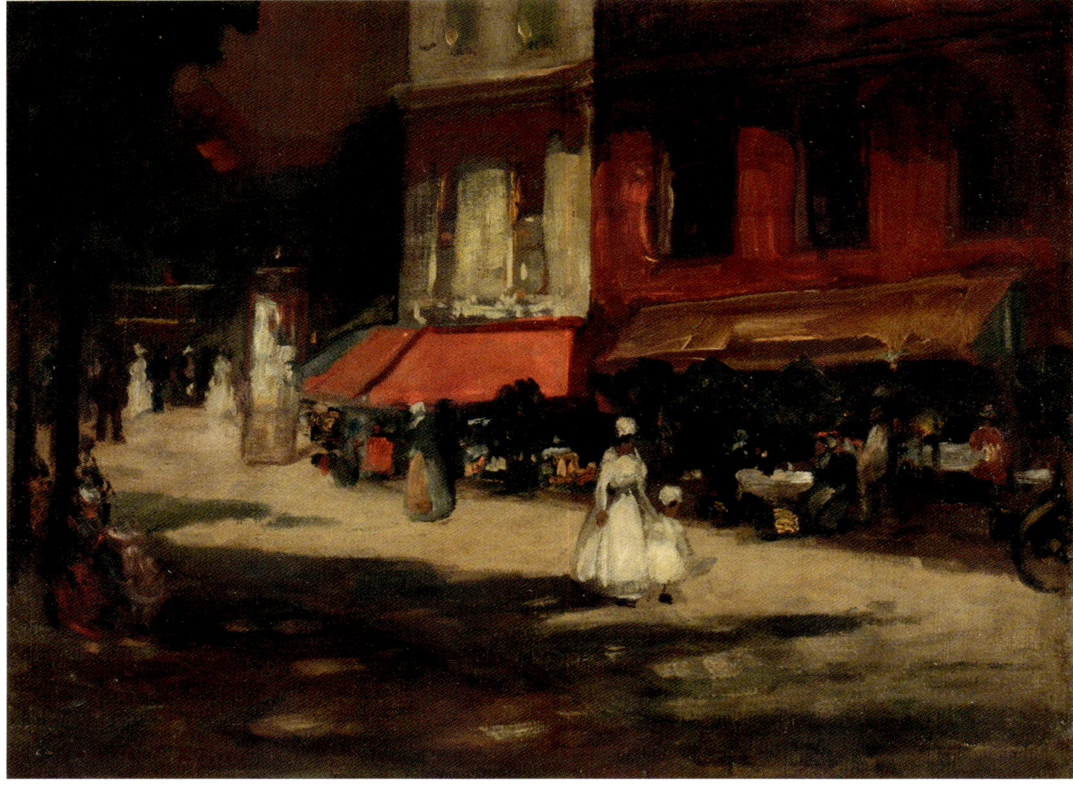

Fig. 23
Robert Henri
American, 1865–1929
Paris Café, Montparnasse, 1898
Oil on canvas
18 ⅜ × 24 ⅜ in. (46.7 × 61.9 cm)
Terra Foundation for American Art, Daniel
J. Terra Collection, 1992.171

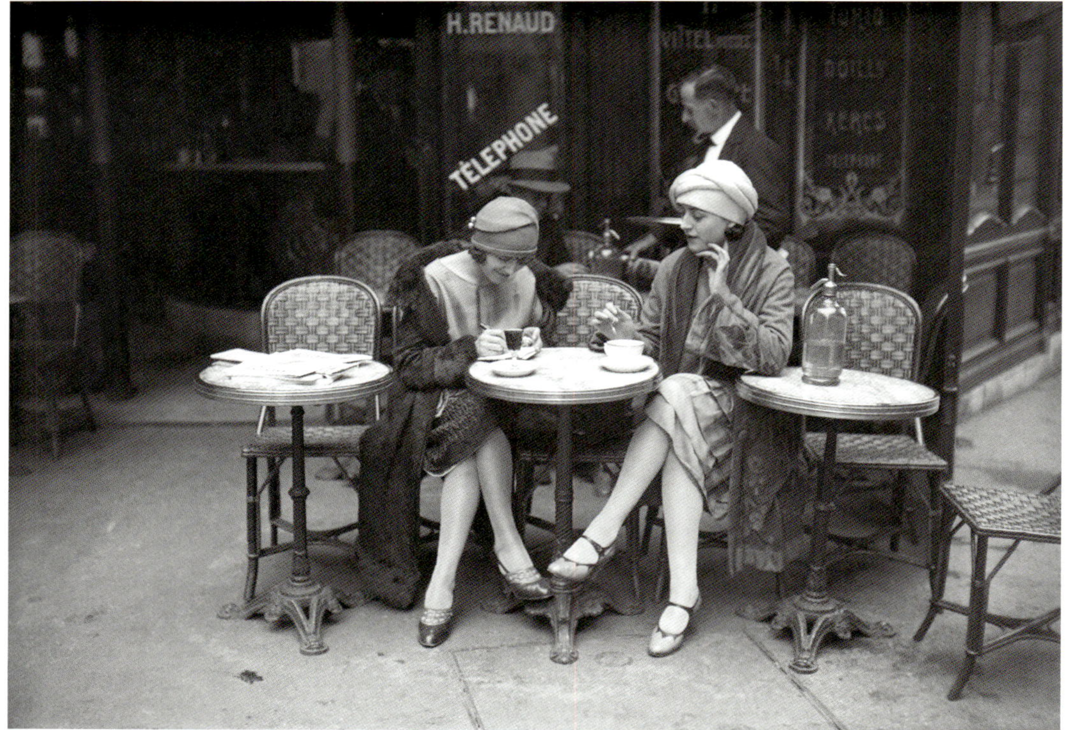

Fig. 24
Maurice-Louis Branger
French, 1874–1950
*Café Terrace, Paris (Djuna Barnes
and Solita Solano)*, ca. 1925
Photograph
Courtesy of Roger-Viollet

That class friction is nowhere more on display than in the fashion people wore to the cafés and which the artists of the day illustrated. To see and be seen at certain cafés in particular outfits was an important way to announce one's social status. The American sociologist Thorstein Veblen coined the term "conspicuous consumption" in his 1899 book *The Theory of the Leisure Class* to describe how the things people bought and did could distinguish them from those lower on the social scale. Money allowed someone to engage in unproductive activities, but the social distinction came from visibly doing these leisurely things. To sit in a café in public view was a way of being conspicuous in one's consumption. And to dress for the occasion—or, as cultural critic Andrew Fiouzi put it, "the non-occasion" of sitting in a café—was key.[28] Pablo Picasso's *Au café* (1901, see cat. 48) in this exhibition shows a trio of women, one with a dog (another sign of disposable income) in their colorful, flowing finery. Maurice Brazil Prendergast's *Woman Drinking Tea* (1893-94, see cat. 38) also captures the importance of showing off elegant fashion and leisure time.

Henri Evenepoel's *In the Café d'Harcourt in Paris* (1897, see cat. 44) captures the practice of "conspicuous consumption." The café, located next to the Sorbonne, was a frequent haunt for students and intellectuals. A young woman in a brilliant red dress adorned with a rose fills the center of the canvas. She coquettishly swirls her outfit to reveal the white lining underneath, suggesting there is much more to be seen. Her hat matches her dress in its color and bold style in a room full of eye-catching millinery. However, she does not attract the gaze of anyone else in the room. Like her, everyone in the café seems to be at leisure, doing no productive work but merely passing the time in drink or conversation. Yet her reason for dressing so brightly is that she is, in fact, working, as likely are the other solitary women in the scene. The café was a place where "Parisian bohemians and ladies of easy virtue pass the time smoking and drinking."[29] Evenepoel, who would die only two years later at the age of twenty-seven, seems to be critiquing the conspicuous consumption of everyone in the café who makes a visible display of their leisure yet leaves women like the one in the red dress unable even to sell her body. "Here, Evenepoel describes turn-of-the-century Paris as a jaded and decadent society."[30]

The interaction between the café and the urban space helped to make all these social changes visible to the artists who then chronicled them on paper or canvas. Café images are about the modern world of turn-of-the-century Paris and capture the city at a historical turning point. Many of these same artists would also draw or paint railway stations or streetscapes of this era as further meditations on the evolution of Paris. These images of modern life—in the spirit of Baudelaire's flâneur touring the streets of the City of Light—transport us back to a moment when much of the Paris we know today came into existence, and they show us just how much the café was at the center of these transformations.

Endnotes

1. https://artvee.com/dl/cafe-wepler/.

2. Jane Nickerson, "Larue's, a Famous Paris Restaurant, Ends Its History of 75 Years," *New York Times,* July 5, 1954, 8.

3. https://www.clevelandart.org/art/2019.57; Jean-Jacques Lévêque, *Les Années impressionnistes* (Paris: ACR Editions, 1990), 10.

4. A. Roger Ekirch, *At Day's Close: Night in Times Past* (New York: W. W. Norton, 2005), 332–33.

5. https://www.nytimes.com/1996/03/30/style/IHT-forain-a-painter-turned-cartoonist.html.

6. https://www.invaluable.com/auction-lot/felix-vallotton-swiss-french-1865-1925-102-c-c894f0b818; Sasha Newman, *Félix Vallotton* (New Haven, CT: Yale University Art Gallery, 1991).

7. W. Scott Haine, *The World of the Paris Café: Sociability among the French Working Class, 1789–1914* (Baltimore: The Johns Hopkins University Press, 1996); Leona Rittner, W. Scott Haine, and Jeffrey H. Jackson, eds., *The Thinking Space: The Café as a Cultural Institution in Paris, Italy and Vienna* (London: Routledge, 2013).

8. https://www.nasjonalmuseet.no/en/guide/collection/53/221/.

9. https://www.clevelandart.org/art/1925.1409.

10. https://buffaloakg.org/artworks/19571-danseuse-au-caf%C3%A9-dancer-caf%C3%A9.

11. Ibid.

12. https://mbarouen.fr/en/oeuvres/in-a-cafe.

13. Ibid.

14. https://www.christies.com/en/lot/lot-5441544.

15. https://www.manet.org/chez-le-pere-lathuille.jsp.

16. https://www.famsf.org/press-room/new-acquisition-the-absinthe-drinkers-by-jean-francois-raffaelli-welcomes-visitors-to-the-summer-impressionist-exhibition-at-the-de-young-museum.

17. Ibid.

18. https://blog.vangoghgallery.com/index.php/en/2015/01/06/van-goghs-relationship-with-alcohol/.

19. https://www.moma.org/collection/works/81307.

20. Jill Miller, "Les Enfants des Ivrognes: Concern for the Children of Montmartre," in *Montmartre and the Making of Mass Culture*, ed. Gabriel P. Weisberg (New Brunswick, NJ: Rutgers University Press, 2001), 72–93.

21. Jeffrey H. Jackson, "Artistic Community and Urban Development in 1920s Montmartre," *French Politics, Culture, and Society* 24 (Summer 2006): 1–25.

22. Sue Roe, *In Montmartre: Picasso, Matisse, and the Birth of Modern Art* (New York: Penguin Books, 2014), 66.

23. https://www.yaneff.com/products/eldorado.

24. Marcus Verhagen, "The Poster in *Fin-de-Siècle* Paris: 'That Mobile and Degenerate Art,'" in *Cinema and the Invention of Modern Life*, ed. Leo Charney and Vanessa R. Schwartz (Berkeley: University of California Press, 1995), 103.

25. Ben Singer, "Modernity, Hyperstimulus, and the Rise of Popular Sensationalism," in Charney and Schwartz, *Cinema and the Invention of Modern Life*, chapter 3.

26. Verhagen, "The Poster in *Fin-de-Siècle* Paris," 105.

27. https://collection.terraamericanart.org/objects/203/paris-cafe-montparnasse.

28. https://melmagazine.com/en-us/story/cafe-core.

29. https://sammlung.staedelmuseum.de/en/work/in-the-cafe-dharcourt-in-paris.

30. Ibid.

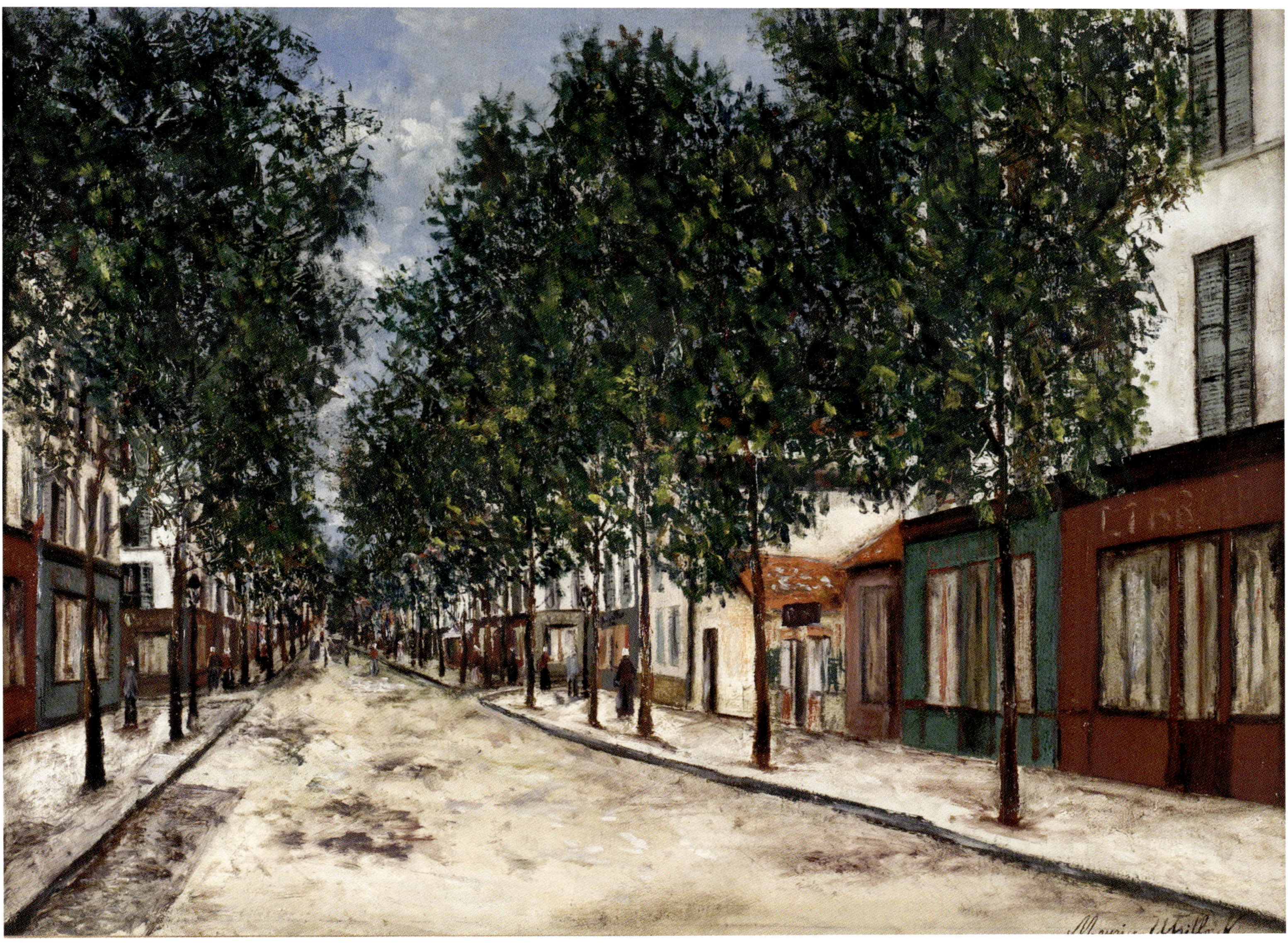

Cat. 66

Maurice Utrillo
French, 1883–1955
Road to Puteaux, 1913–14
Oil on canvas
23 ¾ × 32 ¼ in. (60.3 × 81.9 cm)
Dixon Gallery and Gardens; Gift of Cornelia
Ritchie, 1996.2.17

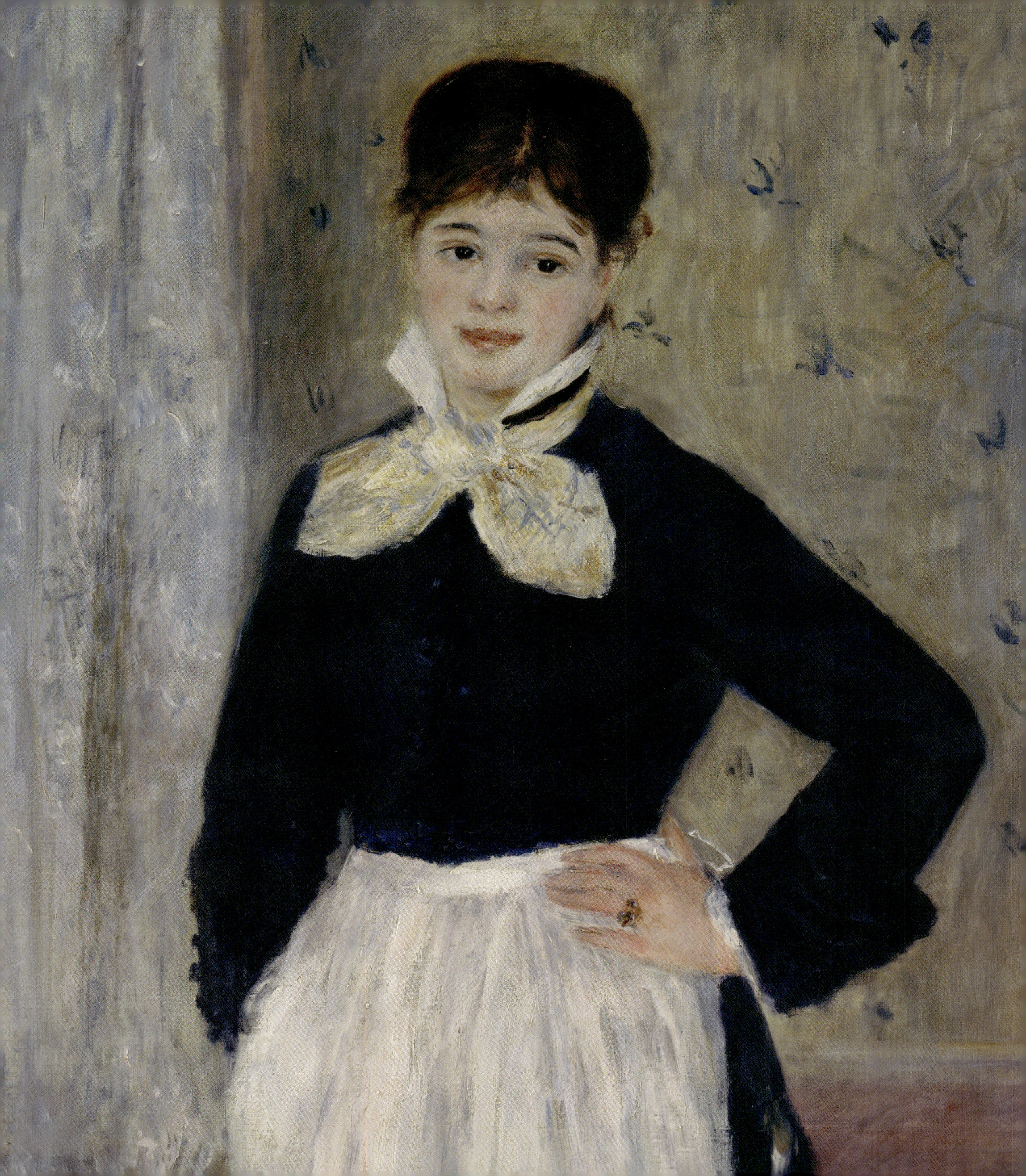

FEMME AU CAFÉ

The Complexities and Evolution of Women's Presence in Parisian Cafés in the Long Nineteenth Century

Julie Pierotti

"Nana and Satin would go down past the church, always following the Rue Le Peletier. Then, a hundred yards short of the Café Riche, as they approached their field of operations, they released the tails of their skirts which they'd been carefully holding up and, letting them sweep the pavement regardless of the dust, they would saunter along, rolling their hips, slowing down when they came into the glare of some large café. Laughing noisily as they swaggered along, glancing back over their shoulders as the men turned to look at them, they were in their element. In the shadow, their whitened faces with the red smudges of their lips and the black patches of their eyelids evoked the disturbing charm of a cheap Oriental bazaar, openly on offer on the public highway."—Émile Zola, *Nana*, 1880

Though women are nearly always depicted in images of Parisian cafés throughout the long nineteenth century, their roles in those spaces were often ambiguous and precarious. Certainly, cafés in Paris and its environs were predominantly male institutions until at least the outbreak of World War I. This fact often led and continues to lead to presumptions about the women who did populate cafés, and indeed cafés were often sites of sexual transactions. But closer examination of the works of art depicting women in cafés from the 1850s through the mid-1910s reveals the myriad of social, political, and intellectual encounters available to women in these new public spaces, the evolution of their functions at cafés, and the subtle nuances in their depictions which helped both contemporary and modern viewers to identify who the women were.

While the majority of paintings and prints set in and around cafés in nineteenth-century Paris cast women in those spaces in a less-than-flattering light, the reality was that a variety of women were

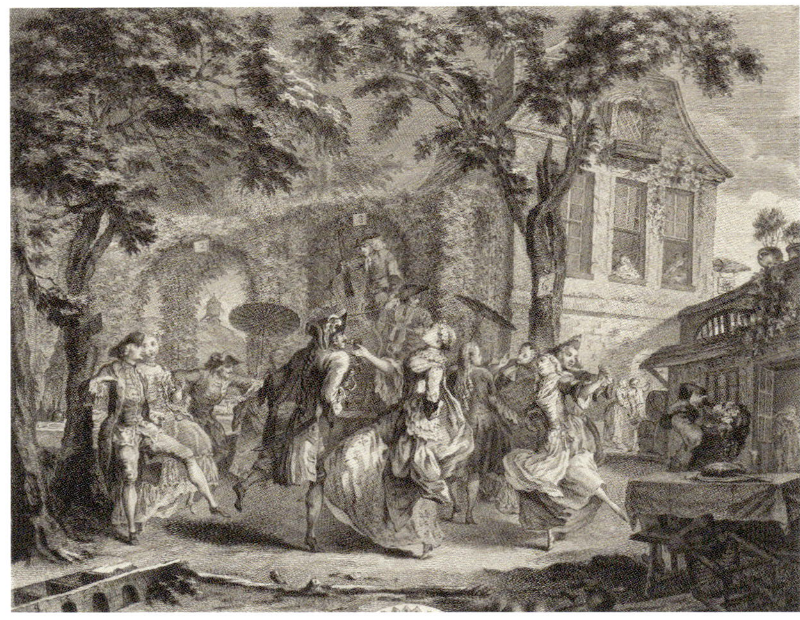

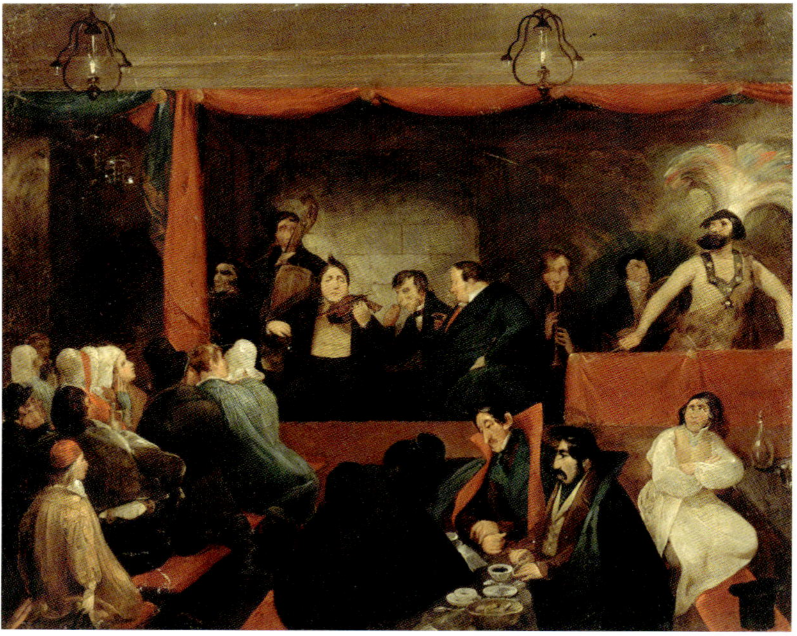

Fig. 25
François Basan (engraver)
French, 1723–1797, after Gabriel de Saint-Aubin, French, 1724–1780
La Guinguette, 1752
Engraving
12 ¾ × 14 ½ in. (32.3 × 37 cm)
The New York Public Library

Fig. 26
Charles-Joseph Traviès
Swiss, 1804–1859
Le Café des Aveugles, au Palais-Royal, ca. 1840
Oil on canvas
15 × 18 ⅛ in. (38 × 46 cm)
Musée Carnavalet, Histoire de Paris

regular patrons at cafés, particularly those catering to the working class, beginning especially around 1850.[1] Throughout the tumult of the Franco-Prussian War and the Paris Commune, cafés became places where perfectly respectable (again, working-class) women could engage in political discussion. But in the aftermath of those upheavals, as Paris was rebuilding itself into a modern, global capital, instances of both organized and clandestine prostitution centered at cafés began to rise sharply. Between 1873 and 1902, more than 6,800 women were arrested at cafés and charged with unlicensed prostitution.[2] The salacious nature of this statistic, coupled with the proliferation of cafés themselves in the French capital in the late nineteenth century, led to a sensationalizing in contemporary art of nearly all women in cafés as sex workers.

Artists concerned with urban realism in late nineteenth-century Paris increasingly looked to the world around them for inspiration, and, as an important source of social and sexual interaction, cafés became a natural subject. Yet this was not an entirely new phenomenon. Seventeenth-century Dutch and Flemish painters, including Adriaen van Ostade, Jan Steen, and David Teniers, often included flirtatious women in their genre paintings of raucous taverns. And women appear in images of public dining establishments by French eighteenth-century artists, too. Gabriel de Saint-Aubin's lively depiction of a *guinguette* (distributed as an engraving by François Basan in 1752, fig. 25) reveals women as leading participants in the singing, dancing, and general merriment that often took place in rural watering holes. Saint-Aubin's image connects to the tradition of lively performance of the *théâtre italien* or *commedia dell'arte* that would have taken place at such a multi-function proto-café, but, in addition to those taking part in the act, other women appear in various situations throughout the scene. In the background, a young woman whispers with a man

holding a jug; just above the couple, another young woman looks out of a second-story window with a man just behind her. Both vignettes allude to the association of guinguettes (and many cafés in more urban areas) with prostitution. But guinguettes, usually located on roads leading into and out of Paris, also filled the role of what would become known as a "rest stop." Therefore, as illustrated in Auguste-Louis Lepère's etching *La Guinguette, route de Billancourt* (1905, cat. 54), working-class women and indeed children in need of a diversion or a place to rest often enjoyed stopping at a rustic guinguette for a drink and socialization.

With their increasing visibility in café spaces, in the early nineteenth century women appear with greater frequency in art and visual culture depicting (and often critically commenting upon) public dining establishments. This rise in prominence coincided with the trend toward realism among French artists. Charles-Joseph Traviès de Villers (a Swiss/French caricaturist commonly known simply as Traviès) presents *Le Café des Aveugles, Palais Royal* (ca. 1840, fig. 26) as a precursor to the café-concert, with a crowded bandstand featuring an all-male orchestra with performers. Much of the clientele in the subterranean café is male, save for a few women whose bonnets immediately identify them as hailing from the working class. Other accounts, both visual and written, of the Café des Aveugles from the period confirm its bawdy reputation: "Formerly the vaults were the favorite meeting place of licensed love merchants. All had their free entrances. The self-respecting man could not venture into these dens; so it was crowded."[3]

From their earliest days, restaurants employed women, particularly young women deemed attractive by contemporary standards, to entice male customers. Initially these women were referred to as *limonadières* due to the fact that many early cafés served lemonade along with coffee and spirits.[4] By the nineteenth century,

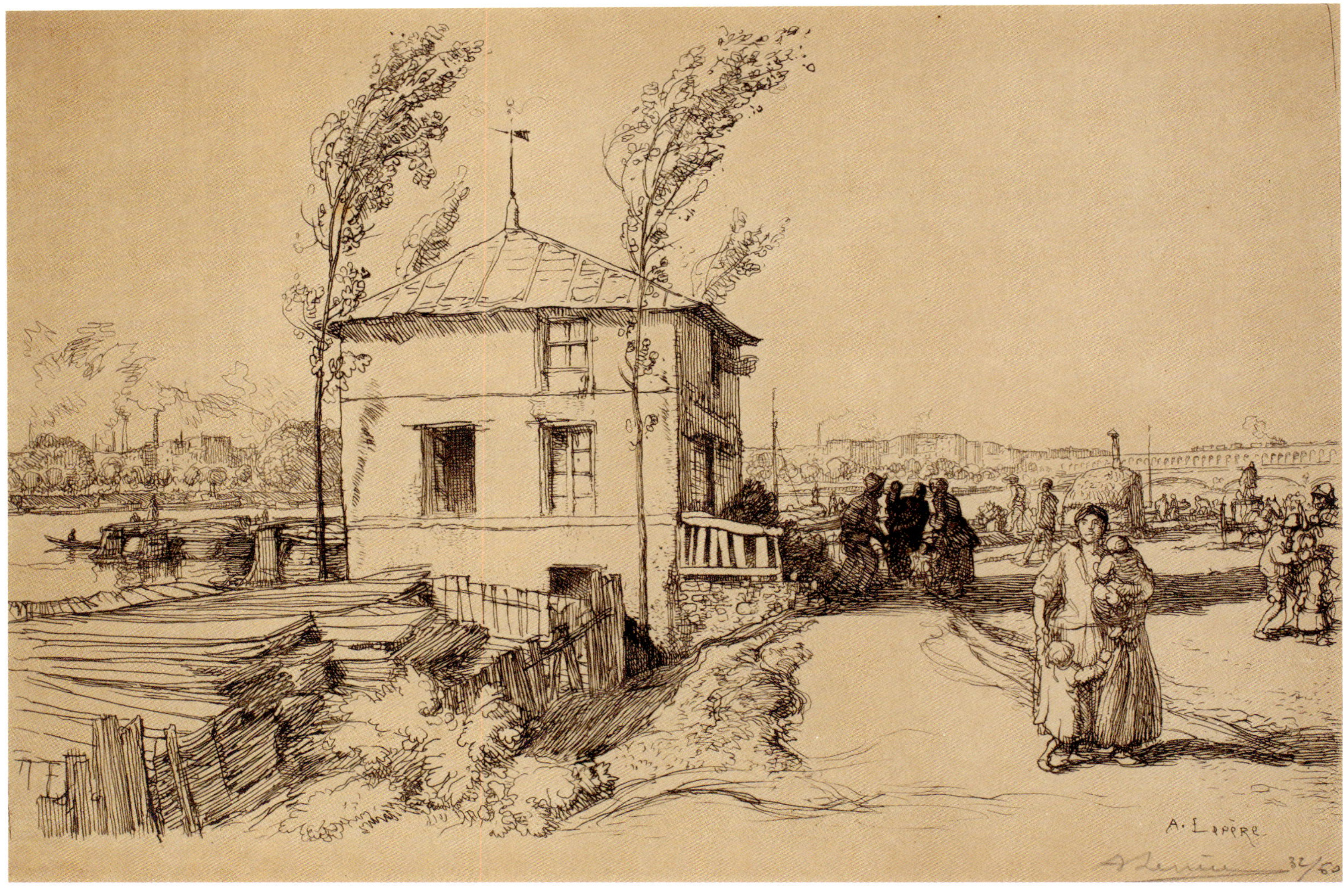

Cat. 54

Auguste Louis Lepère
French, 1849–1918
La Guinguette, route de Billancourt, 1905
Etching
6 ¹⁵⁄₁₆ × 10 ¼ in. (17.6 × 26 cm)
Dixon Gallery and Gardens; Museum
purchase, 2024.3

they had come to be known by the more perfunctory term *dames de comptoir* ("counter ladies") as they often prepared bills and collected money for the owners; however, their most important role was to appear at the entrance to the café to lure and greet customers. The prettiest of these women garnered a kind of celebrity in Paris among natives and tourists alike and were crucial to the financial success of whichever café they presided over, whether it be the more humble *table d'hôte* or a restaurant that catered to a wealthier clientele.

Indeed, the *comédie parisienne* that often played out at the French capital's various dining establishments provided fodder for the city's satirical artists in the mid-nineteenth century. Despite images such as Traviès's, which though humorous tend to suggest that all women in public dining spaces were sex workers, works by other contemporary artists interested in capturing French life reveal that women and, in some cases, children visited restaurants—though often they were tourists. Honoré Daumier's *What is Known as Dining in a Restaurant* (1844, cat. 1), part of his *Les Étrangers à Paris* series, depicts a woman as a restaurant patron, if somewhat clueless as a tourist in Paris, and accompanied by her husband (whom Daumier chooses as the butt of his satire) and child. The title and clear setting identifying this image as a restaurant adds more respectability to the scene, with a restaurant being more formal than the often-ambiguous café. While native Parisian ladies knew that simply appearing in a public dining establishment made their character questionable, the tourists who began to flock to the French capital in the early nineteenth century were often less aware of the social ramifications of just being in such a space.

As Daumier's print illustrates, in the early decades of the nineteenth century, aside from the *dame de comptoir*, men most commonly held serving positions in dining establishments, and perhaps especially cafés,

which were traditionally male-dominated spaces. This idea is echoed in Constantin Guys's painting of a quotidian encounter at a Parisian café in his watercolor simply titled *The Café* (ca. 1860–70, cat. 2). An aproned waiter approaches a table populated by two couples, the men dressed in gentlemen's attire and the women marked by their bonnets and frothy crinoline skirts, which coalesce into one large gray mass under the table. As the quintessential artist fulfilling Charles Baudelaire's call for the painting of modern life, Guys's sharply observed watercolor precedes or foreshadows the work of artists such as Manet, Degas, Forain, and Whistler to come after him. Some of Guys's café subjects border on caricature, but *The Café* walks a fine line—though he, with great economy, relays the expressions and body language of the women for the viewer to ascertain that they are from a lower class, the image forgoes gross exaggeration in favor of simply recording a scene from modern life.

The notion of the *garçon*, also satirized by Daumier (fig. 27) and Jean-Émile Laboureur (see cats. 46 and 50), was a defining characteristic of nearly all types of public dining establishments throughout the nineteenth century and into the twentieth. The *garçon* worked with the *dame de comptoir* to serve diners and deliver the bills once completed (fig. 28), and can most often be seen in the periphery of many works set in cafés (see cats. 2, 6, and 18).

However, around the middle of the nineteenth century, the *garçon* began to have to share space with a new concept in public dining: the waitress. As cafés grew in number, proprietors were increasingly stressed to find affordable labor. Women therefore began to be employed as servers in bars, cafés, taverns, and restaurants: they could be paid less, and, like the *dames de comptoir*, had the added advantage of attracting male customers with encouraged flirtatious behavior.[5] Early cafés of this sort were contemporarily

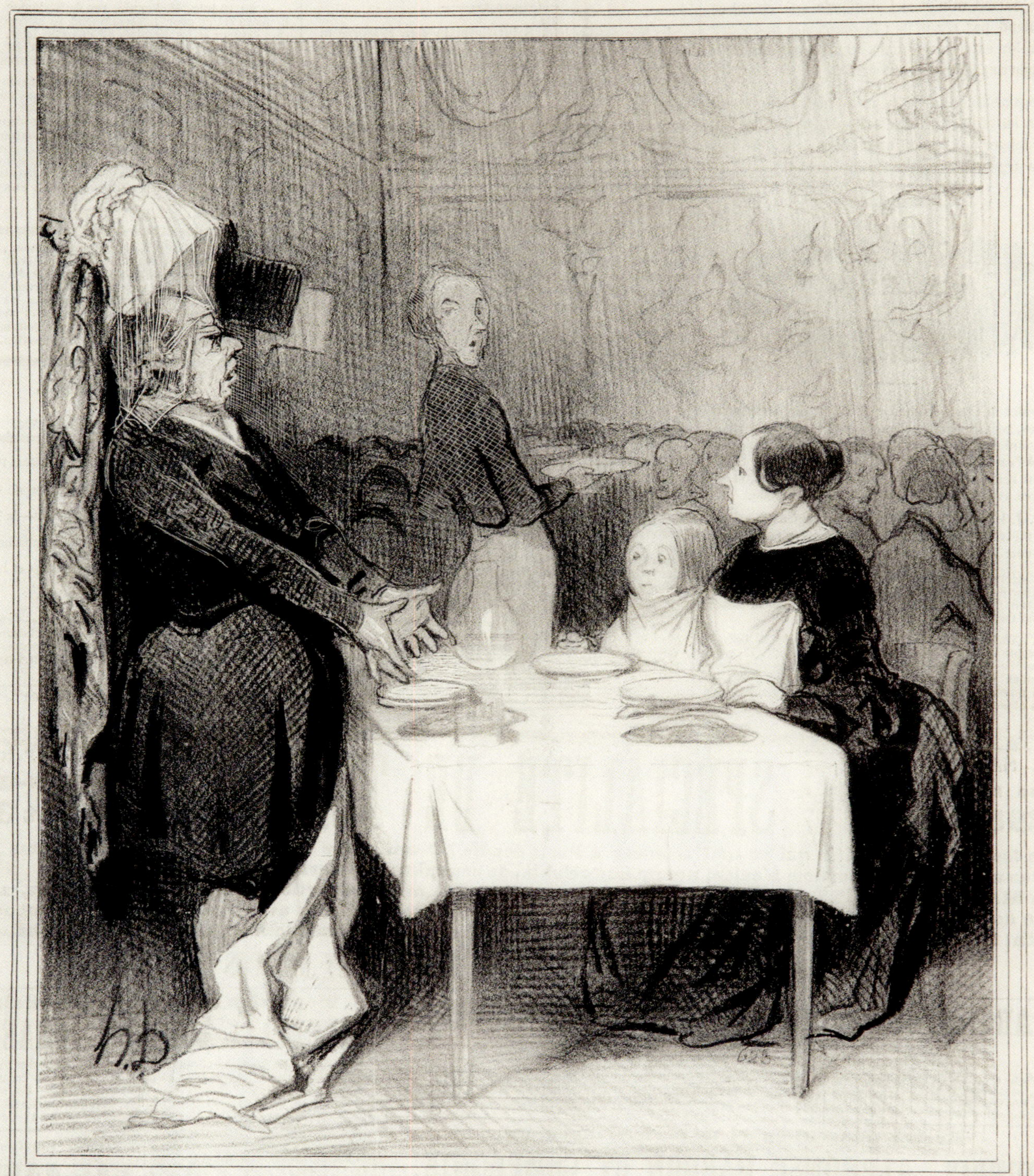

— Garçon !.. voilà une heure et quart que je suis dans votre établissement sans chaise…. et vous n'avez encore servi que des cure-dents à mon épouse qui meurt de faim…. vous me ferez sortir de mon assiette ordinaire, et je finirai par mettre les pieds dans le plat…. entendez-vous, garçon !
— Voilà, monsieur…. voilà, voilà, voilà !!!

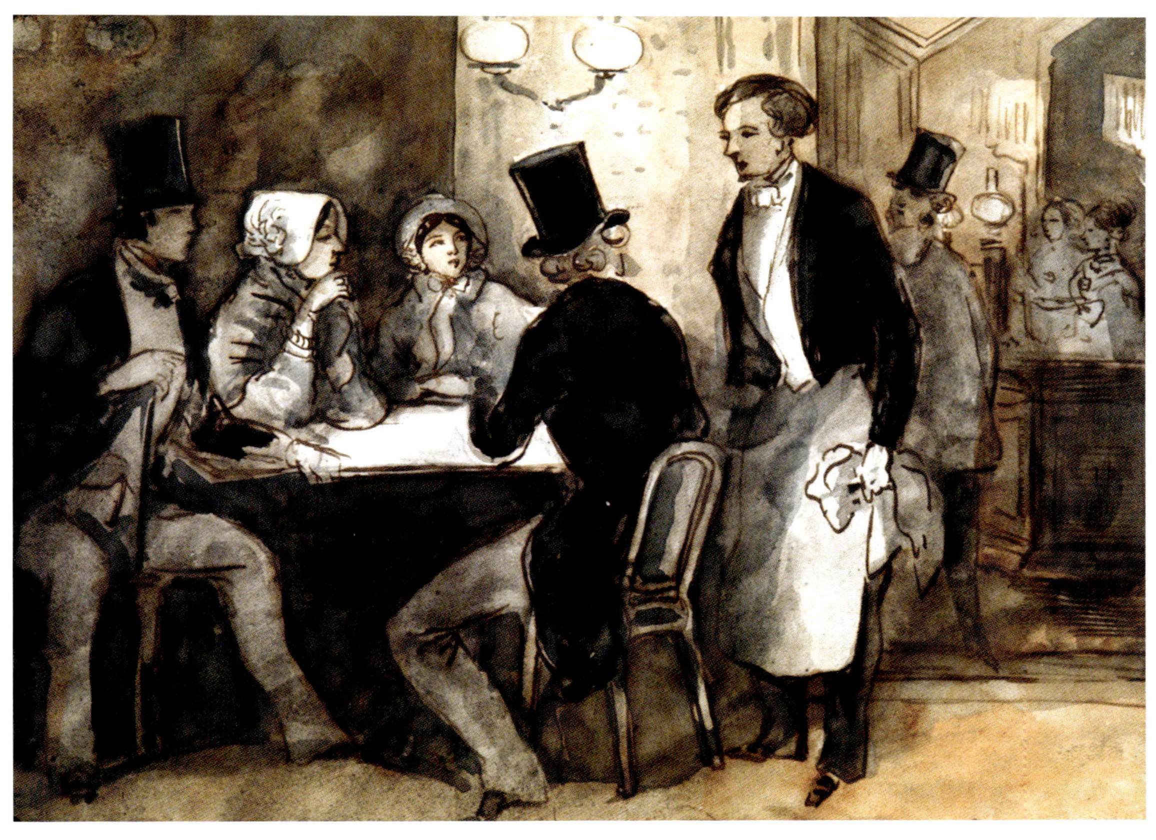

Cat. 1

Honoré Daum er
French, 1808–1879
*What is Known as Dining in a
Restaurant*, 1844
Lithograph on newsprint
11 ⁹⁄₁₆ × 8 ⁹⁄₁₆ in. (29.4 × 21.7 cm)
Dixon Gallery and Gardens;
Gift of The Armand Hammer
Foundation, 1987.40

Cat. 2

Constantin Guys
French, 1805–1892
The Café, ca. 1860–70
Watercolor on paper
7 ¼ × 9 ⅞ in. (18.4 × 25.1 cm)
Denver Art Museum; The T. Edward
and Tullah Hanley memorial gift
to the people of Denver and the
area, 1974.373

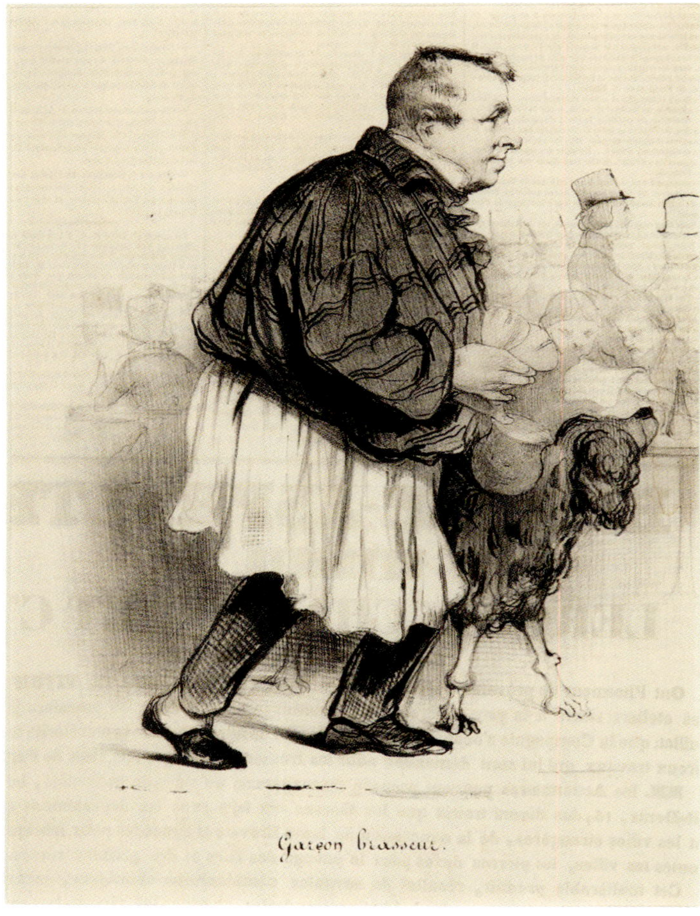

Fig. 27
Honore Daumier
French, 1808–1879
Garçon Brasseur (*Waiter in a Pub*), 1844
Lithograph on newsprint
12 ¹³⁄₁₆ × 9 ½ in. (32.5 × 24.1 cm)
Dixon Gallery and Gardens; Gift of The
Armand Hammer Foundation, 1987.25

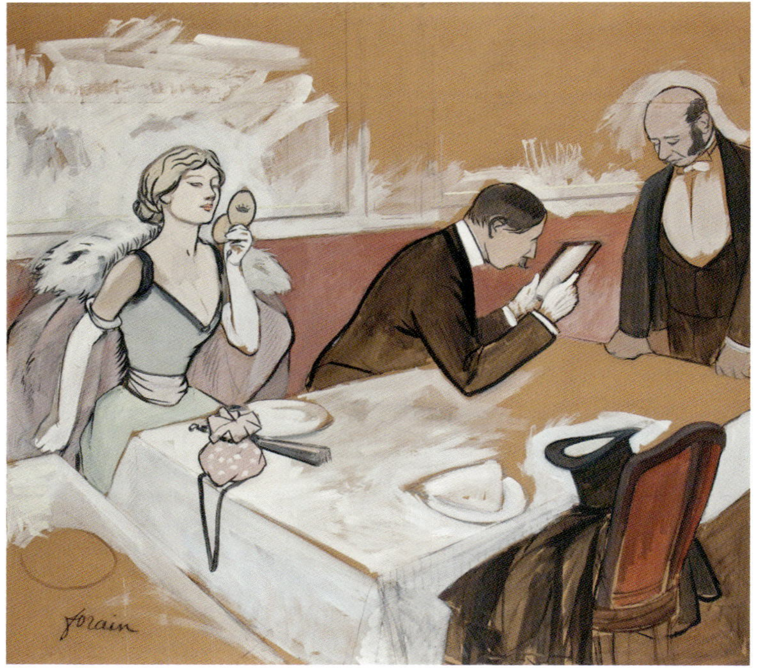

Fig. 28
Jean-Louis Forain
French, 1852–1931
Le Souper, 1894
Gouache on brown paper (design
for a mosaic)
66 ¾ × 72 ⅞ in. (169.5 × 185 cm)
Musée des Arts Décoratifs, Paris

referred to as *caboulots*, and they were relatively rare until the mid-1860s, when in the excitement leading up to the 1867 Exposition Universelle, so many cafés (temporary or otherwise) of various sizes and various levels of respectability began to pop up in Paris and its outskirts that a new type of establishment emerged: the *brasserie à femmes*, a type of restaurant that chiefly employed attractive young women to serve food and drink to male customers.

If women appearing in cafés up to that point were suspicious, the *brasserie à femmes* brazenly opened a new level of ambiguity to their characters. Though these female servers (known as *serveuses* or *inviteuses*) were encouraged to coquettishly project an air of purity and innocence, the labor in the *brasserie à femmes* was often strenuous, required long hours for little pay, and left them vulnerable to the advances of men emboldened by alcohol. Often their uniforms revealed their arms, legs, or décolletages, attracting men in great number. Over the span of just fifteen years, from the time of their introduction at the 1867 Expo to 1882, the number of *brasseries à femmes* rose to more than 180 in the city of Paris alone, employing more than 800 young women.[6] It comes as no surprise that *brasseries à femmes* became common sites for clandestine prostitution, so much

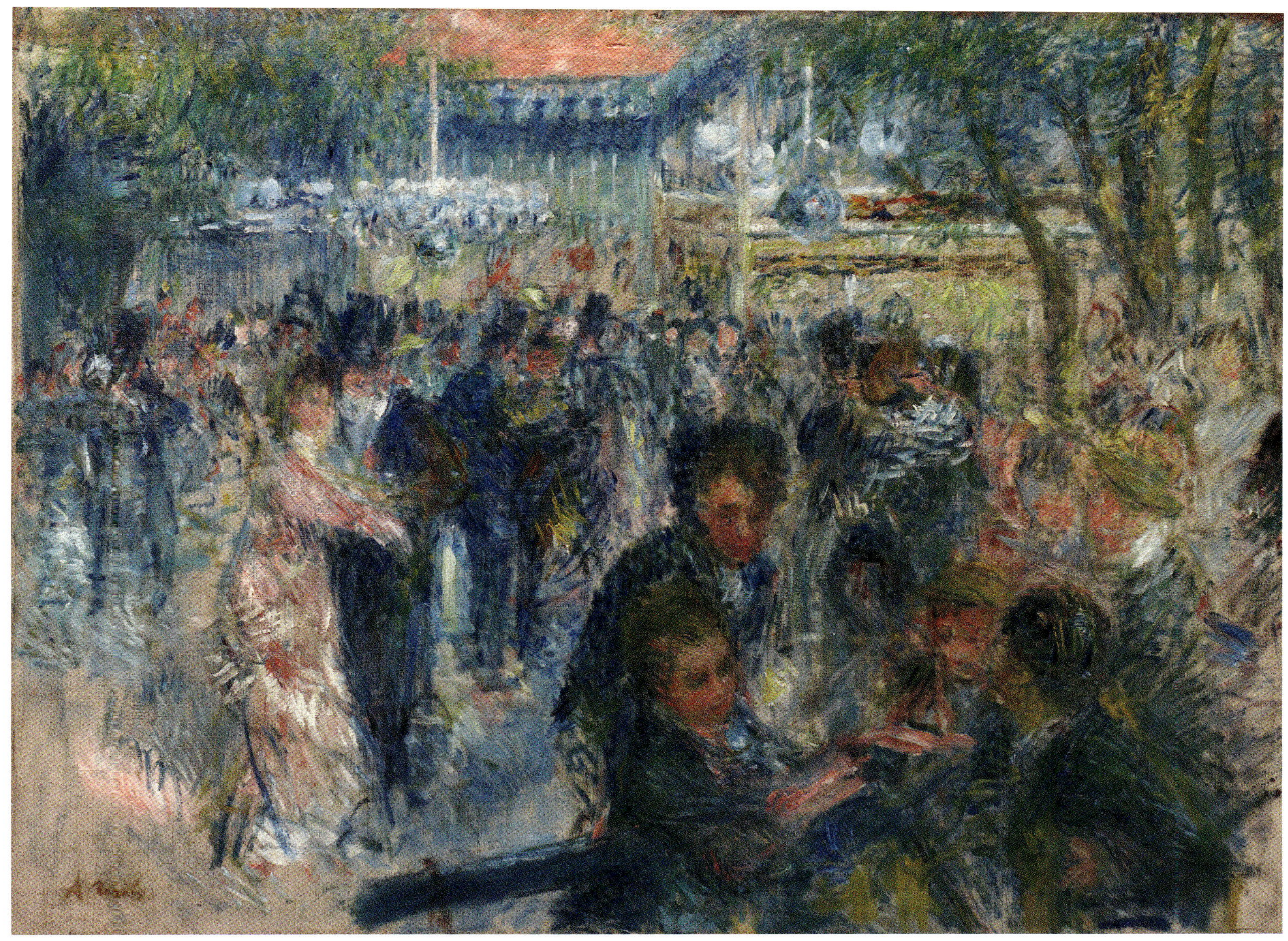

Cat. 8

Pierre-Auguste Renoir
French, 1841–1919
Le Moulin de la Galette, Sketch, 1875–76
Oil on canvas
25 ⅝ × 33 ½ in. (65 × 85 cm)
Ordrupgaard, Charlottenlund

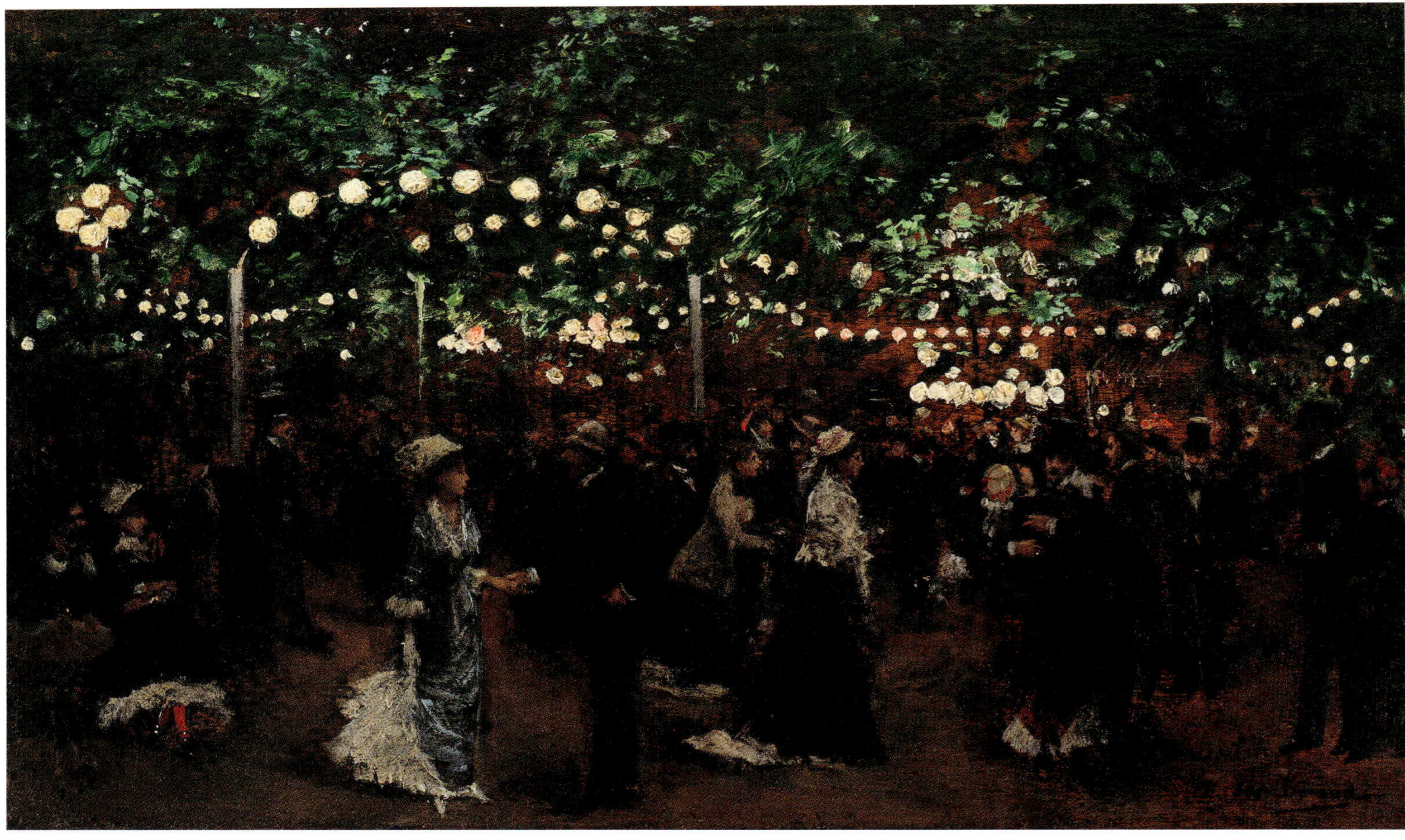

Cat. 4

Jean Béraud
French, 1849–1935
The Bal Mabille near the Champs-Élysées,
ca. 1870–75
Oil on panel
5 ⅝ × 9 ¼ in. (14.3 × 23.5 cm)
Private collection

Cat. 7

Pierre-Auguste Renoir
French, 1841–1919
Young Woman (La Servante), ca. 1875
Oil on canvas
39 ½ × 28 ⅛ in. (100.3 × 71.4 cm)
The Metropolitan Museum of Art; Bequest
of Stephen C. Clark, 1960

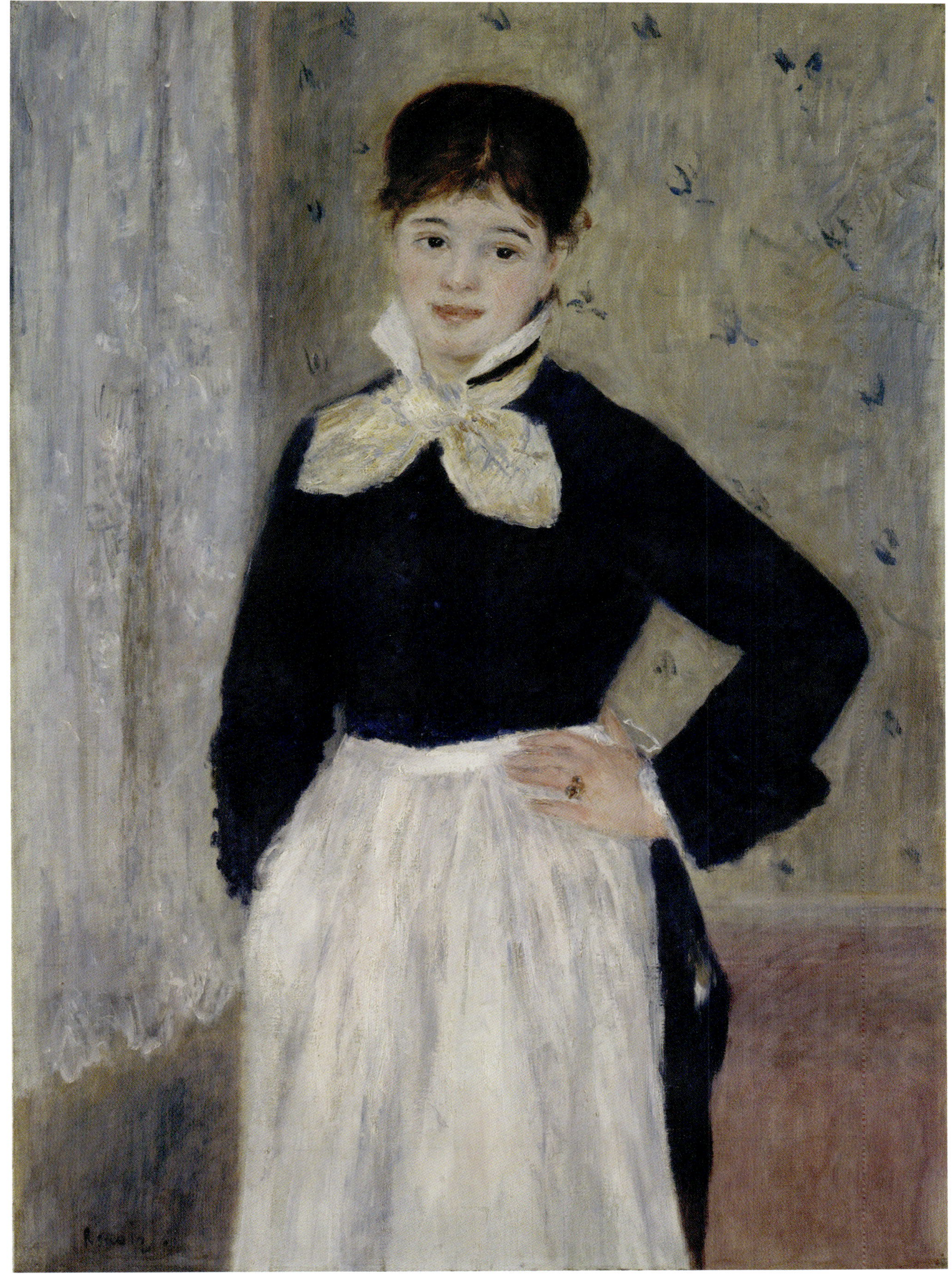

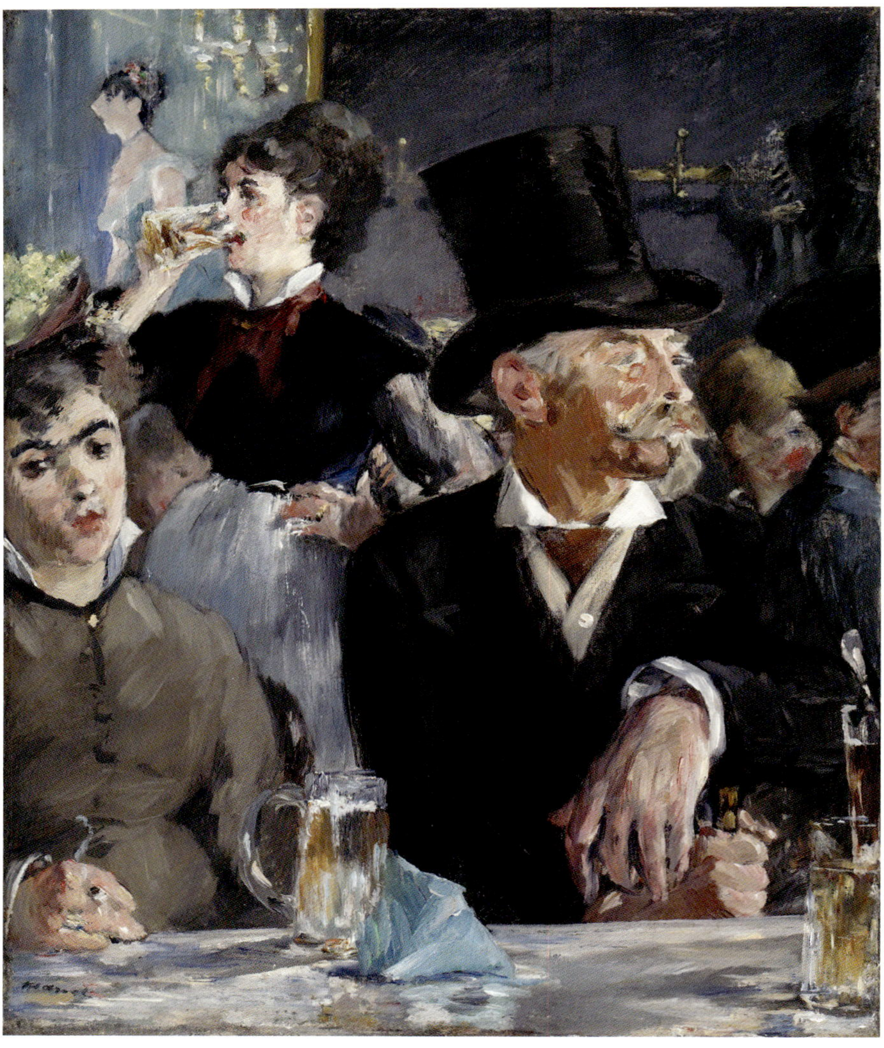

Fig. 29
Édouard Manet
French, 1832–1883
The Café-Concert, ca. 1879
Oil on canvas
18 ⅝ × 15 ⅜ in. (47.3 × 39.1 cm)
Walters Art Museum, Baltimore; Acquired
by Henry Walters, 1909-10, 37.893

so that, in May 1887, police in Paris raided dozens of *brasseries à femmes* to crack down on the proliferation of prostitution in those spaces.[7] Yet, despite attempts such as this to tamp down the type of sex work prevalent in public dining establishments, in the 1890s café prostitution reached a peak.[8]

In many ways influenced by artists such as Daumier and Traviès, a younger generation of artists, coming of age in the 1860s, committed themselves to realism as opposed to historicism and looked to the shifts occurring in Paris (both physically through Haussmannization and socially) as inspiration for their work. Led by Édouard Manet, these artists quickly came to see the ubiquitous Paris café as a multifaceted

source of inspiration: the architecture, the food, the conversation, the entertainment, the sounds all provided opportunities for observation and escape from the solitude of artistic practice.

After a decade or more of gathering daily at cafés such as Tortoni's, the Café Guerbois, and the Café de la Nouvelle Athènes, in the 1870s artists began to mine the creative potential of the café with great fervor. These same artists, including Manet, Degas, Gervex, Béraud, Forain, and many others, had made sexual politics a theme in their work to that point, but the café provided the quintessential Parisian venue for bringing images of women out of the boudoir and into daily public life. Pierre-Auguste Renoir's glimmering *Le Moulin de*

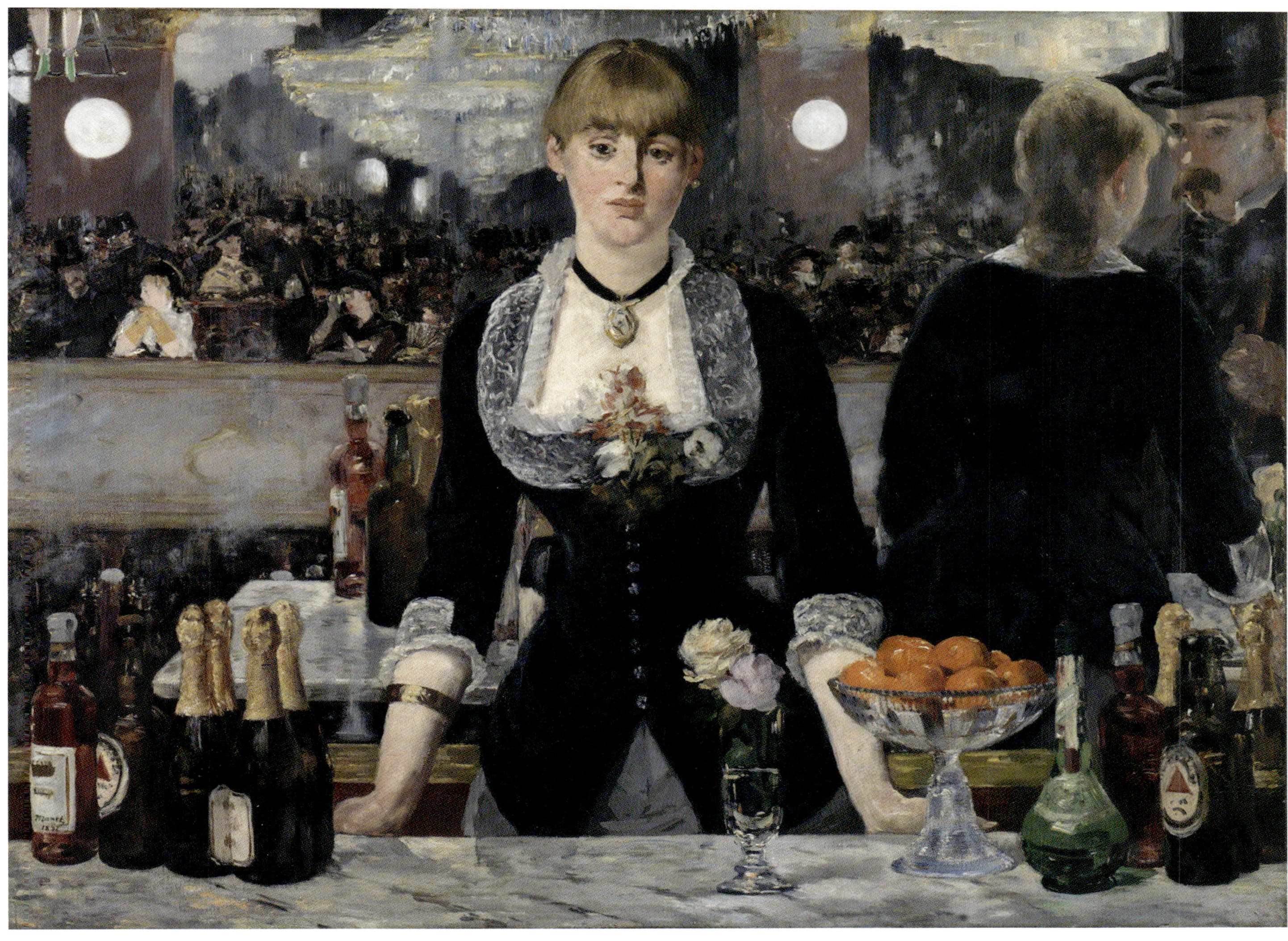

Fig. 30
Édouard Manet
French, 1832–1883
A Bar at the Folies-Bergère, 1882
O l on canvas
37 ¾ × 51 ⅛ in. (96 × 130 cm)
The Courtauld, London (Samuel
Courtauld Trust)

la Galette, Sketch of 1875–76 (cat. 8), a preparatory rendering of the iconic *Dance at the Moulin de la Galette* (ca. 1876; Musée d'Orsay, Paris), offers an earlier example of this slice-of-life at one of Montmartre's most notable establishments. Men and women dance and mingle in the garden of the café, Renoir's exceptionally loose brushwork aiding the sense of a swirling and joyful atmosphere. Though only men are seated at the tables in the foreground, women are peppered throughout the sketch, coquettishly interacting with the men they encounter. And, indeed, women commonly attended the kind of Sunday afternoon *bals* seen in Renoir's paintings, which were noted as a "precious monument to Parisian life, of rigorous exactitude"[9] and today beam with the optimism of a city eager, perhaps desperate, to move forward after the physical and emotional devastation of the Franco-Prussian War and the Commune. Similarly, Jean Béraud's depiction of the Bal Mabille (cat. 4), a long-established outdoor dance and entertainment venue, is crowded with men and women dancing under strings of lanterns, reveling in a reinvigorated postwar Parisian social scene. In a sly nod to reality, Béraud included at the left of the composition a woman revealing red stockings flanked by two men who seem to be vying for her attention for the evening.

Artists dedicated to realism and contemporary urban life found the notion of the waitress irresistible. As early as the mid-1870s, Auguste Renoir had the model for *Young Woman (La Servante)* (cat. 7) pose dressed in a uniform common to female servers; indeed, it has been supposed (accurately or not) that the painting depicts a server from the early Parisian restaurant chain Duval's.[10] Renoir's portrait takes the "pretty waiter girl"[11] out of the café and offers to celebrate and perhaps legitimize her through traditional portraiture. As the leader of the new painters, Édouard Manet completed several, now-iconic, images of female servers, particularly in the late 1870s (fig. 29).[12] His depictions of these proto-waitresses range from the detached to the debauched, but no matter their disposition, they figure so prominently in each composition that their mere presence signaled their contemporaneity and therefore modernity.

Manet's paintings of *serveuses* were not received as warmly as he might have hoped—none gained acceptance to the Paris Salon and, when shown in 1880 at La Vie Moderne gallery, received mixed reviews.[13] Nonetheless, he returned to the theme of female workers in cafés with the monumental and

mystifying *A Bar at the Folies-Bergère* (1882, fig. 30). This time, the painting was selected for the 1882 Salon, where it was one of the exhibition's most provocative paintings. By the time Manet showed the painting, the Folies-Bergère had been open as a café-concert for more than a decade and was widely recognized as the quintessential Parisian pleasure ground.[14] Guests came to experience musical, theatrical, and acrobatic performances while imbibing alcoholic beverages alongside other members of the *haute bourgeoisie*.

In other contemporary paintings of the Folies-Bergère, women appear in serving roles.[15] The barmaid in Manet's image displays much the same indifference as the *serveuses* in his café paintings of the late 1870s, but she is less a woman of action than a woman on display, an item for temptation, consideration, and perhaps purchase just like the bottles and clementines that line the bar counter. As in most nineteenth-century paintings featuring women in café spaces, the distinction between server and sex worker is blurred.

Further distorting the view in *A Bar at the Folies-Bergère* is the question of the mirror, which reveals the glimmering gaiety of the café-concert. Reflected in Manet's mirror is the large ensemble of patrons/spectators who have crowded into the Folies-Bergère. And clearly visible within the crowd are at least two women: one is seated at the bar wearing a white blouse and yellow gloves and is accompanied by a gentleman; another has brought binoculars with her to better observe the entertainment and survey the crowd. Completed just two years before Manet's magnum opus, Jean-Louis Forain's etching *Les Folies-Bergère* (cat. 15), included in Joris-Karl Huysmans's *Croquis parisiens*, chooses as its focus the women who patronize (or trawl?) the famed café, not those who are employed there. A woman in a spotted dress and flamboyant hat appears to have secured company for the evening in one of the top-hatted

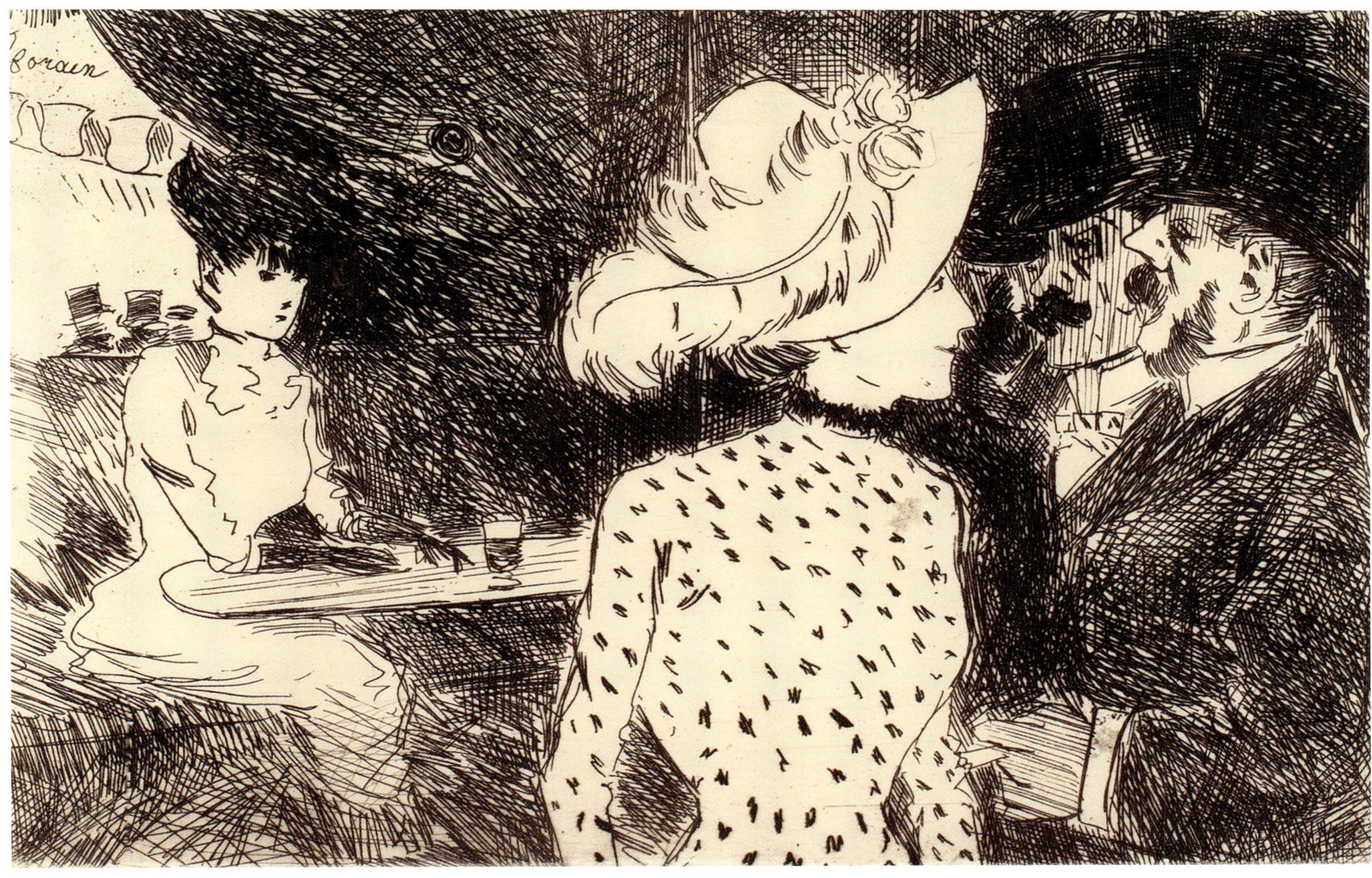

Cat. 15

Jean-Louis Forain
French, 1852-1931
Les Folies-Bergère, 1880 and 1886
Etching
image: 3 ⅝ × 5 ¾ in. (9.2 × 14.6 cm)
sheet: 8 ¾ × 11 in. (22.2 × 27.9 cm)
Dixon Gallery and Gardens; Museum
purchase, 2C22.7

gentlemen to the right of the scene, while another woman sits alone at a table drinking and waiting to be engaged.

What are we to make of these "café women"[16] and the many others like them who appear in fine art at the fin de siècle? Were they perfectly respectable women who were only seeking a place to rest and enjoy a simple meal, or were there other, less savory motives? In the 1860s, the French historian Jules Michelet wrote sympathetically:

> How many irritations for the single woman! She can hardly ever go out in the evening; she would be taken for a prostitute. There are thousands of places where only men are to be seen, and if she needs to go there on business, the men are amazed and laugh like fools. For example, if she should find herself delayed at the other end of Paris and hungry, she will not dare to enter a restaurant. She would constitute an event. She would be a spectacle. All eyes would be constantly fixed on her and she would overhear uncomplimentary and bold conjectures.[17]

Michelet's observation (or is it a warning?) that the presence of a woman in a café would constitute a spectacle finds clear representation soon after in the work of realist painters. In nineteenth-century Paris, there was, in the eyes of the public and often the law, a "direct connection between a public place and a 'public woman.'"[18] Jean-Louis Forain included a woman (seen only from the back) walking through the otherwise all-male etching of the consequential Café de la Nouvelle Athènes (ca. 1876, see cat. 9). A few years later, Forain's *Café Interior* (ca. 1879, cat. 14), exhibiting the

artist's trademark wit, contends more directly with what happens when a single woman enters a café. She is indeed a spectacle in her blue dotted dress as she looks around boldly, a hint of a smile on her lips. A group of three men at the right of the composition size her up, while a couple seated at a table in the foreground turn their heads to see her. In giving her an attention-grabbing dress and a bold singularity, Forain clearly intends to identify his subject as a *fille insoumise*, a somewhat ambiguous or nuanced term for a clandestine sex worker who often trawled for company in cafés.[19]

There existed in nineteenth-century French vocabulary a myriad of terms and expressions to describe the kind of women who frequented cafés to secure sexual exchanges (see the glossary in this volume for some of those terms). Though she draws the attention of many in her vicinity, Forain's *femme au café* still retains an air of ambiguity (is she or isn't she?) that was common in nineteenth-century Paris. Where were the respectable (read: upper-class) women, then? They limited their social interactions to private spaces, hosting salon-type gatherings in their large homes or perhaps seated in a loge at the Opéra. But the café was seen as the "salon of the working man."[20] Therefore, it was mainly working-class Parisian women that would dare enter a café.

Café Interior is one of a series of works Forain made in the late 1870s set against what Huysmans had described as the "muted red background"[21] of the Folies-Bergère. Many of these works, including *Café Interior*, were shown at the 1879 Impressionist exhibition, the first of four in which he would participate. The intimate watercolor, cropped closely compositionally

Cat. 14

Jean-Louis Forain
French, 1852–1931
Café Interior, ca. 1879
Watercolor and gouache on paper
13 ⅛ × 10 ⅛ in. (33.3 × 25.7 cm)
Dixon Gallery and Gardens; Museum purchase with funds provided by Brenda and Lester Crain, Hyde Family Foundations, Irene and Joe Orgill and the Rose Family Foundation, 1993.7.2

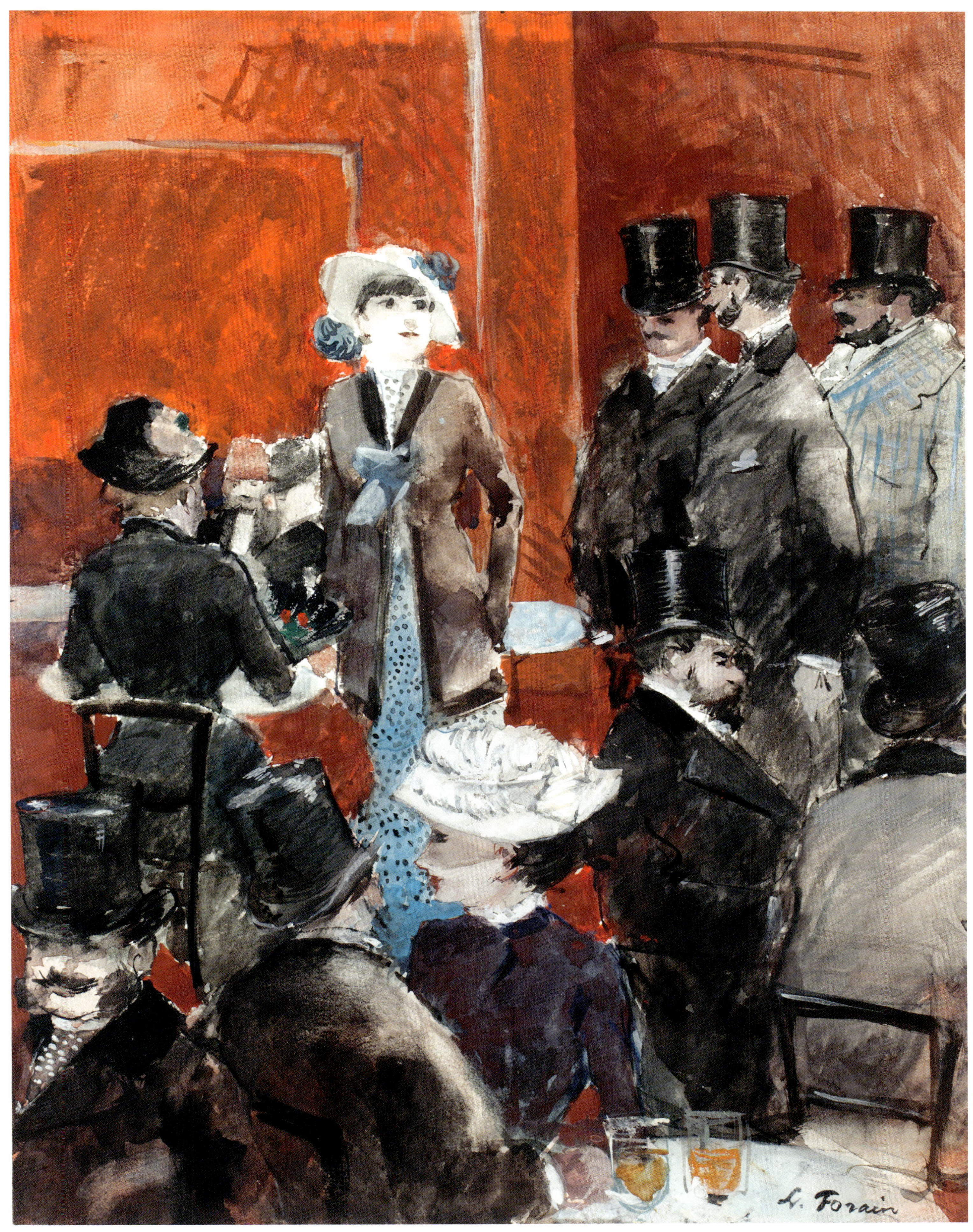
L. Forain

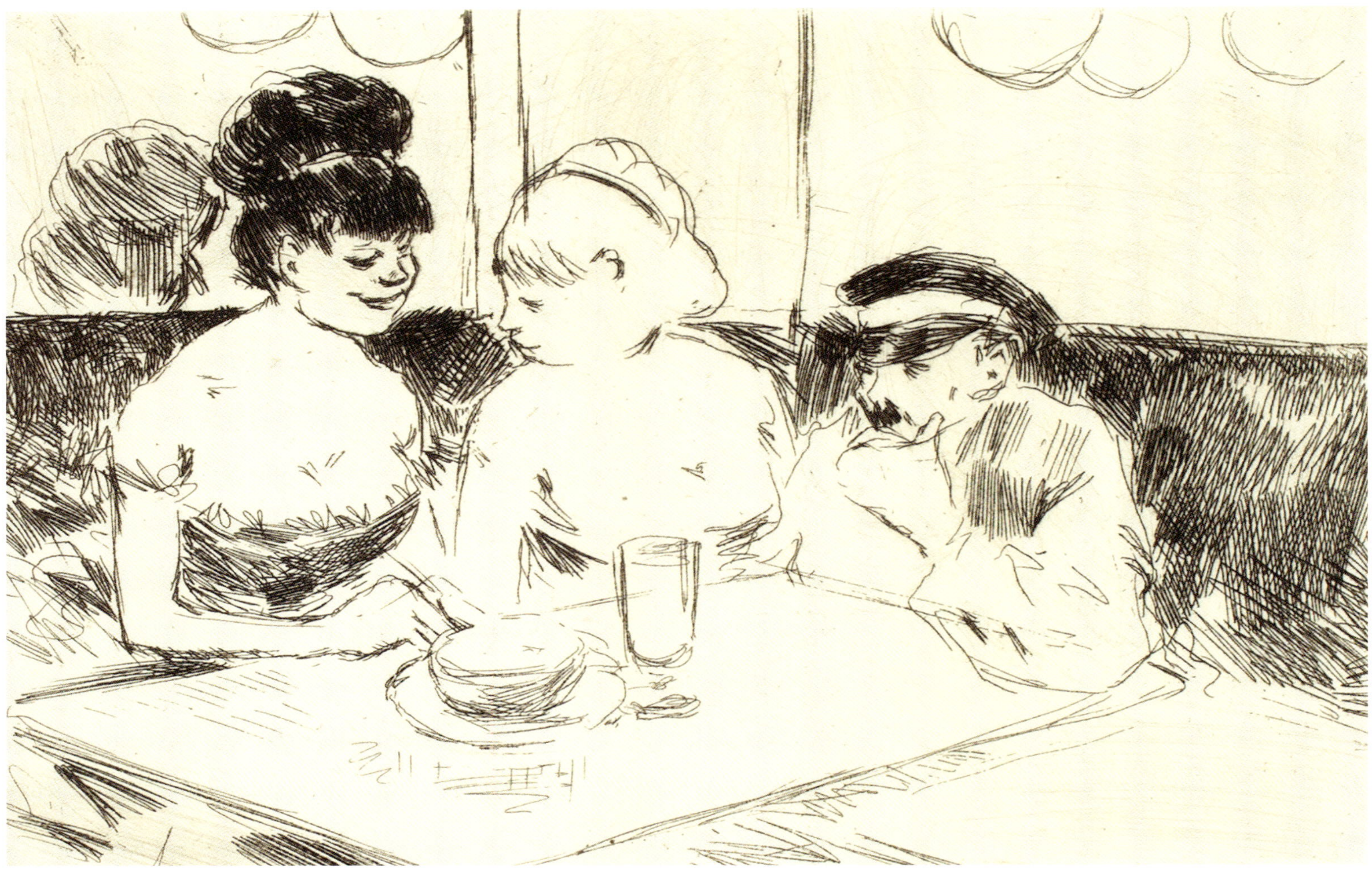

Cat. 16

Jean-Louis Forain
French, 1852–1931
Maison close, 1880 and 1886
Etching
image: 3 ⅞ × 5 ⅞ in. (9.8 × 15 cm)
sheet: 9 ¼ × 12 ⅝ in. (23.5 × 32.1 cm)
Dixon Gallery and Gardens; Museum
purchase, 2023.8

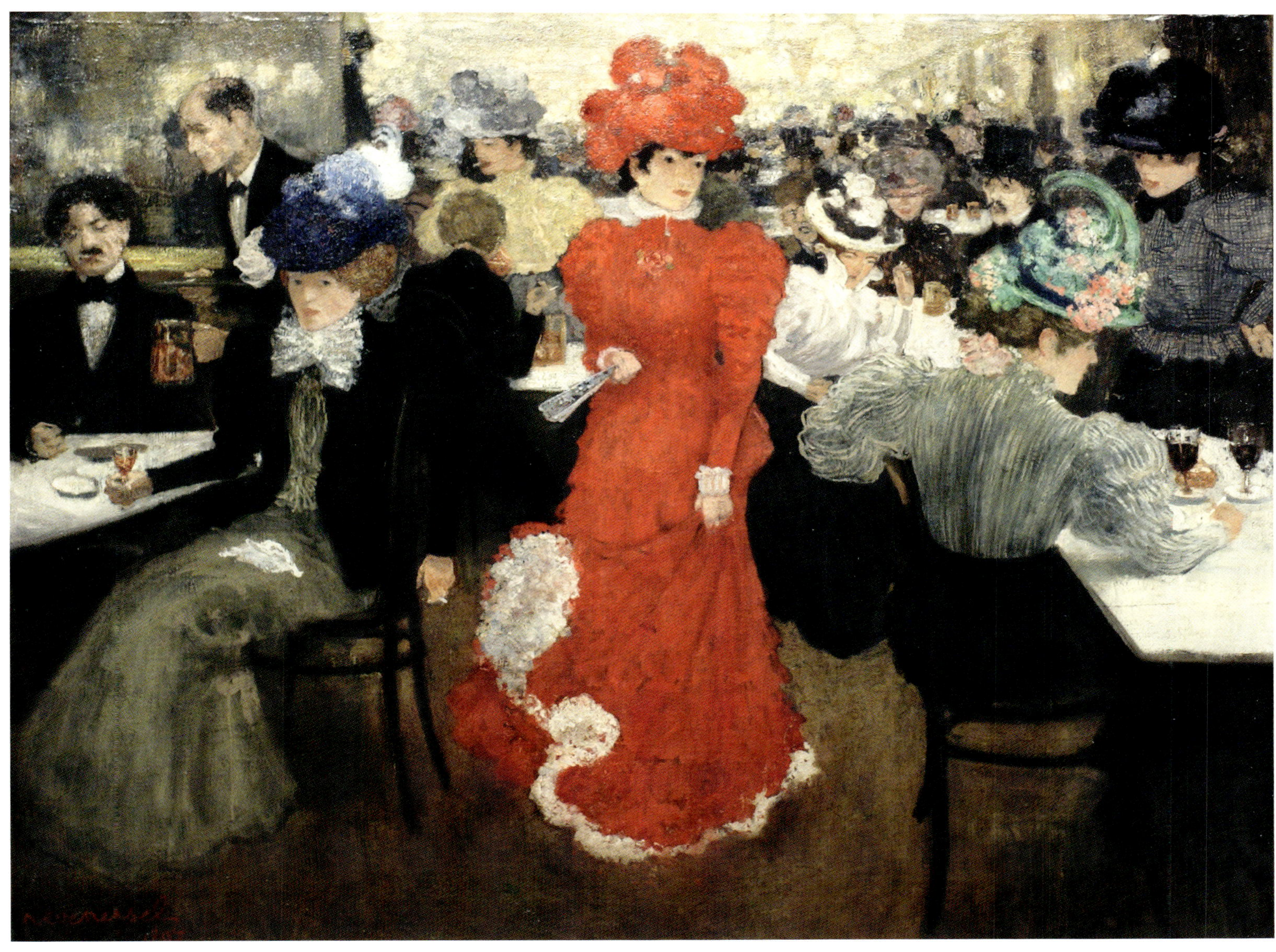

Cat. 44

Henri Evenepoel
Belgian, 1872–1899
In the Café a'Harcourt in Paris, 1897
Oil on canvas
44 ⅞ × 58 ¼ in. (114 × 148 cm)
Städel Museum, Frankfurt, 1811

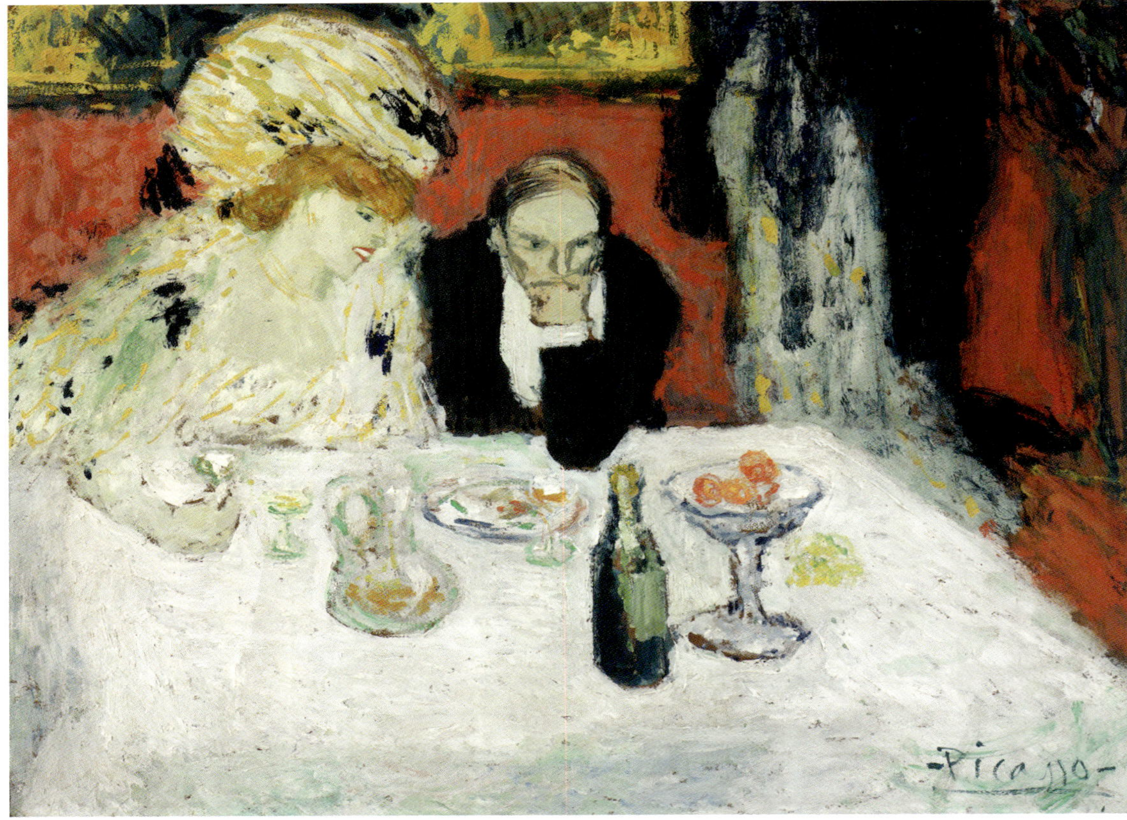

Fig. 31
Pablo Picasso
Spanish, 1881–1973
The Diners (*Les Soupeurs*), 1901
Oil on cardboard
18 ⅝ × 24 ⁹⁄₁₆ in. (47.3 × 62.4 cm)
Courtesy of the RISD Museum,
Providence, RI; Bequest of George
Pierce Metcalf, 57.237

to add to the drama of the scene, was a bold declaration of the artist's adaptation of the *indépendant* aesthetic of Manet and Degas. While *Café Interior* and many of Forain's other works from the period have a tinge of caricature to them, they were described by Huysmans in a review of the 1879 exhibition as "little marvels of Parisian elegance and reality."[22]

In addition to its reliance on the *dame de comptoir* and the *serveuse*, there was another crucial aspect of café culture in the eighteenth and nineteenth centuries that depended on women: the *cabinet particulier*, akin to the modern concept of the restaurant "private room" where illicit sexual activity often took place. Nearly every restaurant and café in Paris had at least one, often several, private rooms for male diners to satisfy their sexual appetites while taking their fill of food and drink as well.[23] In keeping with the establishments

to which they were connected, the *cabinet particulier* ranged from the sparse and rudimentary to the luxurious, but always included a table and chairs and a sofa where men could lounge with their lovers. The women who joined men in these rooms were sometimes their lovers—never their wives, as it would be indecent for a nineteenth-century Parisian lady to appear in a restaurant, even with her husband. Just as often, the women in *cabinets particuliers* were sex workers, and in some circumstances it was customary for them to receive kick-backs in the form of free food and drink from restaurant proprietors for encouraging their companions to spend lavishly over the course of an evening.

As the principal artist chronicling sexual politics in late nineteenth-century Paris, Jean-Louis Forain produced many images of women interacting with men in café spaces, including in the *cabinet particulier*. While Forain worked in a variety of media for a variety of purposes, it is the etchings he made in the late 1870s that walk a line between eyewitness illustration, fine art, and caricature. Forain, along with the realist painter Jean-François Raffaëlli, created a series of etchings to accompany the 1880 edition of his friend Joris-Karl Huysmans's collection of essays on contemporary life, *Croquis parisiens*. Of these prints, *Maison close* (cat. 16) depicts the kind of *cabinet particulier* that might exist in a more working-class café in Paris.[24] Though the title of this work translates to a brothel, the globe light, mirrored walls, and banquette seating in Forain's scene indicate that the location was most likely a more public one. In keeping with the setting, the man in *Maison close* can also be identified as working-class by his workman's cap; he cuts a side-eye at the two women beside him, scrutinizing their ample bosoms and pondering which one he might engage for the evening.

As the nineteenth century came to a close, the social taboo of a woman appearing in a restaurant alone may have loosened somewhat, but artists were still inspired by women seeking to attract attention and company in café spaces. The central figure of Henri Evenepoel's 1897 painting *In the Café d'Harcourt in Paris* (cat. 44) can be identified as a prostitute by her bold red dress and red-plumed hat.[25] The Café d'Harcourt was located in the Place de la Sorbonne in the Quartier Latin and therefore attracted a relatively young and lively clientele. Though the Harcourt was known to employ women as *serveuses*, it was also commonly populated by *grisettes*, or young working-class women who attached themselves to male students.[26] Some of the women who appear seated at the tables in Evenepoel's painting are likely intended to be *grisettes*. The woman at the center of the composition, however, is not a *grisette*; as in Forain's *Café Interior*, she is of a superior ranking

in the hierarchy of Parisian sex workers: a *soupeuse*. *Soupeuses* often wore flashy clothes and appeared at restaurants that stayed open late at night.[27] Just a few years later, in his 1901 painting *The Diners* (fig. 31), Pablo Picasso captured a man seated on a red banquette in what could possibly be the *cabinet particulier* of a café, his hand at his chin in deep contemplation of his options for the evening. When taking into account the work's French title, *Les Soupeurs*, it becomes (even more) evident that the woman seated next to the man is a *soupeuse*. She was such an integral aspect of nightlife in Paris that, in Picasso's painting, she begins to blend in with the white starched linen covering the table. It is possible that Picasso's woman would have been described in her day as a *flibocheuse*, a slang subclassification of *soupeuses* that was particularly aggressive.[28]

Evenepoel positions his *soupeuse* at the center of the composition, but her resigned expression fails to match the panache of her clothing and the liveliness of the Harcourt's atmosphere. Both Forain and Evenepoel's images seem to simultaneously celebrate and question, though not necessarily condemn, the social climate amidst which it was created, revealing what contemporary Belgian critic Octave Maus (1856–1919) aptly articulated as "high life masking empty hearts."[29] Evenepoel himself wrote to his father about the painting: "I am now working on my *Harcourt Café* which is giving me a lot of trouble and which now pleases me and disgusts me."[30]

The theme of a woman seated at a café table, drinking alone and somewhat dejected—just as disreputable a figure as a woman entering a restaurant alone—appeared with some regularity in Parisian art from the 1870s into the 1890s. Though cafés in theory provided a space for socializing, they also served as places where men (and some women) could go to be alone or at least blend in with an anonymous crowd.

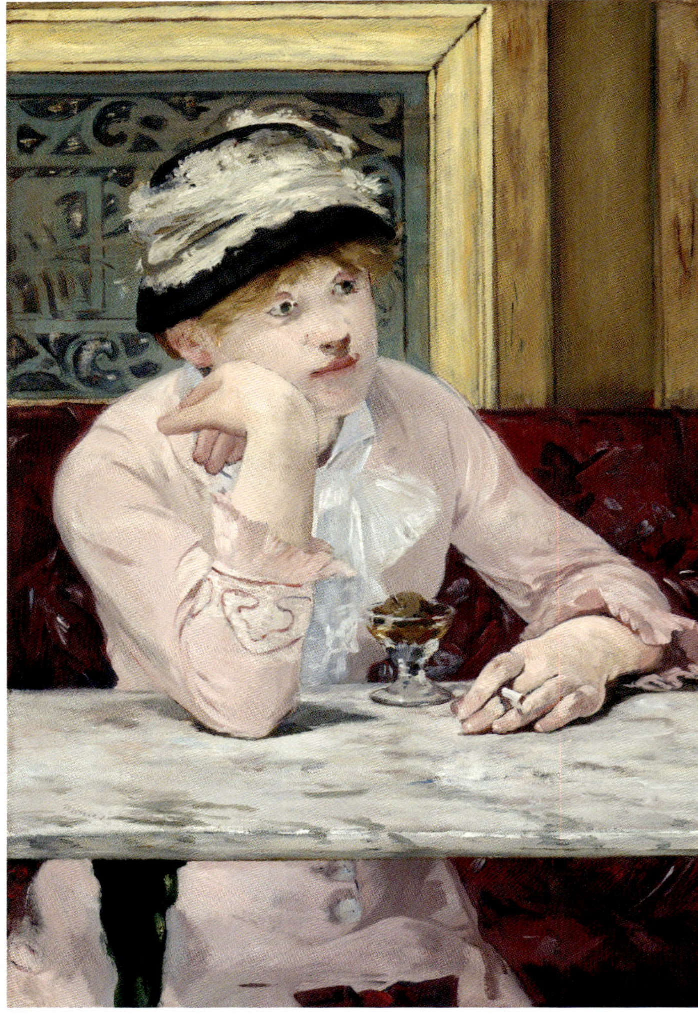

Fig. 32
Édouard Manet
French, 1832–1883
Plum Brandy, ca. 1877
Oil on canvas
29 × 19 ¾ in. (73.6 × 50.2 cm)
National Gallery of Art, Washington,
DC, Collection of Mr. and Mrs. Paul
Mellon, 1971.85.1

Fig. 33
Edgar Degas
French, 1834–1917
Dans un café, 1875–76
Oil on canvas
36 ¼ × 27 in. (92 × 68.5 cm)
Musée d'Orsay, Paris, RF 1984

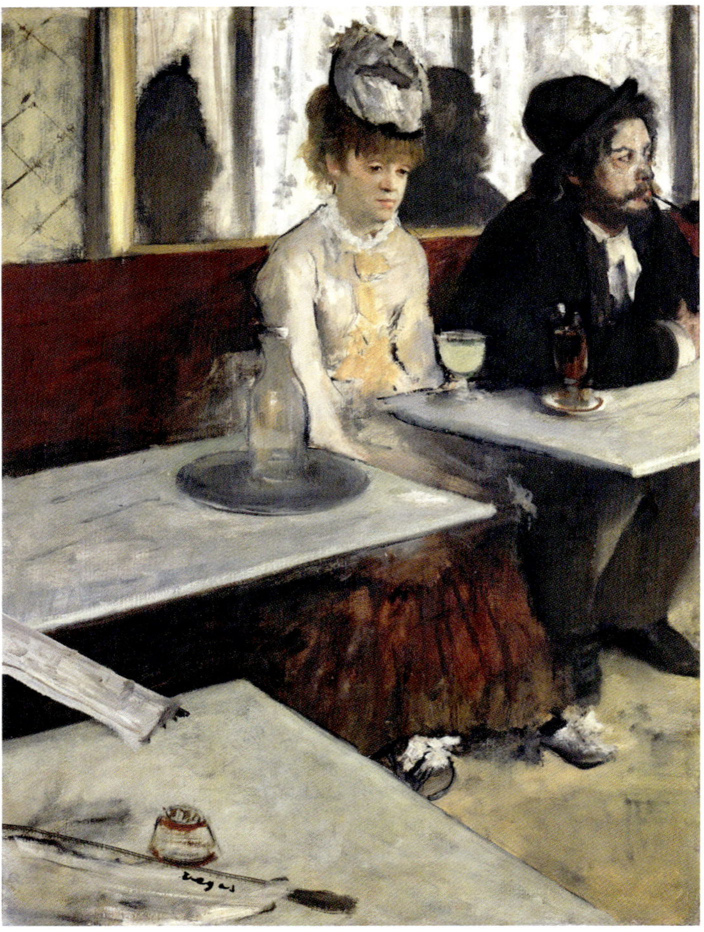

Edgar Degas explored the theme of the single woman
in the café first with his *Dans un café* (1875–76, fig. 33),
quickly followed by Manet through *Plum Brandy*
(ca. 1877, fig. 32), while Forain followed suit a few years
later with *Woman in a Café* (ca. 1885, cat. 19). Unlike
the women in the paintings by his mentors, Forain's
femme au café appears to be expecting someone, and
quite lacks the air of dejection or ennui that marks the
earlier images. When working in oil, Forain tended to pull
back on the satire that defined his work in watercolor
and garnered him the moniker "the youngest and most
incisive of the Impressionists"[31] in favor of more elegant

Cat. 19

Jean-Louis Forain
French, 1852–1931
Woman in a Café, ca. 1885
Oil on panel
18 × 14 ½ in. (45.7 × 36.8 cm)
Dixon Gallery and Gardens; Museum
purchase by the Life Members Society in
honor of John and Lucy Buchanan, 1994.1

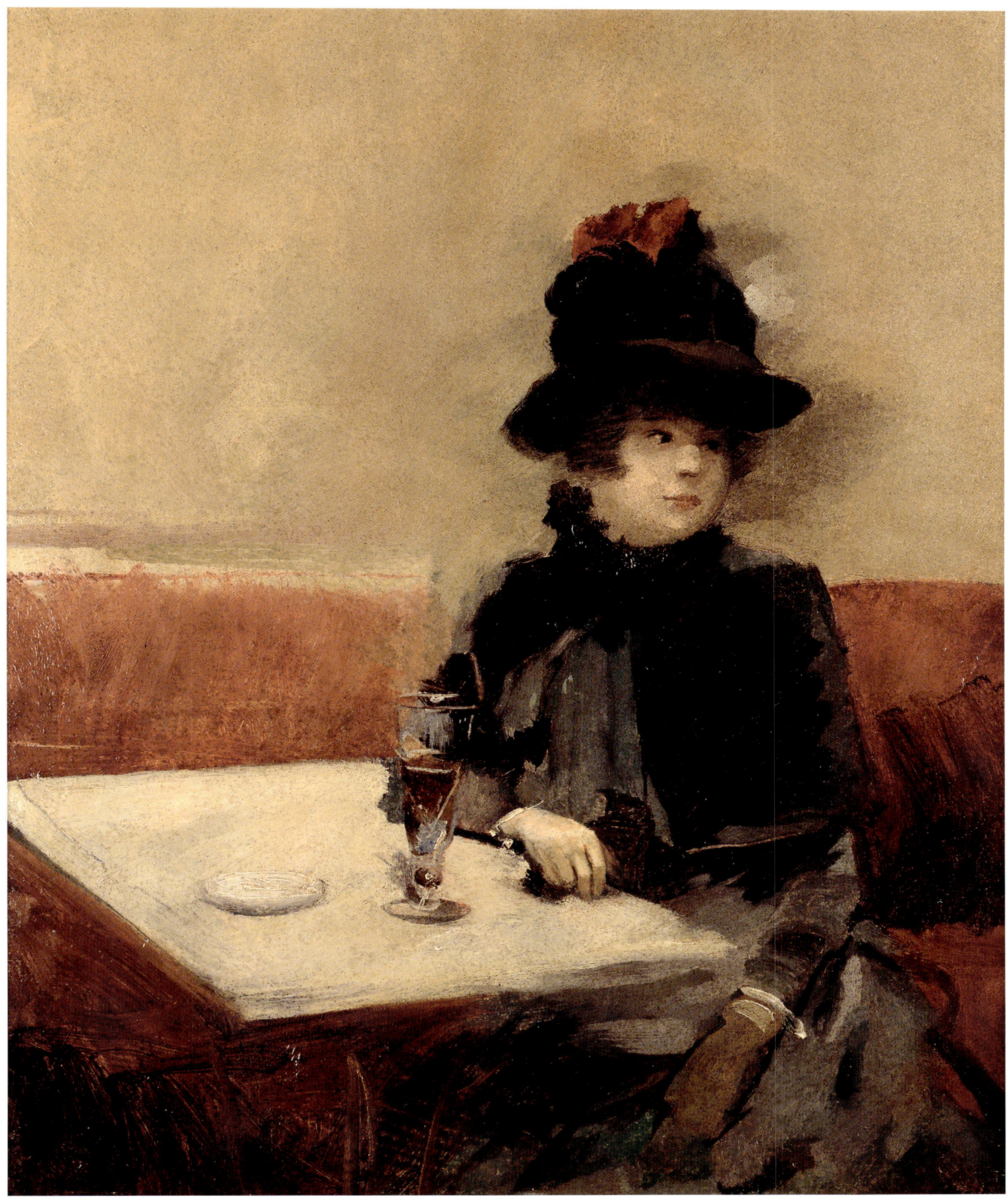

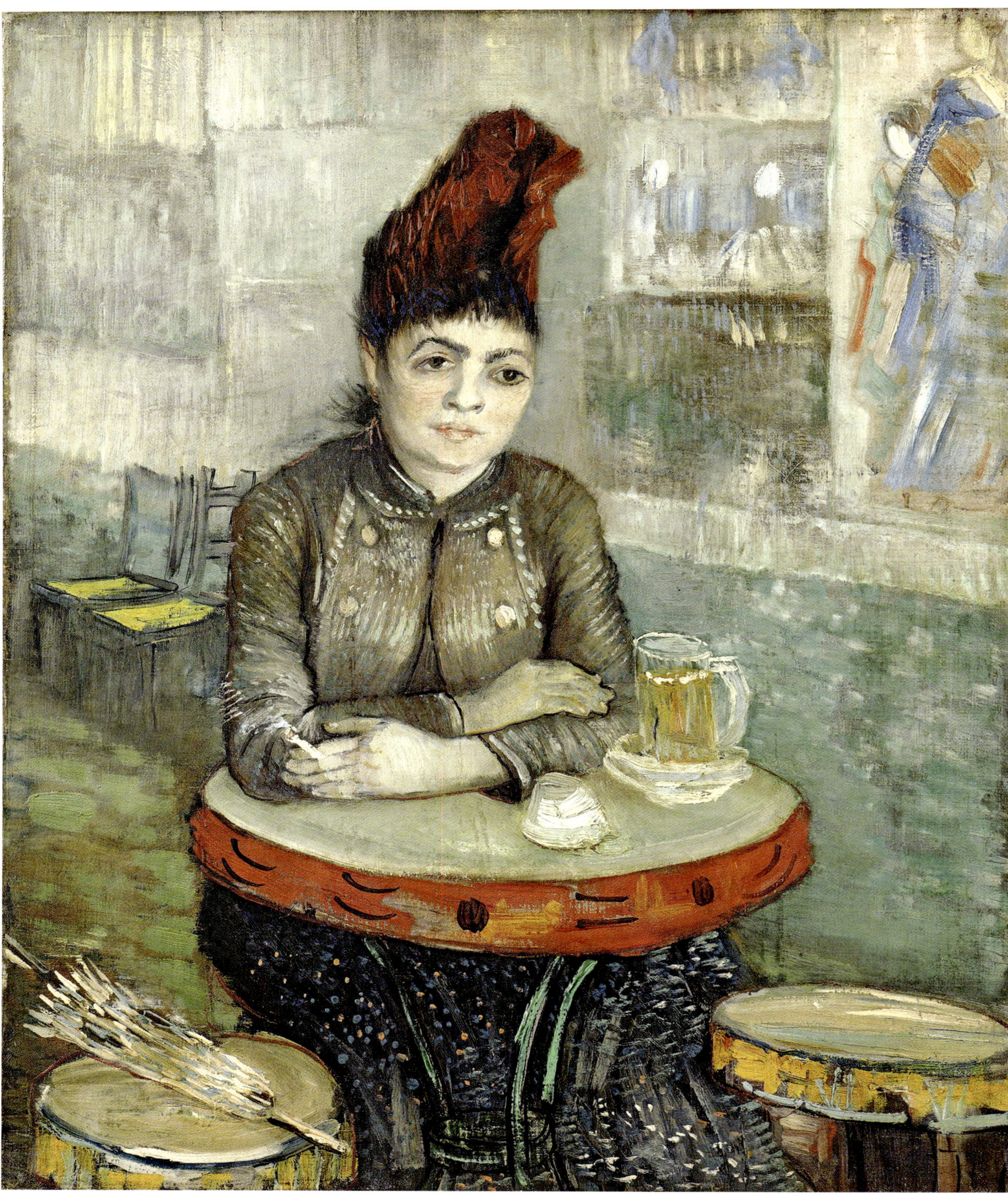

Cat. 25

Vincent van Gogh
Dutch, 1853–1890
*In the Café: Agostina Segatori in
Le Tambourin*, January–March 1887
Oil on canvas
21 ⅞ × 18 ½ in. (55.5 × 47 cm)
Van Gogh Museum, Amsterdam (Vincent
van Gogh Foundation)

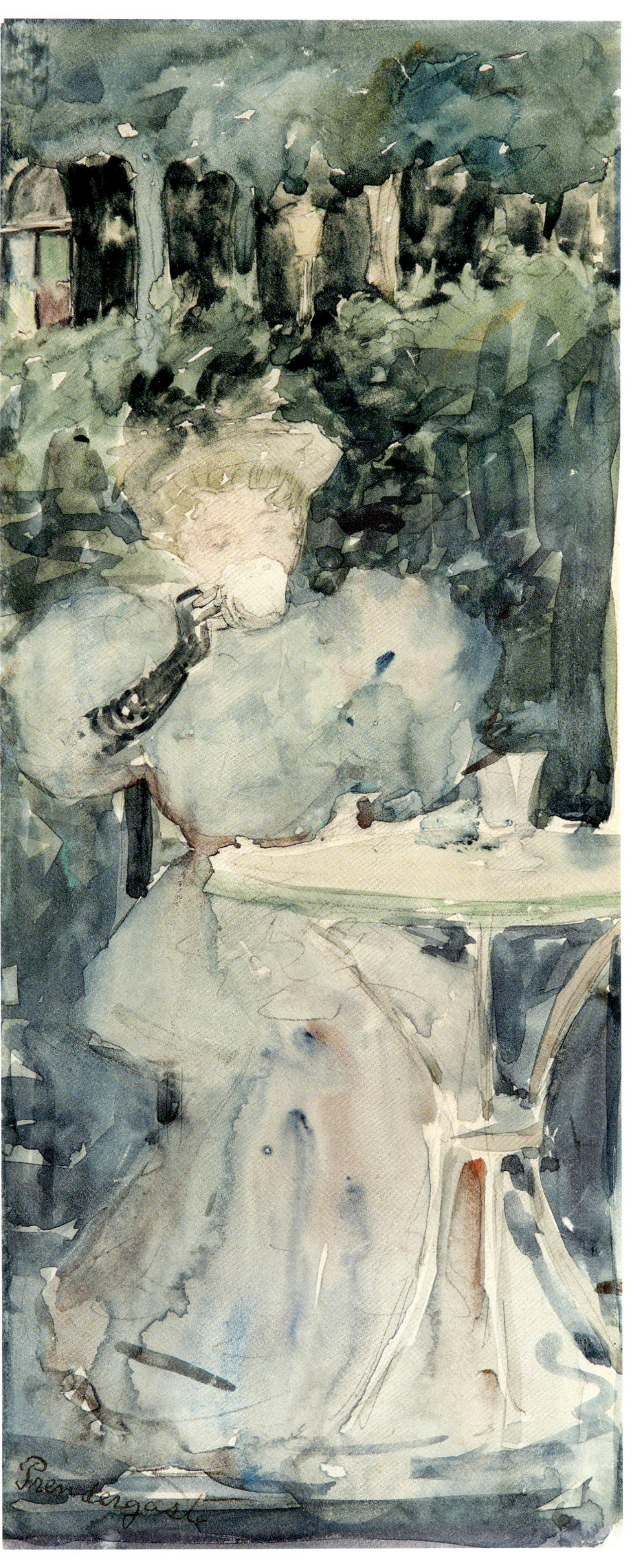

Cat. 38
Maurice Brazil Prendergast
American, 1858–1924
Woman Drinking Tea, 1893–94
Watercolor on paper
10 ½ × 4 ½ in. (26.7 × 11.4 cm)
Dixon Gallery and Gardens; Gift of
Montgomery H. W. Ritchie, 1996.2.11

and objective depictions of contemporary life. Though she is likely hoping to pick up a man for the evening—the fact that she is unescorted and drinking alone signals her status and intentions—she appears slightly understated compared to other depictions of café prostitution.

The taboo of sitting alone also extended to women who worked or even owned public dining establishments. Almost every woman associated with a café, whether a waitress or proprietor, was subject to assumptions of sexual availability. These stereotypes were often perpetuated in the popular press through illustrations, but also in fine art of the era concerned with modern life. Some artists, however, seemed more sympathetic to the plight of female café workers. Vincent van Gogh's early 1887 painting *In the Café: Agostina Segatori in Le Tambourin* (cat. 25) shows the owner of the Montmartre café seated alone at a drum-shaped tabletop (a hallmark of the restaurant), smoking and drinking a beer—both habits that signaled promiscuity and lower class. Van Gogh was an *habitué* of Le Tambourin, organized a couple of art exhibitions there, and also developed a brief romantic relationship with Segatori (1841–1910), the Italian-born artist's model who purchased the café and made it a haven of sorts for artists and writers living in Paris.

Of the various images of women alone in cafés by Degas, Manet, Forain, and Van Gogh discussed above, the latter's depiction remains the most compassionate. "La Segatori," as she was sometimes referred to, appears exhausted, pausing during what was likely a grueling day for a smoke and a few beers. To be sure, work in a café in the nineteenth century required long hours, difficult conditions, physical labor, and a steady stream of harassment from male patrons. Partaking in the alcohol served at the café was common for women, though being seen drinking and smoking in public would have further sullied their reputation. Segatori, however, was by all accounts a progressive woman, and even

before she took over Le Tambourin had a considerable history of being involved with artists.[32]

Similarly, the woman who delicately sips her tea during an afternoon at an outdoor café in the Canadian/American artist Maurice Brazil Prendergast's intimate watercolor *Woman Drinking Tea* (1893–94, cat. 38) appears to be doing so alone. This quickly executed but closely observed painting was made on one of Prendergast's first visits to Paris, and the image therefore bears none of the cynicism typical of French artists depicting similar themes. Prendergast seems so dazzled by the scenic atmosphere of the outdoor café, by the woman's fashionable clothing and accessories, and by the ritual of taking tea that he overlooks or disregards her being seated at her café table alone. Even during the daytime, a woman in late nineteenth-century Paris risked her reputation by sitting alone at a café.

Certainly, for a woman to be seen seated alone at a café table was to risk her reputation. Only slightly safer was for a woman to be seated in a café in the company of other women, in which case the assumption of the women's sexual availability became only ambiguous. They could be waiting flirtatiously for male company for the evening, which was likely the case in the American artist Fernand Lungren's painting *In the Café* (1882–84, cat. 18), or they could simply be socializing or relaxing, a possible interpretation of Edgar Degas's enigmatic, unfinished painting *Au Café* (ca. 1875–77, see fig. 2). Degas's painting bears a much more melancholy tone. The two women are seated together on a café terrace, surrounded by what Degas suggests might be a few trees and possibly the soaring form of the Luxor Obelisk in the Place de la Concorde in the distance. Though loosely painted, *Au Café* was thoughtfully executed and epitomizes Degas's approach to realism—naturalistic poses and expressions. While the women do not appear jovial, neither are they totally separate, and their poses belie

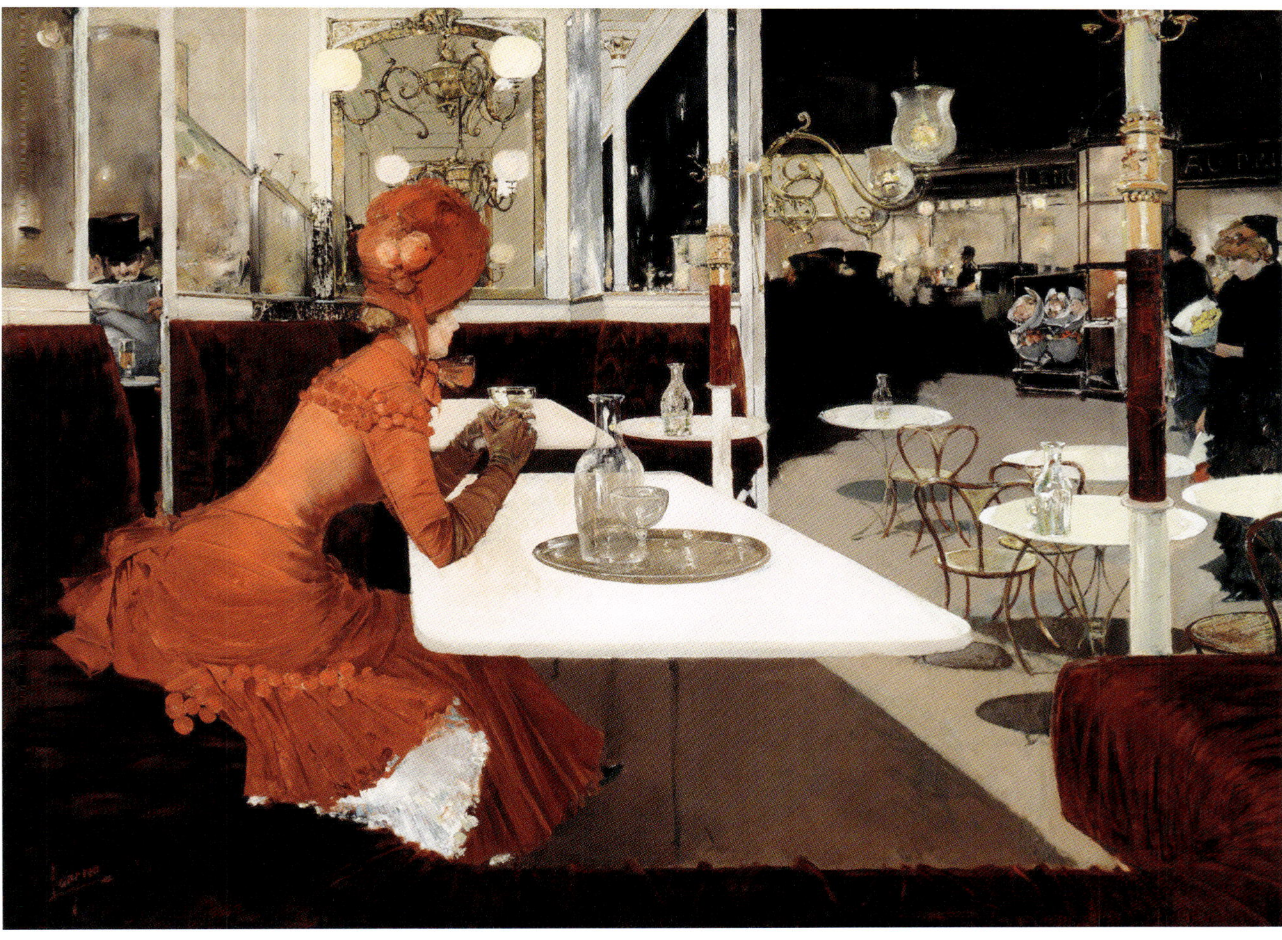

a certain familiarity or ease that suggests they have been in this basic situation many times before.[33] Degas's muted and diluted palette evokes a certain weariness that leads to more questions: are the two women merely relaxing at the end of a long day, or are they resignedly anticipating how the afternoon and evening will unfold?

The lassitude of *Au Café* stands in stark contrast to the "terrifying realism"[34] of other café subjects by Degas and to the dazzle of Fernand Lungren's *In the Café*, made just a few years after the Degas. As a young American artist on an extended visit to Paris, Lungren, not surprisingly, approached the theme of two women in a café from a different angle than Degas, a Parisian more than twenty years his senior. Lungren arrived in Paris in the summer of 1882 along with fellow American painters James Carroll Beckwith, Robert Blum, and William Merritt Chase, among others.[35] Much

Fig. 34
Fernand Lungren
American, 1857–1932
In the Café, 1882–84
Oil on canvas
31 ⅜ × 41 ¼ in. (79.7 × 104.8 cm)
The Art Institute of Chicago, Charles H. and
Mary F.S. Worcester Collection, 1947.85

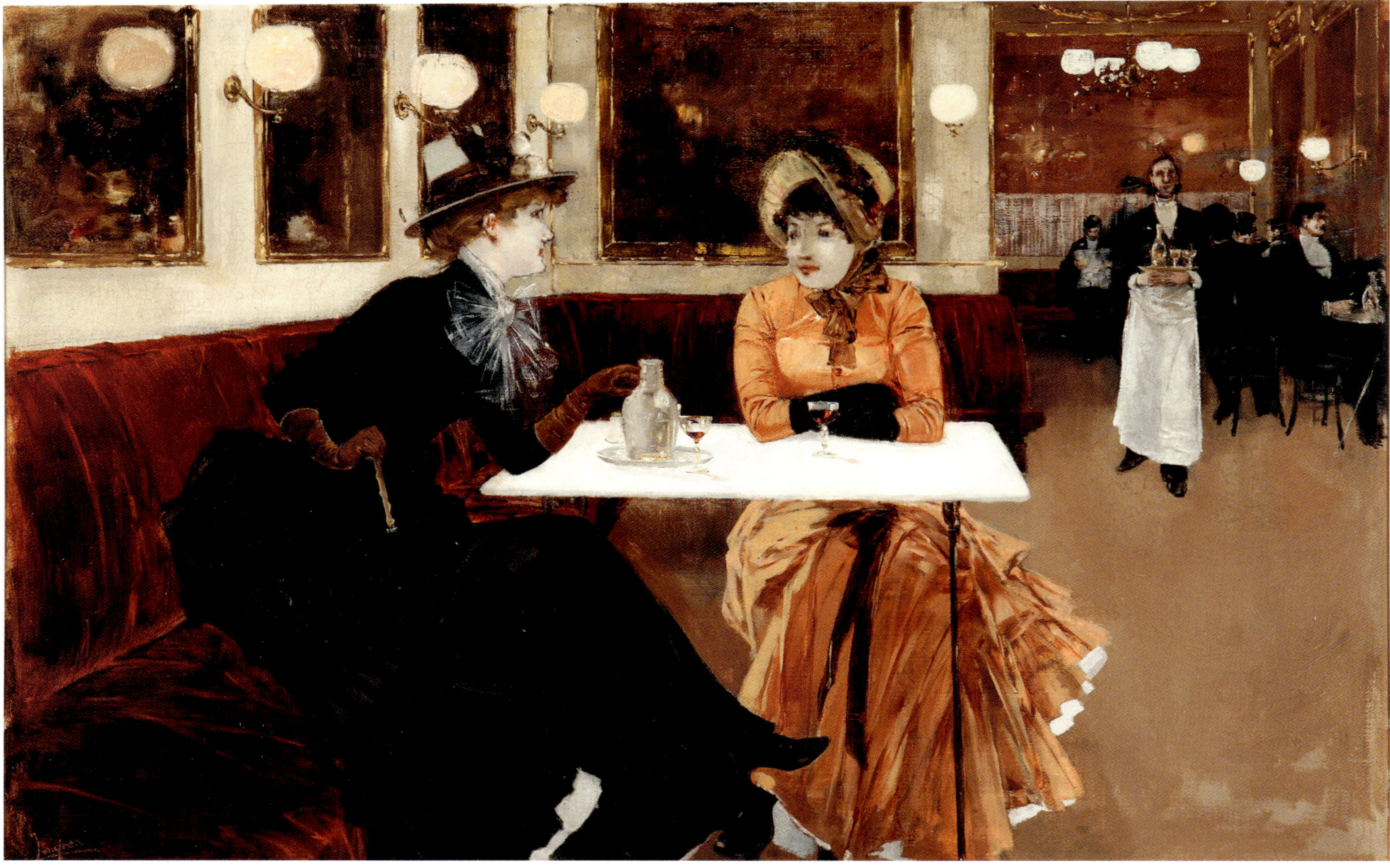

Cat. 18

Fernand Lungren
American, 1857–1932
In the Café, 1882–84
Oil on canvas
17 ⅝ × 26 ½ in. (44.8 × 67.3 cm)
Dixon Gallery and Gardens; Museum
purchase with funds provided by the estate
of Cecil Williams Marshall, 2018.2

of the group stayed at the Hôtel de l'Université in the Quartier Latin, where they would have been surrounded by a multitude of options for public dining and entertainment.[36] After attempting semi-formalized study at the Académie Julian, Lungren rather quickly walked out, choosing instead to let the city of Paris itself guide his painting practice.

Inspired perhaps by the atmosphere of sociability in his neighborhood, Lungren undertook a couple of café paintings during his time in Paris. *In the Café* depicts two women seated together in a typical Parisian café complete with red velvet banquettes, gilded mirrors lining the walls, and the golden glow of globed lighting.[37] The women appear amused and enjoying each other's company. Although Hollis Clayson's research suggests that pairs or groups of women seated together in cafés could maintain respectability, the two women in Lungren's *In the Café* retain an ambiguity that makes them difficult to define.[38] In a larger related painting (fig. 34), Lungren chose to paint a woman, dressed in an attention-grabbing red dress and plumed hat, in a similar café setting seated alone, all but labeling her as a prostitute.[39] And while the two women that dominate the Dixon's version of *In the Café* are relaxed, they do not appear to be exactly off-duty either. One woman wears a pumpkin-orange dress and the other, facing outward, an oversized diaphanous bow; they both have powdered faces and painted lips. Lungren intimates that they are not just in this café for the pleasure of the other's company, but perhaps instead to secure a man's company for the evening. Regardless, the camaraderie between the two women in Lungren's painting is relatively rare in late nineteenth-century Euro/American art, especially by a male artist.

It remains important for twenty-first century viewers to consider the author of the majority of café paintings in the Belle Époque: they were almost always male. So it is through the male gaze that we encounter women in café spaces. The women in these paintings are often stereotyped and objectified, subjected to the gender-disparaging societal rules of nineteenth-century Europe. With a few exceptions, including the expatriate painter Elisabeth Epstein (see cat. 64), women artists were fighting enough prejudice to have their work shown that they dared not subject themselves to further criticism by painting café subjects.

As the twentieth century dawned, Parisian café culture, including its sexual mores, remained largely as it had been in the previous decades. But the art being produced in the French capital, still the center of the international art world, was changing, led by increasingly rebellious young artists coming onto the scene, including Pablo Picasso. When Picasso initially arrived in Paris in 1900, he was drawn to the cabarets of Montmartre, including the Moulin de la Galette, which was a favorite gathering spot for Spanish expatriates.[40]

With his archetypal male gaze, Picasso's images of Parisian cafés from his first years in the city obsessively focus on the women present in those spaces and are more explicit in communicating their sexuality than the recent work of his French peers. These pictures forgo the social commentary of artists such as Daumier and Forain in favor of capturing a more raw desire. Picasso's *Au café* (cat. 48) from 1901, a colorful pastel recording of three women seated at a café table (one distracted by a stray dog), while displaying a fascination with its subject, borders on caricature in the exaggeration of the women's poses and the looseness with which the scene is captured. Despite the swirling gaiety, there is a certain uncomfortable or even ominous tone to *Au Café*, enhanced by the dark shadows that frame or lurk behind the women. The time-worn face of the figure at the right of the composition particularly stands out as the artist's target. Picasso is keenly aware of the reason these women are in the café for the evening: he objectifies them, and, in the exaggeration

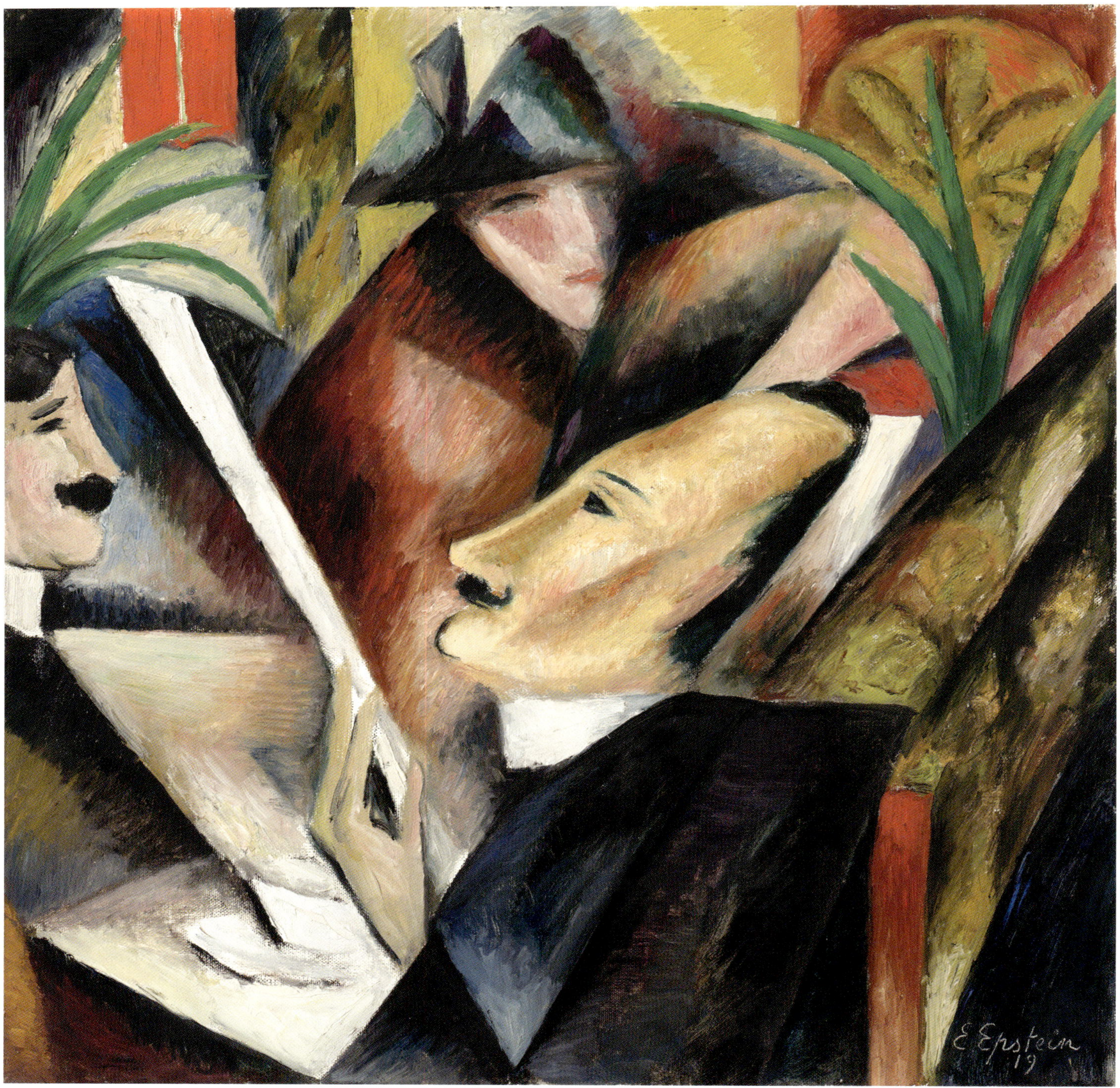

Cat. 64

Elisabeth Epstein
Russian (now Ukraine), 1879–1956
People on a Café Terrace, 1913
Oil on canvas
22 × 22 in. (58.9 × 58.9 cm)
National Gallery of Art, Washington,
DC, Collection of Arnold and Joan Saltzman,
2020.112.9

of their forms, would almost seem to ridicule them were it not for the palpable anticipation of his gaze.

∾

If women entering cafés alone was problematic, and women in the company of other women in public dining establishments ambiguous, what then of women seen in cafés accompanied by men? Did men provide the escort or chaperone that would have made their presence "respectable" by contemporary standards? How were they framed by the art of the late nineteenth and early twentieth centuries? We have already seen in Daumier's series *Les Étrangers à Paris* the common opinion of female tourists dining in the French capital, but other artists target native women in the company of men in restaurants.

In the manner of Daumier, French printmaker Félix Buhot created some of the most innovative and complex prints of the nineteenth century, many of which are marked by a sharp wit. Buhot's view of the Place Pigalle (1878, cat. 12) at the foot of Montmartre initially offers a complacent view of a bustling section of Paris. But closer examination of the print, including its margins and inset image (pp. 110-11), a device Buhot termed "symphonic margins," reveals two women and a gentleman sharing a drink at a sidewalk table outside the Rat Mort, a café known as a gathering spot for writers and artists.[41] The Café de la Nouvelle Athènes is just across the plaza behind the Fontaine Pigalle. Being seated at a sidewalk table out in the open makes these two women even more "public." They exist somewhere between the *filles de joie* or *soupeuses* seen in paintings by Forain and Fernand Lungren, and the *filles de boulevard*, or streetwalkers, who strolled outside of cafés to pick up company for the evening. In Buhot's image, rendered in such a small space that most details were omitted, the woman at the center

of the table has a cigarette dangling from her lips, another indicator of "lewd" behavior.

Henri Gervex, soon to become one of Paris's most controversial painters, completed *Café Scene in Paris* (cat. 11) in 1877, at the same moment that Manet, Degas, and Forain were feverishly mining the world of the café for subject matter.[42] While Gervex's painting may initially seem like a simple recording of an everyday gathering at a neighborhood café, a second look illuminates the painting's complex spatial arrangement, incongruous elements, and enigmatic unfinished areas. These peculiarities converge to create the central tension or melodrama between the figures seated around the stereotypical red banquette.

Where in this café are the figures seated? Are they facing the street? What does the large column that separates the two groups of people delineate—indoor versus outdoor space? It is known that Gervex painted himself into the scene as the man lighting his pipe.[43] In doing so he declares his own modernity as an artist/flâneur, one who both observes and participates in public life. He is part of a quartet of men (or at least a trio if the man at the right is not included in their party) who have gathered at this café, but do not actually interact with one another.[44] The man to the right of Gervex reads the newspaper, a seemingly quotidian act, but one that, in light of the French Ministry of the Interior's 1877 decree that forbade the reading of newspapers aloud in cafés for fear of spreading radical politics, automatically makes the gathering more political.[45]

Though they are joined by two women, none of the men seem to interact with either of them. The woman dressed in the shimmering pink ensemble commands attention at the same time as she has her back to the viewer. She appears to watch the men, her head tilted in longing or anticipation as she lets the glass of absinthe, identifiable by its slight green

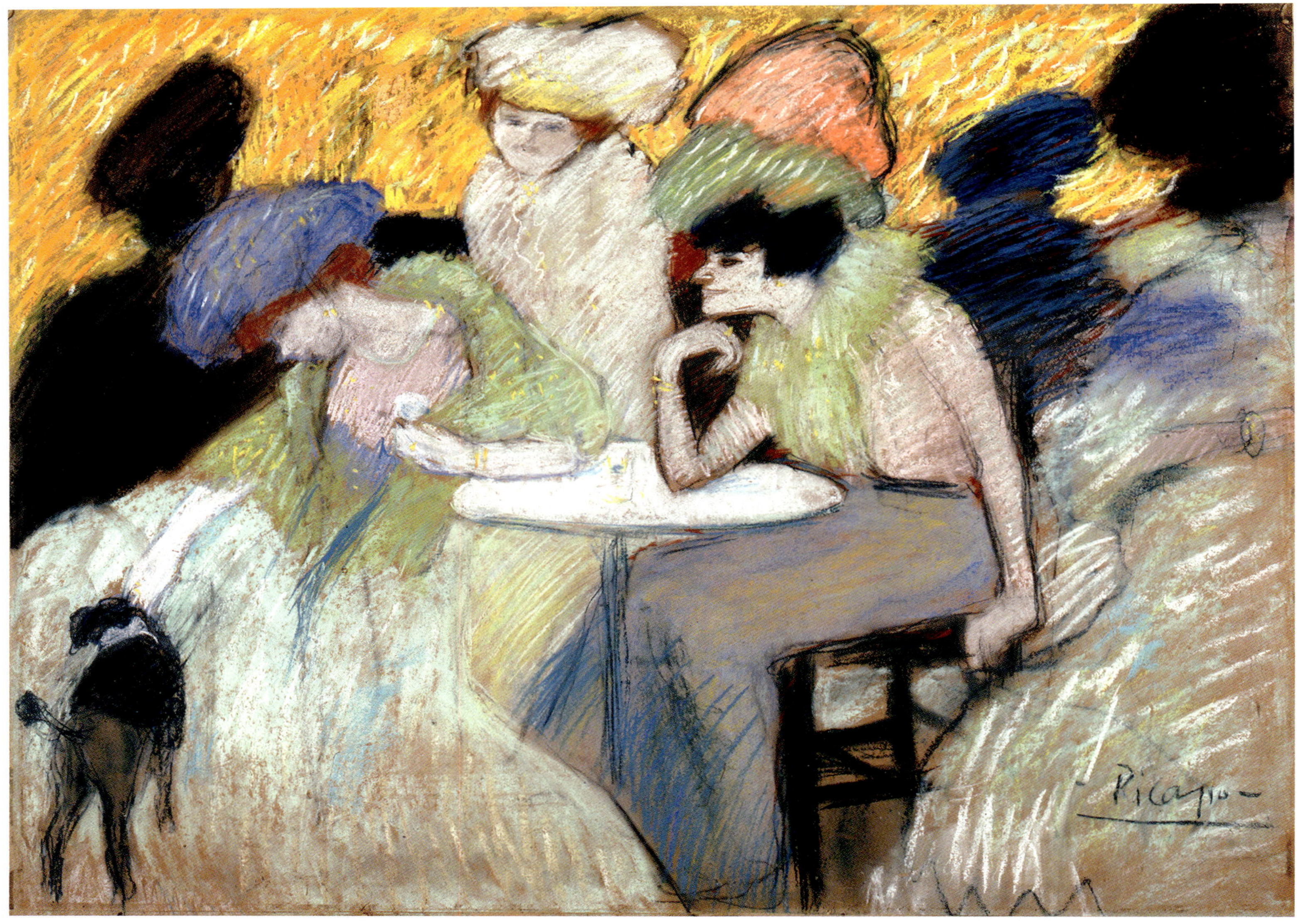

Cat. 48

Pablo Picasso
Spanish, 1881–1973
Au café, 1901
Pastel on cardboard
21 ½ × 29 ½ in. (54.6 × 74.9 cm)
Norton Museum of Art, West Palm Beach;
Gift of R. H. Norton, 53.150

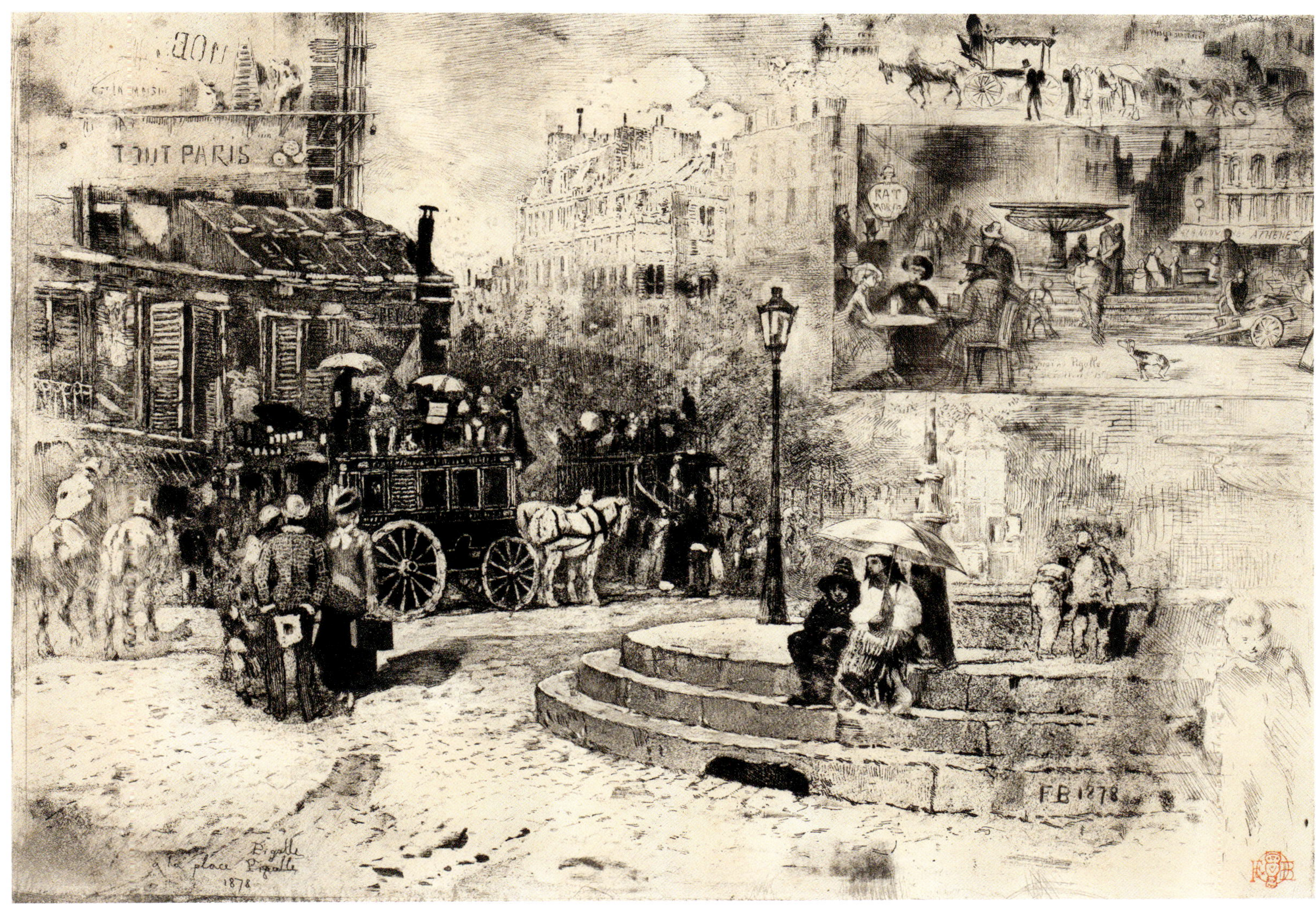

Cat. 12

Félix-Hilaire Buhot
French, 1847–1898
La Place Pigal'e en 1878, 1878
Etching, aquatint, and drypoint; sixth
state of six
17 × 20 ½ in. (43.2 × 52.1 cm)
Private collection

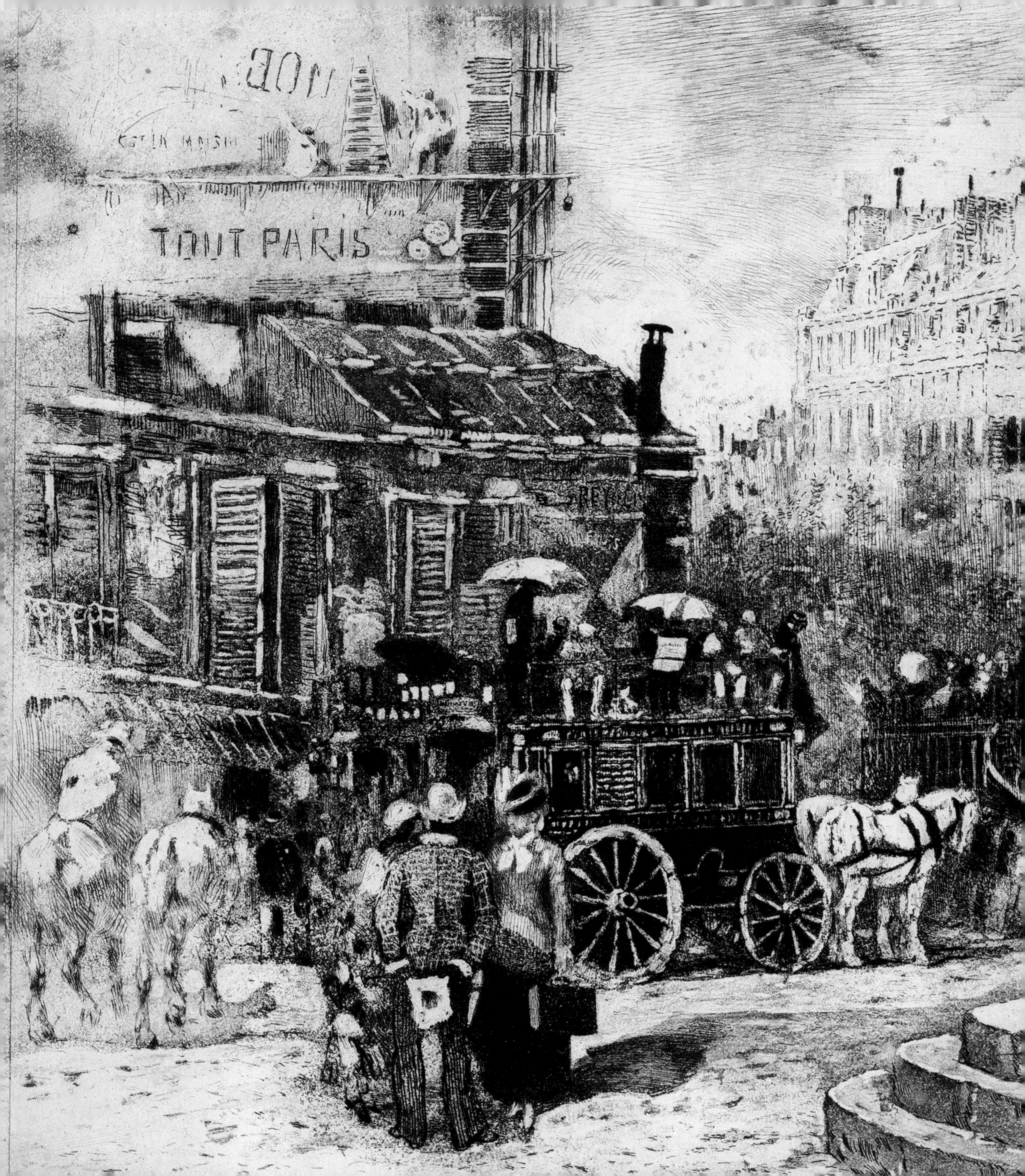
TOUT PARIS

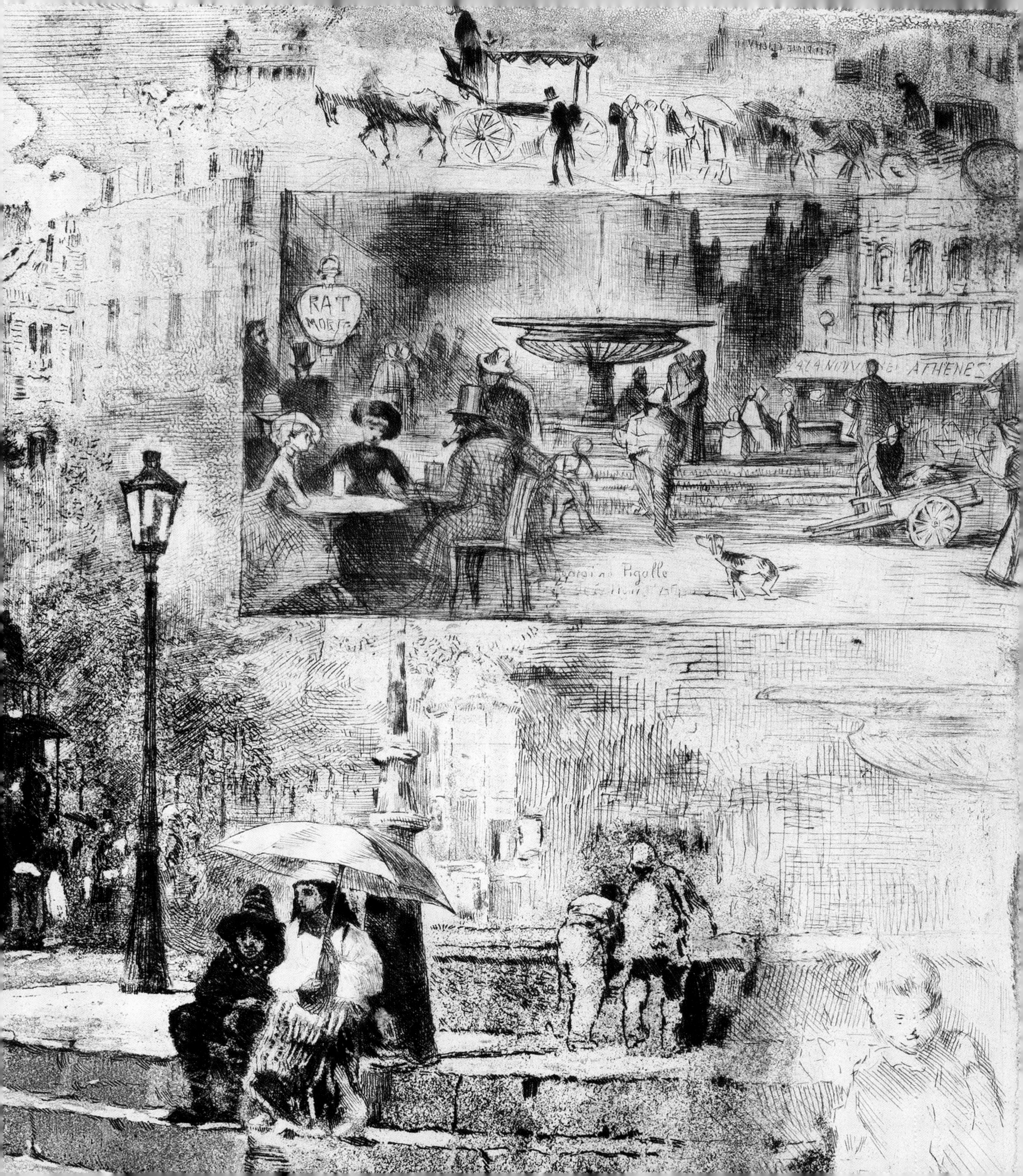

RAT
MORT
À LA NOUVELLE ATHÈNES
Pigalle

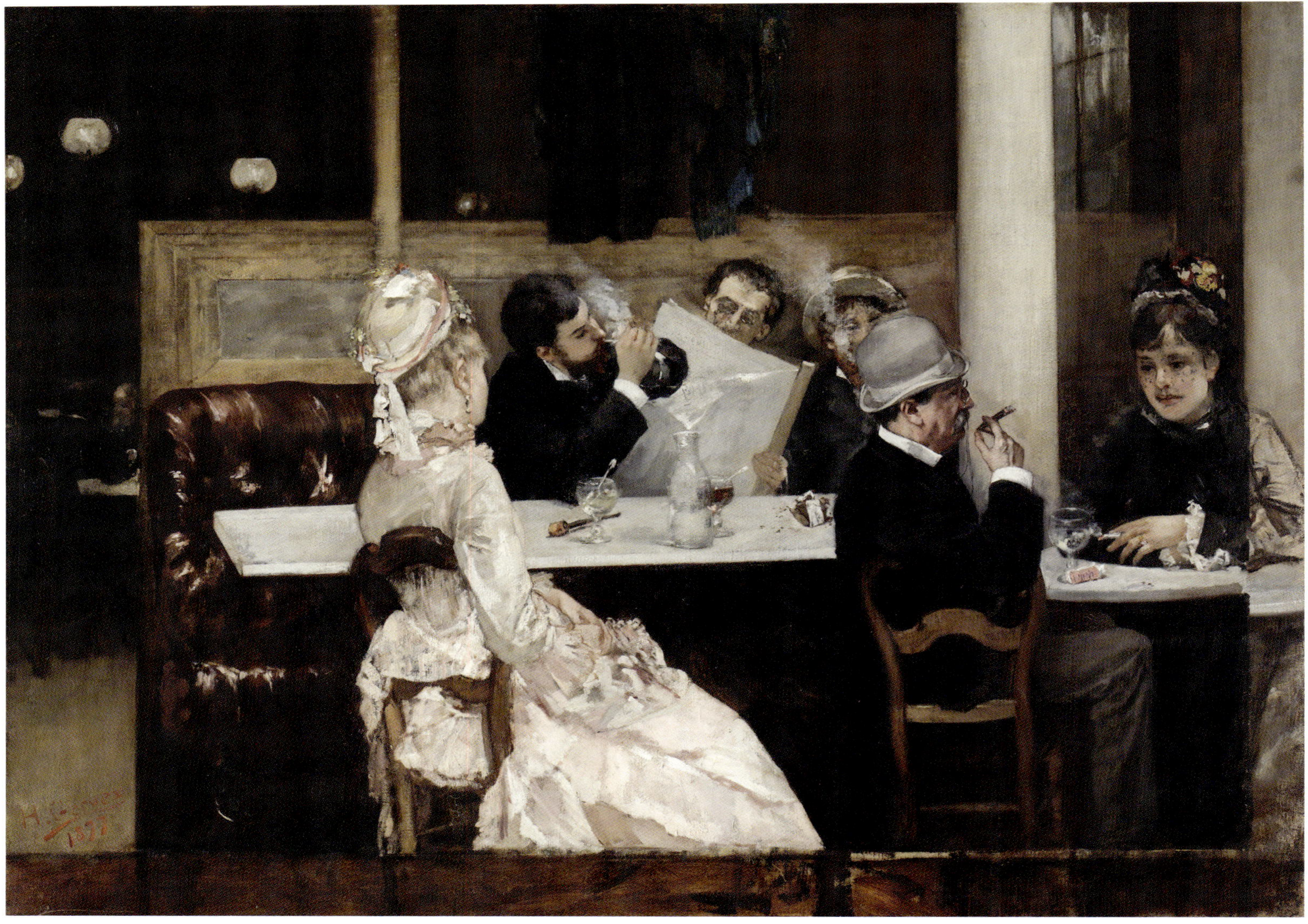

Cat. 11

Henri Gervex
French, 1852–1929
Café Scene in Paris, 1877
Oil on canvas
39 ⅝ × 53 ½ in. (100.6 × 135.9 cm)
Detroit Institute of Arts; Founders Society
Purchase, Robert H. Tannahill Foundation
Fund, 1992.8

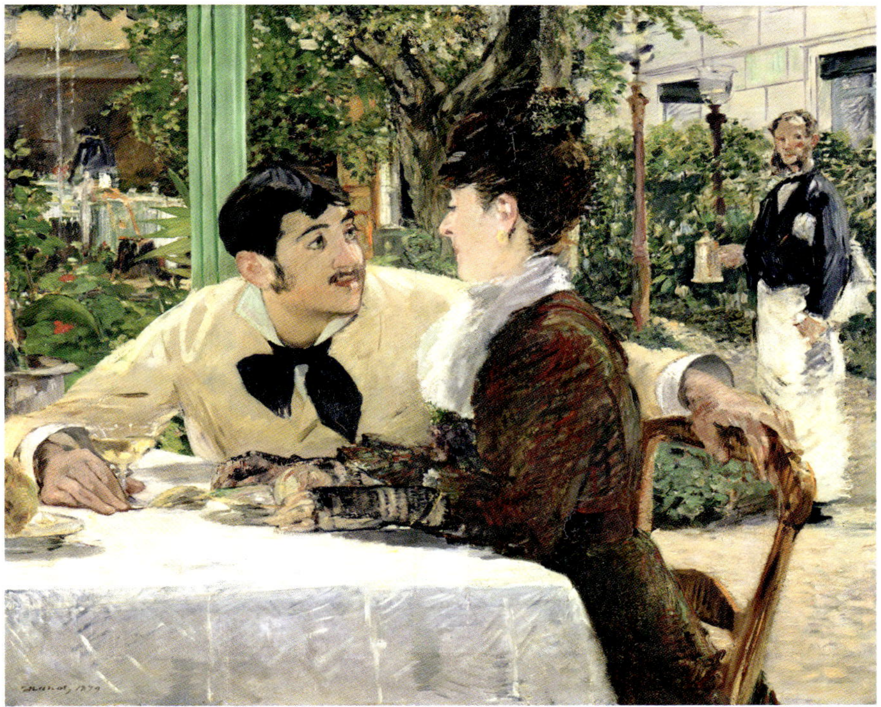

Fig. 35
Édouard Manet
French, 1832–1883
Chez le Père Lathuille, 1879
Oil on canvas
36 ¼ × 44 ⅛ in. (92 × 112 cm)
Musée des Beaux-Arts, Tournai, Belgium

tinge and its spoon, take effect. In her static state, she appears to be as decorative to the scene as the items along the marble-topped table. Conversely, the woman at the right of the composition, only partially rendered due to Gervex's original cropping of the scene, faces the older gentleman seated across from her with some dejection. She belongs to the same group of disillusioned "café women" seen in contemporary paintings such as Manet's *Plum Brandy* and Degas's *Dans un Café*. By showing them in public with these men, drinking liquor and especially smoking, Gervex lets the viewer know that they are women of loose morals.

Not long after Gervex completed *Café Scene in Paris*, a number of works by his contemporaries likewise depicted women in the company of men in restaurants in Paris. Manet's *Chez le Père Lathuille* (1879, fig. 35), unlike many café images, is set on a café terrace or garden on a sunny afternoon, as a young man confidently attempts to charm the lady seated with him, perhaps encouraged by the bottle of champagne that has been opened at the table. Located on the Avenue Clichy near the Café Guerbois, Chez le Père Lathuille was a popular bourgeois restaurant that Manet himself was known to

frequent. The woman in the painting, for which both the actress Ellen Andrée and Judith French (a relative of the popular composer Jacques Offenbach) modeled, is dressed in line with the status of the restaurant.[46] Her younger companion, however, appears more bohemian, and therein lies the central drama of the painting—the circumstances that led a conservatively dressed bourgeois woman to be eating and drinking in public with a younger, charmingly aggressive man, in broad daylight or *en plein air* no less. Even the *garçon* in the background observes their rendezvous with amusement tinged by a hint of derision. Manet's loose, impressionistic brushwork and bright palette tames the impropriety of the scene and perhaps emphasizes the fleeting nature of this potential couple's relationship just as much as it does Manet's own modernity as a painter.[47] While some contemporary writers criticized the painting as vulgar, Armand Silvestre described it "a breath of fresh air," and Huysmans deemed it, "by virtue of its very truth, a masterpiece."[48]

The woman in Manet's *Chez le Père Lathuille* retains a certain respectability, enhanced by the fact she is turned away from the viewer, as she considers the

Cat. 13

Édouard Manet
French, 1832–1883
Le Bouchon, 1878
Ink and pencil on paper
sheet: 8 ¾ × 11 ⅝ in. (22.2 × 29.5 cm)
Dallas Museum of Art, The Wendy and
Emery Reves Collection

Cat. 40

James Abbott McNeill Whistler
American, 1864–1903
The Little Café au Bois, 1894
Lithograph in black on laid paper
image: 10 ¼ × 7 ¼ in. (26 × 18.4 cm)
sheet: 11 ⅛ × 9 in. (28.3 × 22.9 cm)
Dixon Gallery and Gardens; Museum
purchase, 2023.1

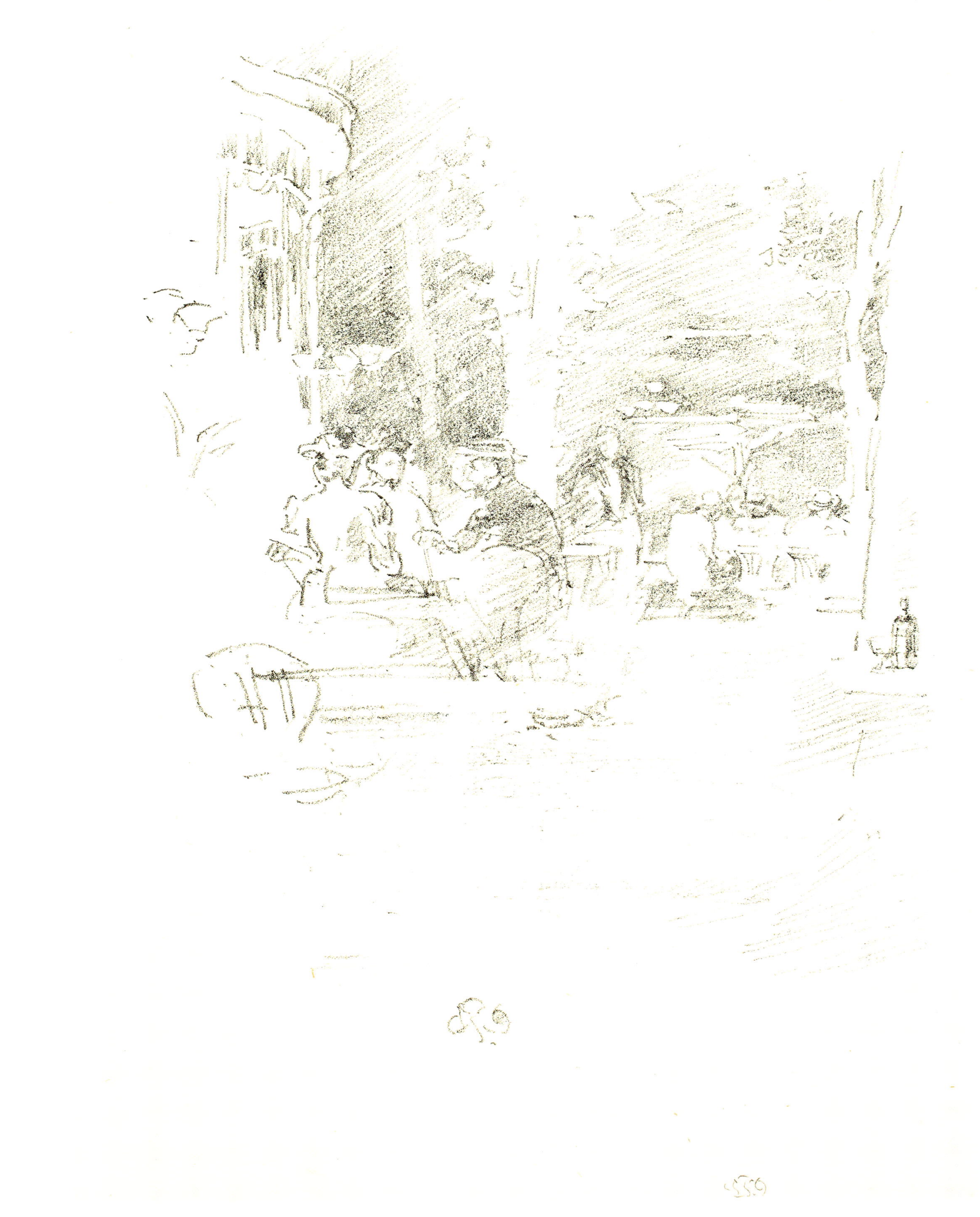

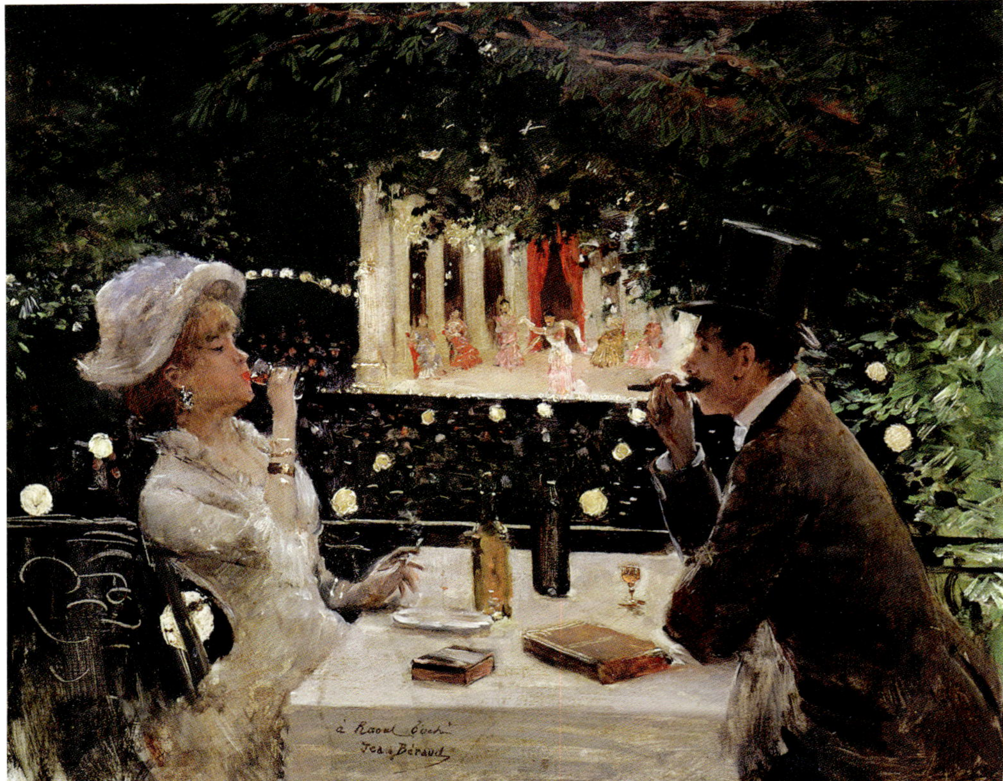

Fig. 36
Jean Béraud
French, 1849–1935
Dîner aux Ambassadeurs, ca. 1880
Oil on canvas
14 ¾ × 17 ¾ in. (37.5 × 45 cm)
Musée Carnavalet, Histoire de Paris, P1736

ardent advances of her male companion. In contrast, Manet's own brush drawing *Le Bouchon* (cat. 13) depicts, with brilliant economy, a female figure slumped over on a terrace café table, likely exhausted and presumably intoxicated, accompanied by a man in a workman's cap and smock.[49] Though quickly executed and loosely rendered, the debauchery of both figures, but especially the woman, is evident. Other contemporaries of Manet were likewise not complimentary of women dining in public in the company of men. Jean Béraud's *Dîner aux Ambassadeurs* (ca. 1880, fig. 36) is satirical almost to the point of caricature in its depiction of a couple seated at a table during one of the nightly performances at the Ambassadeurs, one of the more popular café-concerts in Paris. Disregarding the ambience of glowing lanterns, music, and dancers on stage, the couple seems to be absorbed in their own amusements. The gentleman puffs on his long cigar while gazing knowingly at his female companion. Despite his presence and despite her fine clothing and jewelry, Béraud's decision to represent her in the act of drinking

and smoking, leaning back in her chair in pleasure as the glass of wine touches her rouged lips, marks her out as a courtesan, albeit one of a certain rank.

Artists such as Béraud included images of prostitutes in their paintings in their quest to give an honest portrayal of contemporary life in Paris. Cafés were modern spaces, and the question of the propriety of women in these spaces was a very modern problem; by depicting the various forms of café prostitution, Béraud, Manet, Degas, Forain, Van Gogh, Toulouse-Lautrec, and Picasso positioned themselves as modern too. As the nineteenth century drew to a close and the twentieth century began, the theme remained relevant. American expatriate James Abbott McNeill Whistler, like Félix Buhot an experimental printmaker, alighted on the idea of the Paris café for the evocative lithograph *The Little Café au Bois* (1894, cat. 40). Whistler's image is less satirical than Buhot's, focusing more on conveying an impression of the gaiety of a night at a café-concert in the Bois de Boulogne.[50] The glow of the bandstand sheds light on a table where two women and two men are enjoying the entertainment in their balloon-backed chairs. An aproned *garçon* stands nearby, observing the couples and perhaps the performance as well. By the time he completed *The Little Café au Bois*, Whistler had been either living in or visiting Paris for nearly forty years. The lithographs he made there in the 1890s, marked by a certain delicacy and economy, depict some of the pleasures of living in the French capital, including an evening spent at a café.

French painter Émile-Othon Friesz, an ardent participant in the Fauvist experiment, brought the theme of a café rendezvous into a new era with *Scene in a Parisian Brasserie* (ca. 1905–6, cat. 56). Friesz captured what appears to be an awkward moment in this trio's encounter—none of them interact with one another. The artist's nervous lines and jarring palette heighten the tension, which one believes will be lifted as they all continue drinking the wine at their table.

Although in many if not most instances, society considered it improper for a lady to be seen dining in public, there were exceptions to this rule. One of these was the festivities surrounding the opening day (*vernissage*) of the annual Paris Salon. It was traditional for the artists participating in the Salon to gather, along with their wives, for luncheon to celebrate their acceptance. Not surprisingly, several artists sought to capture the joy of these gatherings on canvas. French painter James Tissot's *The Artists' Wives* (1885, cat. 20) is perhaps the most iconic of these canvases, a brilliant rendering of the excitement and chaos surrounding this annual meal at the Restaurant Ledoyen in the gardens of the Champs-Élysées.[51] Though he included more than two dozen men and women in the painting, his main focus, as the title indicates, was on the women in attendance: wives of the artists dressed in spring fashions (a constant focus of Tissot's) and eager to socialize with one another. The woman at the center

of the composition looks back toward the viewer, perhaps glimpsing whoever might sit at the vacant (though set) tables behind her. With the protection and security their husbands provide, the women can and do enjoy themselves, smiling as they take in the merry atmosphere from their balloon-backed chairs as aproned waiters frantically serve the crowd. The tradition of the *vernissage* luncheon at Ledoyen was indeed a herald of spring for artistic couples of all nationalities. The Swedish artist Hugo Birger recorded an even more raucous scene inside the pavilion at Ledoyen just one year after Tissot (see fig. 39), which features women partaking in champagne and fruit alongside their husbands (and even a well-groomed dog).

The festivities surrounding the running of the Grand-Prix de Paris at Longchamp offered numerous opportunities for respectable public socializing. One of the hubs for social activity connected to the races was the Pavillon d'Armenonville, which housed a restaurant that attracted well-heeled spectators after the races were completed. Henri Gervex captured an impression of the glimmering gaiety of the Pavillon in *Armenonville, le soir du Grand-Prix* (cat. 55), where men and women dine together amidst the restaurant's grand columns and glowing lights.

The near-complete lack of paintings of Parisian cafés by women artists in this exhibition attests to the limits placed on "respectable" women in nineteenth-century French culture. Yet, after the turn of the century, upper-class women increasingly felt emboldened to enter public dining spaces. By the 1910s, as international war loomed on the horizon, women such as the Russian/Ukrainian expatriate Elisabeth Hefter Epstein were among them. Her painting *People on a Café Terrace* (cat. 64), though officially dated 1913, may have been completed in 1919, after she had settled in Geneva, but the painting testifies to her time spent in Paris before the war.[52] The notion of a female artist painting an image

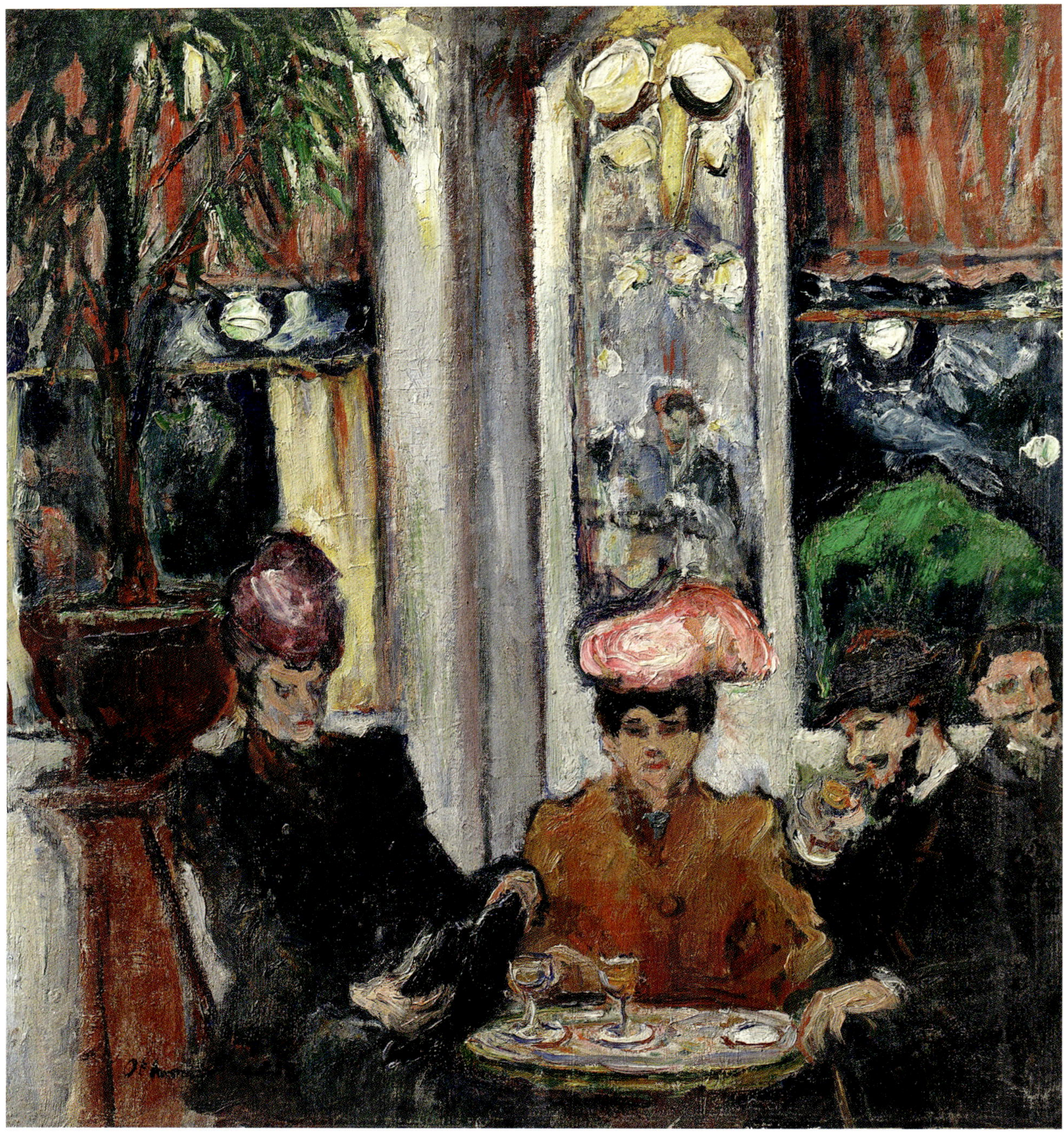

Cat. 56

Émile-Othon Friesz
French, 1879–1949
Scene in a Parisian Brasserie, ca. 1905–6
Oil on canvas
19 ¼ × 17 ⅞ in. (49 × 45.5 cm)
Museum Barberini, Potsdam, MB-Fri-01

Cat. 20

James Tissot
French, 1836–1902
The Artists' Wives, 1885
Oil on canvas
57 ½ × 40 in. (146.1 × 101.6 cm)
Chrysler Museum of Art, Norfolk, Virginia; Gift
of Walter P. Chrysler, Jr., and The Grandy Fund,
Landmark Communications Fund, and "An Affair
to Remember" 1982, 81.153

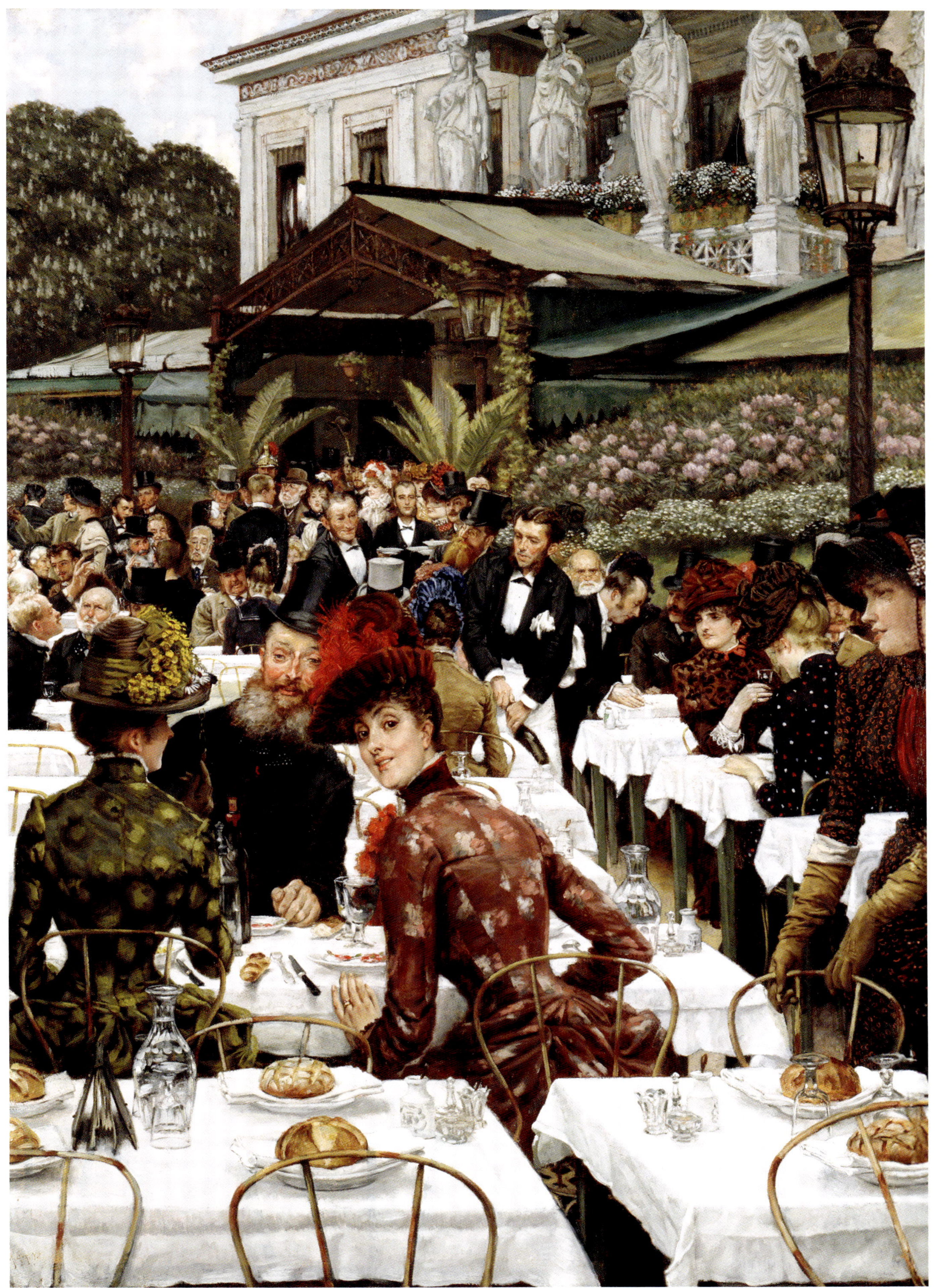

of a woman in a café would have been a shocking subject just a few decades prior, but, in the wake of the atrocities of World War I, the artist's gender, subject, and stylistic approach were undoubtedly less concerning. Around the time she worked on the painting, Epstein herself was newly liberated following a 1911 divorce from her husband, Russian doctor Max Epstein, after years of separation.[53] Painted in a geometric style that stemmed from exposure to Cubism and the approach of artists such as Franz Marc (1880–1916), with whom she exhibited in the landmark 1912 *Der Blaue Reiter* exhibition in Berlin, *People on a Café Terrace* exudes a conscious and international modernity championed by that group.[54] Epstein's bold use of color and mix of curving lines and sharp edges create a simultaneously jovial and noir atmosphere into which the woman in the scene has entered. She approaches the two gentlemen already seated at the table, one perusing a menu, leaving her vulnerable to assumptions about her character.

Half a century after Jules Michelet's statement on the "irritations for the single woman," and forty years after Forain's cocotte boldly sauntered into the Folies-Bergère in *Café Interior*, an image of a woman entering a Parisian café alone still signaled to viewers a kind of loose morality stemming from working-class origins. It would be decades before women would be afforded the same freedoms as men in café spaces, and, even after the upheavals of two world wars and the sexual revolution of the mid- to late twentieth century, cafés, at least as a subject for artists, remained, in a way, unwelcoming to women and women artists until the end of the century.

Cat. 55

Henri Gervex
French, 1852–1929
Armenonville, le soir du Grand-Prix, ca. 1905
Oil on cardboard
19 7/8 × 14 in. (50.5 × 35.5 cm)
Musée Carnavalet, Histoire de Paris, P2708

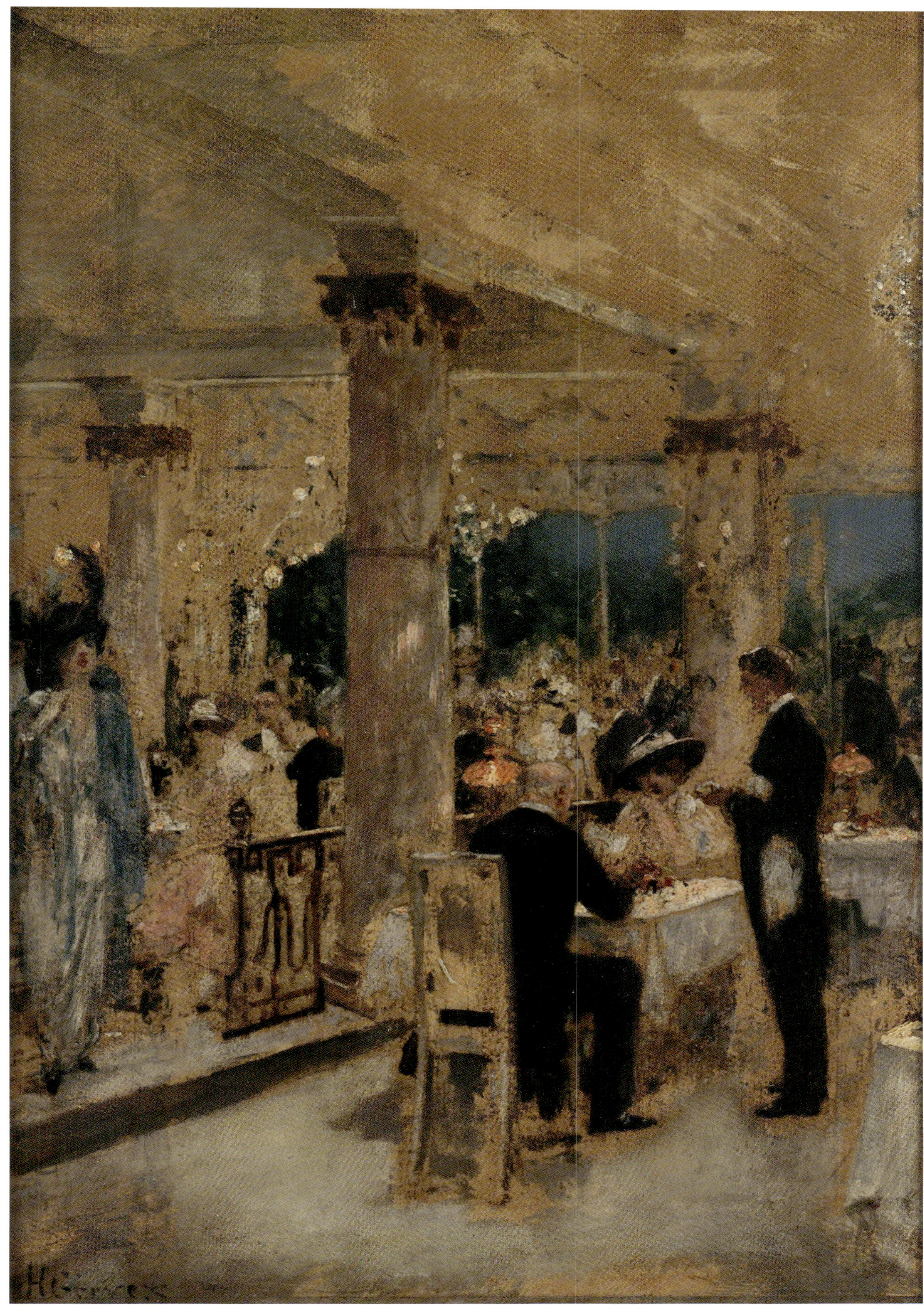

Endnotes

1. W. Scott Haine, *The World of the Paris Café: Sociability among the French Working Class, 1789-1914* (Baltimore: The Johns Hopkins University Press, 1996), 186. The "Women and Gender Politics" chapter in this book offers enlightening data on women in cafés and incidences of prostitution in café spaces.

2. O. Commenge, *Hygiene Sociale: La Prostitution clandestine à Paris* (Paris: Schleicher Frères, 1897), 336.

3. Jules Lovy, "Les cafés de Paris," *Le Tintamarre*, April 18, 1858, 5.

4. Rachel Hope Cleves, *Lustful Appetites: An Intimate History of Good Food and Wicked Sex* (Cambridge: Polity Press, 2025), 35–41. Cleves's research on the association between sex and restaurants in nineteenth-century Paris is crucial and illuminating.

5. Cleves, *Lustful Appetites*, 89.

6. Andrew Israel Ross, "Serving Sex: Playing with Prostitution in the 'Brasseries à femmes' of Late Nineteenth-Century Paris," *Journal of the History of Sexuality* 24, no. 2 (May 2015): 297. The number of *brasseries à femmes* continued to rise until the mid-1890s.

7. Susanna Barrows, "Nineteenth-Century Cafes: Arenas of Everyday Life," in *Pleasures of Paris: Daumier to Picasso*, ed. Barbara Stern Shapiro (Boston: Museum of Fine Arts / David R. Godine, 1991), 24: "Between 11pm and 1am on the night of May 5–6, 1887, Parisian police rushed into forty-eight brasseries with the most notorious reputations."

8. Haine, *World of the Paris Café*, 179.

9. Guillaume Faroult, "These charming masters who reflect the grace and elegance of their time": The Rediscovery of the French Painters of the Eighteenth Century in the Nineteenth Century," in *Renoir: Rococo Revival*, ed. Alexander Eiling (Frankfurt am Main: Städel Museum / Berlin: Hatje Cantz, 2022).

10. The *serveuses* at Duval's were known for wearing more modest black-and-white uniforms.

11. The term "pretty waiter girl" was commonly used in advertisements for cafés to lure in male customers. See Cleves, *Lustful Appetites*, chapter 5.

12. See also Édouard Manet, *The Café-Concert*, ca. 1879, oil on canvas, Walters Art Museum, Baltimore; and Édouard Manet, *The Waitress*, 1878-79, oil on canvas, National Gallery, London.

13. Hollis Clayson, *Painted Love: Prostitution in French Art of the Impressionist Era* (New Haven: Yale University Press, 1991), 144.

14. Bradford R. Collins, "The Dialectics of Desire, the Narcissism of Authorship: A Male Interpretation of the Psychological Origins of Manet's *Bar*," in *12 Views of Manet's "Bar"* (Princeton: Princeton University Press, 1996), 121. See also Barrows, "Nineteenth-Century Cafes," 17-26. The Folies-Bergère was originally established as a home-goods store. It opened a "salle des spectacles" in 1863 that was so successful it expanded in 1869 to become the focus of the enterprise. It changed its name from the Folies Trévise to the Folies-Bergère in 1872 after its proximity to the Rue Bergère.

15. See Jean-Louis Forain, *The Bar at the Folies-Bergère*, 1878, opaque watercolor with graphite underdrawing on paper, Brooklyn Museum.

16. Clayson, *Painted Love*, 99. Clayson notes that the term "café woman," meaning a woman who hung out in cafés, was one of "moral disapprobation" during the late nineteenth century.

17. Quoted in Nicholas Green, *The Spectacle of Nature: Landscape and Bourgeois Culture in Nineteenth-Century France* (Manchester: Manchester University Press, 1993), 40.

18. Haine, *World of the Paris Café*, 203.

19. See Richard Thomson, "Ambiguity, Allure and Uncertainty," in *Splendours and Miseries: Images of Prostitution in France, 1850-1910*, ed. Nienke Bakker, Isolde Pludermacher, Marie Robert, and Richard Thomson (Paris: Musée d'Orsay / Flammarion, 2015), 82.

20. Haine, *World of the Paris Café*, 179.

21. Joris-Karl Huysmans, *Croquis parisiens* (Paris: Henri Vaton, 1880), 12.

22. Ibid., 150.

23. Cleves, *Lustful Appetites*, 9–32. Again, Cleves's research on *cabinets particuliers* is invaluable. Her chapter "Pleasures of the Table" provided essential primary information on the subtleties of these private rooms.

24. Forain's *Maison close* accompanied a chapter in Huysmans's 1880 *Croquis parisiens* entitled "Le Gousset," and it appeared alongside a discussion of the difference between blonde and brunette Parisiennes. See Huysmans, *Croquis parisiens*, 105–8.

25. Lynda Nead, "Fashion and Visual Culture in the 19th Century: Women in Red," lecture delivered March 4, 2014, https://www.gresham.ac.uk/watch-now/women-red.

26. See Clayson, *Painted Love*, 138, and Cleves, *Lustful Appetites*, 42–44. *Grisettes* commonly wore gray cloaks in the mid-nineteenth century, but, by the time Evenepoel created *In the Café d'Harcourt in Paris* at the turn of the century, their dress was less uniform.

27. Cleves, *Lustful Appetites*, 23. In discussing the fashions of the *soupeuses*, Cleves also introduces the idea of the *ogresse*, a woman who sold or rented expensive and flashy clothes to sex workers.

28. Ibid., 25. *Flibocheuse* is a portmanteau of *flibustière* (filibuster or pirate) and *rigolbocheuse* (licentious woman) or *soupeuse*. Ibid., 22–26, gives clear information on the notion of the *soupeuse*.

29. "He is the poet of corruption in evening clothes, of dandyism in the boudoirs, of high life masking empty hearts." Octave Maus, "Les Vingtistes parisiens," *L'Art moderne* [Brussels], June 27, 1886, 201–4, quoted in Ruth Berson, ed., *The New Painting: Impressionism, 1874-1886. Documentation*, vol. 1, 463.

30. Francis E. Hyslop, *Henri Evenepoel: Belgian Painter in Paris, 1892-1899* (University Park: The Pennsylvania State University Press, 1975), 133, n. 15.

31. Joris-Karl Huysmans, "L'Exposition des indépendants en 1880," *L'Art moderne*, 85–123. Paris, G. Charpentier, 1883. Reproduced in *The New Painting*, vol. 1, p. 290.

32. Segatori had a long-term romantic relationship with the French painter Édouard Dantan (1848–1897), for whom she often modeled.

33. Jane Munro, "Painting in Focus: *At the Café*," in *Degas: A Passion for Perfection* (Cambridge: Fitzwilliam Museum / Cambridge University Press, 2017), 138–57. Munro's essay provides interesting information on the theme of *causerie* or chat in Degas's oeuvre.

34. The French engraver and writer Alexandre Pothey (1820–1897) wrote in "Beaux-arts," *Le Petit Parisien*, April 7, 1877: "*Les Femmes devant un café, le soir* are of a terrifying realism. These painted, blighted creatures, sweating vice, who recount to one another the doings and gestures of the day, you have seen them right enough, you know them, and you will come across them again in a little while on the boulevard." Quoted in T. J. Clark, *The Painting of Modern Life: Paris in the Art of Manet and His Followers* (Princeton: Princeton University Press, 1984, rev. ed. 1999), 101.

35. The artists who accompanied Lungren to Paris in 1882 were all members of the Tile Club, an association of American painters interested in the decorative arts. See Elizabeth Brown," *Afterglow in the Desert: The Art of Fernand Lungren* (Santa Barbara: University Art Museum, University of California, Santa Barbara, 2000). See also Ronald G. Pisano, Mary Ann Apicella, and Linda Henefield Skalet, *The Tile Club and the Aesthetic Movement in America* (New York: Harry N. Abrams, 1999).

36. John A. Berger, *Fernand Lungren: A Biography* (Santa Barbara: The Schauer Press, 1936).

37. Lungren found great interest in the effects of the new electric lighting versus gaslight in Paris. See Annelise Madsen, "Fernand Lungren, Illuminated: In the Café and the City of Lights," Art Institute of Chicago, https://www.artic.edu/articles/960/fernand-lungren-illuminated-in-the-cafe-and-the-city-of-lights.

38. Clayson, *Painted Love*, 101.

39. See Madsen's analysis of the Art Institute of Chicago's Lungren, *In the Café*: https://www.artic.edu/articles/960/fernand-lungren-illuminated-in-the-cafe-and-the-city-of-lights.

40. See Pablo Picasso, *The Moulin de la Galette*, 1900, oil on canvas (Solomon R. Guggenheim Museum, New York, Thannhauser Collection, Gift, Justin K. Thannhauser, 1978). See also John Richardson, *A Life of Picasso*, vol. 1, *The Prodigy, 1881–1906* (New York: Knopf, 2007), 167.

41. https://www.nga.gov/collection/artist-info.2408.html.

42. Gervex's 1878 painting *Rolla* (Musée d'Orsay, Paris) would be one of the biggest scandals of the Parisian art world in the nineteenth century. The painting, under the guise of Alfred de Musset's 1833 poem of the same name, depicts a contemporary Parisian man about to commit suicide while the prostitute with whom he has spent the previous night sleeps naked on their shared, rumpled bed.

43. https://dia.org/collection/caf%C3%A9-scene-paris-45816.

44. See *Henri Gervex, 1852–1929* (Paris: Paris-Musées, 1992), 100–3. This retrospective catalogue proposes that the man reading the newspaper in *Café Scene in Paris* is the French poet Albert Mérat (1840–1909), and the man to his right is Gervex's friend, the painter Ferdinand Humbert (1842–1934).

45. See Barrows, "Nineteenth-Century Cafes," 23.

46. Bradley Collins, "Manet's 'In the Conservatory' and 'Chez Le Père Lathuille,'" *Art Journal* 45, no. 1 (1985): 59–66.

47. See Scott Allan, "Faux Frère: Manet and the Salon, 1879–82," in *Manet and Modern Beauty: The Artist's Last Years*, ed. Scott Allan, Emily A. Beeny, and Gloria Groom (Los Angeles: J. Paul Getty Museum, 2019).

48. Reviews of *Chez le Père Lathuille* from the 1880 Salon are quoted in Ronald Pickvance, *Manet* (Martigny: Fondation Pierre Gianadda, 1996), 236.

49. The Dallas Museum of Art's *Le Bouchon* relates to the same artist's *Le Bouchon* (*In the Bar Le Bouchon*), 1878–79, oil on canvas, 72 × 92 cm, Pushkin Museum, Moscow.

50. Thomas R. Way, *Mr. Whistler's Lithographs: The Catalogue* (London: G. Bell & Sons, 1896), 24.

51. Restaurant Ledoyen is today known as Pavillon Ledoyen and remains one of the most historic and revered restaurants in Paris. Its website boasts that it is "the most Michelin-starred independent establishment in the world."

52. I am grateful to Harry Cooper at the National Gallery of Art, Washington, for his candid consultation regarding the dating of Epstein's painting.

53. Hildegarde Reinhart, "Elisabeth Epstein: Moscow–Munich–Paris–Geneva, Waystations of a Painter and Mediator of the French-German Cultural Transfer," in *Marianne Werefkin and the Women Artists in Her Circle*, ed. Tanja Malycheva and Isabel Wünsche (Leiden: Brill, 2017), 165.

54. Ibid., 170.

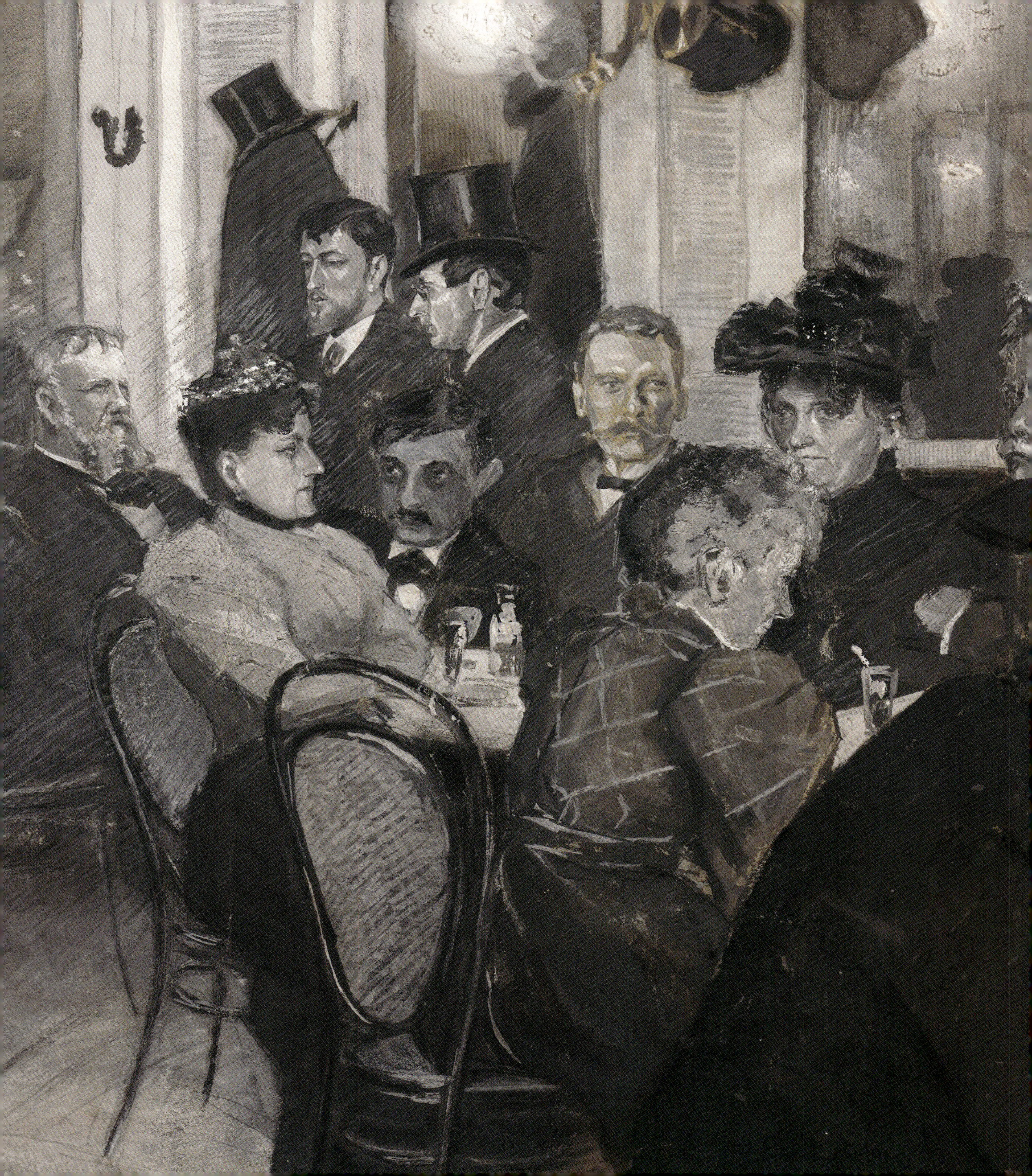

CAFÉ DE LA RÉGENCE

The Paris Haunt of Nordic Artists

Dorthe Vangsgaard Nielsen

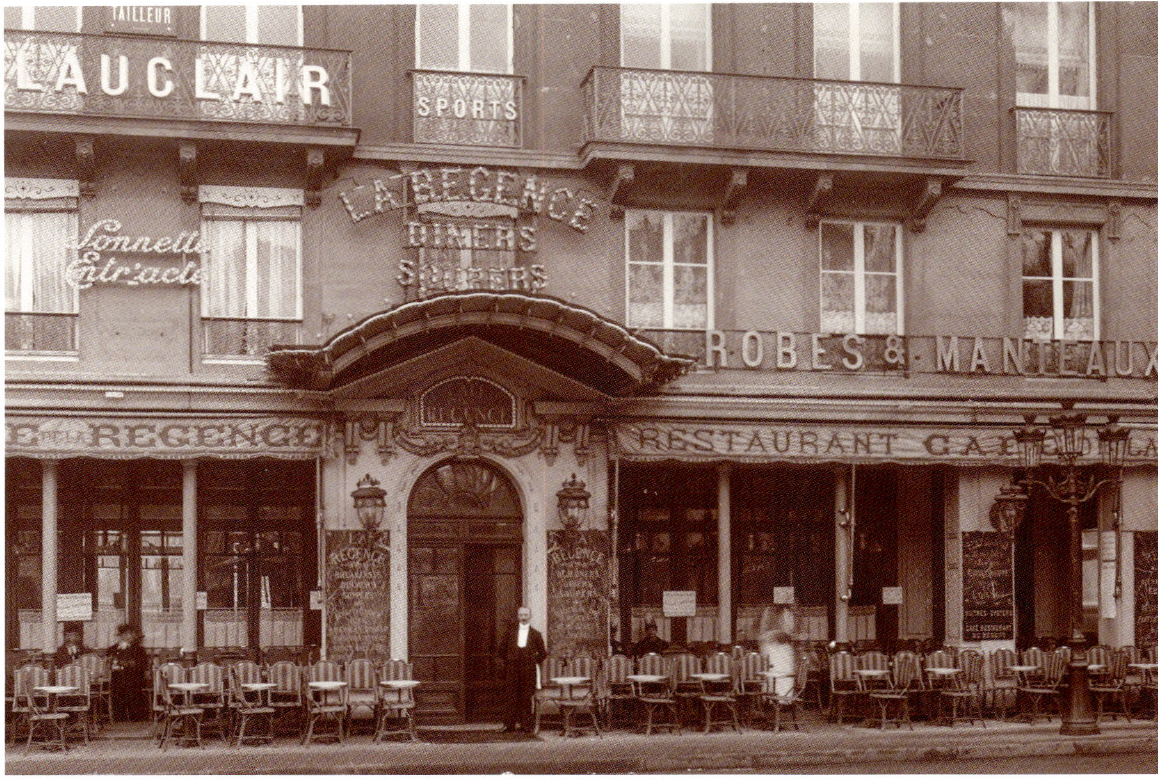

Fig. 37
Café de la Régence, ca. 1911–12
Photograph by Eric
Rafael-Rådberg
The manuscript collection—
National Library of Sweden

"Almost all of Nordic literature and art has, so to speak, passed through the doors of the Café de la Régence. From Vinje to Sigbjørn Obstfelder, from the politician Lerche to August Strindberg, from Georg Brandes to Valdemar Vedel, from the painter Ross to Willumsen and Edvard Munch."[1] This description of late nineteenth-century Scandinavian intelligentsia holding court at the Café de la Régence is provided by the writer Erik Lie, son of the great Norwegian realist writer Jonas Lie, whose dark silhouette appears in the foreground of his countryman Severin Segelcke's portrait of Nordic artists in their Paris haunt (1894, cat. 39). It would hardly be an exaggeration to say that more figures from the Scandinavian cultural scene gathered here than at any other place in the Nordic countries. "The café is like a mirror, eternally shifting, reflecting all the peculiar traits of the North,"[2] said Henrik Cavling, a renowned Danish journalist of the time.

What follows is an introduction to this refuge for Nordic artists and intellectuals, which, being one of the oldest cafés in Paris, has attracted a very great deal of *bel esprit* over the centuries.[3] The essay will then seek to outline the Nordic artistic circles that gathered primarily at the Café de la Régence, though also at other Parisian cafés in the late nineteenth century. This will be done on the basis of selected works from the realms of art and literature alike—and more private media in the form of letters and diaries.

The Revolutionaries' Former Haunt and "the Danes' Coffeehouse"

The Café de la Régence, which first opened its doors in 1718 and relocated to new premises at 161 Rue Saint-Honoré in 1858 (fig. 37), has counted Maximilien Robespierre, Napoleon Bonaparte, and Victor Hugo among its regulars. It famously hosted the pivotal 1844 meeting between the revolutionary socialists Karl Marx and Friedrich Engels. Since the mid-eighteenth century, the café has also been a meeting place for generations

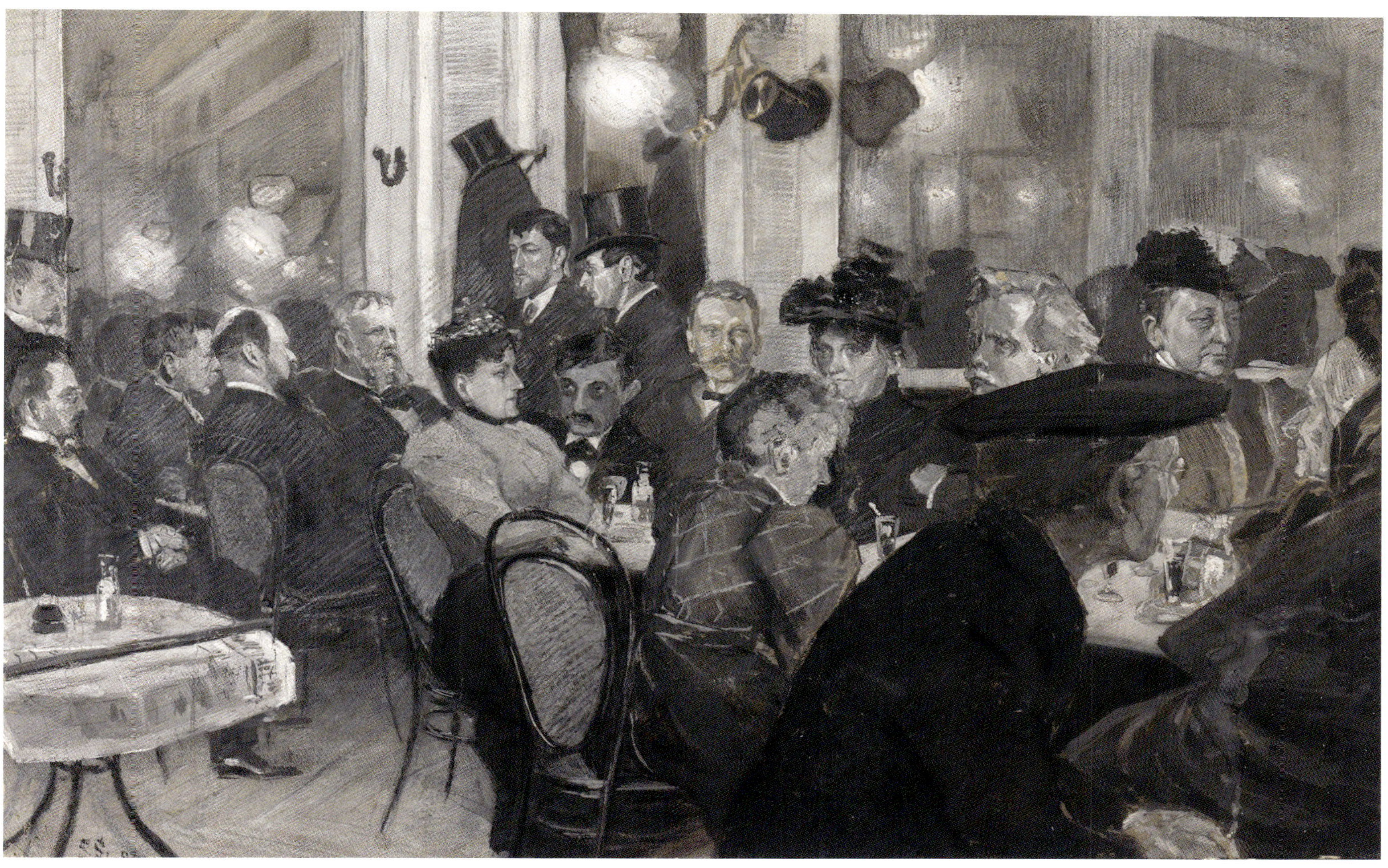

Cat. 39

Severin Segelcke
Norwegian, 1837–1940
Café de la Régence, 1894
Pen, brush, and gouache over
pencil on paper
17 ⅜ × 27 ⅜ in. (44 × 69.5 cm)
Nasjonalmuseet for kunst, arkitektur og
design, Oslo, The Fine Art Collections,
NG.K&H.B.00303

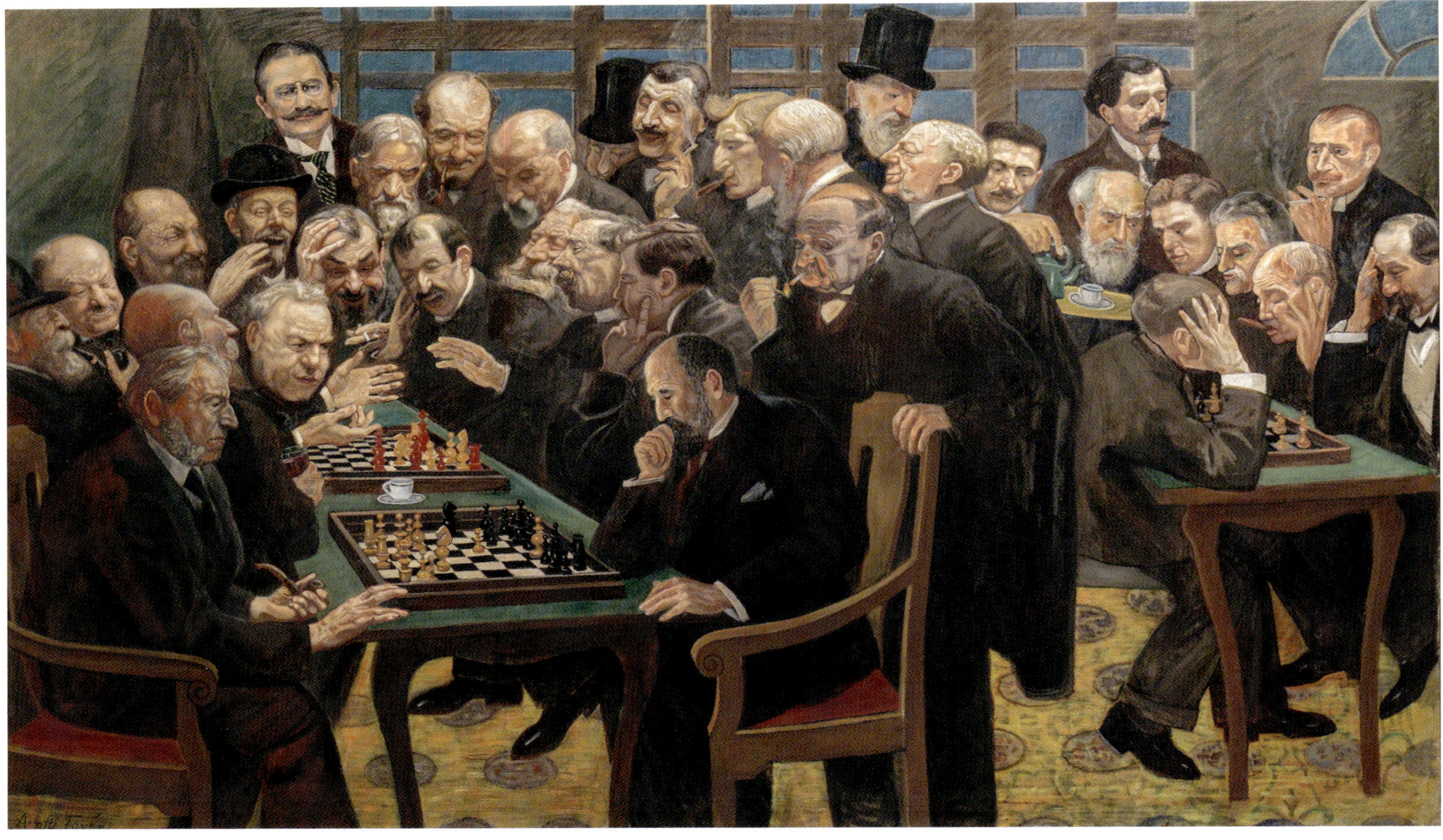

Cat. 65

Antti Favén
Finnish, 1882–1948
The Chess Players, 1913
Oil on canvas
86 ⅝ × 133 ⅞ in. (207 × 343 cm)
Private collection—contributed by the
Nemes Galeria (Budapest)

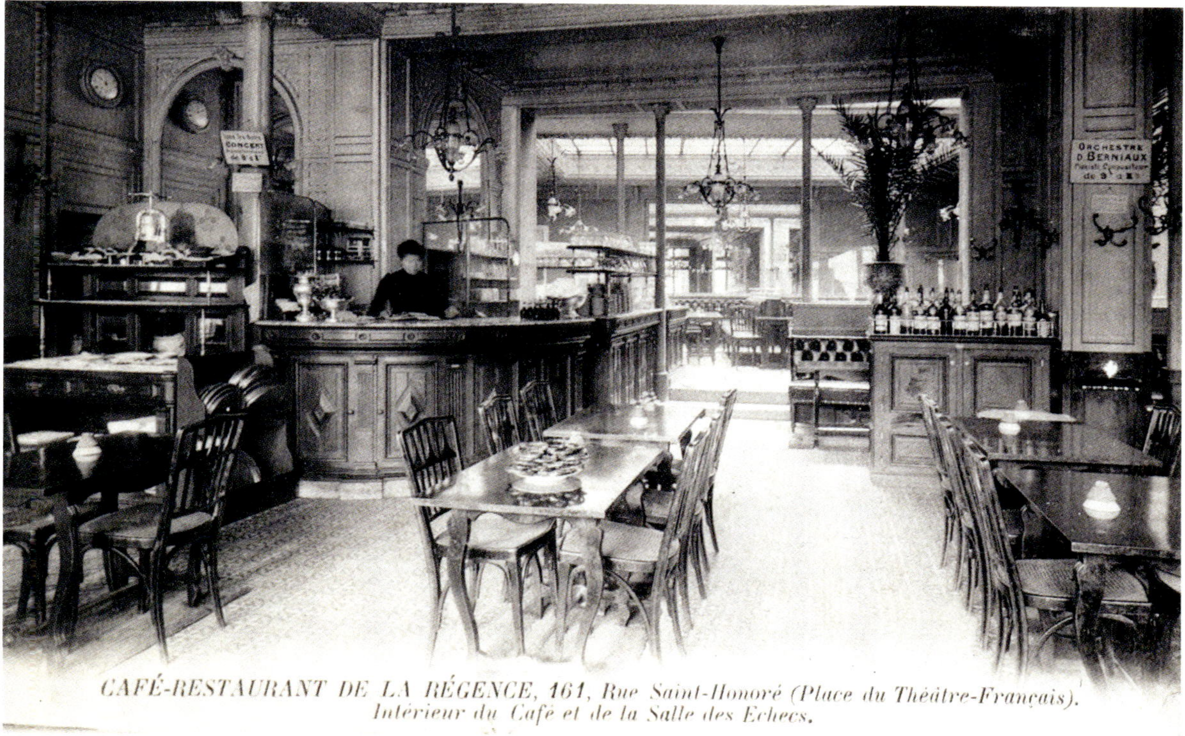

Fig. 38
*Café-restaurant de la Régence, 161,
rue Saint-Honoré (Place du Théâtre-
Français). Intérieur du café et de la salle des
échecs*, ca. 1900
Photograph
Bibliothèque des Arts Décoratifs, Paris

of leading chess players. Henrik Cavling reports how French memoir literature has often dwelled on the fascination with the café's chess-playing clientele:

> As proof of the chessboard's demonic powers of enthrallment, it has been said that none of the great political upheavals ever interrupted the course of a game here. During the Revolution, the condemned being taken to the scaffold were taken past the café's windows on their way from the Palace of Justice to Place de la Concorde, but even on historic days, such as when Marie Antoinette was led to the scaffold, certain chess players could not tear themselves away from their tables. Indeed, even during the

Reign of Terror, Robespierre himself would occasionally enter the café and play a game.[4]

The café's historical air and resonance is often mentioned in the letters of Nordic patrons: "I am writing this at the Régence—the revolutionaries' old café. At a table directly across from me sit some eager chess players—several of them are among the most famous in the world," wrote Edvard Munch to his foster mother in 1889 (fig. 38).[5] The Finnish artist Antti Favén was likewise fascinated by the many chess enthusiasts who sought out the café's legendary premises. In his major breakthrough work *The Chess Players* (1913, cat. 65), he depicts a fictional scene involving many of the renowned figures from the world of chess who frequented the café. Chess rarely finds its way into modern art's many café scenes, but, in a slightly later painting by the Russian artist Aleksandr Yakovlev, *In the Cafe de la Rotonde, Paris* (1921, cat. 69), a chessboard appears in the lower corner. The atmosphere of intense concentration and convivial camaraderie emphasized by Favén seems, however, to have evaporated

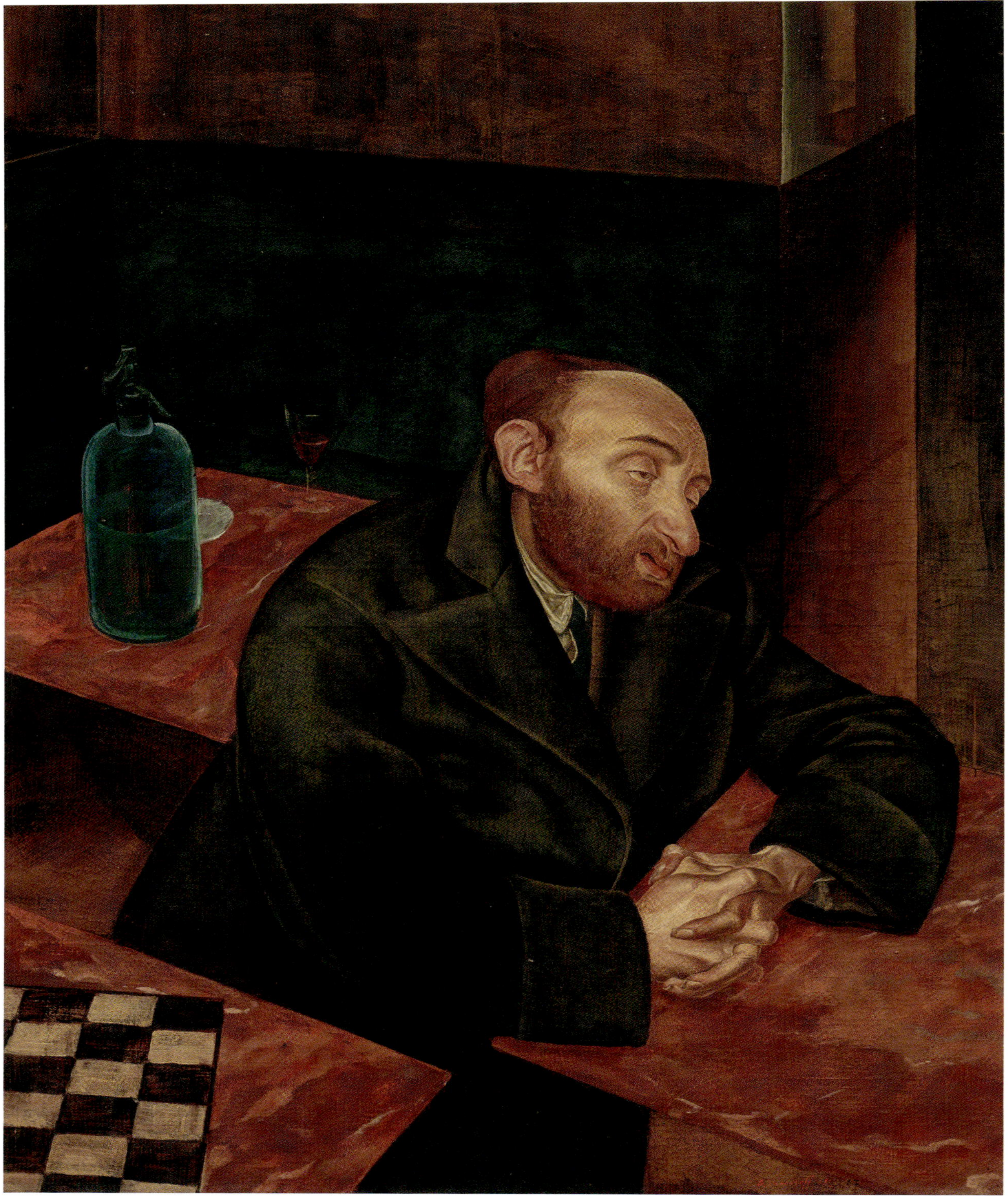

Cat. 69

Aleksandr Yevgeniyevich Yakovlev
Russian, 1887–1938
In the Cafe de la Rotonde, Paris, 1921
Oil on canvas
39 ¼ × 32 ⅛ in. (99.7 × 81.6 cm)
Museum of Fine Arts, Boston, Tompkins
Collection—Arthur Gordon Tompkins Fund, 35.637

in an alcoholic haze in the Russian's painting. Here, coffee has been replaced by alcohol, mental exercise by apathy, and community by solitude.

With its central location on Place du Théâtre-Français, situated between the Tuileries and the Palais Royal, the Café de la Régence lies at the heart of old monarchical Paris. Scandinavians have sought out the place since the early 1800s. Here, among the many shops, restaurants, cafés, gambling halls, brothels, and theaters of the time, wandered the exiled Danish writer P. A. Heiberg and the poet Christian Winther, "who visits the Café de la Régence every day to read the Danish papers."[6] In the play *De Danske i Paris* (The Danes in Paris), staged at the Royal Danish Theater in Copenhagen in 1833, the playwright Johan Ludvig Heiberg, son of the aforementioned P. A. Heiberg, sets the second act in "a coffeehouse in the Palais Royal in Paris," where the servant Mikkel says: "This place is called the Danes' coffeehouse; if that's the case, then at the very least they ought to understand Danish here."[7] In addition to hearing their mother tongue—Danish, Swedish, or Norwegian—in the tastefully furnished rooms, Nordic patrons visiting in the 1880s and '90s could still find Scandinavian newspapers such as *Politiken*, *Verdens Gang*, *Nya Dagligt Allehanda*, and *Morgenbladet* in the café. A copy of the latter, attached to a newspaper holder, appears on the table in the foreground of Segelcke's drawing (see cat. 39).

A Special Occasion

Writing about the Café de la Régence, Erik Lie also states that "[o]n Sunday afternoons and on special occasions—for example, when Grieg's works are to be performed at one of the major concerts, or when Ibsen's dramas are on at *L'Œuvre* [the Théâtre de l'Œuvre], or in springtime when the 'Salon' opens—the place can be so very lively that you might easily believe yourself to be at the Bernina or the Grand."[8] Such a special occasion, one that briefly transported the patron to the Café Bernina in Copenhagen or the Grand Café in Kristiania (now Oslo), likely forms the background for Segelcke's artist portrait. Not least because among those assembled we find the Norwegian composer Edvard Grieg, whose piano compositions were frequently played in Paris, both on the concert stage and by amateur singers and pianists.[9] The white-haired Grieg, who composed the world-famous music to Henrik Ibsen's play *Peer Gynt* (1867), sits with his arms crossed, second from the right in the back row, across from his wife Nina Grieg.

Another major interpreter of Ibsen's drama was the writer and stage director Herman Bang. In 1894—the same year that Segelcke portrayed his Scandinavian colleagues—the Dane's production of Ibsen's international breakthrough and study of gender roles, *A Doll's House* (1879), premiered at the Théâtre du Vaudeville with the celebrated actress Gabrielle Réjane in the role of Nora. That same year, Bang's staging of the Norwegian national poet Bjørnstjerne Bjørnson's *En handske*, variously translated as *A Gauntlet* and *A Glove* (1883), which criticized the double standards—or "glove morality"—that allowed men, but not women, to indulge in erotic experiences outside of marriage, introduced the Nordic sexual morality debate to Paris. The debate, which involved most of the leading authors and cultural critics of the Nordic countries, was a significant aspect of the period in Nordic art known as "The Modern Breakthrough."[10] We find Bang, apparently crouching, in front of the Norwegian author Hans Kinck, the latter wearing a top hat. The small Dane seems to be engaged in conversation with the well-known Swedish actress Olga Björkegren, who, after her marriage in 1887 to the art critic Klas Fåhræus, had retired from the stage.

Bang's great idol and the most widely read novelist in the Nordic region at the time, Jonas Lie, towers in the

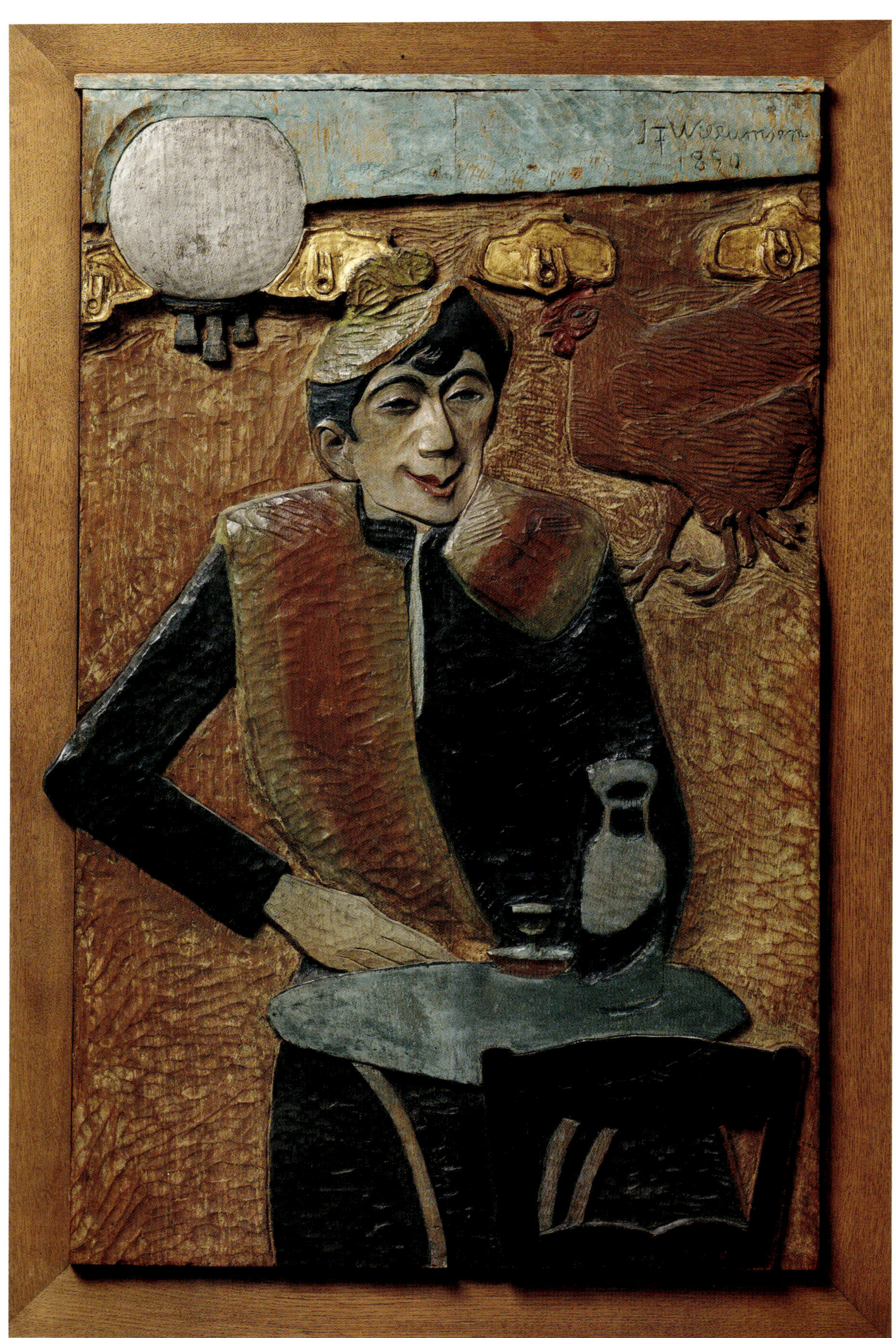

Cat. 32

Jens Ferdinand Willumsen
Danish, 1863–1958
*A Cocotte Hunting in the Montagnes
Russes*, 1890
Polychromed wood
44 ½ × 29 ¼ × 2 ¼ in.
(113 × 74.3 × 5.8 cm)
Willumsens Museum,
Frederikssund, Acc. 507

foreground wearing his characteristic beret. According to Bang, Lie's novels made him a leading figure among the men of the Modern Breakthrough. Alongside the Paris-based Swedish painter August Hagborg, Lie was one of the veterans of the Scandinavian artist colony. Hagborg is shown sitting fourth from the left, viewed in profile, and is easily recognizable by his bald head. The white-bearded figure to his right is the artist Frits Thaulow, one of Norway's leading landscape painters during the naturalistic 1880s. From around 1889, Thaulow also became a well-known and much-admired figure in European art circles. To the left of Hagborg we find his countryman, art superstar Anders Zorn, who resided in Paris in 1894. His brilliant grasp of technique and flamboyant artistic persona won him a clientele not only in France, but also in Sweden, England, and the United States.

If Zorn was the most successful, Carl Larsson was "the most beloved of all Swedish artists. His person and his art warmed and shone like sunshine," wrote art critic Carl G. Laurin later, in all likelihood with Larsson's watercolors from Sundborn in Dalarna, Sweden, in mind—works which were in fact in progress in 1894, and whose publication in *Ett hem* (A Home) in 1899 made Larsson a much-loved figure in Swedish art.[11] Indeed, a particularly warm light appears to fall on his mustachioed face, which Segelcke has placed at the center of the gathering and, uniquely, has rendered frontally so that he faces us, the viewers.

All these painters achieved success at the annual Paris Salon with a naturalistic style that struck a middle ground between academic Salon painting and Impressionism. The Danish artist Jens Ferdinand Willumsen, whose distinctive full beard makes him easy to identify behind Herman Bang and Olga Fåhræus, differs from his Norwegian and Swedish fellow painters in this regard. During the three and a half years he spent in Paris, he changed his style and managed to carve

out a central position within the Symbolist movement. When, in 1891, he exhibited ten works at the Salon des Indépendants—including *A Cocotte Hunting in the Montagnes Russes* (1890, cat. 32)—a French critic hailed him as "the apostle of the new art."[12]

Varnishing Day

The occasion for this gathering of some of the key figures of 1880s and '90s Nordic art at the Café de la Régence might, then, have been one of the major concert performances of Grieg's music or one of Bang's productions of Ibsen's contemporary plays in 1894. Incidentally, Bang's production of the aforementioned play *A Glove* (1883) premiered at the Petit Théâtre— as *Un gant*—on May 1. This was also the day on which the annual Paris Salon opened, making it perhaps more likely that the Scandinavians had arranged to meet for that reason. For Scandinavian artists, the Paris Salon was a highlight of the year and a decisive event in terms of achieving success and receiving new commissions in their native countries and abroad.

On the opening day of the Salon, the cafés in the art capital filled up: "The Scandinavian influx is strongest in the spring months of May and June, which for many reasons—the opening of the Salon and the start of the races—is the most favorable season for a trip to Paris. Then, the Café de la Régence is overflowing with tourists, and the French, who are regulars at the café, often feel as if they have been transported to a foreign place."[13] Sigurd Ibsen, son of the renowned Henrik Ibsen, did not however count himself among the young, hopeful Scandinavians who sought out the Café de la Régence—or other Parisian haunts—for news from home, contacts, or simply a good party in connection with the Salon's opening. During his stay in Paris in 1883, Ibsen junior wrote home to his father: "I want as little as possible to do with other Scandinavians:

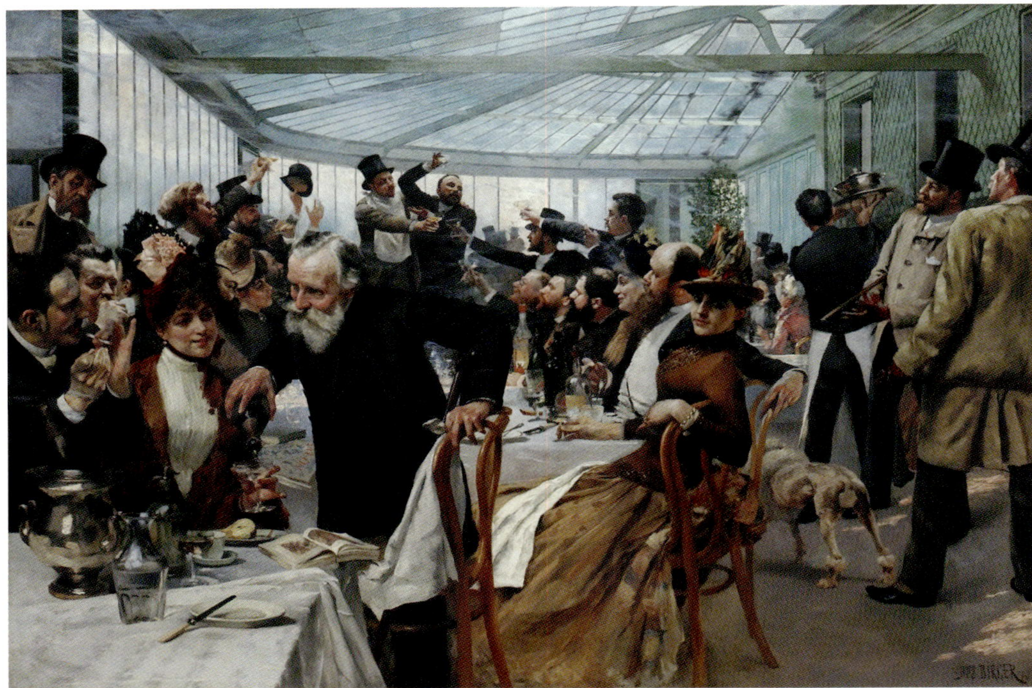

Fig. 39
Hugo Birger
Swedish, 1854–1887
The Scandinavian Artists' Lunch at Café Ledoyen, Paris: Varnishing Day 1886, 1886
Oil on canvas
36 × 44 in. (183.5 × 261.5 cm)
Göteborgs Konstmuseum, Sweden, GKM 0204

therefore I patronize neither Café de la Régence nor Café de l'Ermitage." In the same letter, he describes the so-called "varnishing day," which he did not attend himself but had heard about from his travel companion, the art historian and later professor Lorentz Dietrichson:

> On the day before the Salon's opening, the so-called "varnishing day," it is customary for the artists of each country to gather for a celebration. Indeed, the Scandinavians did so this year as well: 40–50 painters, men and women alike. Dr. Axel Munthe and his wife, along with a few other visitors, had arranged a dinner. I preferred to go to the theater that evening, and I did well to do so, for Dietrichson told me the next day that things had gotten out of hand and the mood had been ruined. The speeches especially did not go well. . . . Worst off was Dietrichson himself, who began a speech about "humanity," but the artists offered ample practical demonstration that this was not the place to talk about such things: they bombarded him with bones and chunks of bread, smashed

his glass so the wine spilled over his clothes, called him an idiot ("which I must say was quite rude," as he put it), and it all ended with him having to take his hat and leave.[14]

The Swedish artist Hugo Birger's celebrated *The Scandinavian Artists' Lunch at Café Ledoyen, Paris: Varnishing Day, 1886* (fig. 39) depicts the lead-up to the kind of rowdy atmosphere Ibsen reports. In contrast to James Tissot's painting *The Artists' Wives* (1885, see cat. 20), which also portrays artists and their wives gathered at Ledoyen for the Salon's varnishing day, Birger has moved the scene indoors, into the restaurant's pavilion. As in Tissot's painting, Birger has placed a fashionably dressed woman in the center of the foreground. She is the only figure in the gathering to look directly at us, the viewer, and so she commands our particular attention. Unlike the male artists in the painting, we do not know her identity. She appears instead to embody the distinctive type that Tissot excelled at portraying: the elegant and feminine Parisienne, who, in the work of painters of modern life such as Édouard Manet and Pierre-Auguste Renoir,

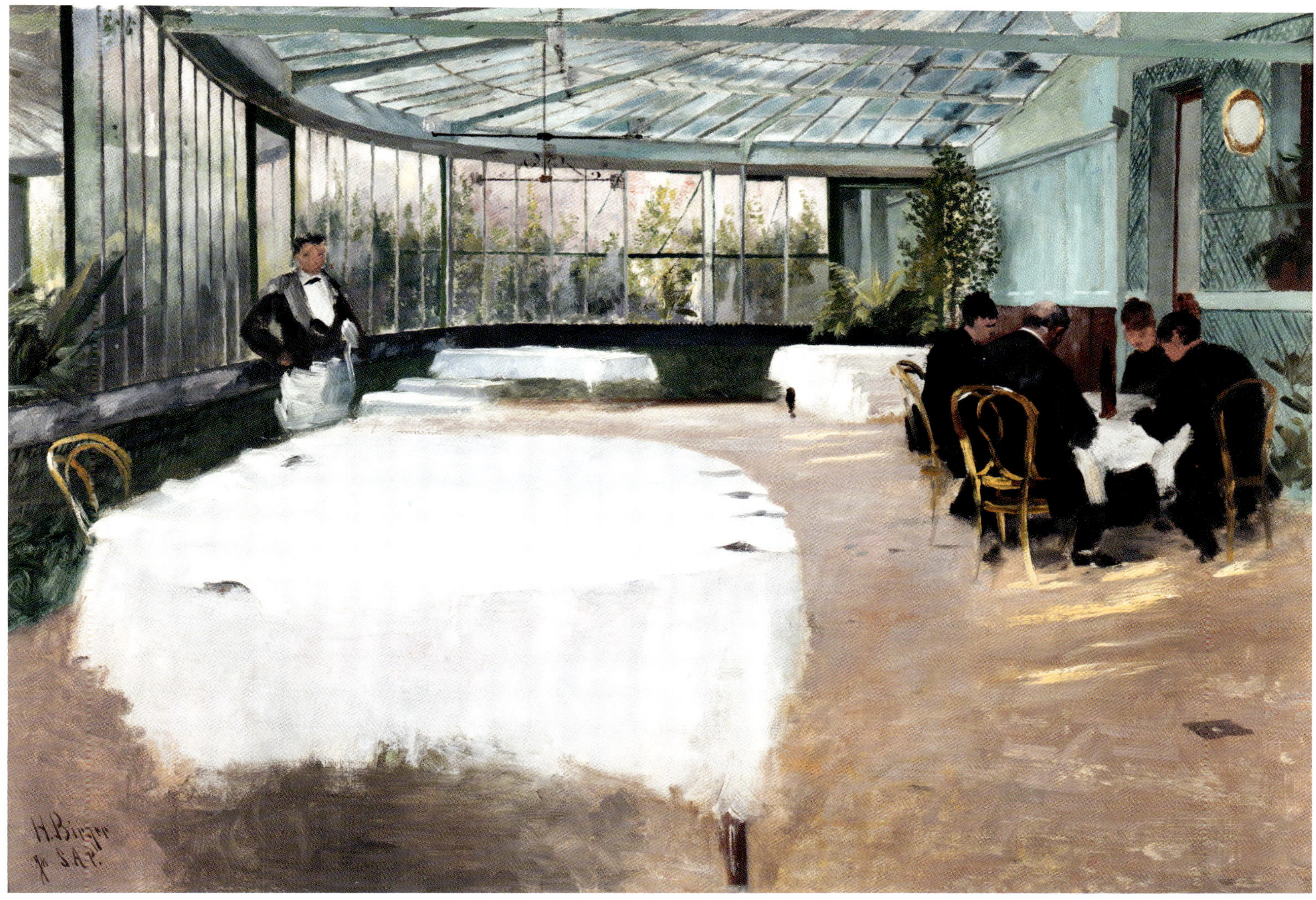

Cat. 33

Hugo Birger
Swedish, 1854–1887
*Interior from Restaurant Ledoyen
(Study for The Artists' Lunch)*, undated
Oil on canvas
18 ⅛ × 25 ½ in. (46 × 65 cm)
Collection of Helene Schmitz

symbolized urban modernity. From letters, we know that Birger considered this festive scene from the Salon's opening to be a distinctly modern subject, and that the two unknown models' matching golden-brown dresses in the foreground were intended to harmonize with the painting's dominant "champagne tone."[15] As one of the studies for his *magnum opus* illustrates, Birger also worked on creating an airy, delicate color tone in the rendering of the restaurant's glass rotunda (cat. 33). In this light-filled pavilion he succeeded, in his own words, in capturing "that peculiar absinthe-green tone that is pervasive in Ledoyen's restaurant."[16]

Representatives of the many female Scandinavian artists living in Paris in 1886 are conspicuously absent from the lively scene in the final version of the painting. Out of at least fifty Swedish female artists who resided in the city and exhibited at the Salon in the 1880s,[17] here we find only the sculptor Antoinette Vallgren, who was married to the Finnish artist Ville Vallgren. The latter's *mention honorable*, awarded by the exhibition jury, served as the official occasion for the festivities in Birger's painting. Vallgren is thus the focal point and is seen toasting, wearing a top hat and with a cloth napkin tied around his neck, while Antoinette Vallgren sits at the central table, second from the left. From the letters of Swedish artist Hanna Hirsch-Pauli sent from Paris, we know that she also attended the Salon's opening day in 1886, in the company of her future husband, the painter Georg Pauli. However, only Pauli is represented in Birger's gathering; he is seen sitting at the central table with his arm extended in a toast with Ville Vallgren. In his 1926 book *Pariserpojkarna* (The Paris Boys) about the Parisian activities of the Swedish artist group Opponenterna (The Opponents), including the secessionist grouping's many meetings at the city's cafés, Pauli makes no mention of the group's female members—not even his own wife![18]

Absinthe Drinkers, Bohemians, and Cocottes

The men and women of the Modern Breakthrough who gathered at the Café de la Régence for celebrations and day-to-day socializing were, for the most part, inspired by the Danish writer and critic Georg Brandes's credo of "bringing problems up for debate." Even before artists including Willumsen and Munch arrived in Paris in 1889, they were already fascinated with the social realism of Jean-François Raffaëlli, whose work they had seen in Copenhagen at the French art exhibition held there in the summer of 1888. Raffaëlli enjoyed great success in the 1880s and was praised by leading critics of the time for expanding the subject matter of painting—particularly in his depictions of *les déclassés*, the "fallen" or marginalized people of the proletariat, who find themselves on the lower rungs of the social ladder.

Raffaëlli exhibited *The Absinthe Drinkers* (1881, see cat. 17) at the sixth Impressionist exhibition in 1881 under the title *Les Déclassés* and again at the 1889 Exposition Universelle in Paris, where it appears to have made a strong impression on the young Munch, who was closely associated with the so-called "Kristiania Bohemians" Christian Krohg and Hans Jæger—two artists for whom art and social commitment went hand in hand. In 1890, when Munch ran out of money and left Paris for the suburb of Saint-Cloud, he also portrayed one of these suburban men in shabby clothes (*In the Tavern*, cat. 30). Like Raffaëlli's lost souls, Munch's figure is depicted wearing an inscrutable expression. The absinthe-drinking laborer or "déclassé" stands notably alone and appears lost in the middle of the tavern floor. There is no interaction between him and the *patron*, and a mood of human isolation and disillusion pervades the painting, which, like Raffaëlli's work, is rendered in hues of gray and brown. *In the Tavern* and *The Absinthe Drinkers* (cat. 31), from the same year, are among the first works in which Munch focuses on the high-proof alcoholic

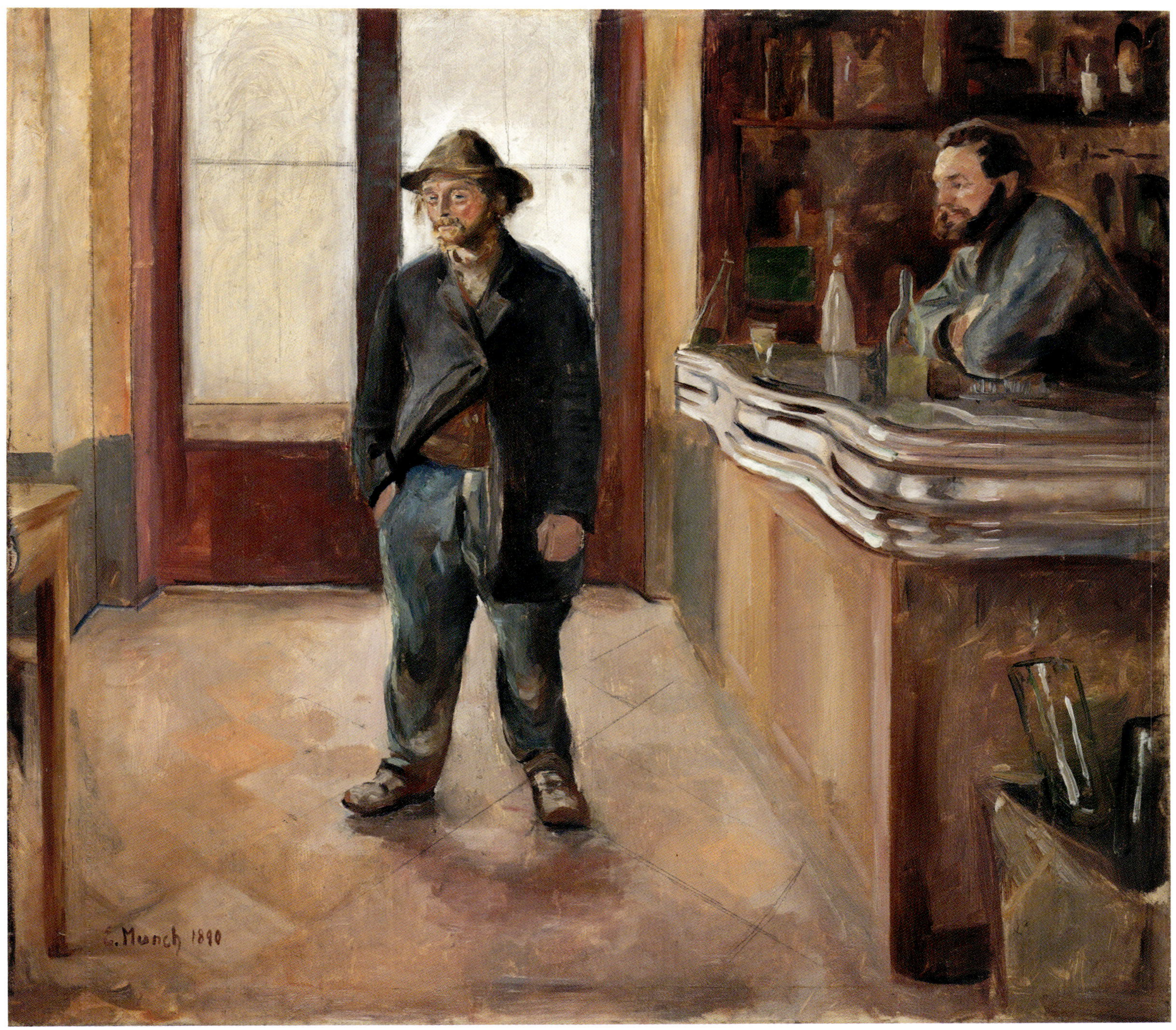

Cat. 30

Edvard Munch
Norwegiar, 1863–1944
In the Tavern, 1890
Oil on canvas
25 ⅜ × 28 ¼ in. (64.5 × 71.7 cm)
Städel Museum, Frankfurt, SG365

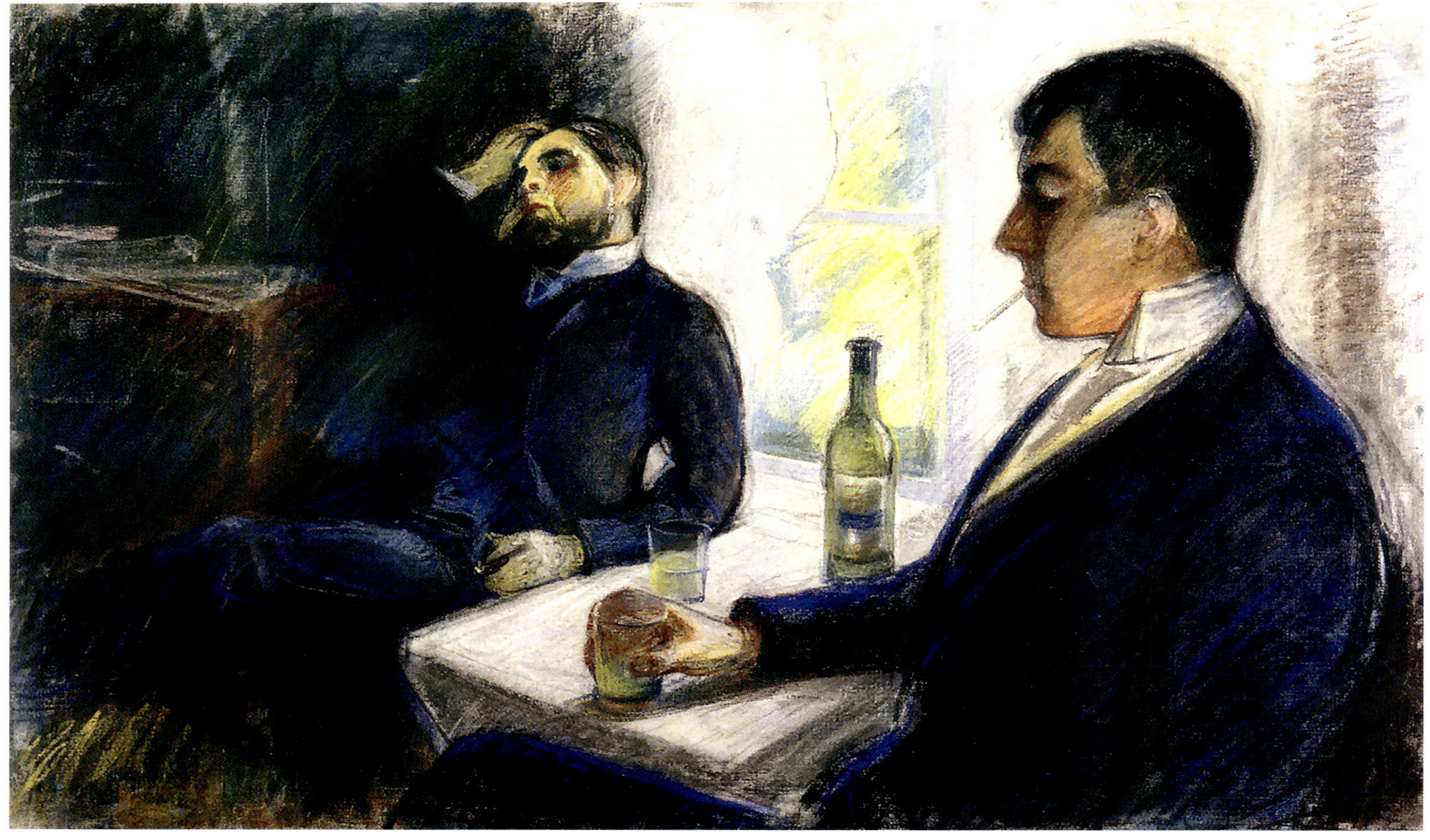

Cat. 31

Edvard Munch
Norwegian, 1863–1944
The Absinthe Drinkers, 1890
Pastel on canvas
22 ⅞ × 37 ¾ in. (58 × 96 cm)
Siem Group

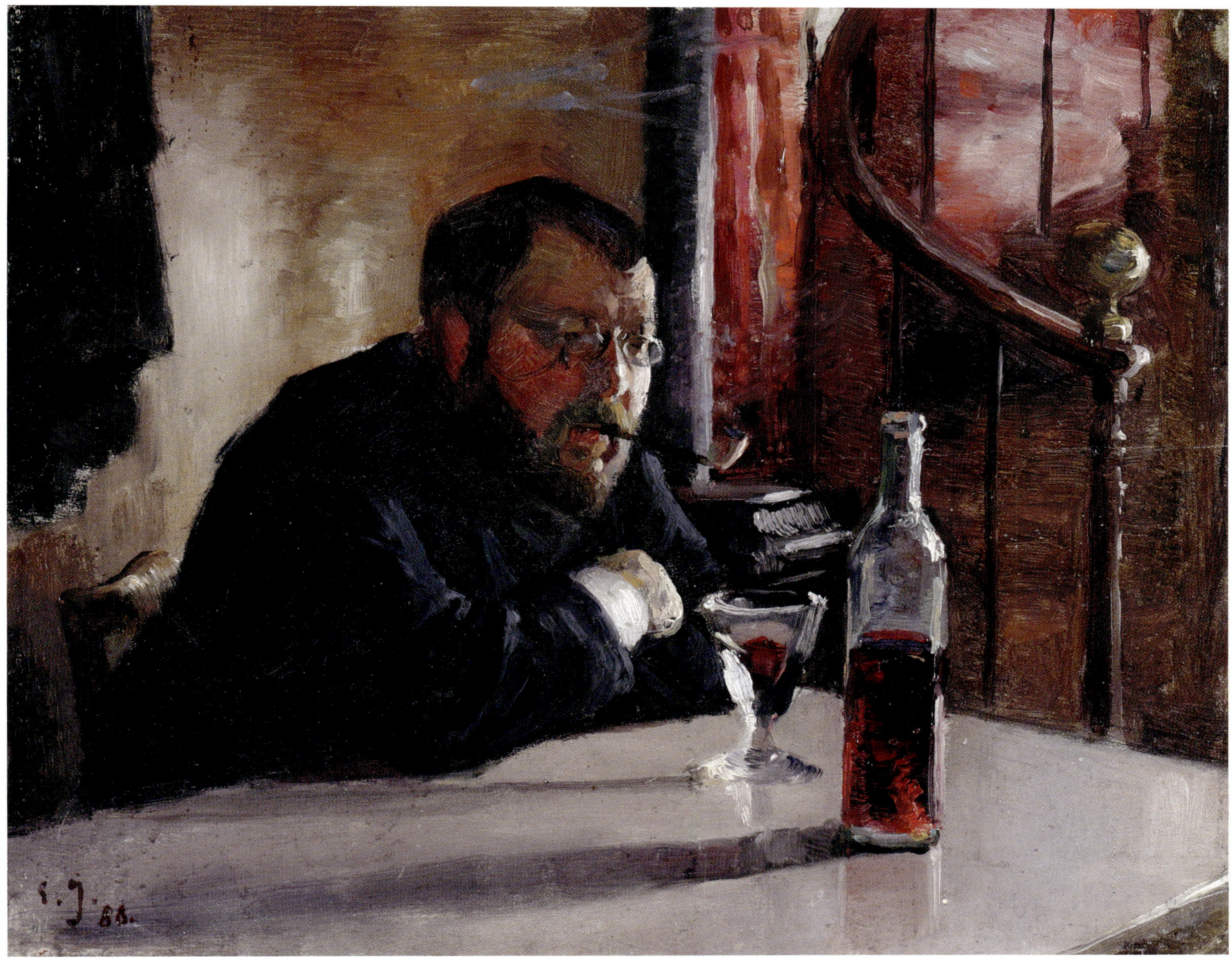

Cat. 29

Sven Jørgensen
Norwegian, 1861–1940
Portrait of Hans Jæger, 1888
Oil on canvas
8 ½ × 10 ⅝ in. (21.8 × 27.1 cm)
Oslo Museum, OB.00481

beverage absinthe—also known as "the green fairy" because of its color and the hallucinations it was said to induce after a glass or two too many. In *The Absinthe Drinkers*, the figure in the foreground has been identified as the poet and fellow Norwegian Jappe Nilssen, while the other is believed to be the aforementioned Jæger, as both were living in Paris in 1890.

Two years previously, a reflective Jæger accompanied by a bottle of wine had been painted by the Norwegian artist Sven Jørgensen in *Portrait of Hans Jæger* (1888, cat. 29). The small picture is clearly inspired by Finnish artist Eero Järnefelt's *French Wine Bar* (1888, cat. 28), which, in terms of composition and character portrayal, borrows elements from the groundbreaking works by Edgar Degas and Manet depicting isolated and alcoholic individuals amid the modern café society of the metropolis (see fig. 19). In contrast to Järnefelt's image, no bartender appears in Jørgensen's work: the focus is solely on Jæger, this central figure of the bohemian life of Kristiania. Jæger was a gifted, anarchistic thinker who challenged the prevalent morals and power structures of his time, and he was also an advocate for free erotic expression. In 1885 he published the novel *Fra Kristiania-Bohêmen* (From the Kristiania Bohemia), which was immediately confiscated for blasphemy and offences against decency. Jæger was fined and sentenced to sixty days in prison. In the autobiographical *Syg kærlighed* (Sick Love), with the subtitle *Bohemens erotiske bekendelser* (The Erotic Confessions of a Bohemian), Jæger describes his passionate but unhappy love affair with Oda Krohg. The plot is heavily informed by Jæger's many visits to the Café du Cardinal, Café de la Régence, and the wine bar Lefranc on Boulevard de Clichy, which also serves as the setting for the café scenes painted by Järnefelt and Jørgensen. Jæger's new book was likewise confiscated in the Scandinavian countries upon its publication in 1893. In Jørgensen's image from 1888, Jæger is already staged as *le bohème*

maudit, alone and immersed in thought, an image that reinforces the perception of him as an intellectual outsider who, like Raffaëlli's and Munch's marginalized figures, has also fallen in social esteem and status.

Jæger's friend, the young Finnish painter Akseli Gallen-Kallela, also came to Lefranc to paint and discuss current social issues, and is said to have been the model for the pipe-smoking bartender in Järnefelt's painting. Gallen-Kallela, the "most radical Finn" according to his friend August Strindberg,[19] was interested in the Swede and Norwegian's criticism of the petty-bourgeois lifestyle. With the overtly erotic painting *Démasquée* (1888, Ateneum Art Museum, Helsinki) of a naked fallen woman on a typical Finnish rya rug in his Paris studio, Gallen-Kallela had also outraged the bourgeoisie in his home country. "They are radical, brave and daring, it is just a shame that they philosophize more than they paint,"[20] wrote the painter Albert Edelfelt about his compatriot and the Norwegian artists with whom Gallen-Kallela surrounded himself in the French capital. The limited production of works from Paris includes *In a Café in Paris* (1886, cat. 22), which depicts an elegant gentleman in the company of a masked lady who apparently does not want her identity revealed after the masked ball they have been attending. In his choice of motif and aesthetics, Gallen-Kallela was clearly inspired by Manet and the Impressionists' bar and café paintings. However, with his modest clothing and hat in hand, the begging man also seems to reflect the social consciousness of the young Finnish artist, thus aligning himself with the Nordic writers who, led by Georg Brandes, put social issues up for discussion.

Another type besides the bohemian frequently encountered by Nordic artists in the cafés was the prostitute, the so-called *cocotte*. At the end of the nineteenth century, prostitution was a widespread phenomenon that transcended class divisions, and cocottes were found in cafés and on boulevards

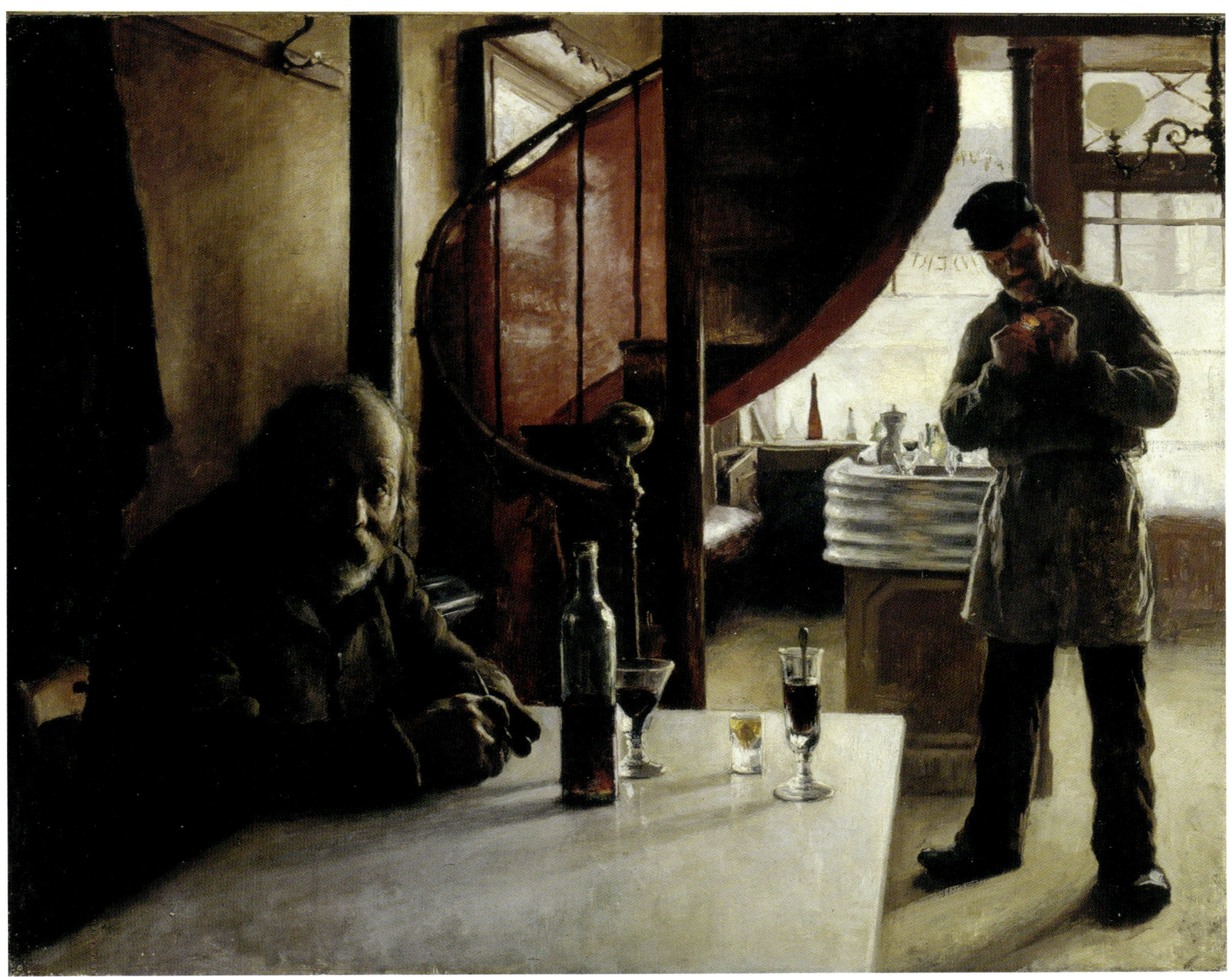

Cat. 28

Eero Järnefelt
Finnish, 1863–1937
French Wine Bar, 1888
Oil on canvas
24 × 29 ⅛ in. (61 × 74 cm)
Finnish National Gallery Collection,
Ateneum Art Museum, A II 1278

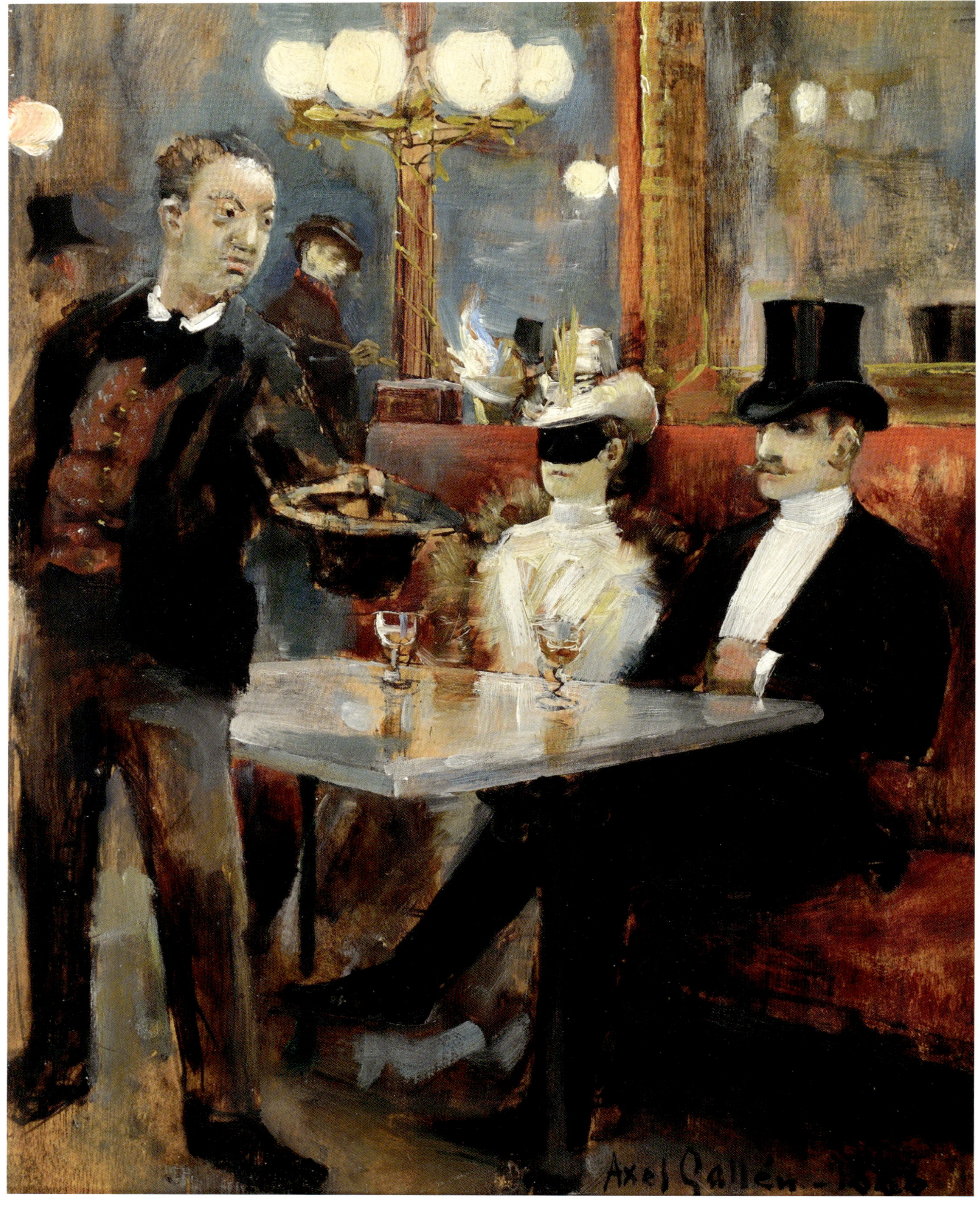

as well as in theater boxes and at the opera. For the Scandinavian (male) artists, they became a subject that could not be ignored, as they were very much considered the embodiment of the modern metropolis. Willumsen recounts how, at the Montagnes Russes entertainment venue on Boulevard des Capucines, they sat "in rows at the tables. Only men would enter the place, and moments later each one would have a girl around his neck. It was amusing to watch and very picturesque."[21] He recorded the experience in the painted wooden relief *A Cocotte Hunting in the Montagnes Russes* (1890, cat. 32), where the prostitute is poised for action, ready to sink her claws into her next prey underneath the glow of the lamps and the hens "on display in the establishment."[22] It should be added here that in French, "cocotte" is the diminutive and feminine form of "coq," which means rooster and is an old-fashioned term for a prostitute.

Alongside the Danish Symbolist writer Sophus Claussen, Willumsen entered the circle of poets, critics, and artists who, led by Paul Verlaine and Stéphane Mallarmé, cultivated decadent poetry and Symbolism, and who often met at the editorial office of the periodical *La Plume* or at the Café Voltaire and Café de la Régence.[23] Late-night venues like the Café d'Harcourt in the Latin Quarter and Café du Rat Mort in Montmartre, which especially attracted poets and writers, also held a strong appeal for the Scandinavian artists, including Munch, Strindberg, and Claussen, as these served simultaneously as places of indulgence and hijinks and as forums for discussion and artistic inspiration. Claussen, who along with the writer Johannes Jørgensen was one of the foremost

representatives of Symbolism in Denmark, writes in his travelogue, *Antonius i Paris* (Antonius in Paris, 1896), about visits to the cafés on the left bank of the Seine, frequented by artists, poets, cocottes, and students. For example, near the Sorbonne he visited "the café called *D'Harcourt*, which is a veritable Sodom and Gomorrah with doors that never close and a constant flow of beer and girls." Here,

> the ugly, young men enter quietly . . . to continue their elevated discussions at a solitary table or write a sentimental poem to one of the beautiful ones who saunter in and out. Wisdom and folly, art and joy always seek a common café here in France. And God knows how many lovely sonnets have been written in the Latin Quarter about some frivolous and cheap beauty, encountered in some café or in one of those cellars where the neighborhood's ballad singers come to sing their songs.[24]

Around the same time, the Belgian artist Henri Evenepoel, who was said to spend his days at the Louvre and his nights at the Moulin Rouge,[25] painted one of the café's "frivolous and cheap beauties" dressed in a striking red dress and feathered hat, her gaze assessing the venue's clientele in the search for her next client (1897, see cat. 44). Anders Zorn also devoted a relatively large canvas to "one of the beautiful ones who saunter in and out" of cafés in one of his well-known paintings, *Night Effect* (fig. 40), for which he executed a number of preliminary studies in order to properly capture the artificial evening light produced by the cafés' novel electric lamps (1892, cat. 34). In one of the early masterpieces of Swedish modernism, *Night Café* (1906, cat. 57), Zorn's compatriot Axel Törneman offers a slightly later insight into the city's decadent café society of which he was a part, specifically at the

Cat. 22

Akseli Gallen-Kallela
Finnish, 1865–1931
In a Café in Paris, 1886
Oil on wood
12 ¾ × 9 ⅞ in. (32.5 × 25 cm)
Gösta Serlachius Fine Arts Foundation,
Mänttä, Finland

legendary Rat Mort on Place Pigalle. The almost
absinthe-green color recurring in the background
interior and in the dress of the woman seen from behind
in the foreground spreads and diffuses throughout
the room due to the artificial lighting. Indeed, the
painting's original title is *Lumière artificielle*, and
the lighting does play a prominent role: it seems
to draw a venomous greenish veil over this nocturnal
underworld, where flamboyant ladies of the night
in colorful dresses and hats drink champagne and flaunt
themselves in uninhibited dances for male observers
in their top hats.

The "Parisian Life" of Women Artists

Such painterly records of the metropolis's cocottes
are hard to find in the work of the large number
of Nordic women artists who stayed in Paris at the end
of the nineteenth century. From private letters and
diaries, however, we know that they too participated
in "Parisian life," even if they are conspicuously absent
from Birger's and Segelcke's scenes of artist gatherings
in cafés. In 1888, for instance, Danish Marie Triepcke
wrote in her diary: "The cafés and restaurants here are
splendidly vibrant, always teeming. We also went to the
Café la Régence, I read a copy of *Politiken* again, it was
truly quite touching. Then, in the evening, we went
to the Variétés [Théâtre des Variétés]."[26] Alongside
a slew of other artists, including the Norwegian painter
Kitty Kielland, the Lies, the Danish Skagen painters
Anna and Michael Ancher, and Peder Severin Krøyer, she
formed a club that met every Wednesday at "la Régence"
and afterwards went out to dinner. Her acquaintance
with the esteemed Danish painter P. S. Krøyer would
lead to marriage the following year, and today she is best
known beyond the Nordic countries by the surname
Krøyer, especially in the role of the white-clad figure

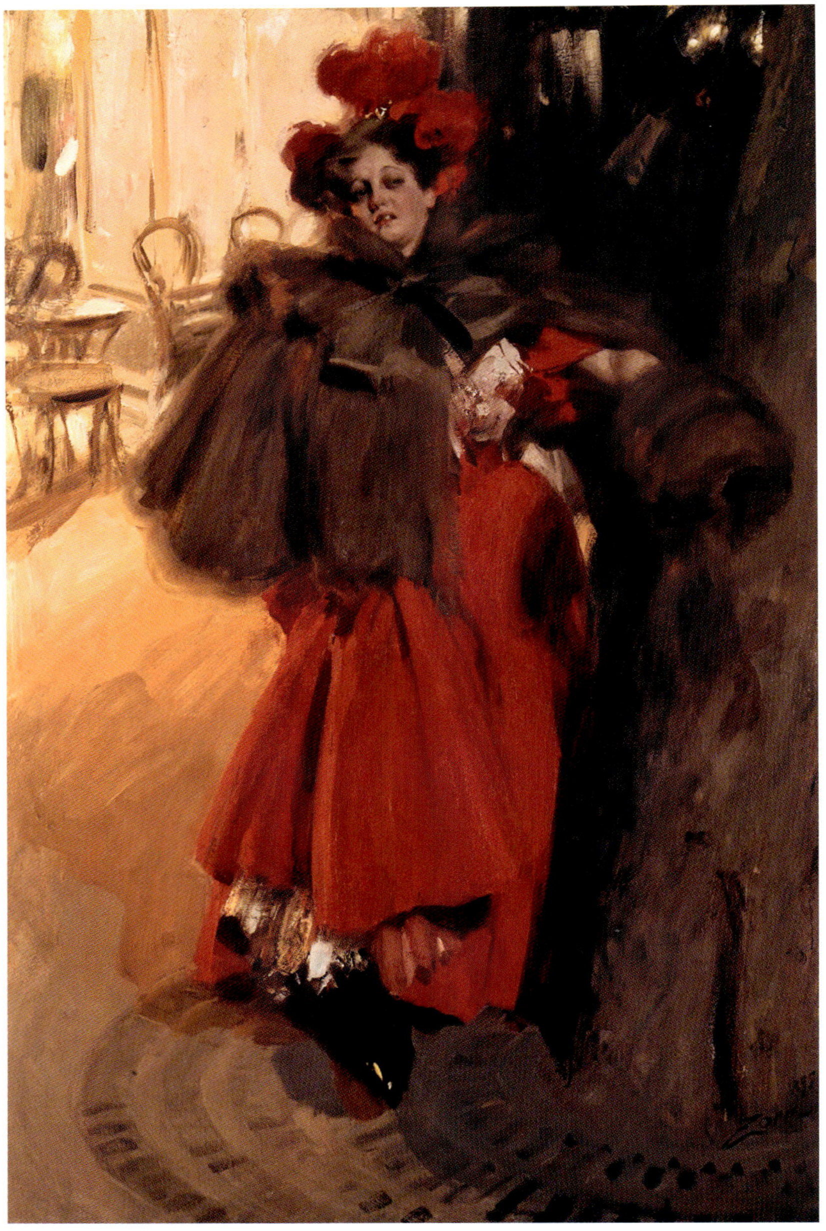

Fig. 40
Anders Zorn
Swedish, 1860–1920
Night Effect, 1895
Oil on canvas
63 ⅜ × 41 ¾ in. (161 × 106 cm)
Göteborgs Konstmuseum, F 161

Cat. 34

Anders Zorn
Swedish, 1860–1920
Study for Night Effect, 1892
Watercolor on paper
9 ⅝ × 6 ¼ in. (24.5 × 16 cm)
Zorn Museum, Mora

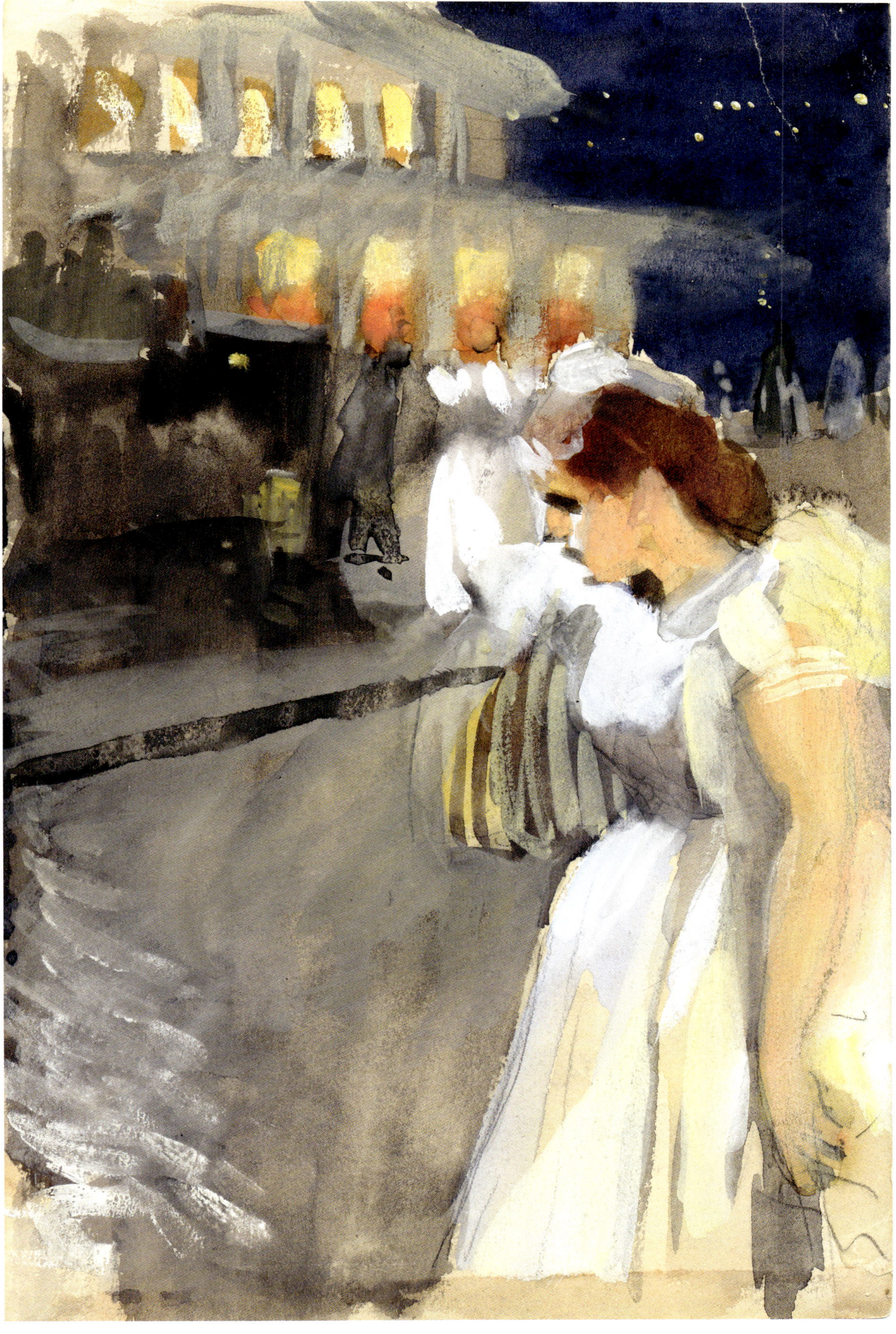

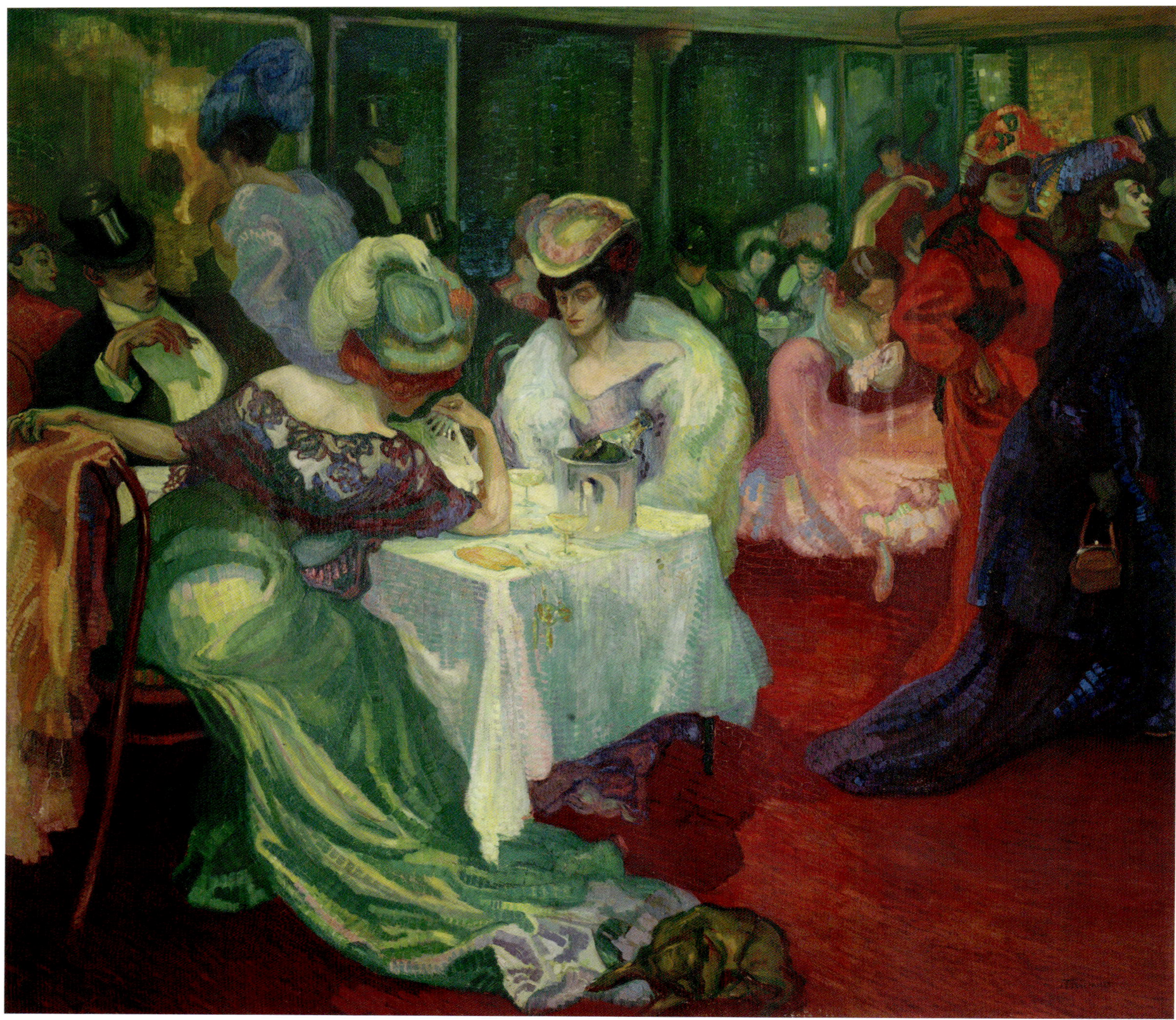

Cat. 57

Axel Törneman
Swedish, 1880–1925
Night Café, 1906
Oil on canvas
70 ½ × 78 ¾ in. (179 × 200 cm)
Thielska Galleriet, Stockholm, TG 361

promenading along the shoreline on long summer nights captured in her husband's paintings. It was in Skagen, Denmark's northernmost town, that the Krøyers settled in the summers from 1891 onwards, becoming a prominent artist couple in the artists' colony alongside Anna and Michael Ancher and Oda and Christian Krohg. In 1888, however, Marie Krøyer was doing her promenading in the theater in Paris:

> On Christmas Day I was at the Eden [Éden-Théâtre] together with Krøyer and a couple of others, we went up to promenade during the intermission. Eden is a place where the refined cocottes belong, though not the most refined. There were a number of them, but one in particular made a powerful impression on me—there was something so petrified, despairingly cool, cold, chilling, and frozen about her, yes, it was quite moving, there was a distinct Max Klinger mood about her—yes, I feel tempted to paint a picture based on that mood; if I could only fully express what I felt, then it might become a most excellent painting. There she stood, so alone and isolated, displaying herself.[27]

Compared to her male colleagues, here we find a different, harsher, and more empathetic depiction of the cocotte, who made such a profound impression on Marie Krøyer that it inspired her to paint "a most excellent painting," which, however, never saw the light of day. Most likely because such a subject from the city's nightlife was not deemed appropriate for a woman artist of the upper middle class in the late nineteenth century.

For many of the Nordic women artists who, like Marie Krøyer, traveled to Paris to study at one of the city's private art schools, the encounter with "Parisian life" brought about a personal revolution. The café and entertainment scenes offered a space of great freedom, far removed from the social control of family and the constricting conventions of the time. In addition to describing her visit to the opening day of the Salon with Georg Pauli, Hanna Hirsch-Pauli, for example, relates how, in 1885, her friend took her for a walk along the grand boulevards, where he wanted to "show [her] the nice cocottes."[28] In the evening they visited the famous Folies-Bergère cabaret music hall near Montmartre, where they "got to see that kind of people both on and off stage."[29] Later, in March 1886, Hirsch-Pauli recounts her participation in the carnival on Boulevard Saint-Michel and subsequently at Bal Bullier, which, however, turned out to be just a bit too well-behaved in the eyes of the avid young woman: "There was laughter, talk, and dancing right in the middle of the street, everything is allowed. We got tired and went into a café for a while to warm up. Later, we went to the Bal Bullier; beautiful legs and beautiful costumes; but so darn decent, no cancan at all!"[30]

Danish, Swedish, Norwegian, and Finnish women artists sought out the pleasures of Parisian nightlife, but, as Marie Krøyer's diary and Hirsch-Pauli's letters show, they could typically only frequent such public places in the company of a chaperone. According to Tulla Larsen from Norway, who had a turbulent relationship with Edvard Munch, the Café de la Régence was "unfortunately the only place in Paris where we can go alone without being at risk of trouble."[31] However, her friend "Mrs Krohg" refused to limit herself to "la Régence." She was considered a particularly independent woman of her time and, in the words of Jæger, "une vraie princesse de Bohême [*sic*],"[32] who remained unrestricted by prevailing conventions and might well go alone to the city's other cafés.

Christian Krohg's famous portrait depicts her with suitable informality (fig. 41). She smiles at us with a direct gaze and is unconventionally dressed in theatre costume or a summer dress rather than the kind of evening wear typically worn by women on the boulevard or in cafés. Munch too was fascinated by the portrait of Oda Krohg and was inspired by it in *Kristiania Bohemians II* (fig. 42), where she is presented as an iconic *femme fatale* who seduces and hypnotizes all the men she meets: her first husband Jørgen Engelhart, her current husband Christian Krohg, her lovers Jappe Nilssen, Hans Jæger, and Gunnar Heiberg, as well as Munch himself in the foreground at right.

Oda Krohg's own artistic endeavors have often been eclipsed by her role as the bohemian princess of the 1880s and the *femme fatale* of the 1890s. Nevertheless, *Night Birds. Bokken Lasson and Sten Drewsen* (1902, cat. 49) is an important work in Nordic art, depicting a scene from urban nightlife and the world of entertainment—a subject that never made it onto the canvases of Marie Krøyer, Hanna Hirsch-Pauli, or any of the other women artists from Scandinavia. In the painting, acquired by Norway's National Museum of Art, Architecture and Design in 2021, Bokken Lasson is portrayed as an artist in her true element, in the midst of performing a number on the guitar accompanied by the lute-playing young Danish writer Sten Drewsen. She is, in fact, Oda's sister Charlotte, called "Bokken" since childhood, who was a cabaret singer (fig. 43) and later, in 1912, the founder of the cabaret Le Chat Noir in Kristiania, inspired by the famous Parisian establishment of the same name. The painting of the two artistic bohemians was likely created in the Norwegian capital after their return from a three-year tour of the United States in the company of the Danish poet Holger Drachmann.

With Oda Krohg and other likeminded artists, the "migratory birds of art" who, in Erik Lie's words, found "a warm shelter" in the Café de la Régence, which served

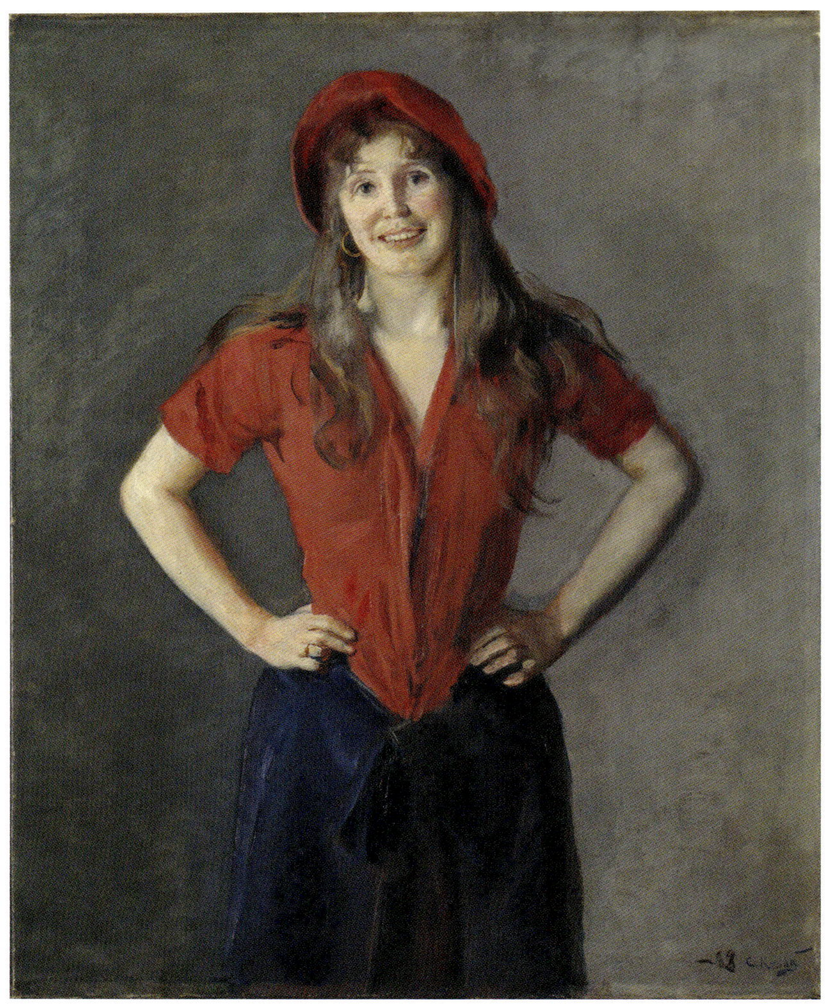

Fig. 41
Christian Krohg
Norwegian, 1852–1925
The Painter Oda Krohg, 1888
Oil on canvas
34 × 27 ⅛ in. (86.4 × 68.8 cm)
Nasjonalmuseet for kunst, arkitektur og design, Oslo, The Fine Art Collections, NG.M.02147

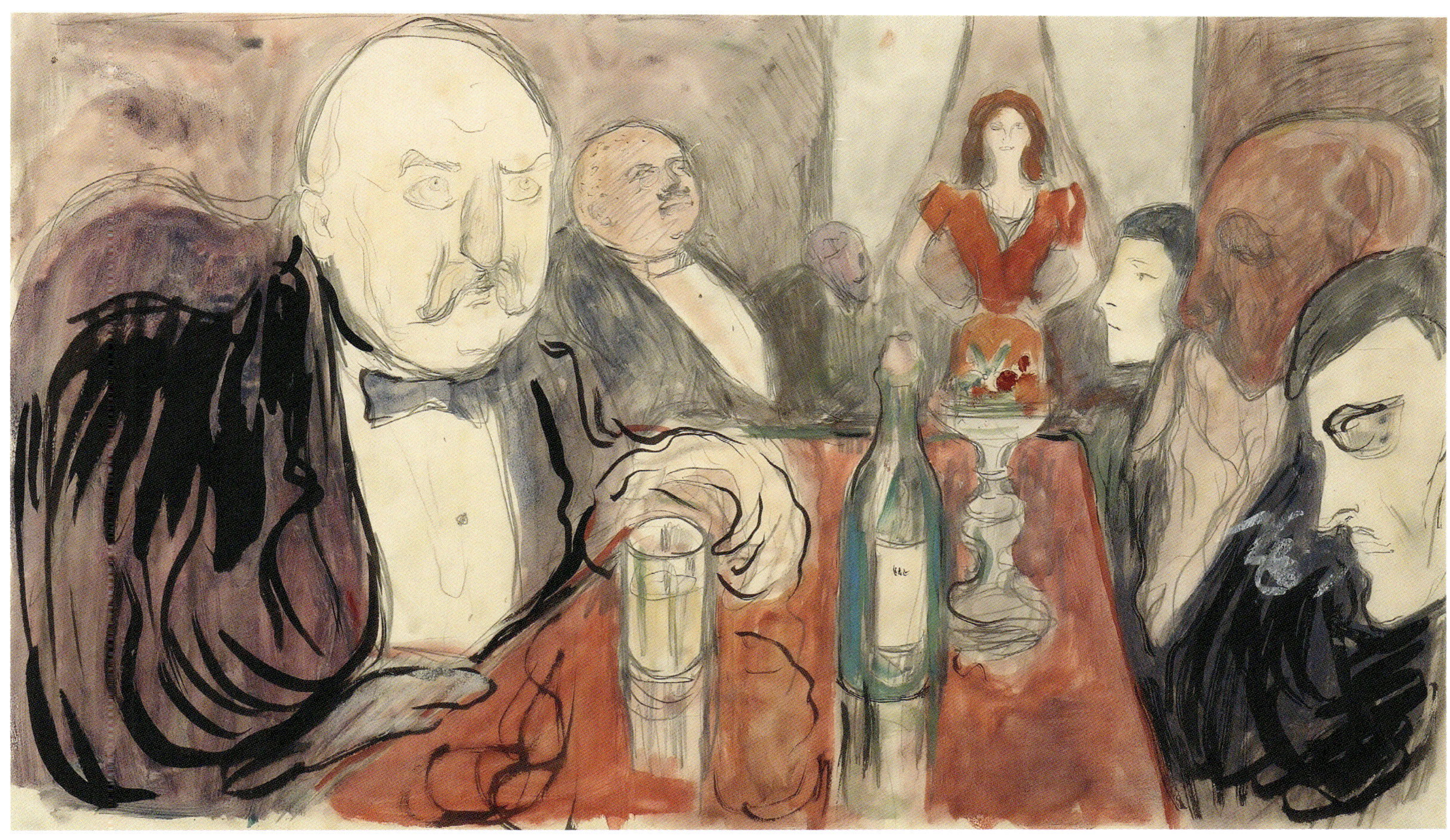

Fig. 42
Edvard Munch
Norwegian, 1863–1944
Kristiania Bohemians II, 1895
Watercolor and pencil on paper
9 ⅞ × 16 ⅜ in. (25 × 41.5 cm)
Munchmuseet, Oslo, MM.T.02383

as "one of the unmissable stations on the outbound journey,"[33] thus returned to their native Kristiania and became night owls. Although many of the returning Scandinavian artists came to be seen as instrumental to the establishment of a modern national art scene related to key locales—for example, Skagen in Denmark, Varberg in Sweden, Fleskum in Norway—the café's importance, both abroad and at home, cannot be overstated. If the Café de la Régence was the Nordic artists' refuge in Paris, then the Grand Café in Kristiania

and Café Bernina in Copenhagen were cultural meeting places with a continental air. Christian Krohg's famous portrait of the artist Gerhard Munthe in the Grand Café (1885, cat. 21) thus transports us to the Paris of Manet and the Impressionists. Munthe is not represented in a painter's shirt, but as a cosmopolitan and dandy in a fashionable black coat with a fur collar, a neat moustache, and intellectual glasses.

For the men and women of the Modern Breakthrough in the 1880s and, later, the circle of

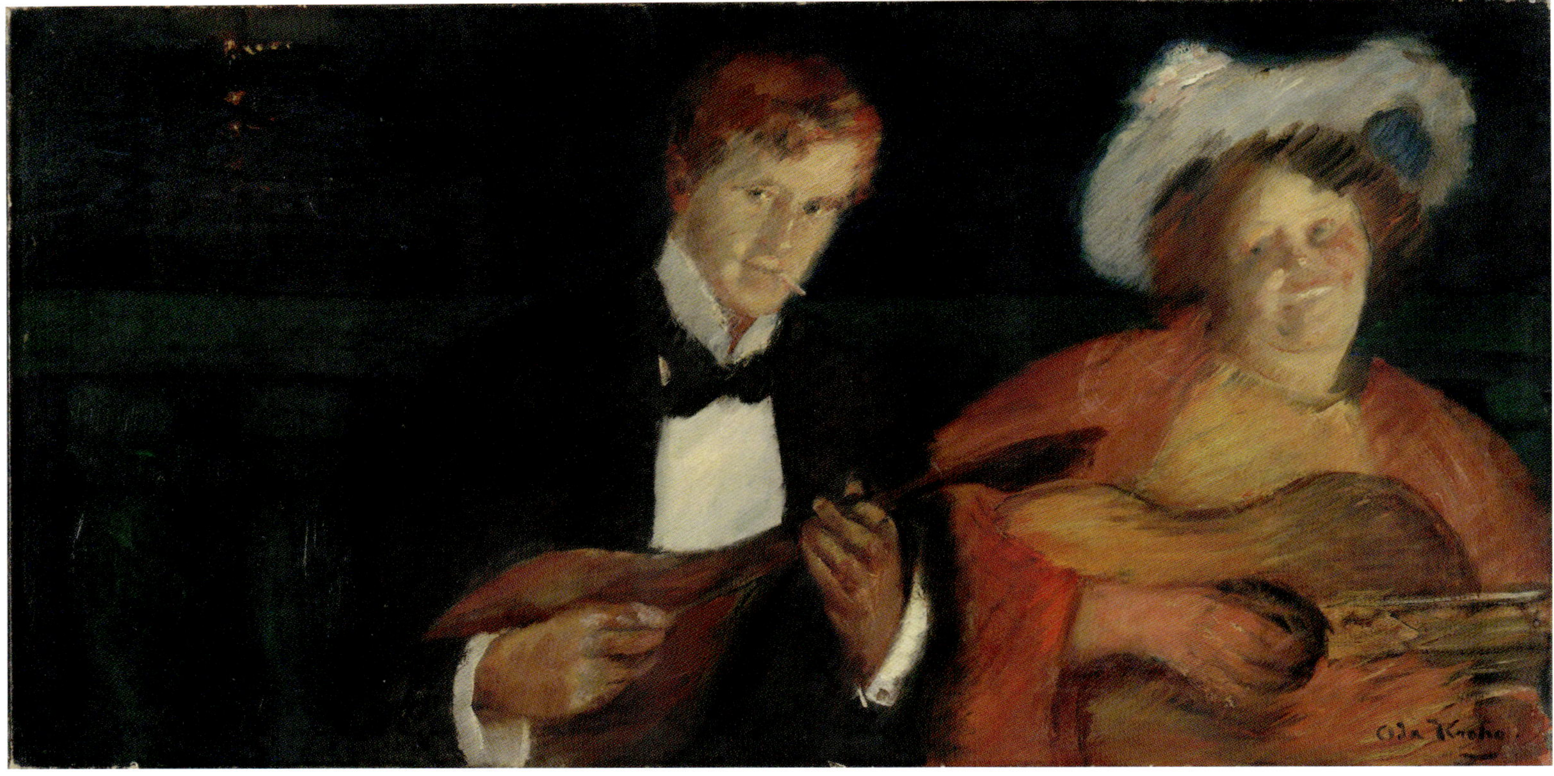

Cat. 49

Oda Krohg
Norwegian, 1860–1935
Night Birds. Bokken Lasson and Sten Drewsen, 1902
Oil on canvas
19 ¾ × 38 ⅜ in. (50.2 × 97.5 cm)
Nasjonalmuseet for kunst, arkitektur og design, Oslo, The Fine Art Collections, NMK.2021.0182

Cat. 21

Christian Krohg
Norwegian, 1852–1925
Portrait of the Painter Gerhard Munthe, 1885
Oil on canvas
59 ⅛ × 45 ¼ in. (150 × 115 cm)
Nasjonalmuseet for kunst, arkitektur og design, Oslo, The Fine Art Collections, NG.M.01555

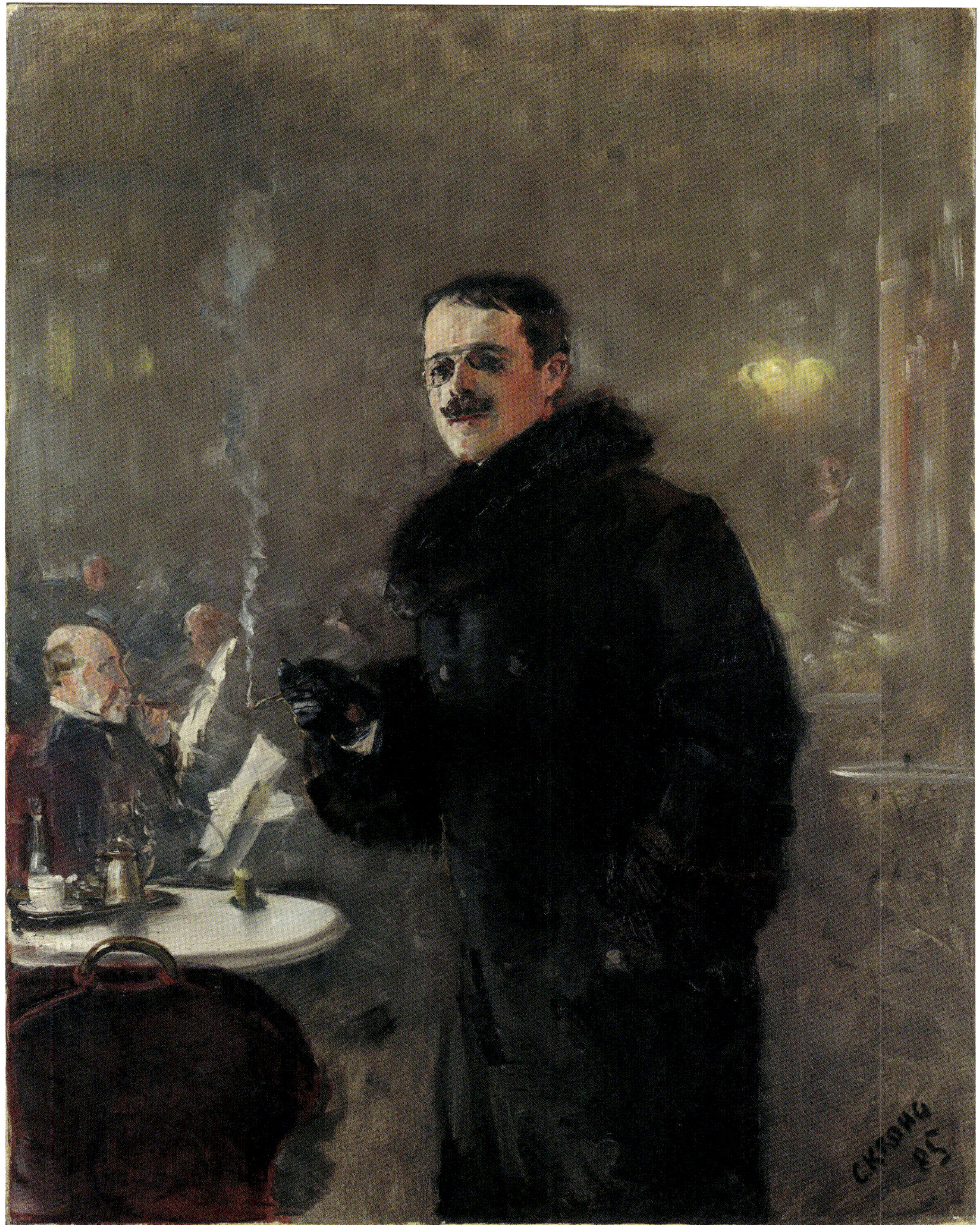

C.KRØHG
85

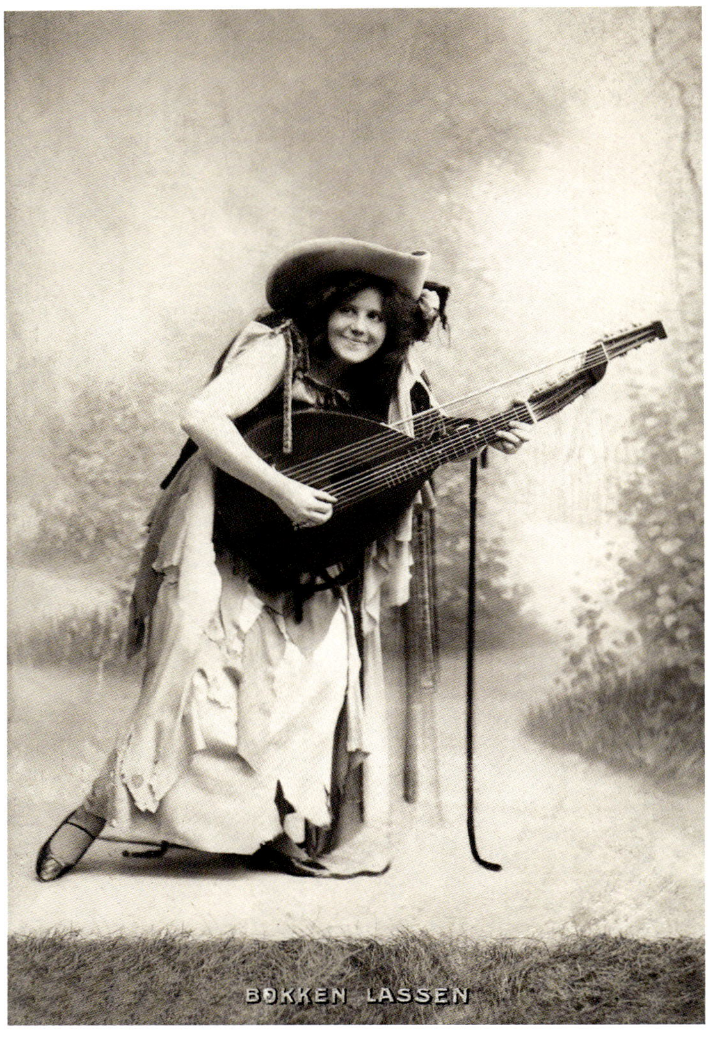

Fig. 43
Bokken Lasson, 1903
Photograph
Oslo Museum

younger artists and writers around Hans Jæger and the Krohgs in the 1890s, the cafés were more than social hubs, they were also incubators of artistic freedom and new ideas—especially at a time when the art academy was either considered outdated, long remained closed to women, or, as in Norway, was non-existent until 1909.

Endnotes

1. Erik Lie, "Fra 'Café de la Régence,'" in *Juleaften* (Stockholm, Kristiania, and Copenhagen: Hjalmar Biglers forlag, 1895), n.p.

2. Henrik Cavling, *Paris: Skildringer fra det moderne Frankrig* (Copenhagen: Gyldendal, 1899), 450.

3. George Walker, *Chess and Chess-Players: Consisting of Original Stories and Sketches* (London: Charles J. Skeet, 1850), 151.

4. Cavling, *Paris*, 451–52.

5. Edvard Munch to Karen Bjølstad in a letter dated 30.11.1889, Munchmuseet, Oslo, MM N 741.

6. "Brev fra Paris," *Illustreret Tidende*, no. 867 (1876): 313.

7. Johan Ludvig Heiberg, *De Danske i Paris: Vaudeville* (Copenhagen: Schubothe, 1833), act 2, scene 4.

8. Lie, "Fra 'Café de la Régence.'"

9. Jean-Michel Nectoux, "Grieg. The Paris Stay of 1903," paper given at the International Edvard Grieg Society conference in Bergen, May 25–27, 2000, https://griegsociety.com/wp-content/uploads/2015/09/Jean-Michel-Nectoux-paper-2000.pdf.

10. In art, the Modern Breakthrough is a period typically said to last from 1870 to 1890. The designation is applied to Scandinavian literature, especially those Nordic writers who, led by the prominent writer and critic Georg Brandes, put controversial issues up for discussion. For the so-called "gauntlet" or "glove" morality and the Nordic sexual morality debate, see Lene Bøgh Rønberg's essay "Handsken i hånden – Handsker og handskemoral i portrætter af gennembruddets kvinder," in *Kvindernes moderne gennembrud, 1880–1910*, ed. Inge Lise Mogensen and Lene Bøgh Rønberg (Aarhus: Aarhus University Press, 2024), 210–27.

11. Carl G. Laurin, *Nordisk konst: Sverige och Finlands konst från 1880 till 1926* (Stockholm: P. A. Norstedt & Söners förlag, 1926), 46.

12. Henrik Wivel, *Jeg er en anden: En biografi om J.F. Willumsen* (Gylling: Strandberg Publishing, 2024), 98.

13. Cavling, *Paris*, 450.

14. Bergliot Ibsen, *De Tre: Erindringer om Henrik Ibsen, Suzannah Ibsen, Sigurd Ibsen. Samlet og gjenfortalt av Bergliot Ibsen* (Oslo: Gyldendal Norsk Forlag, 1949), 95.

15. Charlotta Nordström, "Från Champs-Élysées till Göteborg. Sociala rum i konstens närhet," in *Ett eget rum: Konstnärsrollen under det sena 1800-talet*, ed. Carina Rech and Karin Sidén (Stockholm: Prins Eugens Waldemarsudde, 2021), 94.

16. Author's translation. Quoted from Bukowskis' entry on the work, lot 421, https://www.bukowskis.com/sv/auctions/H056/421-hugo-birger-interior-fran-restaurant-ledoyen-studie-till-frukosten.

17. Barbro Werkmäster, "Frigjord eller bunden? De kvinnliga konstnärerna och 1880-talets emancipationssträvanden," in *De drogo till Paris: Nordiska konstnärinnor på 1800-talet*, ed. Bo Särnstedt and Louise Robbert (Stockholm: Liljevalchs Konsthall, 1988), 11.

18. Sylvain Briens, *Paris: Laboratoire de la littérature scandinave moderne, 1880–1905* (Paris: L'Harmattan, 2010), 145.

19. Author's translation. Timo Martin, *Akseli Gallen-Kallela: Elämäkerrallinen rapsodia* (Helsinki: Watti-kustannus Oy, 1984), 30.

20. Ibid.

21. Wivel, *Jeg er en anden*, 103.

22. J. F. Willumsen in a letter to Johan Rohde dated ca. 1892, Royal Danish Library, Manuscript Collection, Tilg. 392.

23. Wivel, *Jeg er en anden*, 101.

24. Sophus Claussen, *Antonius i Paris: Valfart*, ed. and with an afterword by Jørgen Hunosøe (Copenhagen: Det Danske Sprog- og Litteraturselskab / Borgens Forslag, 1990 [1896]), 105.

25. Marie-Claude Delahaye and Benoît Noël, *Absinthe, muse des peintres* (Paris: Les éditions de l'Amateur, 1999), 117.

26. Diary of Marie Triepcke (later Krøyer) from her time in Paris, 1888–89, Royal Danish Library, Manuscript Collection, NSA8-A05025 / Acc. 1987/95, 4.12.1888–15.1.1889.

27. Ibid.

28. Carina Rech, "A City of One's Own: The Parisian Letters of the Swedish Painter Hanna Hirsch-Pauli," *Nineteenth-Century Art Worldwide* 23, no. 1 (Spring 2024), https://doi.org/10.29411/ncaw.2024.23.1.4.

29. Ibid.

30. Ibid.

31. Tulla Larsen in a letter to Edvard Munch (date illegible), Munchmuseet, Oslo, MM K 501.

32. Hans Jæger, *Syk Kjærlihet* (Paris: Imprimerie Adolphe Reiff, 1893), 13.

33. Erik Lie, "Fra 'Café de la Régence.'"

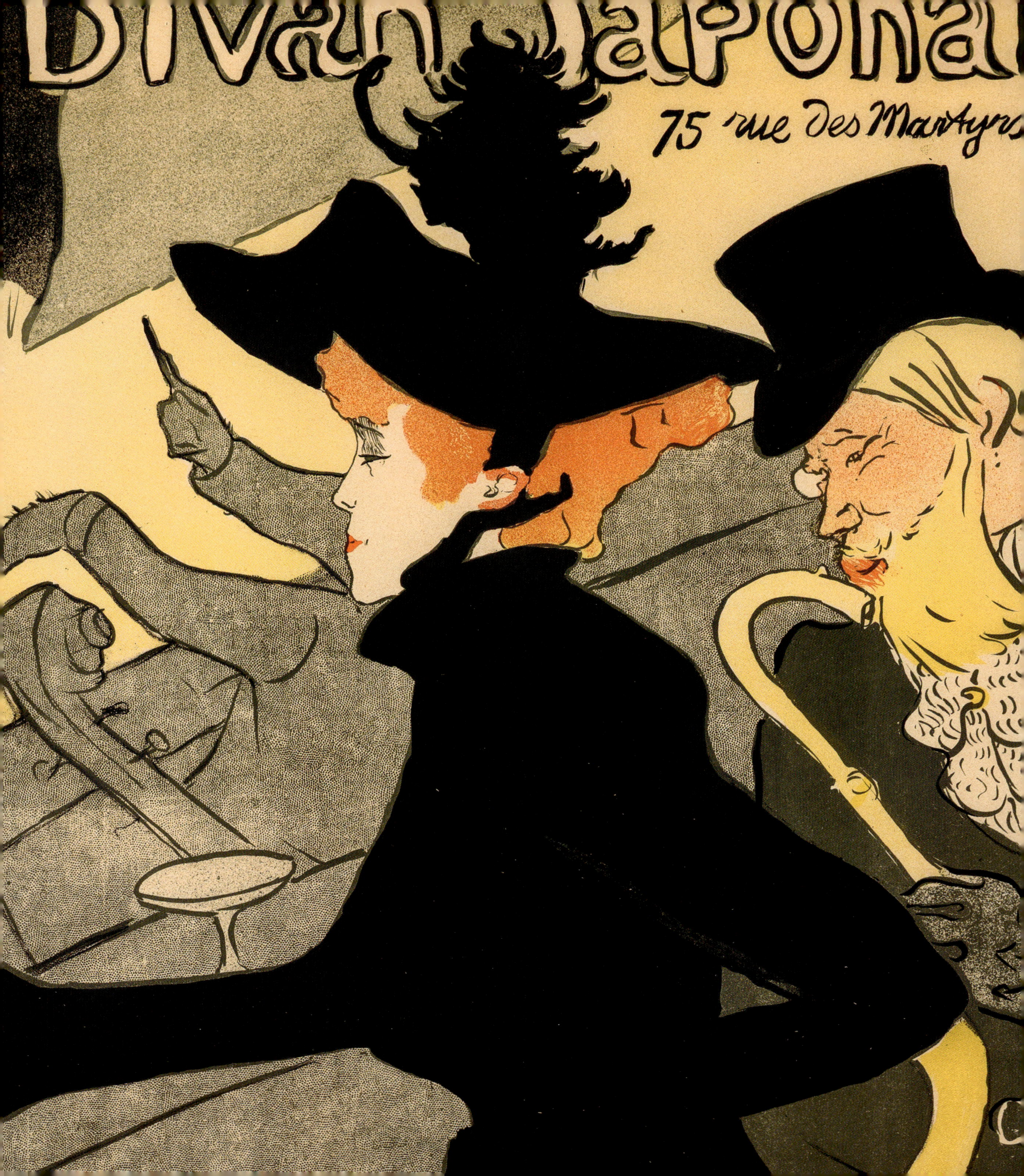

DIVAN JAPONAI
75 rue des Martyrs

MODERN ICONS

Lithography and the Making of Café Society

Taylor J. Acosta

Jane Avril raises her leg, poised to perform an energetic cancan dance at the Jardin de Paris. Loïe Fuller swirls in a voluminous silk costume beneath the multicolored lights of the Folies-Bergère. Donning her signature black gloves, Yvette Guilbert enthralls the audience at the Café des Ambassadeurs. A cast of colorful players animate the music hall of the Eldorado. The notable characters and famed cafés depicted in prints and posters by artists such as Edgar Degas, Henri de Toulouse-Lautrec, Théophile Alexandre Steinlen, and Jules Chéret suggest the fantasies and realities of a time and place variously described as *la belle époque*, the *fin de siècle*, and *Paris nouveau*.

These wonderfully evocative terms refer to a period of French history often associated with leisure, recreation, and pleasure. As the opening of a section titled "useful information" from Cassell's 1884 illustrated guide to the city of Paris related: "No people in the world are so fond of amusements—or *distractions*, as they term them—as Parisians. Morning, noon, and night, summer and winter, there is always something to be seen and a large portion of the population seems absorbed in the pursuit of pleasure."[1] Intended to prepare and instruct the visitor, this guidebook also seems to already confirm what is evident in so many representations of the city: by the final third of the nineteenth century, Paris had become a complex urban space to be seen and experienced. Various activities and sites of interest are thereafter enumerated, including cafés, which the guidebook describes as being a national institution, abundant, and deriving from the peculiarities of the French character.[2] Indeed, the very plan of the city, transformed under the direction of Baron Haussmann, encouraged a proliferation of cafés that opened onto the wide boulevards, filled the garden areas of the Champs-Élysées, and dotted the bohemian neighborhood of Montmartre.

While cafés had operated in Paris in the late seventeenth century, when coffee was introduced in Europe, and flourished in the eighteenth century, it was in the second half of the nineteenth century that cafés became a defining feature of the Parisian cityscape and of public life. Nineteenth-century cafés, in their many variations—cafés-concerts, music and dance halls, and cabarets—were important centers of sociability, venues for entertainment, and subjects of visual culture. The rise of cafés coincided with a creative boom for lithography, spurred by a resurgent interest in the graphic arts, innovations in printing technology, lessened restrictions for printed materials in public spaces, and a growing network of publishers, printers, dealers, and collectors. The present essay addresses the significance of prints and posters as self-consciously modern and popular forms of art particularly well suited to convey, chronicle, and perpetuate café culture. It endeavors to trace the dynamic, dialogical relationship between cafés, artists, performers, and prints and suggests that lithographic prints and posters not only captured and represented the new café society, they also helped to produce it.

The technique of lithography was invented in Germany in 1789. Conceived as an inexpensive, mass-printing technique for commercial purposes, the method relies on the mutual repulsion of oil and water. In traditional lithography, a drawing made with a greasy crayon or liquid on a specially prepared limestone block is bonded to the stone using a chemical solution. The stone is then inked and put through a printing press, resulting in a reverse image transfer to the sheet. In the early nineteenth century, Paris was a site of robust printing activity, with lithography presses producing advertisements, magazines, and broadsides. The artistic possibilities of the technique were recognized by early

Cat. 10

Edgar Degas
French, 1834–1914
The Song of the Dog (*La Chanson du chien*), 1876–77
Transfer crayon lithograph
image: 14 × 9 ⅛ in. (35.6 × 23.2 cm)
sheet: 14 ¹⁵⁄₁₆ × 10 ¹⁵⁄₁₆ in. (37.9 × 27.8 cm)
Cincinnati Art Museum, The Albert P. Strietmann Collection, 1996.461

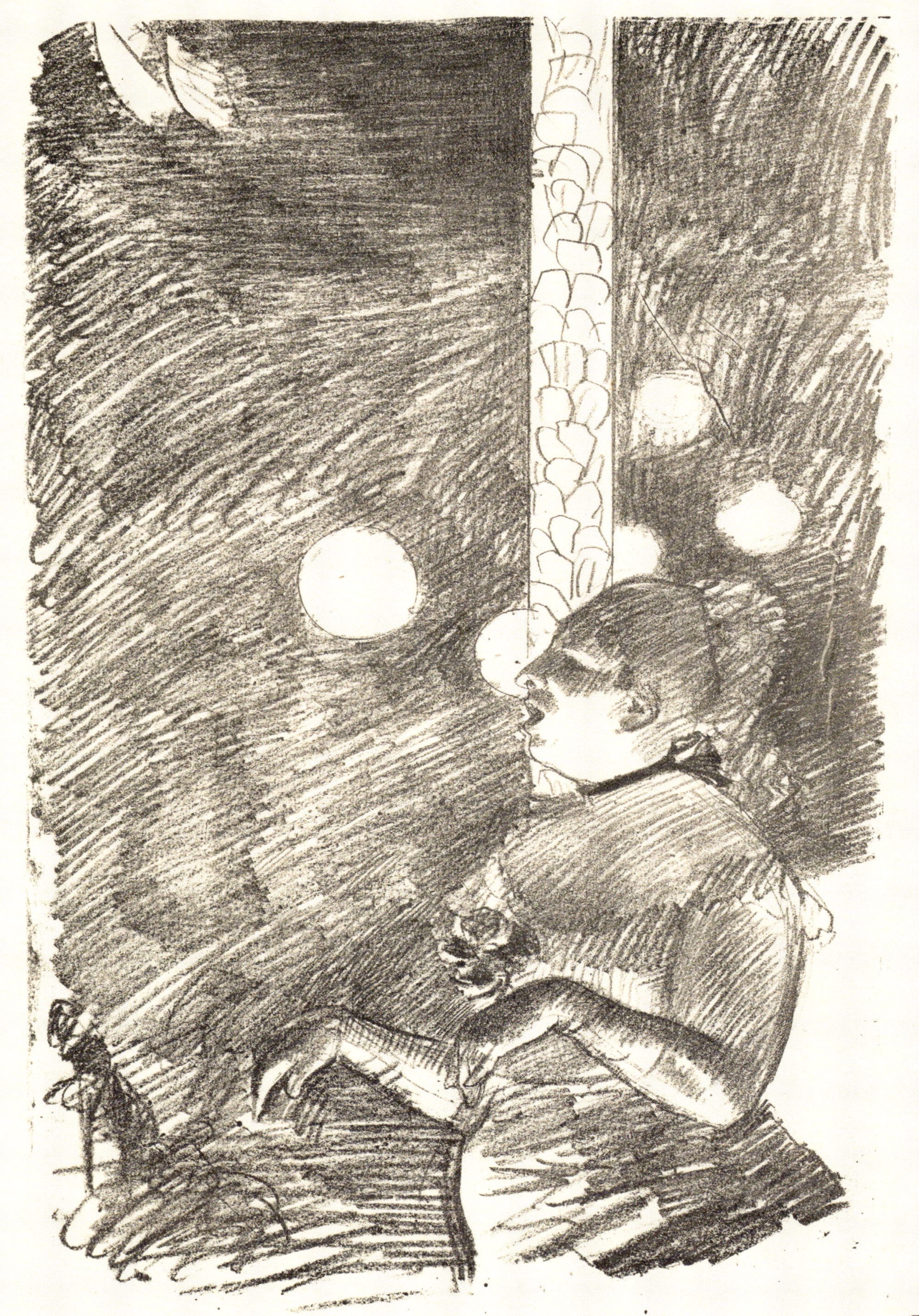

practitioners, including Eugène Delacroix and Théodore Gericault. Prominent artists such as Pierre Bonnard, Maurice Denis, and Édouard Vuillard adopted a persona of the *peintre-graveur*, embracing both mediums with equal dedication. Toward the end of the century, artists increasingly appropriated and transformed lithography for original art making, and café culture was a favored subject.

The adaptation of cafés and brasseries to cafés-concerts (known colloquially as *caf'-conc'*), where patrons could smoke, drink, and dine while performers offered song, dance, and comedy, began in the 1840s; growing substantially in number in the 1850s and 1860s, cafés-concerts reached the height of their popularity in the 1870s. Live entertainment could be found on the small indoor stages of these fashionable cafés or, in the summer, in the gardens and open-air pavilions of the Alcazar-d'Été and the Café des Ambassadeurs, both on the Champs-Élysées. Extensive gas lighting made these venues more festive for evening and late-night engagements. The program could be quite varied but typically followed a three-part format featuring singers and comics. The music was lively and occasionally bawdy, including popular tunes familiar to a diverse audience comprising all classes of Parisian society. Following a visit to one of the cafés-concerts on the Champs-Élysées, the art and literary critic Edmond de Goncourt noted, "An enthusiasm, an electricity, a fraternization of the audience joining in the refrain, as if it was a truly patriotic anthem."[3] Edgar Degas captured this form of merriment in a monotype with pastel (1875–77, formerly Havemeyer Collection) and lithograph, *The Song of the Dog* (1876–77, cat. 10). Moving the viewer from the loges to the main floor and stage of the Café des Ambassadeurs, Degas portrayed the famous performer Thérésa (born Emma Valadon). Occupying a significant portion of the composition, the singer stands with her arms and wrists bent in a pawlike

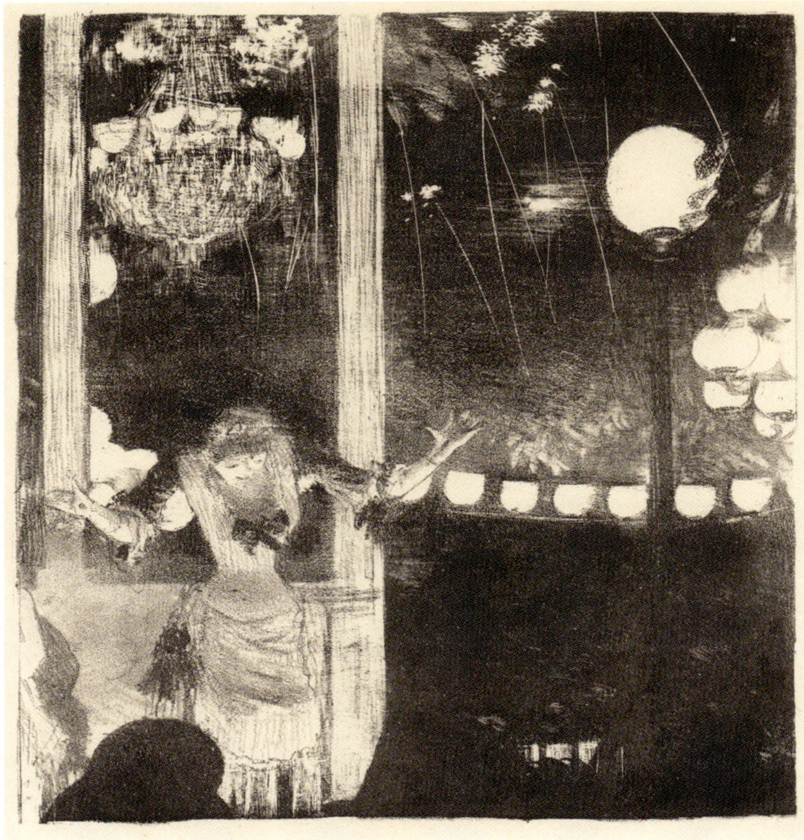

Fig. 44
Edgar Degas
French, 1834–1914
Mademoiselle Bécat at the Café des Ambassadeurs, Paris, 1877–78
Lithograph
image: 8 1/8 × 7 5/8 in. (20.6 × 19.4 cm)
sheet: 13 1/2 × 10 3/4 in. (34.3 × 27.3 cm)
The Metropolitan Museum of Art, New York, Rogers Fund, 1919

gesture. Her head is tilted upward, and her mouth open as she mimics a barking dog. In a letter of 1883 to the painter Henry Lerolle, Degas described Valadon's voice as "the most natural, the most delicate, and the most vibrantly tender."[4] Seen from a close vantage point, the figure dominates the scene. The background, hazily illuminated by scattered globes, is highly suggestive. Degas created the lithograph using crayon on paper, which was then transferred directly to the lithographic stone and printed.

Degas was one of the first in the circle of French Impressionists to portray the café-concert, treating the subject in a manner quite distinct from contemporary popular prints and illustrated weeklies. Images inspired by these cafés, primarily featuring singers, appeared in Degas's work around 1876 with a number of monotypes, some of which, reworked with pastel, were exhibited in 1877. Émilie Bécat, who made her debut at the Café des Ambassadeurs in 1875, also caught Degas's eye. The famed chanteuse had a formidable voice but was better known for her extraordinary dance repertoire that included frenzied movements and jumps described as "le style épileptique."[5] The lithograph *Mademoiselle Bécat at the Café des Ambassadeurs, Paris* (fig. 44) is exemplary of the artist's new printmaking direction around 1877-78.[6] In this work, the spotlighted Bécat stands with her arms raised and fingers splayed. The print also includes several of the artist's frequent motifs, including prominent, vertical architectural elements as well as cropped double basses and gentlemen's hats in the foreground. Extensive work in lithographic crayon is evident in the final print, demonstrably in the chandelier and fireworks, which appear to have been scraped with a tool. Here, as in other works, the artist pursued an experimental technique to capture modern subject matter.

The Ambassadeurs was a landmark, and some twenty years later it attracted the attention of Henri de Toulouse-Lautrec. In a lithograph made for *L'Estampe originale*, a quarterly print portfolio published by André Marty, Lautrec took on a similar scene. The contraction of space and prominent verticals in Lautrec's *At the Ambassadeurs—Café-Concert Singer* of 1894 (cat. 43) indicate an admiration for Degas, though the resulting print is markedly different. The composition employs a tripartite division typical of Japanese ukiyo-e woodcuts. A balustrade in the foreground effectively compresses all the visual information into the upper portion of the image, which appears quite flat with unmodulated, abutted areas of color. Only a few elements help establish the location: chandelier, trees, and clouds of smoke. While Degas situated the viewer among the audience, Lautrec positioned the viewer behind the performer, who gestures in her low-backed dress to an unseen crowd of spectators. The print also demonstrates Lautrec's experimentation with the medium. Lithography permits a great range of mark-making with a wide variety of tools, and Lautrec was especially well known for his *crachis*, a splatter effect achieved by raking the bristles of a brush across the stone, as seen in this print of the café-concert singer.

A great number of prints and portfolios celebrated the café-concert and its luminaries, but it was really through the artistic poster that artists came to not only reflect but help create this site of modern culture. The artistic poster occupied a unique position at the intersection of fine art, design, and advertising.[7] It was instrumental in the development of a modernist visual language comprising word and image. In its reproducibility and accessibility, it constituted an adaptation of fine art to an era of mass media and led to an unprecedented circulation of visual representations that could document, promote, and distill the image of the modern Parisian café.

Jules Chéret is credited with the invention of the artistic poster, bringing the more refined aesthetic and decorative sensibility of artistic lithography to the format of the commercial poster. When the French state made him chevalier in the Legion of Honor in 1890, the commendation was for "creating a new industry by applying art to commercial and industrial printing."[8] Chéret, and other innovative artists, were drawn to the poster as a site for experimentation, for representing modernity, for communicating with a broad audience, and for embracing an ephemerality that responded to a public interest in novelty and

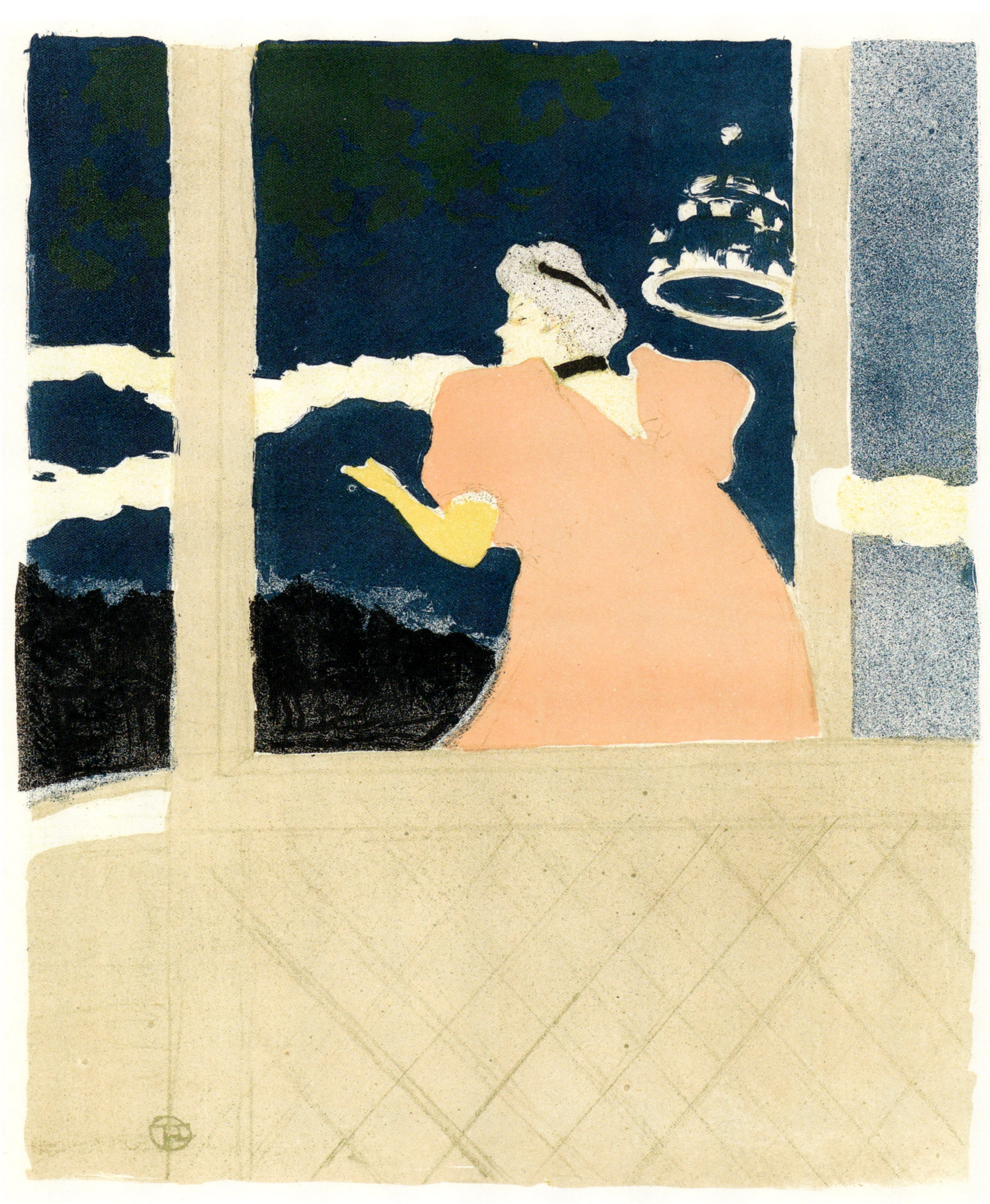

rapid change. Many contemporary texts discussed the role played by such posters in casting the café and its celebrities as modern icons while also transforming the city into an outdoor gallery.[9] As Lautrec declared, "The poster, that's all there is!"[10] The artistic poster was not just a casual and accessible medium: it was, like the café, a cultural phenomenon. Belonging both to the art world and to the world of the street, posters were the most visible and ubiquitous manifestations of a culture formed within the new café, a culture that prioritized the visual, and which, by the twentieth century, became identified as a culture of spectacle.

Henri de Toulouse-Lautrec understood the potential of the medium and its natural affiliation with café culture. His formal innovations—areas of broad, flat color, bold outlines, striking silhouettes, unusual points of view, and clever integration of text and image—could evoke the atmosphere of the café-concert and elevate the reputation of its program and performers. The artist strategically adapted his composition and style to complement specific venues and individuals, depicting the eclectic décor of a particular café and the defining gestures, costumes, and expressions of its habitués. Enthralled by certain performers for a single season or an entire career, Lautrec developed personal and professional obsessions, which he termed his *furias*, focused on particular figures.[11] He was especially drawn to individuals who excelled in crafting unique public personae—those who truly inhabited their roles, both on stage and off.

Jane Avril began her dancing career at the Moulin Rouge in 1889. Within a few years, she was the headline performer at its summer outpost, a café-concert on the Champs-Élysées known as the Jardin de Paris. Avril's mode of performance distinguished her from other dancers. She developed her own improvisational choreography, integrating her movements with the multilayered and colorful costumes she designed. She acquired the nickname La Mélinite, denoting a type of explosive.[12] An active agent in the construction of her own image, Avril commissioned Lautrec to design her first poster in the spring of 1893. As she had not yet signed a contract with a particular café-concert, the first edition of the poster included only Avril's name (fig. 45). At Avril's request, Lautrec made twenty impressions of the poster and signed them individually.[13] The highly inventive composition features Avril performing a cancan kick, framed within a musical border. Lautrec extended the neck of the double bass up and around to create a slightly irregular outline, culminating at the lower right with a caricatured bass player, brow furrowed in concentration while he holds the instrument. At the center, Avril appears wearing her signature bonnet. Her black-stockinged legs contrast sharply with the yellow and white undergarments of her orange skirt, which coordinate with the color of her hair. While this costume may have been Lautrec's invention, such carefully orchestrated color combinations were certainly in keeping with Avril's practices. Moreover, the representation evidences Lautrec's admiration for Avril and the aesthetic sophistication of her act. The critic Arsène Alexandre regarded the poster as one of Lautrec's finest works, commending the artist's ability to evoke the spectacle of Avril's performance, which was a blend of brazenness and finesse.[14] Soon after the initial printing, Avril began performing at the Jardin de Paris and obtained the café's approval to use the design to promote her show there. The name of the establishment, "Le Jardin de Paris," was added to the poster and a larger print run was ordered.[15] While

Cat. 43

Henri de Toulouse-Lautrec
French, 1864–1901
At the Ambassadeurs—Café-Concert Singer, 1894
Color lithograph (crayon, tusche, and splatter)
image: 12 ⅛ × 9 ¹¹⁄₁₆ in. (30.6 × 24.6 cm)
Cincinnati Art Museum; Bequest of Herbert Greer French, 1943.685

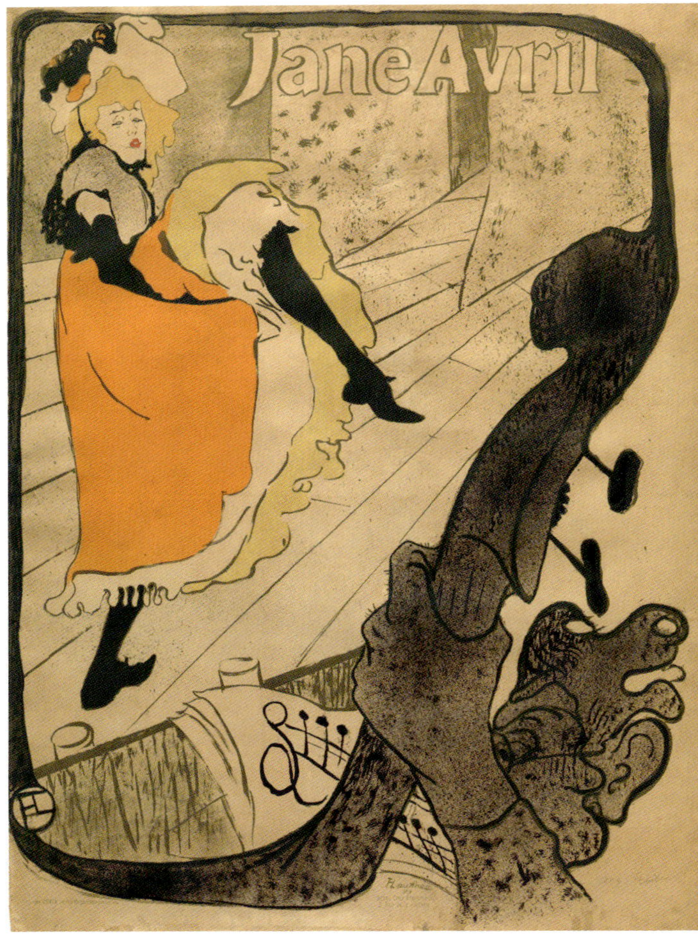

Fig. 45
Henri de Toulouse-Lautrec
French, 1864–1901
Jane Avril, 1893
Lithograph
image: 48 ¹³⁄₁₆ × 34 ¹⁵⁄₁₆ in. (124 × 88.8 cm)
sheet: 49 ⅝ × 36 ⅛ in. (126 × 91.8 cm)
The Museum of Modern Art, New York; Gift
of A. Conger Goodyear, 456.1954

the Moulin Rouge had been a premier venue for entertainment, Avril's performances at the Jardin helped to entice customers from Montmartre, who could travel in a bus organized by the proprietor, Charles Zidler.

In the 1893 poster *Divan Japonais* (cat. 36), Lautrec portrayed Avril as a fashionable patron taking in a performance by Yvette Guilbert. Avril is seated next to Édouard Dujardin, the critic, editor, and founder of the literary journal *La Revue wagnérienne* and of *La Revue indépendante*, whose attention is fixed on Avril rather than Guilbert. Decorated with lanterns and bamboo chairs, the Divan Japonais capitalized on the vogue for *japonisme*—a fascination with Japanese art and design—that had taken hold in Paris in the 1860s. Located on the Rue des Martyrs in Montmartre, the Divan Japonais opened in 1882 and transformed into a café-concert under the direction of Édouard Fournier by 1892. Yvette Guilbert began her career at the venue, and the stage was later graced by Jane Avril. The Divan Japonais attracted aesthetes, such as Dujardin, an advocate of *japonisme* in his own writings. Much of this information is conveyed in Lautrec's poster, which operates on multiple levels. Avril's figure dominates the composition, with Dujardin appearing partially cropped in the right margin and Guilbert depicted headless, though easily identifiable by her long black gloves and lithe form, in the background. Dujardin may be interpreted as a flâneur—that Parisian type, like his peers in dress in demeanor, yet distinguished by his refinement and connoisseurship. Yet it is less the people or place portrayed than the brilliant compositional structure that makes this image an emblem of modern spectatorship and sociability within the café. Avril, appearing self-possessed and yet also on display, focuses

Cat. 36

Henri de Toulouse-Lautrec
French, 1864–1901
Divan Japonais, 1893
Lithograph (printer: Edward Ancourt, Paris)
31 ¹⁵⁄₁₆ × 23 ¾ in. (81.2 × 60.3 cm)
Joslyn Art Museum; Gift of the Estate of
Lenore Polack, 2022.17.19

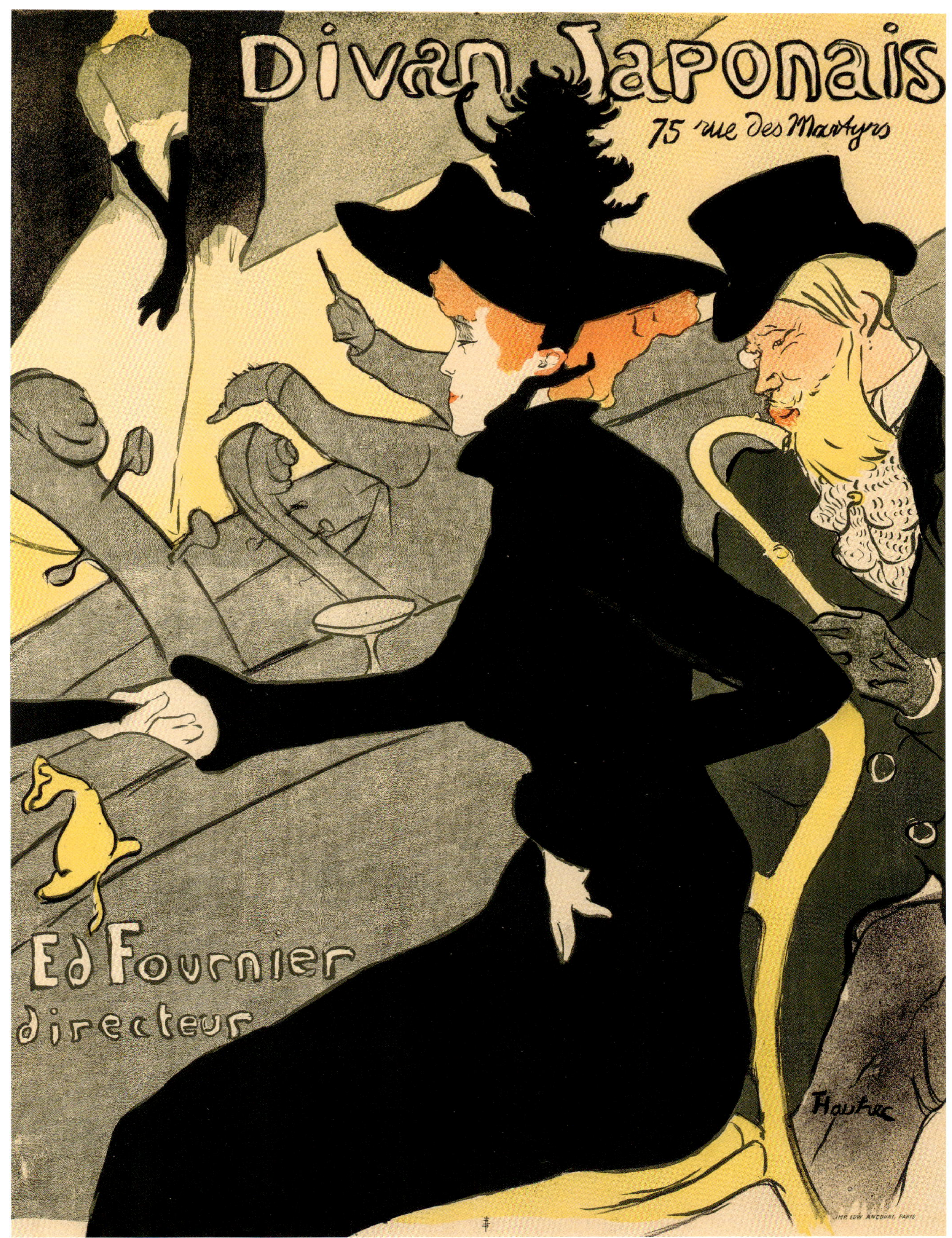

Divan Japonais
75 rue des Martyrs
Ed Fournier
directeur

her gaze on the performance, while Dujardin sets his own on her, and indirectly on the viewer, emphasizing the multiple misdirected attentions. Dujardin is at once a spectator and part of the spectacle.[16] The perceptiveness required to orchestrate the narrative and symbolic logic of a poster such as *Divan Japonais* was immediately recognizable to contemporary critics. As André Mellerio wrote, "[Lautrec] has mastered the science of particular behaviors, which he had dressed in the garb of our epoch, known as the *fin de siècle*."[17] Lautrec's posters helped to foment the café as the true theater of modern life.

Lautrec's obsession with a performer would often manifest in a series of images. One of the artist's longtime *furias* was the acclaimed stage performer Yvette Guilbert, hailed at the time as "the most brilliant star in the café-concert firmament today," who had "completely revolutionized the style of presentation of songs."[18] After her Paris theater debut at the age of twenty, Guilbert became a star of the café-concert scene, performing at the Moulin Rouge and Divan Japonais. Rather than singing, she spoke her songs, often laced with obscenities, in a low tone. She delivered the lyrics while standing completely still without gesture or expression. She created a stage look quite distinct from that of her contemporaries: dyed red hair, pale skin, formfitting gowns to accentuate her slender figure, and elbow-length black gloves. Recalling the donning of her trademark accessory, she wrote: "I was looking out for a silhouette. . . . I took care to wear them with light-colored dresses and to wear them so long that they exaggerated the willowiness of my arms and made my shoulders and neck seem even more slender and slim."[19] This stage persona was memorialized in an 1894 album comprising seventeen lithographs by Lautrec and accompanying text by Gustave Geffroy, elaborating the performer's character and the milieu of the café-concert.

In 1894, Guilbert brought her popular act to the Café des Ambassadeurs. Lautrec's initial design for

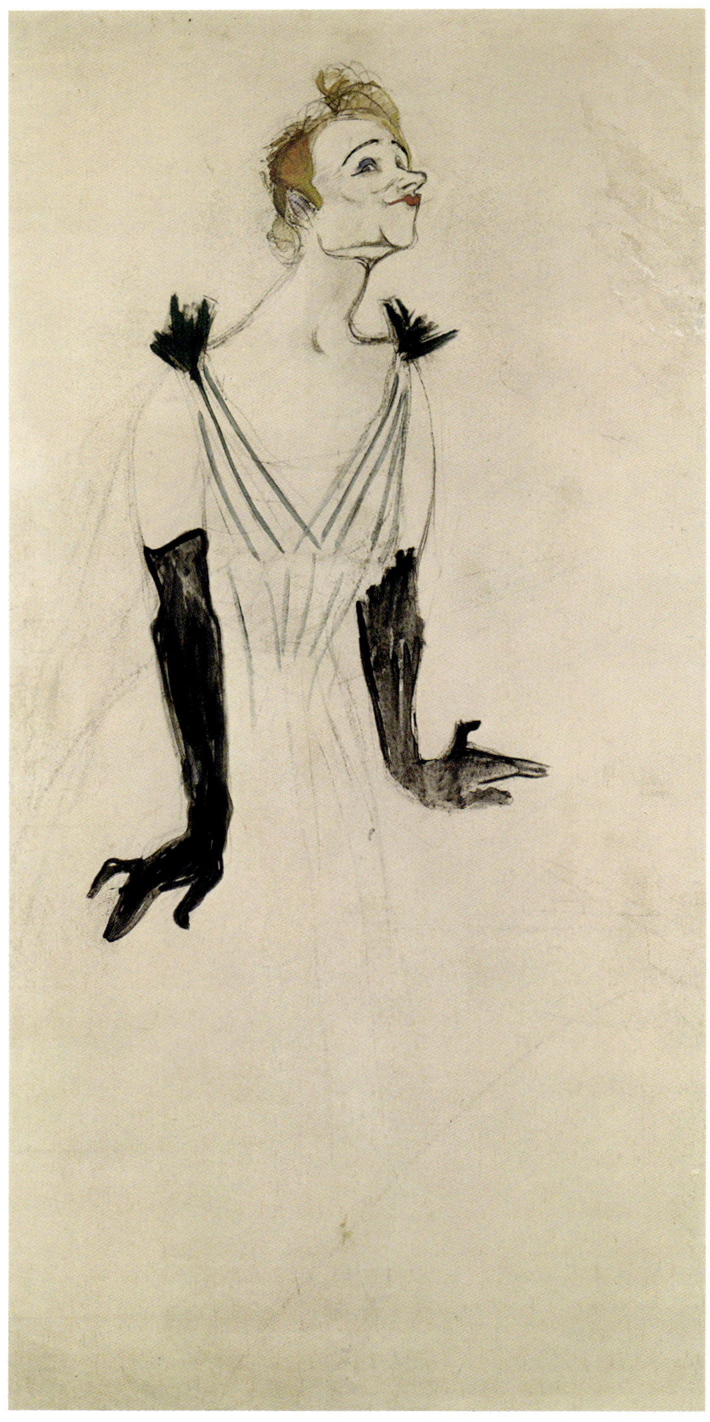

Fig. 46
Henri de Toulouse-Lautrec
French, 1864–1901
Yvette Guilbert, 1894
Gouache and charcoal on paper
73 ¼ × 36 ⅝ in. (186 × 93 cm)
Musée Toulouse-Lautrec, Albi

a poster to promote her upcoming season at the more upscale café shows the performer standing at the edge of the stage, her neck extended and other features quite exaggerated (fig. 46). Guilbert found the rendering rather unpleasant, recalling, "For the love of heaven don't make me so atrociously ugly! Just a little less!"[20] After rejecting Lautrec's sketch, she turned to another prominent poster artist and fixture of the café scene, Théophile Alexandre Steinlen. The two-sheet poster *Yvette Guilbert / Ambassadeurs* (cat. 42) presents an almost life-size image of its subject. Steinlen cleverly employed the poster's vertical format to emphasize Guilbert's tall, slender form. She appears at the edge of a curtain, poised to go on stage in an elegant floor-length dress and black gloves. The right side of the poster depicts the orchestra led by the conductor, who raises his baton, and the audience, arranged in rows, many in white shirts and top hats. Above the crowd, the artist sketched the globe lights of the garden. Steinlen produced a poster with an elegant design and a flattering likeness befitting the venue.

Cafés-concerts that hosted evening entertainment also competed with music halls such as the Folies-Bergère and the Eldorado. This variation of the café establishment functioned in many ways as a variety-entertainment theater, boasting a repertory that encompassed musical comedies and revues, short operettas, select vaudeville and circus acts, commercial ballets, and popular and modern dance performances. Jules Chéret's fluid line, exuberant color, and artful lettering were particularly well suited to convey the grandiose spectacles of the Parisian music hall. In the eyes of discerning critics and the general public alike, Chéret's lithographic work appeared to replace the hard, mechanical character of earlier commercial posters with a "vaporous impression" that evoked the delicate and powdery quality of pastel.[21] His innovative printing techniques made it possible for him to create these artistic posters swiftly and inexpensively. The lithographic process traditionally

involves discrete colors applied with a separate stone. Chéret developed a process of printing from three stones—one red, one black, and one with a background that progressed from orange to blue. The process became more sophisticated when he expanded his workshop and, in 1881, merged his press with the printing company Imprimerie Chaix. As artistic director, he managed a team of artists and a fleet of steam-powered presses and was able to print with four or even five colors. Despite his growing operation and prolific output, Chéret maintained a unique and recognizable style, which commentators described as dynamic, in motion, and full of life.[22]

Jules Chéret's ability to convey the energy of his subjects is exemplified in the posters promoting the Paris debut of the innovative American performer Loïe Fuller. Born in a suburb of Chicago, Marie Louise Fuller began her career as a child actress and later choreographed and performed dances in burlesque, vaudeville, and circus shows. She conceived revolutionary routines in which her movements, set to the music of Debussy, Chopin, and Schubert, were amplified by elaborate costumes and novel lighting schemes. In Fuller's own words, she "created something new, something composed of light, color, music, and the dance."[23] Bamboo poles attached to her garments allowed her to manipulate dozens of yards of lightweight silk that billowed around her. Her production design included a darkened stage and early electric lights with hand-turned colored gels over bulbs that created kaleidoscopic effects. For her act at the Folies-Bergère in 1892, she performed her signature serpentine dance, butterfly dance, violet dance, and the so-called white dance, in which she twirled swiftly, enveloped in white fabric under lights that continuously shifted color. Arsène Alexandre described Fuller as "the marvelous dream-creature you see dancing madly in a vision swirling among her dappled veils, which change ten thousand times a minute."[24] Fuller was the

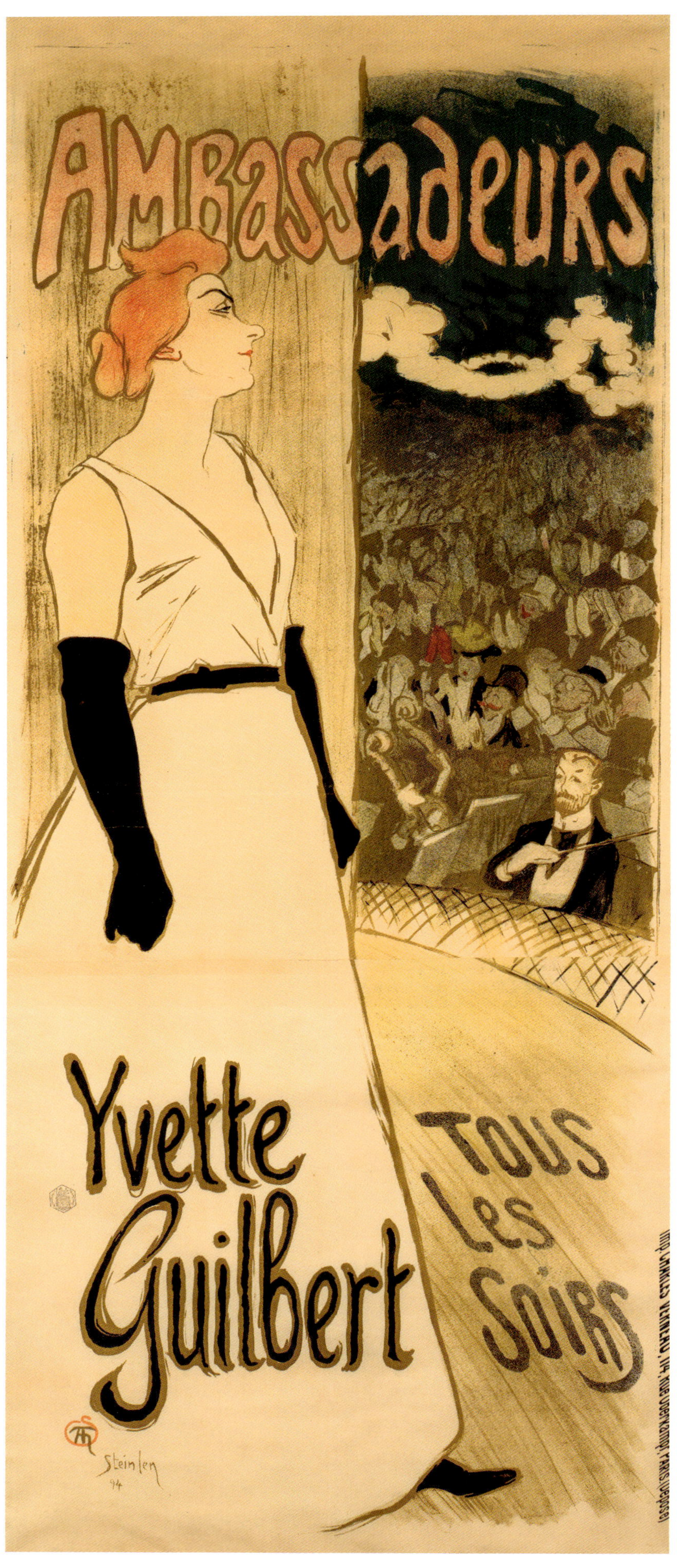

Cat. 42

Théophile Alexandre Steinlen
Swiss, 1859–1923
Yvette Guilbert / Ambassadeurs, 1894
Lithograph (printer: Charles Verneau, Paris)
71 ¾ × 31 ⅛ in. (182.3 × 79.1 cm)
Joslyn Art Museum; Gift of the Estate of
Lenore Polack, 2022.17.18

first performer to offer an afternoon program, and she was affectionately called the "Fairy of Light" by the mothers and children who attended the matinees. While the Lumière brothers would later attempt to capture her style of dance on film, Jules Chéret managed to convey a cinematic effect in lithography through a progressive series of images, including *Folies-Bergère / La Loïe Fuller* (1893, cat. 37). In this poster, the outline of Fuller's body is visible beneath a transparent gown, and swirling curves intimate motion. With her head thrown back, the viewer has a sense of the drama of her movements. Her dainty feet and slim arms peeking out from the folds of fabric suggest the volume of her trademark costume. To convey the brilliant and varied colors she achieved with her lighting effects, Chéret printed the same image in four color combinations. The series demonstrated the very effective application of conventions closely associated with product advertising, including commercial printing and seriality, to create a distinct brand, as much for the performer and the venue as for the artist.

While Jules Chéret astutely depicted recognizable café performers and venues, he also invented a clever and resolutely modern iconography that captured the Parisian café society in all its frivolity, gaiety, and sensuality.[25] The *chérette* (named after him) was a popular, fantasy figure the artist enlisted to promote commercial products and various entertainments, admiringly described by the British critic Joseph Thacher Clarke as "an elusive and evanescent vision."[26] Critics discerned Chéret's art historical references, namely rococo and classical art, which led them to regard the *chérette* as charming, delicate, or a "Parisian Aphrodite," even as she was highly sexualized.[27] Chéret also developed a cast of colorful types, including acrobats, musicians, and clowns, to capture the excitement and variety of the performances staged at a particular venue. Redeployed across prints, these

figures became a visual shorthand, comprehensible by passersby, and enticing enough to encourage them to seek out the amusements and experience them for themselves. Chéret used this strategy in his 1894 poster for the Eldorado (cat. 41). Located on the Boulevard de Strasbourg, the Eldorado was a popular music hall boasting a brilliantly decorated interior and varied program. Rather than promote a specific artist or revue, Chéret's poster evokes the lively atmosphere and pageantry that was on offer every night. A leaping woman dressed in a suggestive gown trimmed in gold holds a tambourine in her left hand, while her right arm is thrown up in an exuberant gesture. At the lower right, a clown strums a banjo while another raises his finger to his lips. Their twisted poses and jumps suggest carefree motion, while their arrangement and almost indeterminate placement within space conjure a world of pleasure and escapism. While the generalized characters and scene convey the idea that such delights are always on offer, the ephemeral nature of Chéret's chosen medium—a poster that would be posted and then likely covered over or removed in days or weeks—was fitting for a café culture that capitalized on the belief that the city was changing and that modernity had accelerated the pace of daily life.[28]

The Symbolist writer Joris-Karl Huysmans was among the first to laud Chéret in the press, insisting that his "chromos" were more representative of Parisian life than many of the formulaic submissions to the official exhibition of the 1879 Salon.[29] And the art critic Roger Marx praised their documentary quality: "Browse through the lithographic work of Chéret, it will seem to you to be an illustrated chronicle of the era, ready-prepared documentation for historians curious about the details of our way of life."[30] These contemporary assessments attest to a particular criterion for aesthetic achievement in late nineteenth-century Paris that was not grounded in

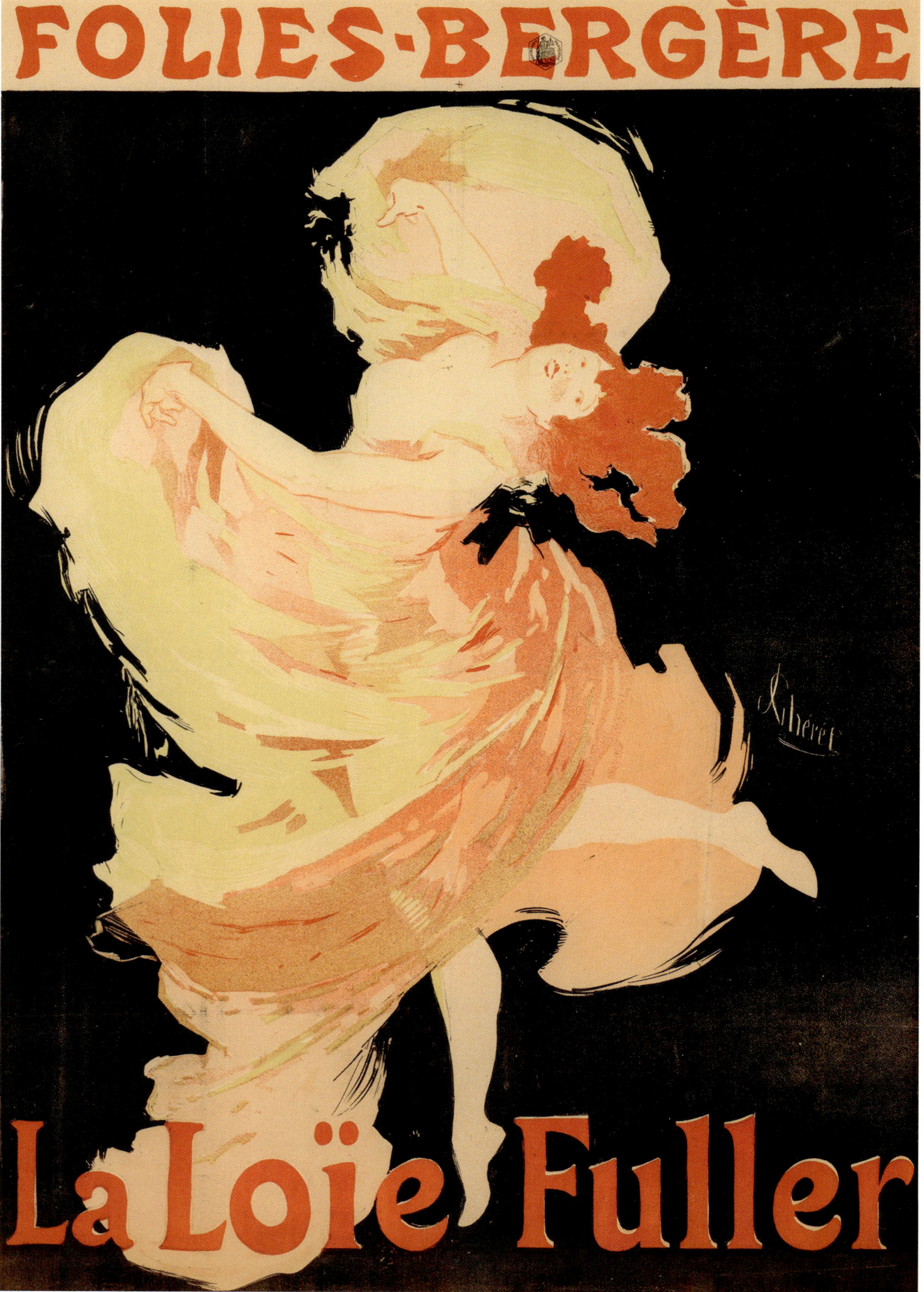

Cat. 37

Jules Chéret
French, 1836–1932
Folies-Bergère / La Loïe Fuller, 1893
Lithograph (printer: Imprimerie Chaix, Paris)
48 ½ × 34 ½ in. (123.2 × 87.6 cm)
Joslyn Art Museum; Gift of the Estate of Lenore Polack, 2022.17.3

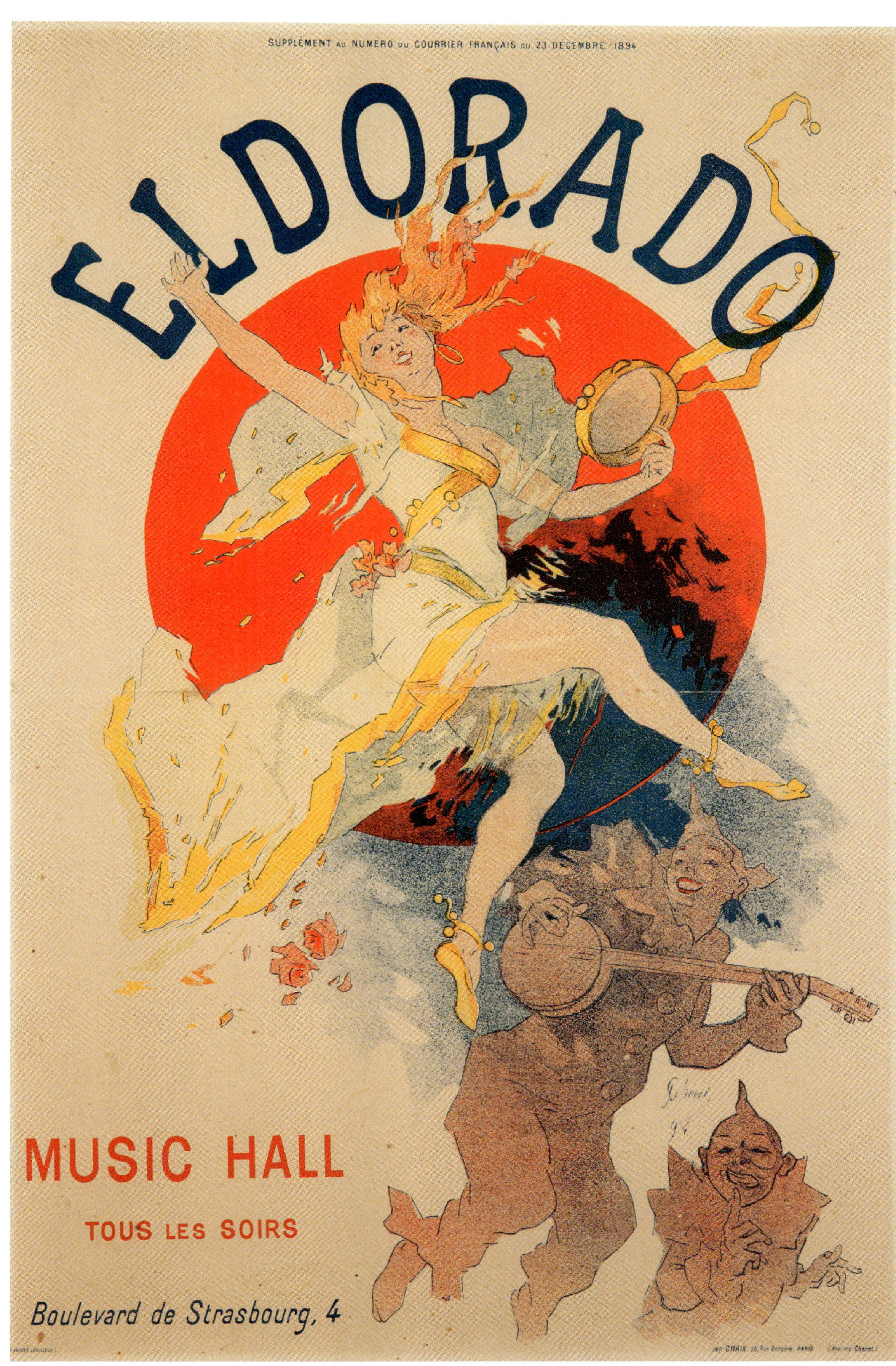

Cat. 41

Jules Chéret
French, 1836–1932
Eldorado, 1894
Color lithograph
22 × 15 in. (55.9 × 38.1 cm)
Dixon Gallery and Gardens;
Museum purchase, Gift of the
Dixon Gallery and Gardens
Staff, 2015 2

timeless, absolute, or universal ideals, but rather in a sense that art should be of its time. The author Félicien Champsaur, who enlisted Chéret to illustrate the printed text of his play *La Gomme* (1889), considered the artist to be the "king of the poster" and the "master of our modernity," proclaiming, "More than any other designer of this genre, Chéret has the distinctive feature of his time; and this time, we love it."[31]

Photographs, prints, and paintings from the last decade of the nineteenth century depicted walls filled with illustrated posters and, notably, with recognizable posters by Chéret.[32] In an 1898 portrait of the Symbolist poet Henri-François-Joseph de Régnier painted by Nicolas Félix Escalier, the subject appears standing confidently in front of a wall plastered with posters (cat. 45). Régnier circulated among the intellectuals, writers, and artists that patronized the city's cafés. He also cultivated a distinct public image and presumably would have impressed upon the painter his desire to be portrayed as a modern aesthete. Régnier appears with his signature monocle, wearing a fashionable suit and top hat, and carrying an umbrella. Cast as the archetype of the boulevardier, he is posed before one of the city's many billboards with posters pasted edge to edge. While the posters appear overlapping, cropped, or partially obscured, four may be identified: Chéret's posters for the Eldorado (1894, cat. 41), the fortified wine Vin Mariani (1894), and the Grands Magasins du Louvre (1897)—a prominent department store on the Place du Palais-Royal—as well as a poster by Jules-Alexandre Grün for the cabaret La Cigale (1898). The painter's accurate representation of specific posters gives the impression that he chose an actual Paris wall to reproduce for the background of the portrait. However, the concentration of posters by a single artist, even Chéret, seems unlikely, as does the presence of posters known to have been printed in 1894 and 1897, which surely would have been removed or pasted over by 1898,

when the painting was made. Instead, one can infer that Escalier consciously selected these posters to convey something more about himself or his subject, whether an appreciation for the work of Chéret, for posters, for café culture, or for the visual character of the modern city. Certainly, their inclusion is a testament to the prominence of lithography in the public imagination.

Artists and writers of the late nineteenth century were concerned with representing and comprehending their contemporary moment, which they perceived to be demonstrably different from even the recent past. The nature of lithography—swift, efficient, inexpensive, and adaptive to new techniques—encouraged many critics to adopt it as a symbol of modernity. The café, in all its iterations, engendered modern concepts of performance and spectatorship that consecrated the stars of the stage and the cafés themselves as modern icons. Café culture inspired visual culture, and, as this essay has argued, some of the most compelling depictions of the café were executed by artists enlisting lithography as a mode of representation preferred for its ephemeral, mutable, and modern qualities. The artistic print and the café, developed in France, and most especially in Paris, were hallmarks of the fin de siècle. These cultural phenomena remade public space, prompted a reassessment of high and low culture, and fostered new forms of sociability for a modern era.

Cat. 45

Nicolas Félix Escalier
French, 1843–1920
Henri-François-Joseph de Régnier, 1898
Oil on canvas
15 ¾ × 11 ¼ in. (40 × 28.6 cm)
Dixon Gallery and Gardens; Museum purchase, 2015.1

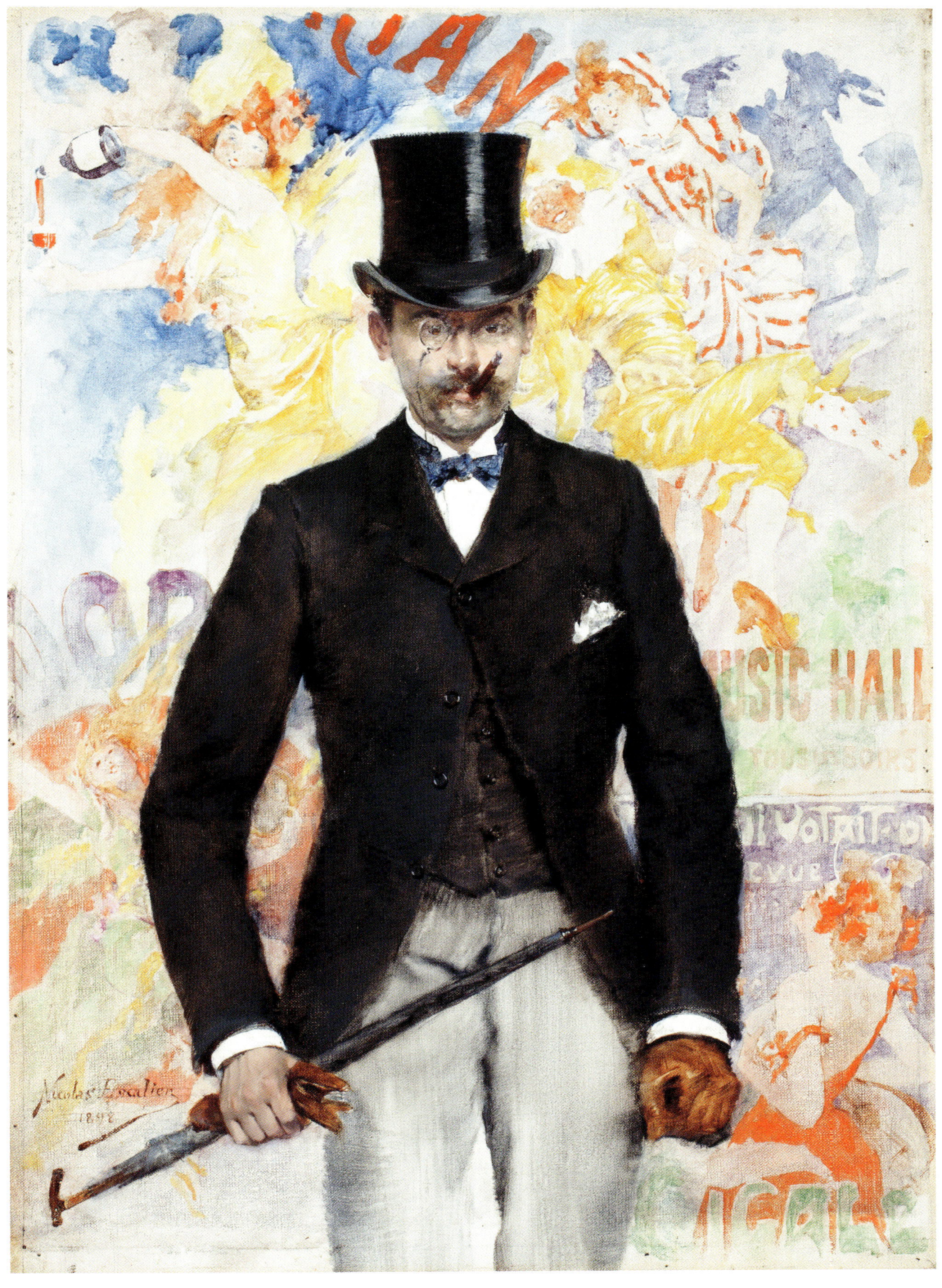

Endnotes

1. *Illustrated Guide to Paris* (London: Cassell, 1884), 111.

2. Ibid., 123.

3. Edmond de Goncourt and Jules de Goncourt, *Journal des Goncourt: Mémoires de la vie littéraire*, vol. 2, *1864–1878*, ed. Robert Ricatte (Paris: Fasquelle and Flammarion, 1956), 1143.

4. Quoted in Jean Sutherland Boggs, *Degas* (New York: Metropolitan Museum of Art / Paris: RMN / Ottawa: National Gallery of Canada, 1988), 291.

5. Anne Joly, "Sur deux modèles de Degas," *Gazette des Beaux-Arts* 69, no. 1180–81 (May–June 1967): 373-74.

6. Degas's technique has been discussed in Theodore Reff, *Degas: The Artist's Mind* (New York: Metropolitan Museum of Art, 1976), 282–88; Sue Reed and Barbara Shapiro, *Edgar Degas: The Painter as Printmaker* (Boston: Museum of Fine Arts Boston, 1985), no. 31; and Boggs, *Degas*, 292-93.

7. For an account of the development, proliferation, and reception of the nineteenth-century poster, see Ruth E. Iskin, *The Poster: Art, Advertising, Design, and Collecting, 1860s-1900s* (Hanover, NH: Dartmouth College Press, 2014).

8. *Journal des artistes* (April 13, 1890), cited in Réjane Bargiel and Ségolène Le Men, *La Belle Époque de Jules Chéret: De l'affiche au décor* (Paris: Les Arts décoratifs and Bibliotèque nationale de France, 2010), 125.

9. See Nicholas-Henri Zmelty, *L'Affiche illustrée au temps de l'affichomanie (1889-1905)* (Paris: Mare & Martin, 2014).

10. Julie Frey, *Toulouse-Lautrec: A Life* (New York: Viking Press, 1994), 357.

11. Ibid., 112.

12. There is much literature on Avril's artistry; see, for example, Catherine Pedley-Hindson, "Jane Avril and the Entertainment Lithograph: The Female Celebrity and *fin-de-siècle* Questions of Corporeality and Performance," *Theater Research International* 30, no. 2 (2005): 107-23.

13. Frey, *Toulouse-Lautrec: A Life*, 325.

14. Arsène Alexandre, "Celle qui danse," *L'Art français*, July 29, 1893, reproduced and translated as "She Who Dances," in *Toulouse-Lautrec and Jane Avril: Beyond the Moulin Rouge*, ed. Nancy Ireson (London: Courtauld Gallery, 2011), 131.

15. Estimated to be one thousand to three thousand. Götz Adriani, *Toulouse-Lautrec: The Complete Graphic Works, a Catalogue Raisonné; The Gerstenberg Collection* (London: Royal Academy of Arts / Thames & Hudson, 1988), 40. See also Iskin, *The Poster*, 88–89.

16. Vanessa R. Schwartz has sensitively argued that the flâneur is not so much a person as *flânerie* is a position of power and privilege through which the individual is able to be part of the spectacle and in command of it at the same time. See Schwartz, *Spectacular Realities: Early Mass Culture in Fin-de-Siècle Paris* (Berkeley, Los Angeles, and London: University of California Press, 1998), 10–11.

17. André Mellerio, *Le Mouvement idéaliste en peinture* (Paris: H. Floury, 1896), 36.

18. Victor Joncières, *Le Figaro* (June 1896), quoted in *Toulouse-Lautrec, 1864-1901* (Montreal: Musée des Beaux-Arts de Montréal, 1968), 17.

19. Yvette Guilbert, *The Song of My Life: My Memories*, trans. Béatrice de Holthoir (London: G. G. Harrap & Co., 1929), 65, 67.

20. Quoted in Theodore B. Donson and Marcel M. Griepp, *Henri de Toulouse-Lautrec: Performers of the Stage and the Boudoir, 1891-1899* (New York: Theodore B. Donson, 1980), no. 22.

21. Camille Mauclair, *Jules Chéret* (Paris: Maurice Le Garrec, 1930), 22.

22. Ernest Maindron, *Les Affiches illustrées, 1886-1895* (Paris: G. Boudet, 1896), 48.

23. Loïe Fuller, *Fifteen Years of a Dancer's Life, with Some Account of Her Distinguished Friends* (New York: Dance Horizons, 1978), 62.

24. Arsène Alexandre, "Le théâtre de la Loïe Fuller," *Le Théâtre* 4 (August 11, 1900): 24.

25. Mauclair, *Jules Chéret*, 77-78.

26. Quoted in Edward Bella, ed., *A Collection of Posters: The Illustrated Catalogue of the First Exhibition* (London: Royal Aquarium, 1894), 9. On the *chérette*, see Marius Verhagen, "The Poster in *Fin-de-Siècle* Paris: 'That Mobile and Degenerate Art,'" in *Cinema and the Invention of Modern Life*, ed. Leo Charney and Vanessa R. Schwartz (Berkeley: University of California Press, 1995), 103-29.

27. Iskin, *The Poster*, 52; Marius Vachon, *Les Arts et les industries du papier en France* (Paris: Librairies-Imprimeries Réunies, 1894), 200.

28. Nikki Otten has thoughtfully articulated the connection between the ephemerality of Jules Chéret's posters and contemporary ideas about modernity and the experience of time. Otten, "Lithographic Monuments: The Ephemeral as Modern in Chéret's Posters," in *Always New: The Posters of Jules Chéret*, ed. Nikki Otten (Milwaukee: Milwaukee Art Museum, 2022), 15-33.

29. J.-K. Huysmans, "Le Salon de 1879," *L'Art moderne*, June 10, 1879. See also Karen L. Carter, "Joris-Karl Huysmans, a *Dénicheur* of Jules Chéret's Posters," *Nineteenth-Century French Studies* 41, nos. 1-2 (Fall-Winter 2012-13): 122-41.

30. *La Plume*, no. 110 (November 15, 1893): 483-85.

31. Félicien Champsaur, "Le Roi de l'affiche," *La Plume*, no. 110 (November 15, 1893): 481-82.

32. On artworks depicting posters, see Mary Weaver Chapin, *Posters of Paris: Toulouse-Lautrec and His Contemporaries* (Munich: DelMonico Books, 2012), 12-21, and Iskin, *The Poster*, 192-202.

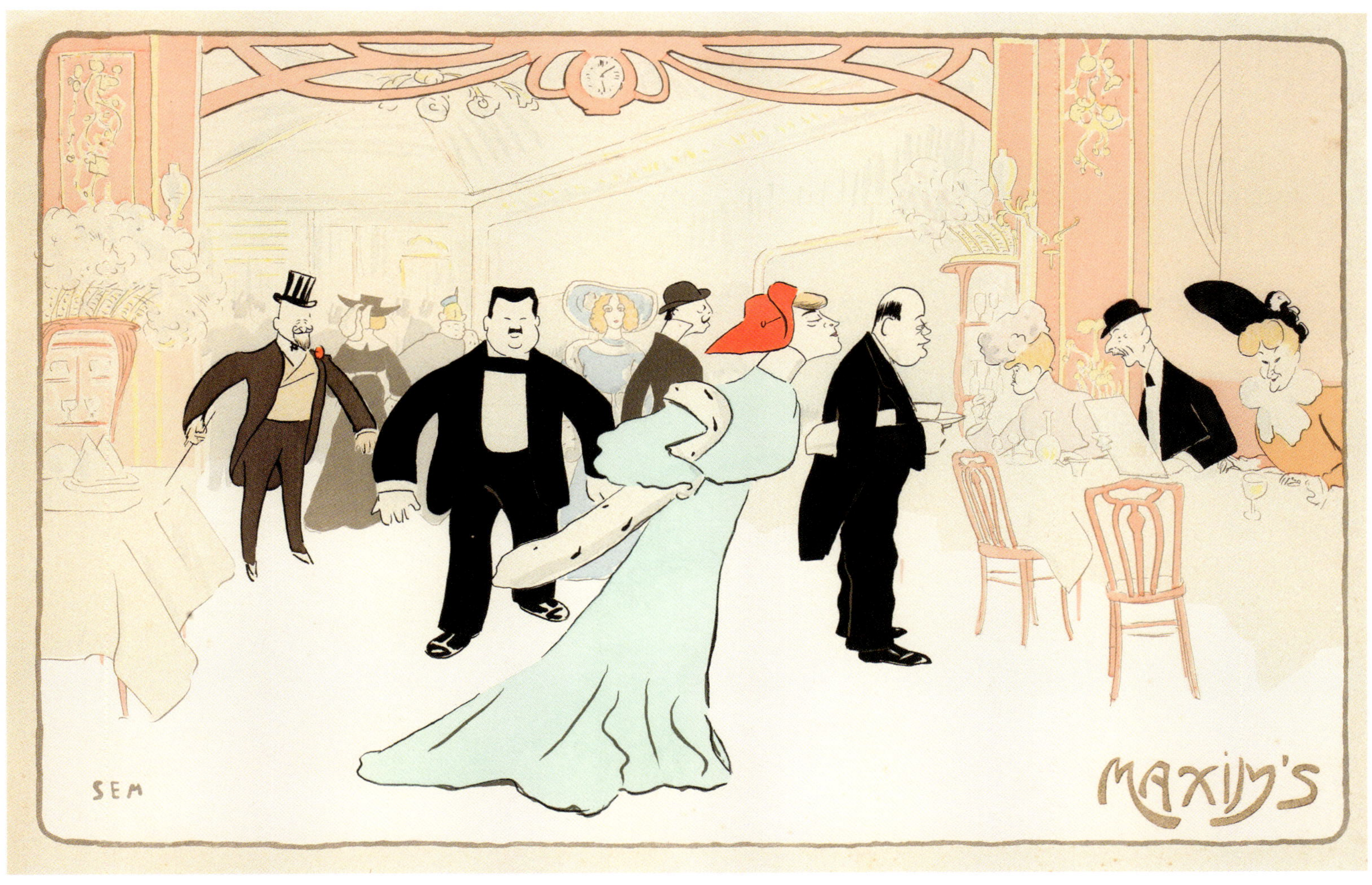

Cat. 53

SEM [Georges Goursat]
French, 1863–1934
Chez Maxim's, 1904
Pochoir and lithograph
11 ¾ × 18 in. (29.8 × 45.7 cm)
Private collection, Memphis

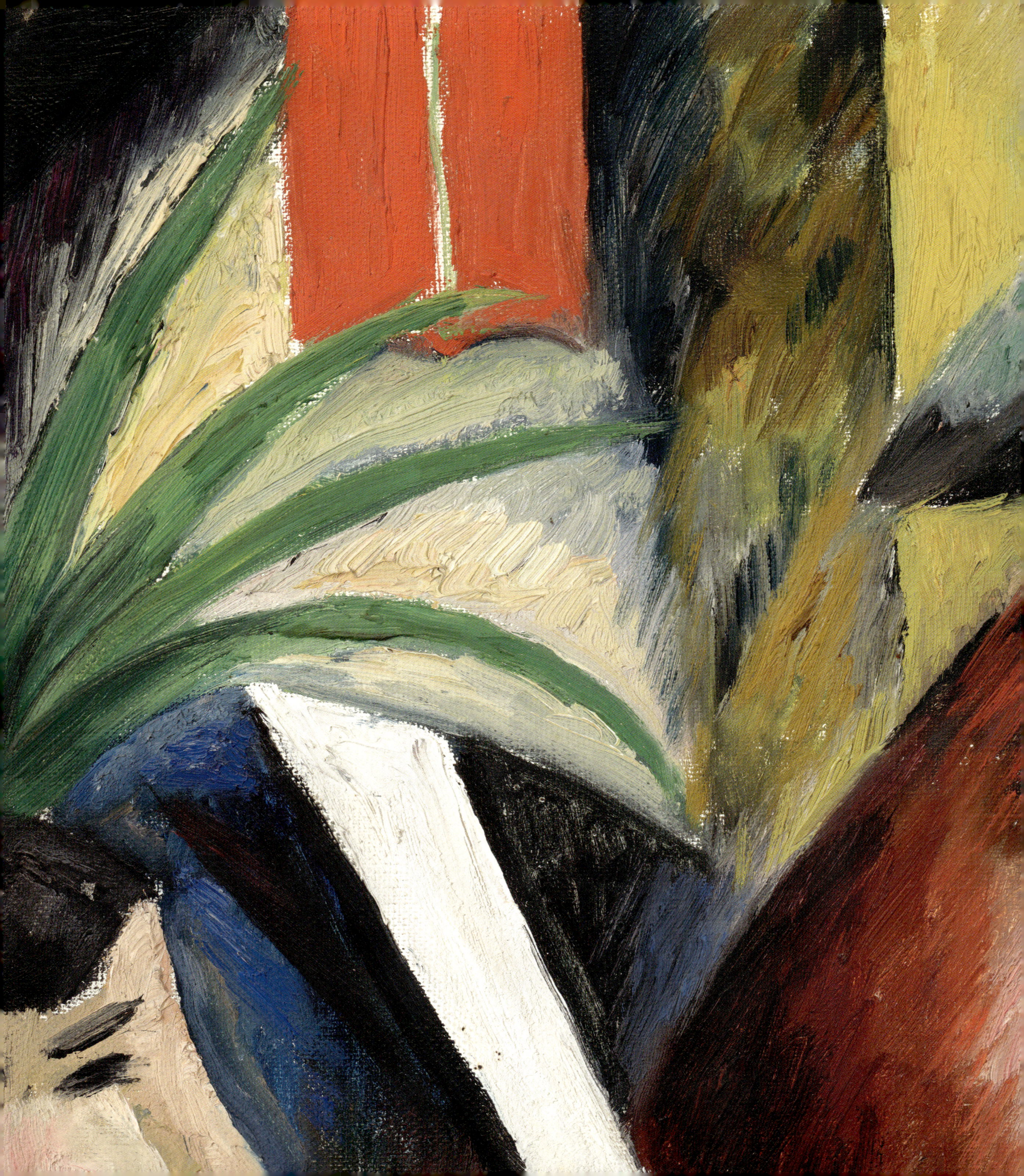

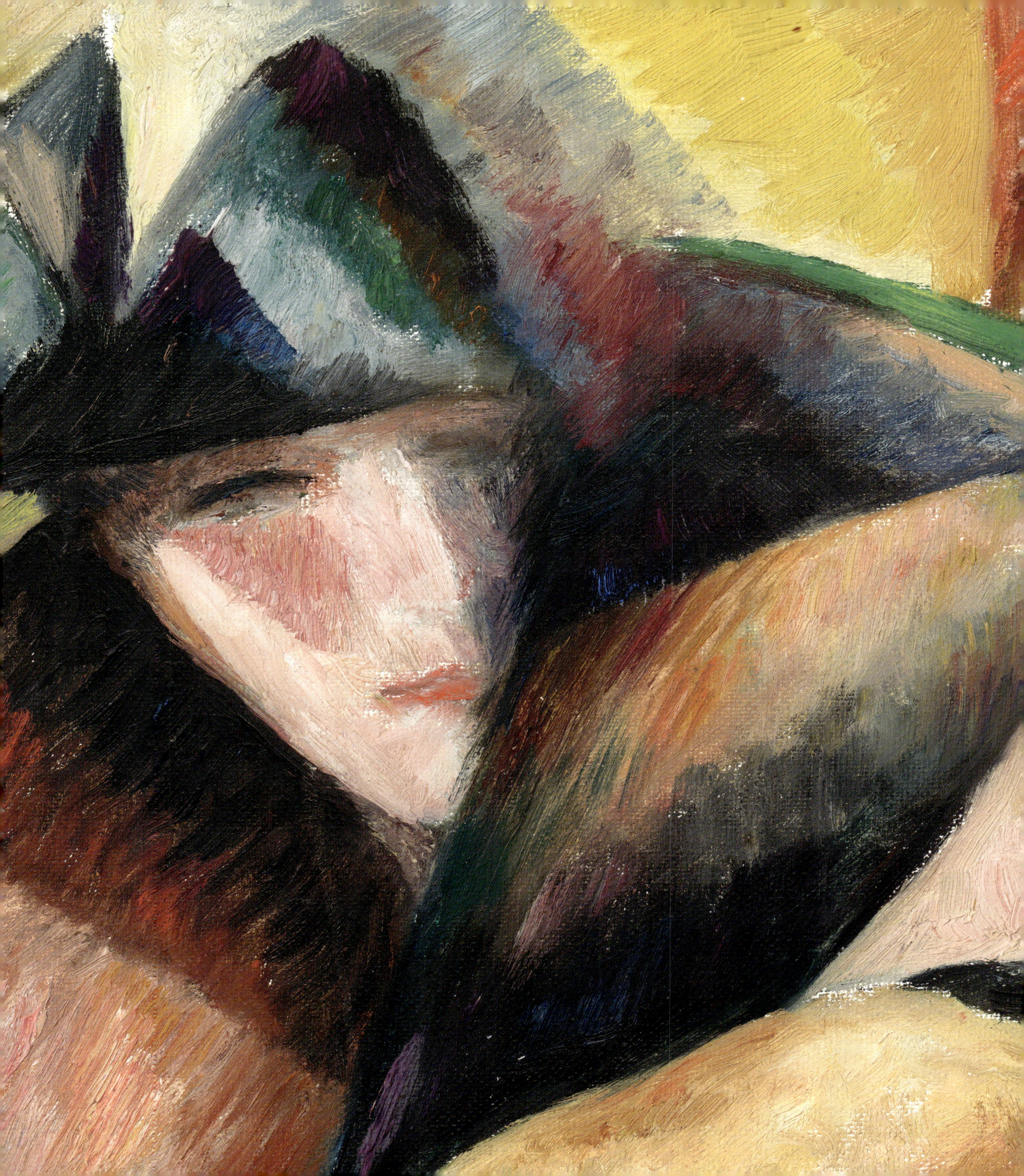

CATALOGUE OF THE EXHIBITION

Cat. 1
Honoré Daumier
French, 1808–1879
What is Known as Dining in a Restaurant, 1844
Lithograph on newsprint
11 ⁹⁄₁₆ × 8 ⁹⁄₁₆ in. (29.4 × 21.7 cm)
Dixon Gallery and Gardens; Gift of The Armand Hammer
Foundation, 1987.40

Cat. 2
Constantin Guys
French, 1805–1892
The Café, ca. 1860–70
Watercolor on paper
7 ¼ × 9 ⅞ in. (18.4 × 25.1 cm)
Denver Art Museum; The T. Edward and Tullah
Hanley memorial gift to the people of Denver and the
area, 1974.373
DIXON AND JOSLYN ONLY

Cat. 3
Honoré Daumier
French, 1808–1879
The Corner of Ravaged Poets, 1864
Lithograph on newsprint
9 ¼ × 10 ³⁄₁₆ in. (23.5 × 25.9 cm)
Dixon Gallery and Gardens; Gift of Dr. Armand
Hammer, 1987.86

Cat. 4
Jean Béraud
French, 1849–1935
The Bal Mabille near the Champs-Élysées, ca. 1870–75
Oil on panel
5 ⅝ × 9 ¼ in. (14.3 × 23.5 cm)
Private collection

Cat. 5
Armand Guillaumin
French, 1841–1927
Banks of the Seine, 1873
Oil on canvas
21 ¼ × 25 ⅝ in. (54 × 65.1 cm)
Private collection

Cat. 6
Édouard Manet
French, 1832–1883
At the Café, 1874
Brush and ink transfer relief plate
image: 10 ³⁄₈ × 13 ⅛ in. (26.4 × 33.3 cm)
sheet: 10 ⅞ × 13 ¹¹⁄₁₆ in. (27.6 × 34.8 cm)
Baltimore Museum of Art; The George A. Lucas
Collection, purchased with funds from the State of
Maryland, Laurence and Stella Bendann Fund, and
contributions from individuals, foundations, and
corporations throughout the Baltimore community, BMA
1996.48.18058
DIXON AND JOSLYN ONLY

Cat. 7
Pierre-Auguste Renoir
French, 1841–1919
Young Woman (La Servante), ca. 1875
Oil on canvas
39 ½ × 28 ⅛ in. (100.3 × 71.4 cm)
The Metropolitan Museum of Art; Bequest of Stephen
C. Clark, 1960
DIXON AND JOSLYN ONLY

Cat. 8
Pierre-Auguste Renoir
French, 1841–1919
Le Moulin de la Galette, Sketch, 1875–76
Oil on canvas
25 ⅝ × 33 ½ in. (65 × 85 cm)
Ordrupgaard, Charlottenlund

Cat. 9
Jean-Louis Forain
French, 1852–1931
Café de la Nouvelle Athènes, ca. 1876
Etching
image: 6 ⅛ × 4 ⅝ in. (15.6 × 11.7 cm)
sheet: 11 ½ × 9 ½ (29.2 × 24.1 cm)
Dixon Gallery and Gardens; Museum purchase, 2022.3

Cat. 10
Edgar Degas
French, 1834–1914
The Song of the Dog (*La Chanson du chien*), 1876–77
Transfer crayon lithograph
image: 14 × 9 ⅛ in. (35.6 × 23.2 cm)
sheet: 14 ¹⁵⁄₁₆ × 10 ¹⁵⁄₁₆ in. (37.9 × 27.8 cm)
Cincinnati Art Museum, The Albert P. Strietmann
Collection, 1996.461

Cat. 11
Henri Gervex
French, 1852–1929
Café Scene in Paris, 1877
Oil on canvas
39 ⅝ × 53 ½ in. (100.6 × 135.9 cm)
Detroit Institute of Arts; Founders Society Purchase,
Robert H. Tannahill Foundation Fund, 1992.8
NOT IN EXHIBITION

Cat. 12
Félix-Hilaire Buhot
French, 1847–1898
La Place Pigalle en 1878, 1878
Etching, aquatint, and drypoint; sixth state of six
17 × 20 ½ in. (43.2 × 52.1 cm)
Private collection

Cat. 13
Édouard Manet
French, 1832–1883
Le Bouchon, 1878
Ink and pencil on paper
sheet: 8 ¾ × 11 ⅝ in. (22.2 × 29.5 cm)
Dallas Museum of Art, The Wendy and Emery Reves
Collection

Cat. 14
Jean-Louis Forain
French, 1852–1931
Café Interior, ca. 1879
Watercolor and gouache on paper
13 ⅛ × 10 ⅛ in. (33.3 × 25.7 cm)
Dixon Gallery and Gardens; Museum purchase with
funds provided by Brenda and Lester Crain, Hyde Family
Foundations, Irene and Joe Orgill and the Rose Family
Foundation, 1993.7.2

Cat. 15
Jean-Louis Forain
French, 1852–1931
Les Folies-Bergère, 1880 and 1886
Etching
image: 3 ⅝ × 5 ¾ in. (9.2 × 14.6 cm)
sheet: 8 ¾ × 11 in. (22.2 × 27.9 cm)
Dixon Gallery and Gardens; Museum purchase, 2022.7

Cat. 16
Jean-Louis Forain
French, 1852–1931
Maison close, 1880 and 1886
Etching
image: 3 ⅞ × 5 ⅞ in. (9.8 × 15 cm)
sheet: 9 ¼ × 12 ⅝ in. (23.5 × 32.1 cm)
Dixon Gallery and Gardens; Museum purchase, 2023.8

Cat. 17
Jean-François Raffaëlli
French, 1850–1924
The Absinthe Drinkers, 1881
Oil on canvas
42 ½ × 42 ½ in. (108 × 108 cm)
Fine Arts Museums of San Francisco; Museum purchase,
Roscoe and Margaret Oakes Income Fund, Jay D. and
Clare C. McEvoy Endowment Fund, Tribute Funds,
Friends of Ian White Endowment Fund, Unrestricted Art
Acquisition Endowment Income Fund, Grover A. Magnin
Bequest Fund, and the Yvonne Cappeller Trust, 2010.16

Cat. 18
Fernand Lungren
American, 1857–1932
In the Café, 1882–84
Oil on canvas
17 ⅝ × 26 ½ in. (44.8 × 67.3 cm)
Dixon Gallery and Gardens; Museum purchase with funds
provided by the estate of Cecil Williams Marshall, 2018.2

Cat. 19
Jean-Louis Forain
French, 1852–1931
Woman in a Café, ca. 1885
Oil on panel
18 × 14 ½ in. (45.7 × 36.8 cm)
Dixon Gallery and Gardens; Museum purchase by
the Life Members Society in honor of John and Lucy
Buchanan, 1994.1

Cat. 20
James Tissot
French, 1836–1902
The Artists' Wives, 1885
Oil on canvas
57 ½ × 40 in. (146.1 × 101.6 cm)
Chrysler Museum of Art, Norfolk, Virginia; Gift of
Walter P. Chrysler, Jr., and The Grandy Fund, Landmark
Communications Fund, and "An Affair to Remember"
1982, 81.153

Cat. 21
Christian Krohg
Norwegian, 1852–1925
Portrait of the Painter Gerhard Munthe, 1885
Oil on canvas
59 ⅛ × 45 ¼ in. (150 × 115 cm)
Nasjonalmuseet for kunst, arkitektur og design, Oslo,
The Fine Art Collections, NG.M.01555
ORDRUPGAARD ONLY

Cat. 22
Akseli Gallen-Kallela
Finnish, 1865–1931
In a Café in Paris, 1886
Oil on wood
12 ¾ × 9 ⅞ in. (32.5 × 25 cm)
Gösta Serlachius Fine Arts Foundation, Mänttä, Finland
ORDRUPGAARD ONLY

Cat. 23
Vincent van Gogh
Dutch, 1853–1890
La Guinguette à Montmartre, October 1886
Oil on canvas
9 ¹¹⁄₁₆ × 25 ⅜ in. (50 × 64.5 cm)
Musée d'Orsay, Paris; Bequest of Pierre Goujon in
memory of his father Dr. Etienne Goujon, 1915
ORDRUPGAARD ONLY

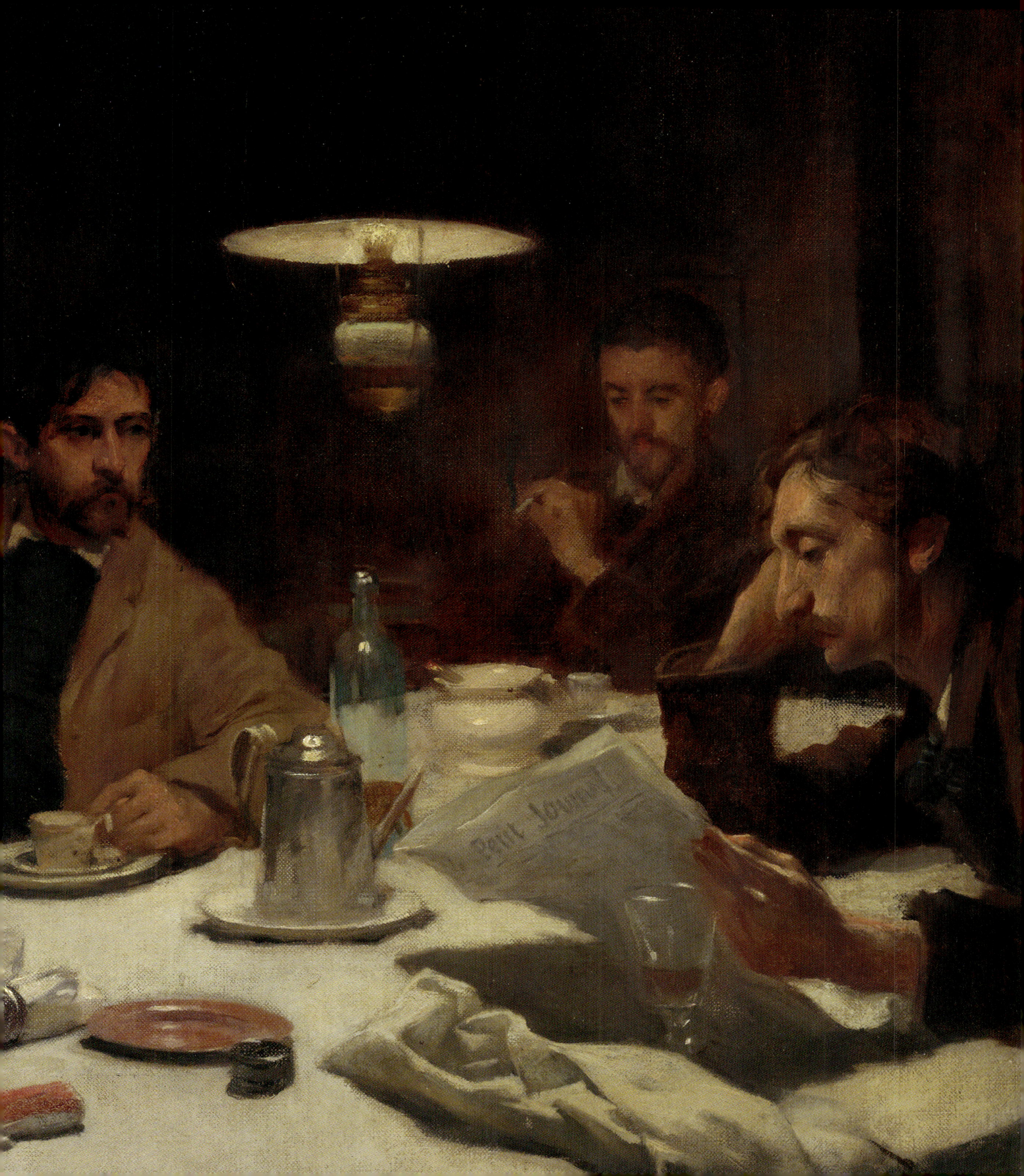

Cat. 24
Vincent van Gogh
Dutch, 1853–1890
Restaurant Rispal at Asnières, 1887
Oil on canvas
28 ⅞ × 23 ⅝ in. (73.3 × 60 cm)
The Nelson-Atkins Museum of Art, Kansas City; Gift of
Henry W. and Marion H. Bloch, 2015.13.10
ORDRUPGAARD AND JOSLYN ONLY

Cat. 25
Vincent van Gogh
Dutch, 1853–1890
In the Café: Agostina Segatori in Le Tambourin, January–
March 1887
Oil on canvas
21 ⅞ × 18 ½ in. (55.5 × 47 cm)
Van Gogh Museum, Amsterdam (Vincent van Gogh
Foundation)
ORDRUPGAARD ONLY

Cat. 26
Willard Leroy Metcalf
American, 1858–1925
The Ten Cent Breakfast, 1887
Oil on canvas
14 ¾ × 21 ½ in. (37.5 × 54.6 cm)
Denver Art Museum; Gift of T. Edward & Tullah Hanley
Collection, 1974.418
DIXON AND JOSLYN ONLY

Cat. 27
Willard Leroy Metcalf
American, 1858–1925
Au café, 1888
Oil on panel
13 ¹¹⁄₁₆ × 6 ¹⁄₁₆ in. (34.8 × 15.4 cm)
Terra Foundation for American Art, Daniel J. Terra
Collection, 1992.10
DIXON AND JOSLYN ONLY

Cat. 28
Eero Järnefelt
Finnish, 1863–1937
French Wine Bar, 1888
Oil on canvas
24 × 29 ⅛ in. (61 × 74 cm)
Finnish National Gallery Collection, Ateneum Art
Museum, A II 1278
ORDRUPGAARD ONLY

Cat. 29
Sven Jørgensen
Norwegian, 1861–1940
Portrait of Hans Jæger, 1888
Oil on canvas
8 ½ × 10 ⅝ in. (21.8 × 27.1 cm)
Oslo Museum, OB.00481
ORDRUPGAARD ONLY

Cat. 30
Edvard Munch
Norwegian, 1863–1944
In the Tavern, 1890
Oil on canvas
25 ⅜ × 28 ¼ in. (64.5 × 71.7 cm)
Städel Museum, Frankfurt, SG365

Cat. 31
Edvard Munch
Norwegian, 1863–1944
The Absinthe Drinkers, 1890
Pastel on canvas
22 ⅞ × 37 ¾ in. (58 × 96 cm)
Siem Group
ORDRUPGAARD ONLY

Cat. 32
Jens Ferdinand Willumsen
Danish, 1863–1958
A Cocotte Hunting in the Montagnes Russes, 1890
Polychromed wood
44 ½ × 29 ¼ × 2 ¼ in. (113 × 74.3 × 5.8 cm)
Willumsens Museum, Frederikssund, Acc. 507
ORDRUPGAARD AND DIXON ONLY

Cat. 33
Hugo Birger
Swedish, 1854–1887
Interior from Restaurant Ledoyen (Study for The Artists' Lunch), undated
Oil on canvas
18 ⅛ × 25 ½ in. (46 × 65 cm)
Collection of Helene Schmitz

Cat. 34
Anders Zorn
Swedish, 1860–1920
Study for Night Effect, 1892
Watercolor on paper
9 ⅝ × 6 ¼ in. (24.5 × 16 cm)
Zorn Museum, Mora

Cat. 35
Félix Vallotton
Swiss, 1865–1925
The Brawl (*La Rixe*), 1892
Woodcut in black on wove paper, sole state
10 ⅝ × 14 ⅛ in. (27 × 35.9 cm)
Memorial Art Gallery, University of Rochester; General Acquisitions Fund, 1984.17

Cat. 36
Henri de Toulouse-Lautrec
French, 1864–1901
Divan Japonais, 1893
Lithograph (printer: Edward Ancourt, Paris)
31 ¹⁵⁄₁₆ × 23 ¾ in. (81.2 × 60.3 cm)
Joslyn Art Museum; Gift of the Estate of Lenore Polack, 2022.17.19

Cat. 37
Jules Chéret
French, 1836–1932
Folies-Bergère / La Loïe Fuller, 1893
Lithograph (printer: Imprimerie Chaix, Paris)
48 ½ × 34 ½ in. (123.2 × 87.6 cm)
Joslyn Art Museum; Gift of the Estate of Lenore Polack, 2022.17.3

Cat. 38
Maurice Brazil Prendergast
American, 1858–1924
Woman Drinking Tea, 1893–94
Watercolor on paper
10 ½ × 4 ½ in. (26.7 × 11.4 cm)
Dixon Gallery and Gardens; Gift of Montgomery H. W. Ritchie, 1996.2.11

Cat. 39
Severin Segelcke
Norwegian, 1867–1940
Café de la Régence, 1894
Pen, brush, and gouache over pencil on paper
17 ⅜ × 27 ⅜ in. (44 × 69.5 cm)
Nasjonalmuseet for kunst, arkitektur og design, Oslo, The Fine Art Collections, NG.K&H.B.00603
ORDRUPGAARD ONLY

Cat. 40
James Abbott McNeill Whistler
American, 1864–1903
The Little Café au Bois, 1894
Lithograph in black on laid paper
image: 10 ¼ × 7 ¼ in. (26 × 18.4 cm)
sheet: 11 ⅛ × 9 in. (28.3 × 22.9 cm)
Dixon Gallery and Gardens; Museum purchase, 2023.1

Cat. 41
Jules Chéret
French, 1836–1932
Eldorado, 1894
Color lithograph
22 × 15 in. (55.9 × 38.1 cm)
Dixon Gallery and Gardens; Museum purchase, Gift of
the Dixon Gallery and Gardens Staff, 2015.2

Cat. 42
Théophile Alexandre Steinlen
Swiss, 1859–1923
Yvette Guilbert / Ambassadeurs, 1894
Lithograph (printer: Charles Verneau, Paris)
71 ¾ × 31 ⅛ in. (182.3 × 79.1 cm)
Joslyn Art Museum; Gift of the Estate of Lenore Polack,
2022.17.18

Cat. 43
Henri de Toulouse-Lautrec
French, 1864–1901
At the Ambassadeurs—Café-Concert Singer, 1894
Color lithograph (crayon, tusche, and splatter)
image: 12 ¹⁄₁₆ × 9 ¹¹⁄₁₆ in. (30.6 × 24.6 cm)
Cincinnati Art Museum; Bequest of Herbert Greer
French, 1943.685

Cat. 44
Henri Evenepoel
Belgian, 1872–1899
In the Café d'Harcourt in Paris, 1897
Oil on canvas
44 ⅞ × 58 ¼ in. (114 × 148 cm)
Städel Museum, Frankfurt, 1811

Cat. 45
Nicolas Félix Escalier
French, 1843–1920
Henri-François-Joseph de Régnier, 1898
Oil on canvas
15 ¾ × 11 ¼ in. (40 × 28.6 cm)
Dixon Gallery and Gardens; Museum purchase, 2015.1

Cat. 46
Jean-Émile Laboureur
French, 1877–1973
*Menu pour le 14 juillet au 65ᵉ régiment
d'infanterie*, 1899
Drypoint
7 ¾ × 4 ¾ in. (19.7 × 12.1 cm)
Georgina Kelman Works on Paper

Cat. 47
Robert Henri
American, 1865–1929
Café Terrace, 1899
Oil on canvas
25 ¾ × 32 ⅛ in. (65.4 × 81.6 cm)
Fayez S. Sarofim Collection, FSC 2022.064
DIXON AND JOSLYN ONLY

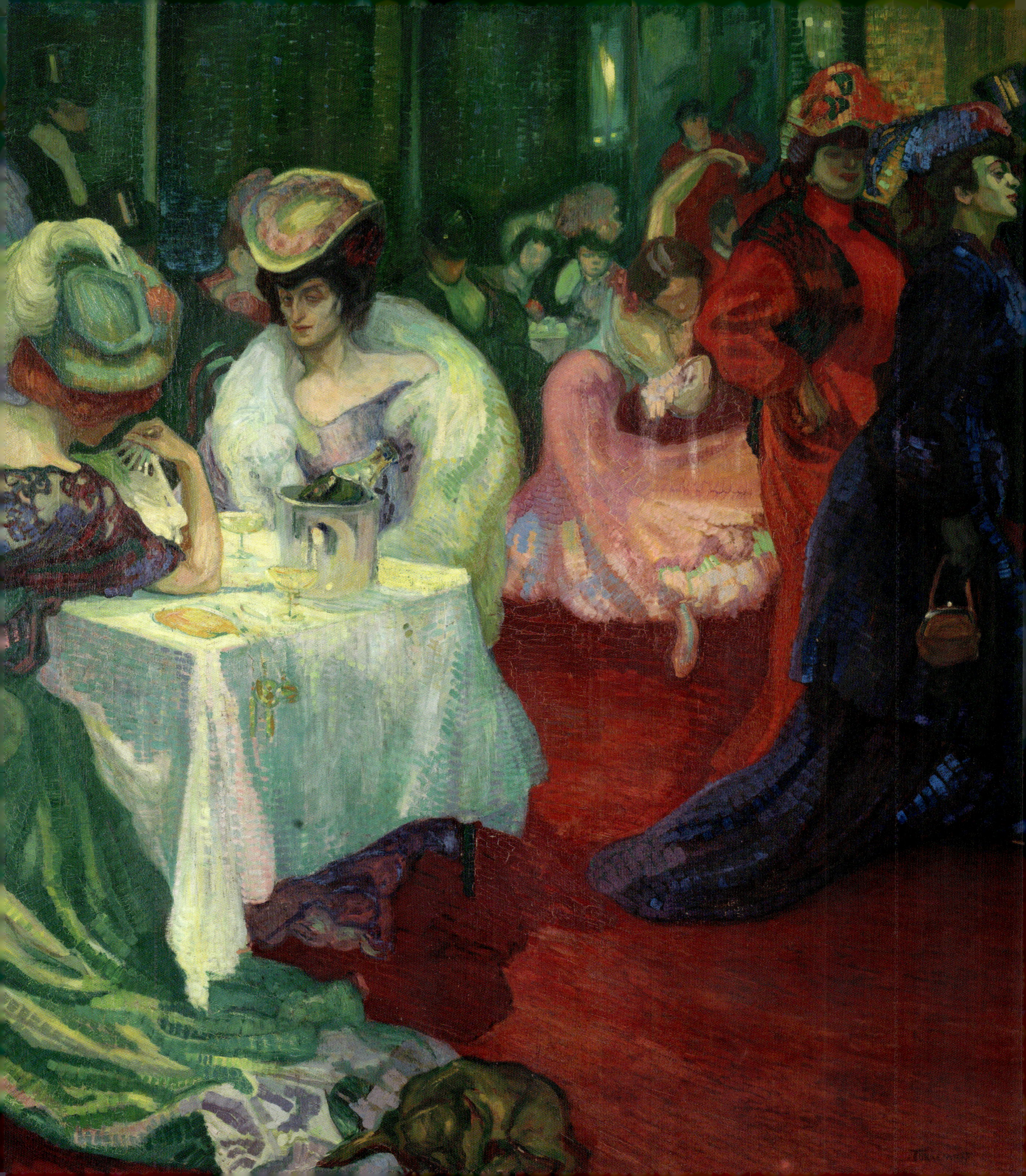

Cat. 48
Pablo Picasso
Spanish, 1881–1973
Au café, 1901
Pastel on cardboard
21 ½ × 29 ½ in. (54.6 × 74.9 cm)
Norton Museum of Art, West Palm Beach; Gift of R. H.
Norton, 53.150
ORDRUPGAARD ONLY

Cat. 49
Oda Krohg
Norwegian, 1860–1935
Night Birds. Bokken Lasson and Sten Drewsen, 1902
Oil on canvas
19 ¾ × 38 ⅜ in. (50.2 × 97.5 cm)
Nasjonalmuseet for kunst, arkitektur og design, Oslo,
The Fine Art Collections, NMK.2021.0182
ORDRUPGAARD ONLY

Cat. 50
Jean-Émile Laboureur
French, 1877–1973
Ernest, garçon de restaurant, 1902–11
Woodcut printed in black with lithographic transfer in
yellow and orange
image: 17 ⅜ × 11 in. (44.1 × 27.9 cm)
Dixon Gallery and Gardens; Museum purchase with funds
provided by Peggy and Keith Kunkel and an anonymous
donor, 2024.9

Cat. 51
George Bottini
French, 1874–1907
Les Rouliers (Southard 56), 1903
Etching printed in colors, edition of 15
5 ⅞ × 8 ½ in. (14.9 × 21.6 cm)
Georgina Kelman Works on Paper

Cat. 52
André Devambez
French, 1867–1944
Les Incompris, ca. 1904
Oil on canvas
36 ¼ × 44 in. (92 × 112 cm)
Musée des Beaux-Arts de Quimper, Bequest of Corentin-
Guyho, 1936

Cat. 53
SEM [Georges Goursat]
French, 1863–1934
Chez Maxim's, 1904
Pochoir and lithograph
11 ¾ × 18 in. (29.8 × 45.7 cm)
Private collection, Memphis

Cat. 54
Auguste Louis Lepère
French, 1849–1918
La Guinguette, route de Billancourt, 1905
Etching
6 ¹⁵⁄₁₆ × 10 ¼ in. (17.6 × 26 cm)
Dixon Gallery and Gardens; Museum purchase, 2024.3

Cat. 55
Henri Gervex
French, 1852–1929
Armenonville, le soir du Grand-Prix, ca. 1905
Oil on cardboard
19 ⅞ × 14 in. (50.5 × 35.5 cm)
Musée Carnavalet, Histoire de Paris, P2708

Cat. 56
Émile-Othon Friesz
French, 1879–1949
Scene in a Parisian Brasserie, ca. 1905–6
Oil on canvas
19 ¼ × 17 ⅞ in. (49 × 45.5 cm)
Museum Barberini, Potsdam, MB-Fri-01
ORDRUPGAARD ONLY

Cat. 57
Axel Törneman
Swedish, 1880–1925
Night Café, 1906
Oil on canvas
70 ½ × 78 ¾ in. (179 × 200 cm)
Thielska Galleriet, Stockholm, TG 361
ORDRUPGAARD ONLY

Cat. 58
Richard E. Miller
American, 1875–1943
Café L'Avenue, Paris, ca. 1906–10
Oil on canvas
44 ⅞ × 57 ½ in. (114 × 146.1 cm)
Cummer Museum of Art & Gardens, Jacksonville,
Florida; Purchased with funds from the Cummer Council,
AP.1985.1.1
DIXON AND JOSLYN ONLY

Cat. 59
Édouard Vuillard
French, 1868–1940
Café Wepler, ca. 1908–10, reworked in 1912
Oil on fabric
24 ½ × 40 ⅝ in. (62.2 × 103.2 cm)
The Cleveland Museum of Art; Gift of the Hanna
Fund, 1950.90

Cat. 60
Pablo Picasso
Spanish, 1881–1973
Mandolin and a Glass of Pernod, 1911
Oil on canvas
13 × 18 ½ in. (33 × 47 cm)
National Gallery, Prague, O 14818
ORDRUPGAARD ONLY

Cat. 61
Georges Lepape
French, 1887–1971
Menu for Restaurant Larue, ca. 1912
Pochoir
6 ¼ × 5 ¹⁵⁄₁₆ in. (15.9 × 15.1 cm)
Private collection, Memphis

Cat. 62
Pablo Picasso
Spanish, 1881–1973
La Glace, January–March 1912
Oil on canvas
9 ½ × 5 ½ in. (24.1 × 14 cm)
Kirkland Family Collection

Cat. 63
Juan Gris
Spanish, 1887–1927
Man in a Café, 1912
Oil on canvas
50 ¼ × 34 ¾ in. (127.6 × 88.3 cm)
Philadelphia Museum of Art, The Louise and Walter
Arensberg Collection, 1950, 1950-134-94

Cat. 64
Elisabeth Epstein
Russian (now Ukraine), 1879–1956
People on a Café Terrace, 1913
Oil on canvas
22 × 22 in. (58.9 × 58.9 cm)
National Gallery of Art, Washington, DC, Collection of
Arnold and Joan Saltzman, 2020.112.9

Cat. 65
Antti Favén
Finnish, 1882–1948
The Chess Players, 1913
Oil on canvas
86 ⅝ × 133 ⅞ in. (207 × 343 cm)
Private collection—contributed by the Nemes Galeria
(Budapest)

Cat. 66
Maurice Utrillo
French, 1883–1955
Road to Puteaux, 1913–14
Oil on canvas
23 ¾ × 32 ¼ in. (60.3 × 81.9 cm)
Dixon Gallery and Gardens; Gift of Cornelia
Ritchie, 1996.2.17

Cat. 67
Albert André
French, 1869–1954
The Café, 1917
Oil on canvas
15 × 18 in. (38.1 × 45.7 cm)
Joslyn Art Museum; Gift of the American Federation of
Arts, 1943.60

Cat. 68
Gen Paul (Paul Trelade)
French, 1895–1975
Le Lapin Agile, ca. 1920
Aquatint
image: 5 ¾ × 8 in. (14.6 × 20.3 cm)
sheet: 9 ¾ × 11 ⅝ in. (24.8 × 29.5 cm)
Private collection
DIXON ONLY

Cat. 69
Aleksandr Yevgeniyevich Yakovlev
Russian, 1887–1938
In the Cafe de la Rotonde, Paris, 1921
Oil on canvas
39 ¼ × 32 ⅛ in. (99.7 × 81.6 cm)
Museum of Fine Arts, Boston, Tompkins Collection—
Arthur Gordon Tompkins Fund, 35.637

Cat. 70
Henri de Toulouse-Lautrec
French, 1864–1901
Moulin de la Galette, 1889
Oil on canvas
35 ⅞ × 39 ⅝ in. (88.5 × 101.3 cm)
Art Institute of Chicago; Mr. and Mrs. Lewis Larned
Coburn Memorial Collection, 1933.458
ORDRUPGAARD ONLY

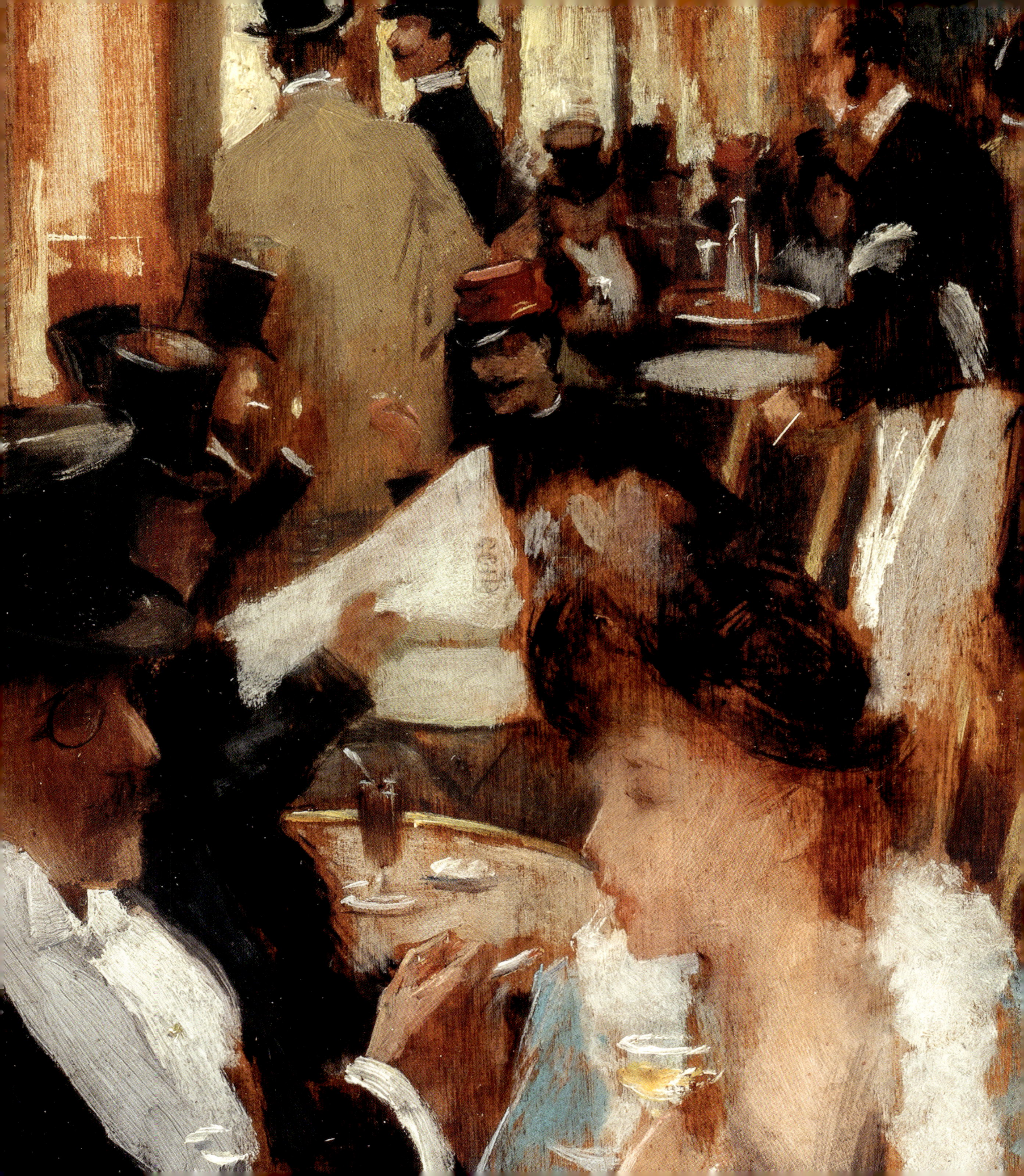

GLOSSARY

ardoise: trans. "slate," a running tab or small loan café patrons could request to tide them over until their next payday

auberge: a rural inn that offered food and drink to travelers

bistro: an eatery that is open continuously morning to night, serves comfort foods at moderate prices, and houses an active bar where locals can gather for a drink and some lively conversation[1]

boîte à femmes: a new type of café dominated by lower-class women[2]

bouge: a dive bar or neighborhood watering hole; see also *rade*, *troquet*

bouillon: a dining venue in Paris originally established to serve workers a single dish—often a soup or bouillon; these venues eventually expanded the menu while maintaining a simplicity and affordability[3]

brasserie: originally designating an establishment where beer is brewed, brasserie can be a synonym for café, usually with a relaxed atmosphere and a small menu

brasserie à femmes: a café where women sold and served food and drink; an ambiguous type of establishment, prone to clandestine prostitution; also known as a *café à femmes*

buvette: a small bar or roadside tavern, generally found in rural areas

cabaret: originally denoting a café or any eating and drinking establishment, the term "cabaret" only came to mean a music hall or nightclub towards the end of the nineteenth century. At a cabaret, most visitors do not dance, but stay at their tables. Cabaret performances could be political, with a singing style characterized by its "rough tone, proletarian slang, and frequent insults aimed at the middle-class clientele in the audience."[4]

cabinet noir: a private room in a café or restaurant associated with prostitution

cabinet particulier: similar to a *cabinet noir*; a private room in a restaurant where a man could dine with a woman who was not his wife and, commonly, engage in sexual activity with her; the accommodations in this room depended on the class of the restaurant and could therefore be sumptuous or sparse[5]

caboulot: a type of café first emerging in the mid-nineteenth century that primarily employed women; a predecessor of the *brasserie à femmes*

café: a public establishment for socializing, drinking, eating, reading the newspaper, etc., it became a fundamental aspect of Parisian culture in the nineteenth century;[6] by 1850, Paris had about 4,000 cafes

café à femmes: see *brasserie à femmes*

café-caveau: a subterranean café popular in the late eighteenth century and early nineteenth century, the "café cavern" or "cellar café" was associated with the area around the Palais Royal. Such establishments featured performances by musicians and acts including ventriloquists and were also noted as sites of prostitution. They were seen as a predecessor of the café-concert.

café-chantant: trans. "singing café," a café that featured musical entertainments; see also cabaret and café-concert.

café-concert: a music and performing establishment, originally an outdoor café where musicians played for the public; also known as a *café-chantant*

canaille: riffraff at cafés

casuel: a passerby who enters a café only by chance; opposite of an *habitué*

cercle: a group of regulars at a café, who meet at the same time on a daily or regular basis to discuss politics, life, etc.; "the bourgeois form of sociability" equivalent to the salon of the aristocracy[7]

corbeille: a cluster of female performers who filled the stage at a café-concert, often perceived as sexually available

dame de comptoir: a woman who greeted patrons to the café or restaurant, prepared bills, and collected payments; akin to a hostess today. Preceding the waitress, *dames de comptoir* also served to attract customers.

débit de boissons: general term for a drinking establishment in nineteenth-century France[8]

débit de vin: a bar or tavern

débitant: a person who frequents a drinking establishment

estaminet: a small café or tavern in France that serves alcoholic drinks; in the nineteenth century, they were a common destination for smoking, with an open entrance to the street, and were known for prostitution[9]

femme de boulevard: a streetwalker; a woman who picks up men on the street, often outside of cafés

fille de joie: trans. "good-time girl," a woman who frequented cafés to solicit for sex

gargote: a cheap cabaret[10]

goguette: a singing and drinking social club that usually met in a room in a café or restaurant; generally suburban, such clubs became somewhat political as the nineteenth century progressed, and were mainly patronized on Sundays, Mondays, and holidays

grisette: a young, working-class woman who went to cafés, usually in the Latin Quarter, to meet young men

guinguette: a suburban tavern, mostly patronized by working-class and lower middle-class Parisians on Sundays, Mondays, and holidays— alcohol was cheaper in the *barrières*. Important guinguettes could be found in Montparnasse, Clichy, Montmartre, and Belleville.

habitué: a regular patron of a café; the opposite of a *casuel*

inviteuse: a waitress in a *brasserie à femmes*; see also *serveuse*[11]

limonadière: another word for a *dame de comptoir*, the term goes back to the early eighteenth century when restaurants served lemonade along with coffee[12]

marchand de vin: a drinking establishment for lower-class Parisians. Any number of activities took place at the *marchand de vin*, including meetings and the hiring of laborers. The owners of the establishments were close with their regulars, and would even organize fundraisers to help them out when they fell on hard times. In a similar way to the café, each *marchand de vin* was like its own mini-community.[13]

police des débits de boissons: a special police task force focused on drinking establishments, which started to appear around the 1830s in larger cities

rade: slang term for a small bar or neighborhood watering hole; see also *bouge*, *troquet*

restaurant: public eating establishment; "eating out" was regularly practiced by all sections of the bourgeoisie by the 1850s;[14] originally, *restaurant* was a type of meat bouillon thought to have restorative powers and a *restaurateur* was someone who made the bouillon[15]

restaurant particulier: private dining room inside a restaurant for illicit rendezvous; see also *cabinet particulier* and *cabinet noir*

serveuse: a waitress or female server in a café, particularly in a *brasserie à femmes*

soupeuse: a prostitute known for frequenting or bringing clients to *cabinets particuliers* in cafés for dinner before their sexual transaction[16]

table d'hôte: trans. "host's table," a small restaurant with a set menu, usually around a communal table; prix fixe; often of the kind served at a modern bed-and-breakfast establishment[17]

tavern: a predecessor of the working-class café, taverns had been around in France since at least the fifth century, and had a history of eliciting consternation from the clergy and regulation from the Crown[18]

troquet: a small café or bar in Paris, sometimes serving food; a neighborhood watering hole; see also *bouge* and *rade*

Endnotes

1. https://www.bbc.co.uk/travel/ article/20180709-is-the-iconic- parisian-bistro-dying.

2. Theresa Ann Gronberg, "Femmes de Brasserie," *Art History* 7, no. 3 (September 1984): 333.

3. Joanie Osburn, *Café Society: Time Suspended: The Cafés & Bistros of Paris* (San Francisco: Goff Books, 2022), 234.

4. Leona Rittner, W. Scott Haine, and Jeffrey H. Jackson, eds., *The Thinking Space: The Café as Cultural Institution in Paris, Italy and Vienna* (London: Routledge, 2013), 8.

5. Rachel Hope Cleves, *Lustful Appetites: An Intimate History of Good Food and Wicked Sex* (Cambridge: Polity Press, 2025), 12.

6. Richard D. E. Burton, *The Flâneur and His City: Patterns of Daily Life in Paris, 1815– 1851* (Manchester: Manchester University Press, 1994), 16.

7. Ibid., 18.

8. Susanna Barrows, "Nineteenth-Century Cafes: Arenas of Everyday Life," in *Pleasures of Paris: Daumier to Picasso*, ed. Barbara Stern Shapiro (Boston: Museum of Fine Arts, 1991), 19.

9. Hollis Clayson, *Painted Love: Prostitution in French Art of the Impressionist Era* (New Haven: Yale University Press, 1991), 29.

10. Rebecca L. Spang, *The Invention of the Restaurant: Paris and Modern Gastronomic Culture* (Cambridge: Harvard University Press, 2000), 11.

11. Gronberg, "Femmes de Brasserie," 336.

12. Cleves, *Lustful Appetites*, 35.

13. Burton, *The Flâneur and His City*, 28–30.

14. Ibid., 23.

15. Spang, *Invention of the Restaurant*, viii; see also Cleves, *Lustful Appetites*, 12.

16. Cleves, *Lustful Appetites*, 23.

17. Ibid., 14.

18. W. Scott Haine, *The World of the Paris Café: Sociability among the French Working Class, 1789–1914* (Baltimore: The Johns Hopkins University Press, 1996), 6.

MAP OF PARIS

A note about the map

Ellen Daugherty
Corkey Sinks

This visual record of Parisian cafés is based on a ca. 1880 map of the city of Paris, *Nouveau plan de Paris divisé en 20 arrondissements*. The original hand-colored lithograph was drawn by L. Sonnet, published by Théodore Lefèvre, and printed by Imprimerie Dufrénoy. It is archived at the Getty Library and is available digitally through the Getty Research Institute Digital Collections website.

These markers approximate the locations of a selection of cafés in operation between the seventeenth and twenty-first centuries. Thus, the map is a fictional construction, bringing together establishments that often did not exist at the same time, may not have been in operation at the moment the original map was published, and may not have been located at the precise spots pinpointed because the city of Paris was reconstructed and rebuilt many times. Over the centuries, street names changed, their courses shifted, and whole streets or even neighborhoods were demolished.

The original map's designers used four colors and bold numerals to help distinguish between the city's twenty administrative districts known as arrondissements, which spiral outward in numerical order from the city's center near the Louvre Palace. These features remain organizational touchstones. The accompanying key lists cafés by arrondissement, the complementary modern postal code, and approximate dates of operation.

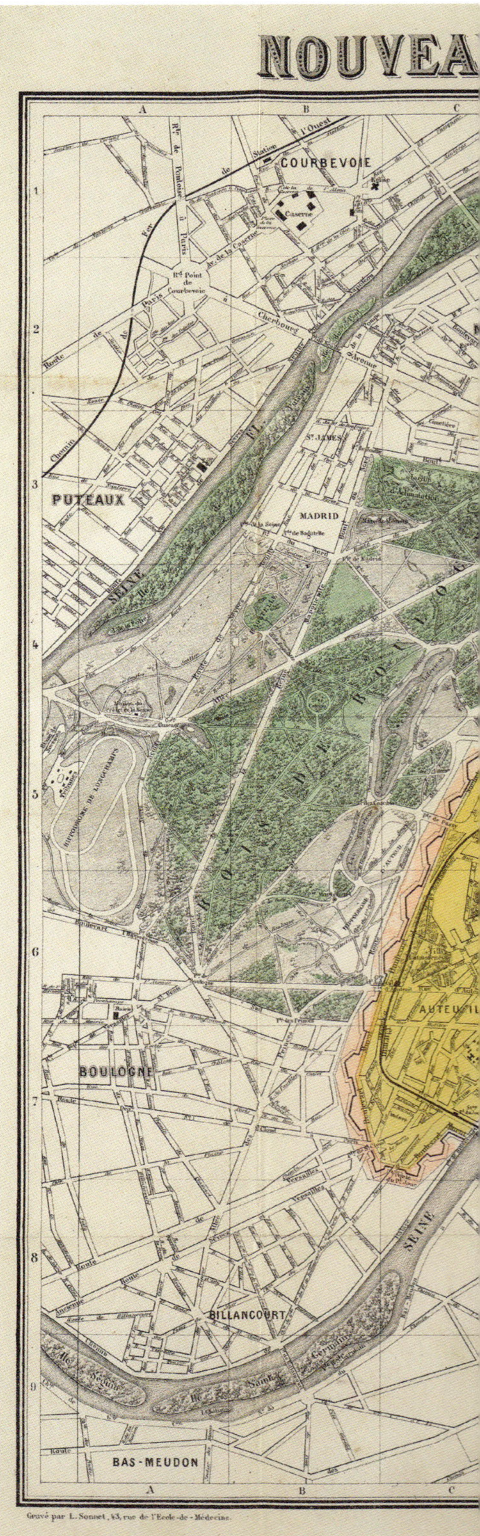

L. Sonnet, engraver
Théodore, publisher
Imp. Dufrenoy, printer
Nouveau plan de Paris divisé en 20 arrondissements / gravé par L. Sonnet, ca. 1880
Hand-colored lithograph
Getty Research Institute, Prints Collection

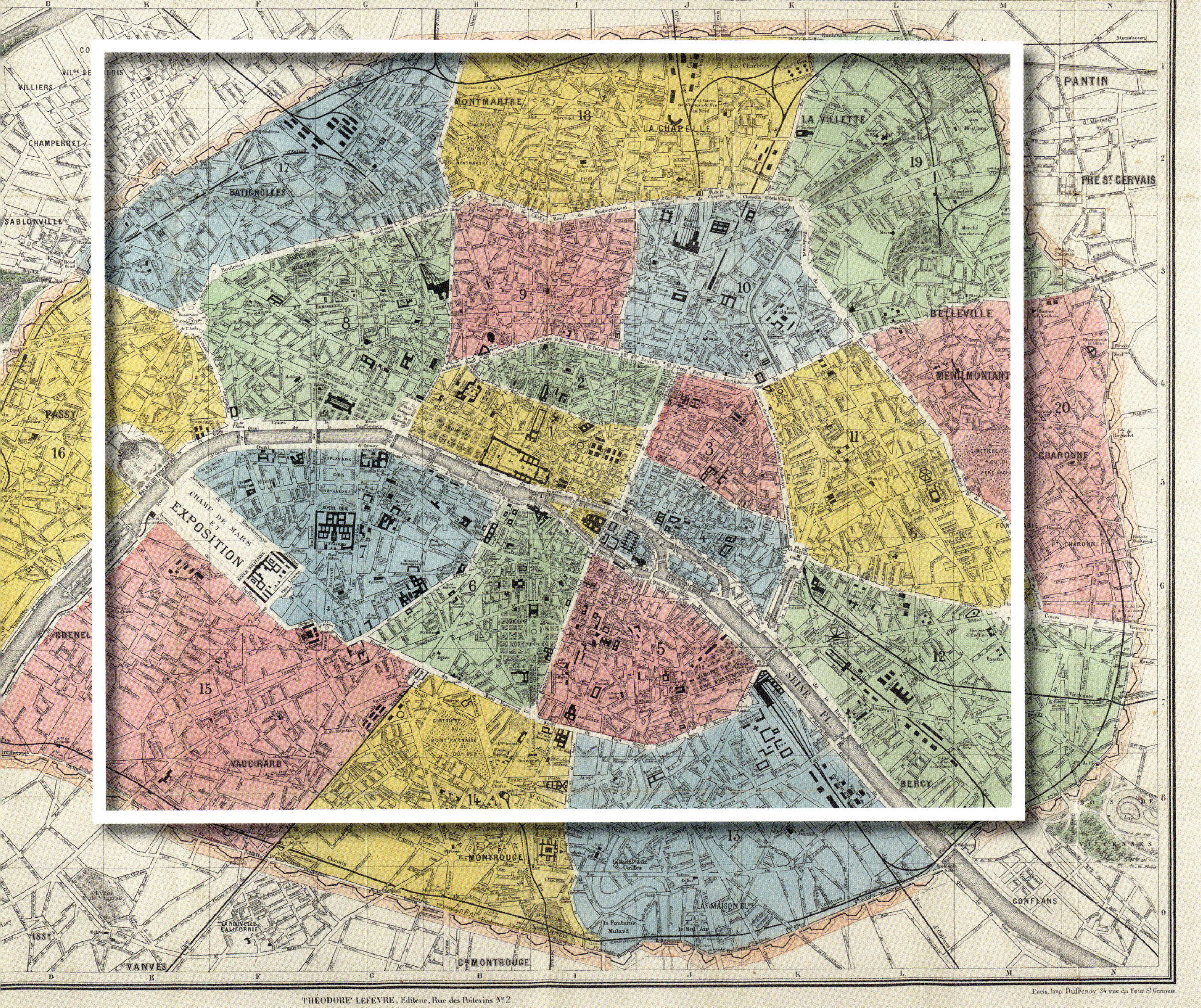
PLAN DE PARIS DIVISÉ EN 20 ARRONDISSEMENTS
VILLIERS
CHAMPERRET
SABLONVILLE
PASSY
GRENEL
ISSY
VANVES
BATIGNOLLES
MONTMARTRE
LA CHAPELLE
LA VILLETTE
PANTIN
PRE ST GERVAIS
BELLEVILLE
MÉNILMONTANT
CHARONNE
CHAMP DE MARS
EXPOSITION
VAUGIRARD
MONTROUGE
CMONTROUGE
LA MAISON BL
CONFLANS
BERCY
SEINE
THÉODORE LEFÈVRE, Éditeur, Rue des Poitevins N.º 2.
Paris, Imp. Dufrenoy 34 rue du Four-St-Germain

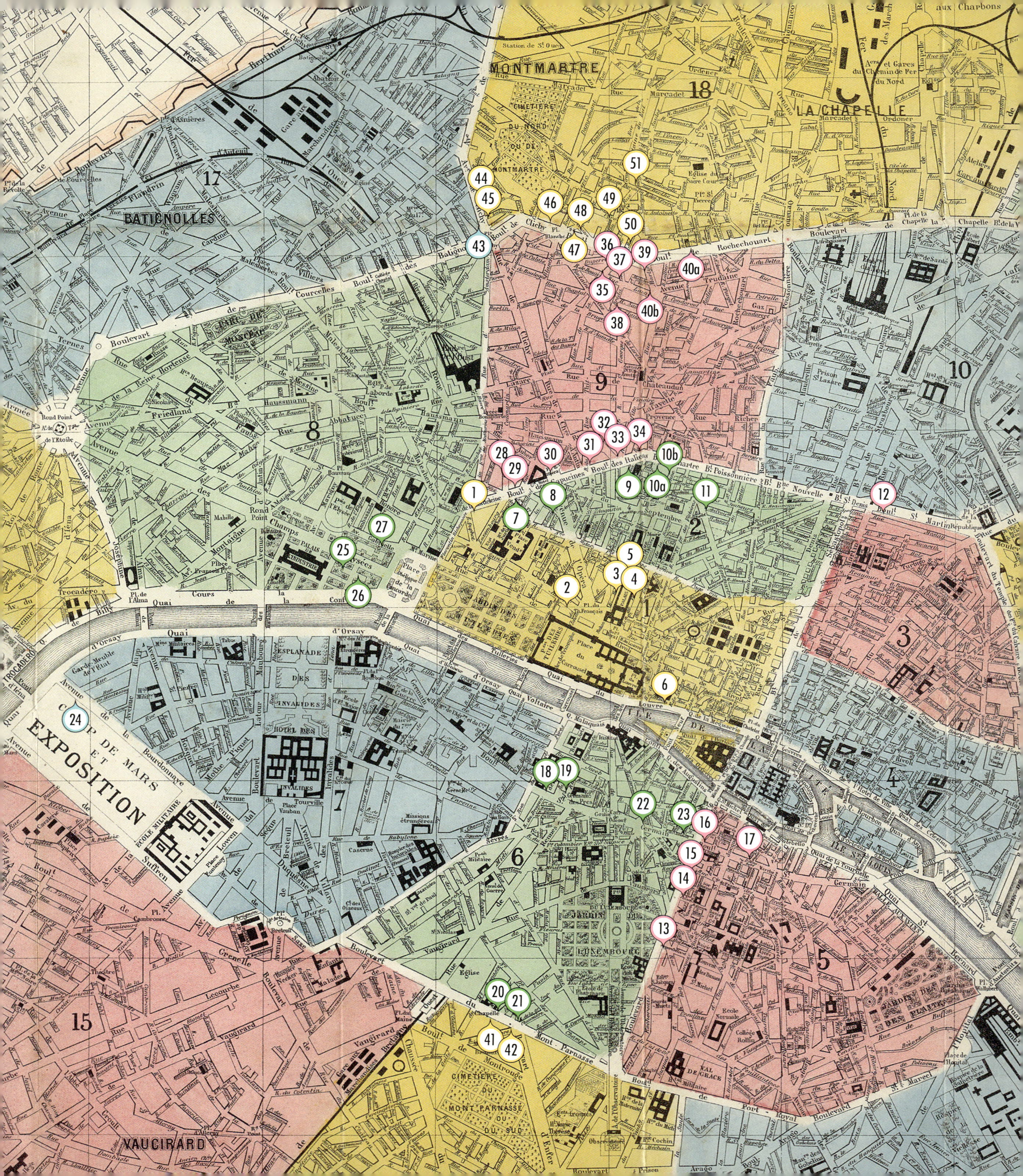

MONTMARTRE
LA CHAPELLE
18
17
BATIGNOLLES
CIMETIÈRE DU NORD OU DE MONTMARTRE
PARC DE MONCEAU
8
9
10
2
CHAMPS ÉLYSÉES
Rond Point de l'Étoile
Rond Point des Champs Élysées
Quai d'Orsay
ESPLANADE DES INVALIDES
HÔTEL DES INVALIDES
CHAMP DE MARS ET EXPOSITION
EXPOSITION
ÉCOLE MILITAIRE
TROCADÉRO
3
4
7
6
JARDIN DU LUXEMBOURG
15
VAUGIRARD
CIMETIÈRE DU MONT PARNASSE OU DU SUD
MONT PARNASSE
VAL DE GRACE

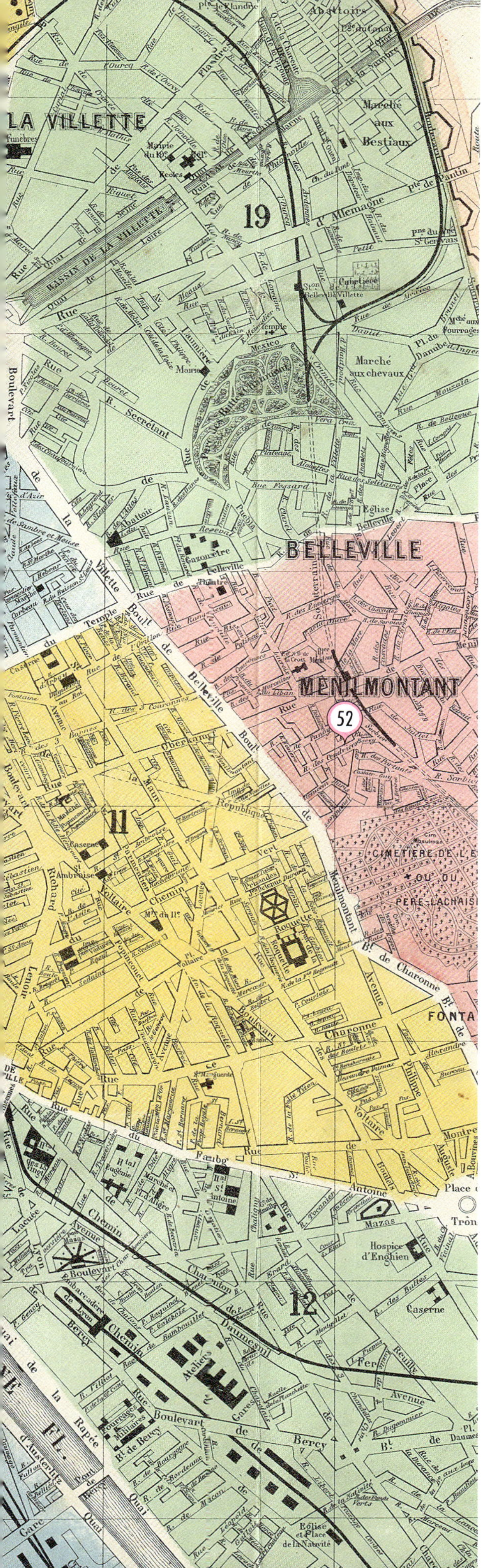

1st arrondissement (75001)

1. Café de Londres (by 1867–?)
2. Café de la Régence (1681–present)
3. Café des Mille Colonnes (by 1814–?)
4. Les Trois Frères Provençaux (1786–1872)
5. Café des Aveugles (eighteenth century–1867 or later)
6. Café Momus (by 1820–1856)

2nd arrondissement (75002)

7. Hill's Tavern (by 1867–?)
8. Café de Paris (1878–early 1950s)
9. Café Anglais (1802–1913)
10. a. Café Frascati (ca. 1789–ca. 1857) b. Café Frascati (ca. 1857–1888)
11. Café du Croissant (1820–present)

3rd arrondissement (75003)

12. Grand Café Parisien (by 1855–?)

5th arrondissement (75005)

13. Café François Ier (by 1892–?)
14. Café d'Harcourt (by 1871–1940)
15. Café Vachette (1878–1913?)
16. Café de Cluny or Café du Musée de Cluny (by 1862–?)
17. Le Père Lunette or Le Cabaret du Père Lunette (by 1840–1908)

6th arrondissement (75006)

18. Café Taranne (?–1877?)
19. Les Deux Magots (1884–present)
20. Le Select (1923–present)
21. Café de la Rotonde (1911–present)
22. Café le Procope (1668–present)
23. Brasserie Andler (1848–1877)

7th arrondissement (75007)

24. Café Volpini or Café des Arts (by 1889–?)

8th arrondissement (75008)

25. Restaurant Ledoyen (1791–present)
26. Jardin de Paris (1885–1914)
27. Café-concert des Ambassadeurs, also known as Les Ambassadeurs or Les Ambass' (1764?–1929)

9th arrondissement (75009)

28. Le Grand Teddy (ca. 1918–?)
29. Montagnes Russes (1889–1893)
30. Café de la Paix (1862–present)
31. Café de Bade (by 1866–?)
32. Tortoni (1798–1893)
33. Maison Dorée (1841–1902)
34. Café Riche (1785–1916)
35. Brasserie Hanneton (ca. 1890s–ca. 1914)
36. Café de la Nouvelle Athènes (ca. 1870–ca. 1914)
37. Le Rat Mort or Café du Rat Mort (1837–1934)
38. Chez Dinochau (by 1860–?)
39. Taverne de l'Ermitage (by 1909–?)
40. a. Le Chat Noir (1881–1885) b. Le Chat Noir (1885–1897)

14th arrondissement (75014)

41. La Coupole (1927–present)
42. Le Dôme, also Café du Dôme (1898–present)

17th arrondissement (75017)

43. Chez le Père Lathuille (1790–1906)

18th arrondissement (75018)

44. Café Guerbois (by 1863–?)
45. Café Wepler (1881–present)
46. Moulin Rouge (1889–present)
47. Lefranc (by 1888–?)
48. Café du Tambourin (1885–1893)
49. Café-Brasserie de Reichshoffen (by 1875–?)
50. Brasserie des Martyrs (1861–1873); Divan Japonais (1873–1901)
51. Le Lapin Agile (ca. 1880s–present)

20th arrondissement (75020)

52. Café Munier (unknown dates)

BIBLIOGRAPHY

Adriani, Götz. *Toulouse-Lautrec: The Complete Graphic Works, a Catalogue Raisonné; The Gerstenberg Collection*. London: Royal Academy of Arts / Thames & Hudson, 1988.

Allan, Scott, Emily A. Beeny, and Gloria Groom, eds. *Manet and Modern Beauty: The Artist's Last Years*. Los Angeles: J. Paul Getty Museum, 2019.

Bakker, Nienke, Isolde Pludermacher, Marie Robert, and Richard Thomson. *Splendours and Miseries: Images of Prostitution in France, 1850–1910*. Paris: Musée d'Orsay / Flammarion, 2015.

Bech, Inge Lise Mogensen, and Lene Bøgh Rønberg, eds. *Women Artists in Denmark, 1880–1910*, trans. David Possen. Aarhus: Aarhus University Press, 2025.

Bella, Edward, ed. *A Collection of Posters: The Illustrated Catalogue of the First Exhibition*. London: Royal Aquarium, 1894.

Boggs, Jean Sutherland, *Degas*. New York: Metropolitan Museum of Art / Paris: RMN / Ottawa: National Gallery of Canada, 1988.

Briens, Sylvain. *Paris: Laboratoire de la littérature scandinave moderne, 1880–1905*. Paris: L'Harmattan, 2010.

Carter, Karen L. "Joris-Karl Huysmans, a *Dénicheur* of Jules Chéret's Posters," *Nineteenth-Century French Studies* 41, nos. 1–2 (Fall–Winter 2012-13): 122–41.

Cavling, Henrik. *Paris: Skildringer fra det moderne Frankrig*. Copenhagen: Gyldendal, 1899.

Chapin, Mary Weaver. *Posters of Paris: Toulouse-Lautrec and His Contemporaries*. Munich: DelMonico Books, 2012.

Claussen, Sophus. *Antonius i Paris: Valfart*, ed. and with an afterword by Jørgen Hunosøe. Copenhagen: Det Danske Sprog- og Litteraturselskab / Borgens Forslag, 1990 [1896].

Clayson, Hollis. *Painted Love: Prostitution in French Art of the Impressionist Era*. New Haven: Yale University Press, 1991.

Cleves, Rachel Hope. *Lustful Appetites: An Intimate History of Good Food and Wicked Sex*. Cambridge: Polity Press, 2025.

Collins, Bradford R., ed. *12 Views of Manet's "Bar"*. Princeton: Princeton University Press. 1996.

Collins, Bradley. "Manet's 'In the Conservatory' and 'Chez Le Père Lathuille,'" *Art Journal* 45, no. 1 (1985): 59-66.

Delahaye, Marie-Claude, and Benoît Noël. *Absinthe, muse des peintres*. Paris: Les éditions de l'Amateur, 1999.

Donson, Theodore B., and Marcel M. Griepp. *Henri de Toulouse-Lautrec: Performers of the Stage and the Boudoir, 1891–1899*. New York: Theodore B. Donson, 1980.

Ekirch, A. Roger. *At Day's Close: Night in Times Past*. New York: W. W. Norton, 2005.

Eiling, Alexander B,. ed. *Renoir: Rococo Revival*. Frankfurt am Main: Städel Museum / Berlin: Hatje Cantz, 2022.

Frey, Julie. *Toulouse-Lautrec: A Life*. New York: Viking Press, 1994.

Fuller, Loïe. *Fifteen Years of a Dancer's Life, with Some Account of Her Distinguished Friends*. New York: Dance Horizons, 1978.

Goncourt, Edmond de, and Jules de Goncourt. *Journal des Goncourt: Mémoires de la vie littéraire*, vol. 2, *1864-1878*, ed. Robert Ricatte. Paris: Fasquelle and Flammarion, 1956.

Guilbert, Yvette. *The Song of My Life: My Memories*, trans. Béatrice de Holthoir. London: G. G. Harrap & Co., 1929.

Haine, W. Scott. *The World of the Paris Café: Sociability among the French Working Class, 1789–1914*. Baltimore: The Johns Hopkins University Press, 1996.

Huysmans, Joris-Karl. *Croquis parisiens*. Paris: Henri Vaton, 1880.

Hyslop, Francis E. *Henri Evenepoel: Belgian Painter in Paris, 1892–1899*. University Park: The Pennsylvania State University Press, 1975.

Iskin, Ruth E. *The Poster: Art, Advertising, Design, and Collecting, 1860s–1900s*. Hanover, NH: Dartmouth College Press, 2014.

Jackson, Jeffrey H. "Artistic Community and Urban Development in 1920s Montmartre," *French Politics, Culture, and Society* 24 (Summer 2006): 1–25.

Joly, Anne. "Sur deux modèles de Degas," *Gazette des Beaux-Arts* 69, no. 1180–81 (May–June 1967): 373–74.

Laurin, Carl G. *Nordisk konst: Sverige och Finlands konst från 1880 till 1926*. Stockholm: P. A. Nordstedt & Söners förlag, 1926.

Lévêque, Jean-Jacques. *Les Années impressionnistes*. Paris: ACR Editions, 1990.

Lie, Erik. "Fra 'Café de la Régence,'" in *Juleaften*. Stockholm, Kristiania, and Copenhagen: Hjalmar Biglers forlag, 1895.

Lloyd, Christopher. "Edgar Degas' 'At the Café,'" https://artuk.org/discover/stories/edgar-degas-at-the-cafe.

Lovy, Jules. "Les cafés de Paris," *Le Tintamarre*, April 18, 1858.

Maindron, Ernest. *Les Affiches illustrées, 1886–1895*. Paris: G. Boudet, 1896.

Mauclair, Camille. *Jules Chéret*. Paris: Maurice Le Garrec, 1930.

Melikian, Souren. "Forain, a Painter Turned Cartoonist," *International Herald Tribune*, March 30, 1996.

Mellerio, André. *Le Mouvement idéaliste en peinture*. Paris: H. Floury, 1896.

Miller, Jill. "Les Enfants des Ivrognes: Concern for the Children of Montmartre," in *Montmartre and the Making of Mass Culture*, ed. Gabriel P. Weisberg, 72–93. New Brunswick, NJ: Rutgers University Press, 2001.

Munro, Jane, ed. *Degas: A Passion for Perfection*. Cambridge: Fitzwilliam Museum / Cambridge University Press, 2017.

Otten, Nikki, ed. *Always New: The Posters of Jules Chéret. Selections from the James and Susee Wiechmann Collection at the Milwaukee Art Museum*. Milwaukee: Milwaukee Art Museum.

Nickerson, Jane. "Larue's, a Famous Paris Restaurant, Ends Its History of 75 Years," *New York Times,* July 5, 1954, 8.

Newman, Sasha. *Félix Vallotton*. New Haven, CT: Yale University Art Gallery, 1991.

Nordström, Charlotta, "Från Champs-Élysées till Göteborg. Sociala rum i konstens närhet," in *Ett eget rum: Konstnärsrollen under det sena 1800-talet*, ed. Carina Rech and Karin Sidén, 92–103. Stockholm: Prins Eugens Waldemarsudde, 2021.

Pedley-Hindson, Catherine. "Jane Avril and the Entertainment Lithograph: The Female Celebrity and *fin-de-siècle* Questions of Corporeality and Performance," *Theater Research International* 30, no. 2 (2005): 107–23.

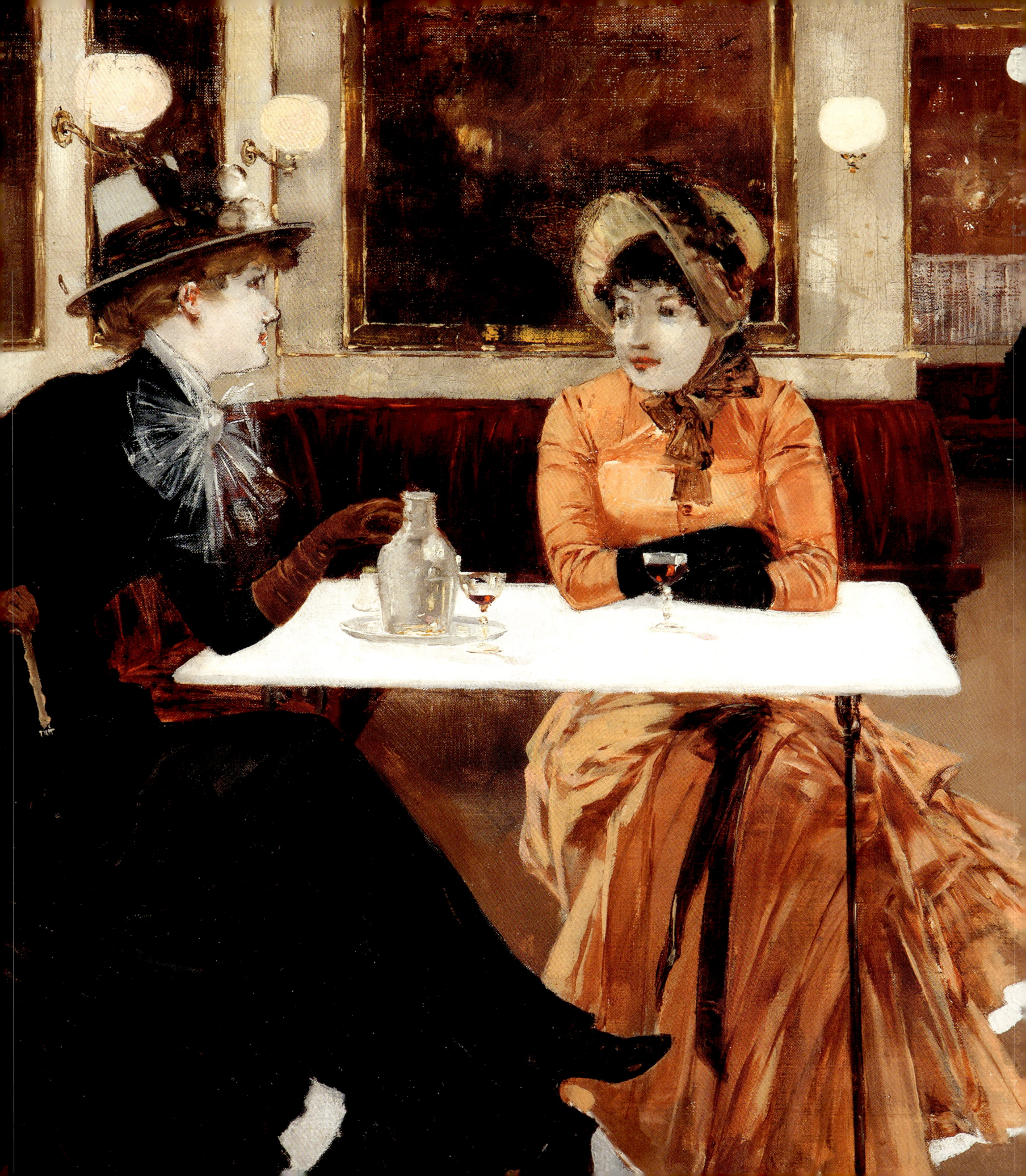

Rech, Carina. "A City of One's Own: The Parisian Letters of the Swedish Painter Hanna Hirsch-Pauli," *Nineteenth-Century Art Worldwide* 23, no. 1 (Spring 2024), https://doi.org/10.29411/ncaw.2024.23.1.4.

Reinhart, Hildegarde. "Elisabeth Epstein: Moscow–Munich–Paris–Geneva, Waystations of a Painter and Mediator of the French-German Cultural Transfer," in *Marianne Werefkin and the Women Artists in Her Circle*, ed. Tanja Malycheva and Isabel Wünsche, 165–74. Leiden: Brill, 2017.

Richardson, John. *A Life of Picasso*, vol. 1, *The Prodigy, 1881–1906*. New York: Knopf, 2007.

Rittner, Leona, W. Scott Haine, and Jeffrey H. Jackson, eds. *The Thinking Space: The Café as a Cultural Institution in Paris, Italy and Vienna*. London: Routledge, 2013.

Roe, Sue. *In Montmartre: Picasso, Matisse, and the Birth of Modern Art*. New York: Penguin Books, 2014.

Ross, Andrew Israel. *Public City/Public Sex: Homosexuality, Prostitution, and Urban Culture in Nineteenth-Century Paris*. Philadelphia: Temple University Press. 2019.

Schwartz, Vanessa R. *Spectacular Realities: Early Mass Culture in Fin-de-Siècle Paris*. Berkeley, Los Angeles, and London: University of California Press, 1998.

Shapiro, Barbara Stern, ed. *Pleasures of Paris: Daumier to Picasso*. Boston: Museum of Fine Arts, Boston / David R. Godine, 1991.

Singer, Ben. "Modernity, Hyperstimulus, and the Rise of Popular Sensationalism," in *Cinema and the Invention of Modern Life*, ed. Leo Charney and Vanessa R. Schwartz, 72–102. Berkeley: University of California Press, 1995.

Valdès-Forain, Florence, ed. *Jean-Louis Forain: La Comédie parisienne*. Memphis: Dixon Gallery and Gardens, 2011.

Vangsgaard-Nielsen, Dorthe, ed. *Impressionism and Its Overlooked Women*. Charlottenlund: Ordrupgaard, 2024.

Verhagen, Marcus. "The Poster in *Fin-de-Siècle* Paris: 'That Mobile and Degenerate Art,'" in *Cinema and the Invention of Modern Life*, ed. Leo Charney and Vanessa R. Schwartz, 103–29. Berkeley: University of California Press, 1995.

Walker, George. *Chess and Chess-Players: Consisting of Original Stories and Sketches*. London: Charles J. Skeet, 1850.

Way, Thomas R. *Mr. Whistler's Lithographs: The Catalogue*. London: G. Bell & Sons, 1896.

Werkmäster, Barbro. "Frigjord eller bunden? De kvinnliga konstnärerna och 1880-talets emancipationssträvanden," in *De drogo till Paris: Nordiska konstnärinnor på 1800-talet*, ed. Bo Särnstedt and Louise Robbert, 11–28. Stockholm: 1988.

Wivel, Henrik. *Jeg er en anden: En biografi om J.F. Willumsen*. Gylling: Strandberg Publishing, 2024.

Zmelty, Nicholas-Henri. *L'Affiche illustrée au temps de l'affichomanie (1889–1905)*. Paris: Mare & Martin, 2014.

INDEX

Page numbers in italics refer to the illustrations

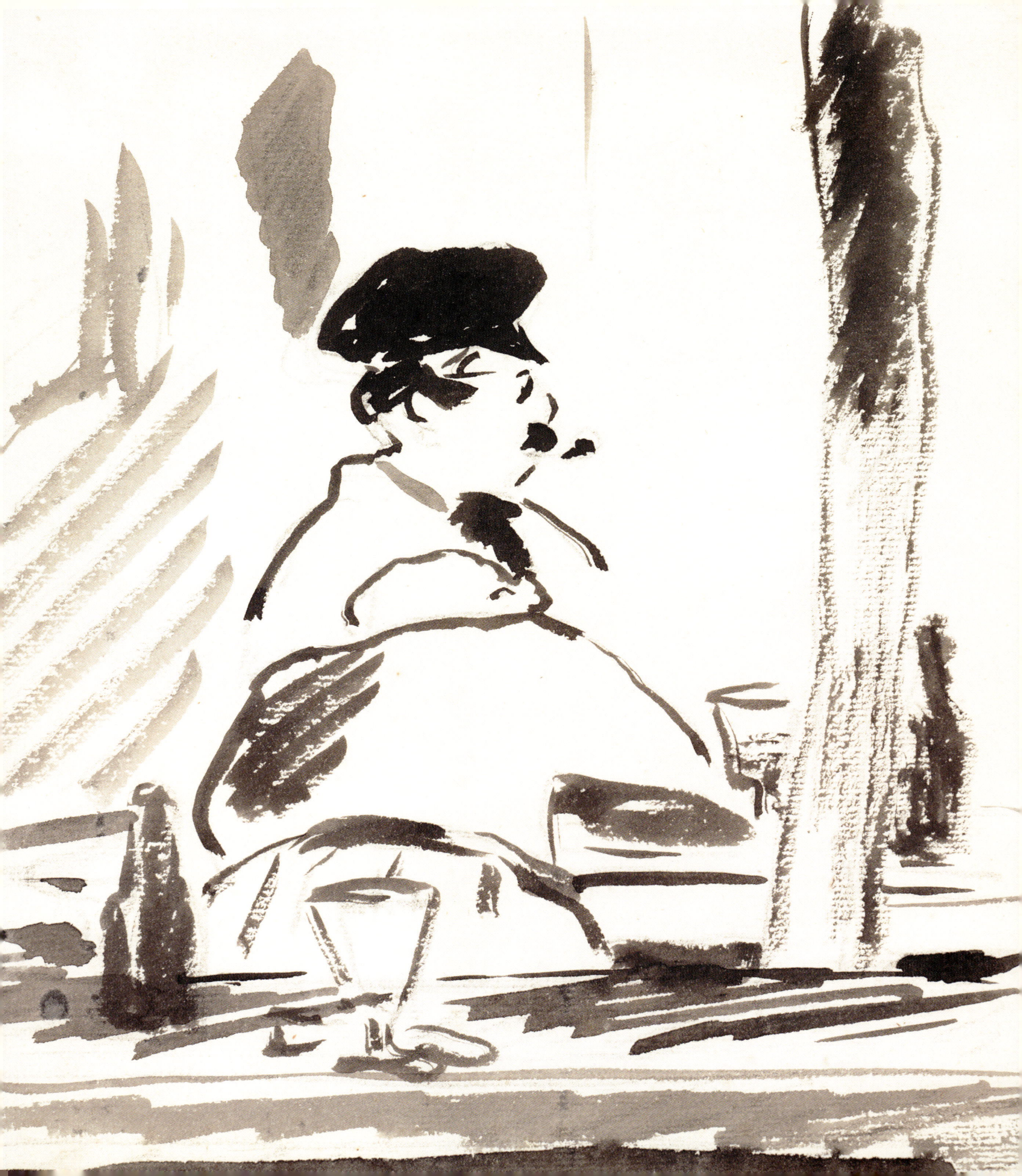

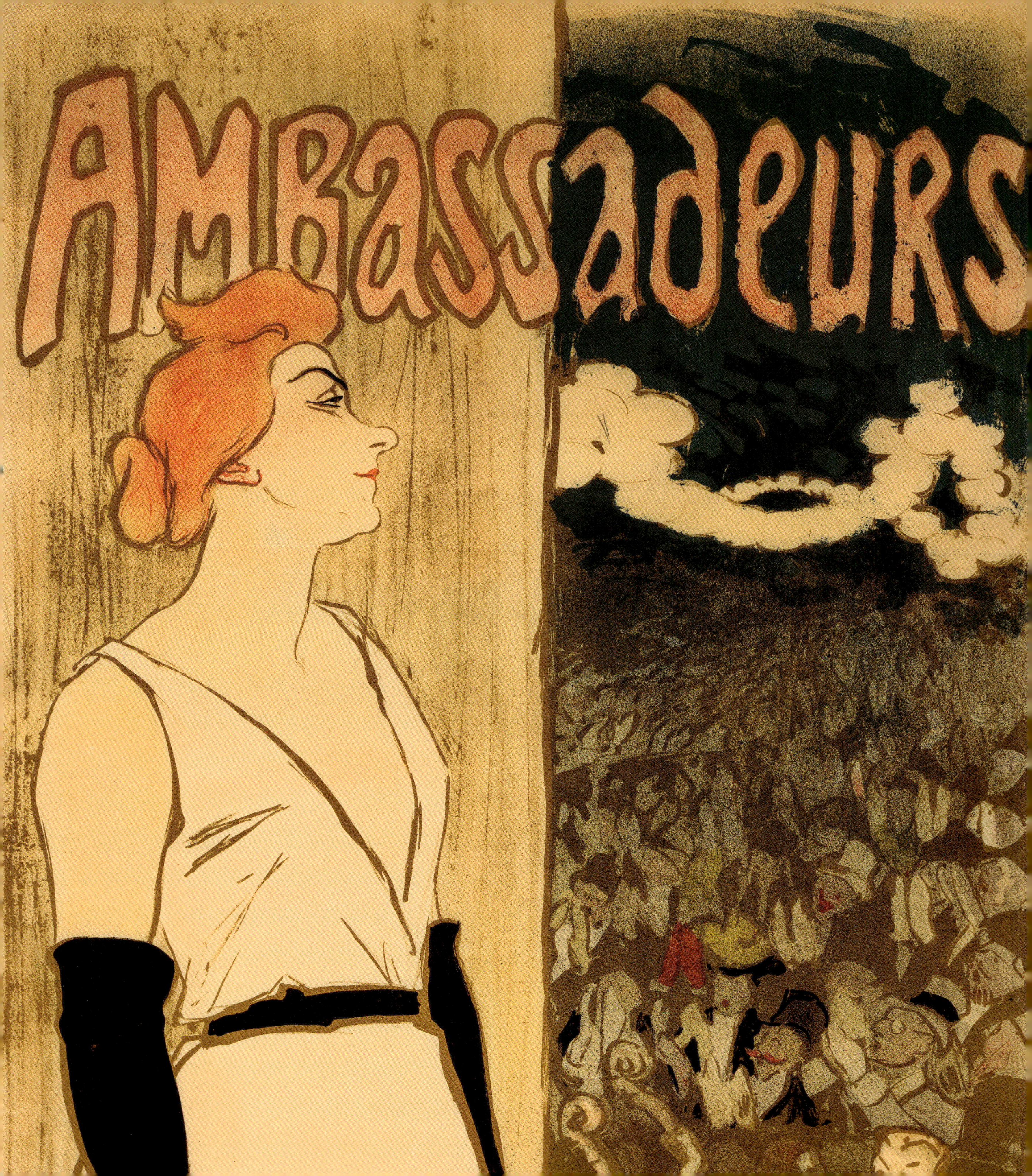

Ambassadeurs

PHOTO CREDITS

Fig. 1 Peter van Evert / Alamy Stock Photo

Fig. 2 © Fitzwilliam Museum / Bridgeman Images

Fig. 5 Private collection / Bridgeman Images

Fig. 6 © RMN-Grand Palais / Art Resource, NY; Photo: Jean-Gilles Berizzi

Fig. 8 © J.F. Willumsen / VISDA [2026]; Photo © O. Vaering / Bridgeman Images

Fig. 10 © Estate of Jean Metzinger / Artists Rights Society (ARS), New York / ADAGP, Paris; Buffalo AKG Art Museum / Art Resource, NY

Fig. 11 Bridgeman Images

Fig. 12 Christie's Images / Bridgeman Images

Fig. 13 Bridgeman Images

Fig. 14 The Picture Art Collection / Alamy Stock Photo

Fig. 15 VTR / Alamy Stock Photo

Fig. 16 Van Gogh Museum, Amsterdam, The Netherlands / Bridgeman Images

Fig. 17 © 2026 Estate of Pablo Picasso / Artists Rights Society (ARS), New York; Digital Image © The Museum of Modern Art / Licensed by SCALA / Art Resource, NY / VISDA

Fig. 18 Everett Collection / Bridgeman Images

Fig. 19 © Musée d'Orsay, Dist. RMN-Grand Palais / Patrice Schmidt; Musée d'Orsay, Paris, France / Bridgeman Images

Fig. 20 © Fine Art Images / Bridgeman Images

Fig. 21 Carnegie Museum of Art, Pittsburgh, PA / Art Resource, NY

Fig. 22 © Collection Kröller-Müller Museum, Otterlo, The Netherlands. Photography by Rik Klein Gotink

Fig. 24 © Maurice-Louis Branger / Robert-Viollet

Fig. 26 Bridgeman Images

Fig. 28 © Les Arts Décoratifs / Jean Tholance

Fig. 30 © The Courtauld / Bridgeman Images

Fig. 31 © 2026 Estate of Pablo Picasso / Artists Rights Society (ARS), New York / VISDA

Fig. 33 © Musée d'Orsay, Dist. RMN-Grand Palais / Patrice Schmidt; Musée d'Orsay, Paris, France / Bridgeman Images

Fig. 34 The Art Institute of Chicago / Art Resource, NY

Fig. 35 Bridgeman Images

Fig. 36 Bridgeman Images

Fig. 37 Reproduction: Lina Löfström Baker / National Library of Sweden

Fig. 38 © Leonard de Selva / Bridgeman Images

Fig. 39 Bridgeman Images

Fig. 40 © Fine Art Images / Bridgeman Images

Fig. 41 Nasjonalmuseet, Oslo / Bridgeman Images; Photo: Nasjonalmuseet / Børre Høstland

Fig. 42 © Munchmuseet

Fig. 43 Hilfing-Rasmussen, Jens Carl Frederik / Oslo Museum

Fig. 44 Courtesy of The Metropolitan Museum of Art, New York

Fig. 45 Digital Image © The Museum of Modern Art/Licensed by SCALA / Art Resource, NY

Fig. 46 Musée Toulouse-Lautrec, Albi, France / Bridgeman Images

Cat. 2 Courtesy of Denver Art Museum

Cat. 4 Bridgeman Images

Cat. 11 © Detroit Institute of Arts / Bridgeman Images

Cat. 13 Courtesy Dallas Museum of Art

Cat. 17 Joseph McDonald, courtesy of the Fine Arts Museums of San Francisco

Cat. 21 Nasjonalmuseet / Børre Høstland

Cat. 22 © Fine Arts Images / Bridgeman Images

Cat. 23 © Photo Josse / Bridgeman Images

Cat. 24 Image courtesy of Nelson-Atkins Digital Production & Preservation, Gabe Hopkins

Cat. 25 Bridgeman Images

Cat. 26 Courtesy of Denver Art Museum

Cat. 28 © Finnish National Gallery, Helsinki / Bridgeman Images; Photo: Finnish National Gallery / Aleks Talve

Cat. 29 Rune Aakvik

Cat. 30 Städel Museum, Frankurt au Main, Germany / Bridgeman Images

Cat. 31 Artepics / Alamy Stock Photo

Cat. 32 J.F. Willumsen / VISDA; photographer: Anders Sune Berg

Cat. 33 Courtesy of Bukowskis

Cat. 36 Courtesy Bill Ganzel, Ganzel Group Communications, Inc.

Cat. 37 Courtesy Bill Ganzel, Ganzel Group Communications, Inc.

Cat. 39 Nasjonalmuseet / Andreas Harvik

Cat. 42 Courtesy Bill Ganzel, Ganzel Group Communications, Inc.

Cat. 44 Städel Museum, Frankfurt am Main, Germany / Bridgeman Images

Cat. 47 © The Museum of Fine Arts, Houston; Thomas R. DuBrock

Cat. 48 © 2026 Estate of Pablo Picasso / Artists Rights Society (ARS), New York / VISDA

Cat. 49 Nasjonalmuseet / Børre Høstland

Cat. 52 © Fine Art Images/ Bridgeman Images

Cat. 55 Bridgeman Images

Cat. 56 © Fine Art Images / Bridgeman Images

Cat. 57 Thielska Galleriet, Stockholm / Bridgeman Images; Photographer: Per Myrehed / Thielska Galleriet

Cat. 59 The Cleveland Museum of Art

Cat. 60 © 2026 Estate of Pablo Picasso / Artists Rights Society (ARS), New York / VISDA

Cat. 62 © 2026 Estate of Pablo Picasso / Artists Rights Society (ARS), New York / VISDA

Cat. 67 Photograph © Bruce M. White, 2019 © 2025 Artists Rights Society (ARS), New York / ADAGP, Paris

Cat. 69 © 2026 Museum of Fine Arts, Boston